Databases and Information Systems

Databases and Information Systems

Fourth International Baltic Workshop, Baltic DB&IS 2000 Vilnius, Lithuania, May 1–5, 2000 Selected Papers

Edited by

Janis Barzdins

Institute of Mathematics and Computer Science,
University of Latvia, Riga

and

Albertas Caplinskas

Institute of Mathematics and Informatics,
Vilnius

KLUWER ACADEMIC PUBLISHERS

DORDRECHT / BOSTON / LONDON

A C.I.P. Catalogue record for this book is available from the Library of Congress.

ISBN 978-90-481-5657-3

Published by Kluwer Academic Publishers,
P.O. Box 17, 3300 AA Dordrecht, The Netherlands.

Sold and distributed in North, Central and South America
by Kluwer Academic Publishers,
101 Philip Drive, Norwell, MA 02061, U.S.A.

In all other countries, sold and distributed
by Kluwer Academic Publishers,
P.O. Box 322, 3300 AH Dordrecht, The Netherlands.

Printed on acid-free paper

Table of contents

Part 5: Information Systems and Software Engineering

Part 6: Knowledge Bases, Artificial Intelligence, and Information Systems

Part 7: Activity Modelling and Workflow Management

Preface

This volume contains revised versions of best papers presented at the 4th IEEE Baltic Workshop on Databases and Information Systems (BalticDB&IS'2000). The indented audience for this book is researchers and practitioners interested in current database and information system issues. The papers cover a wide range of topics including foundations of databases, knowledge bases, knowledge management, data mining, data warehousing, distributed information systems, mobile computing, agent technologies, network-based information systems, software engineering, activity modelling, and workflow management.

The BalticDB&IS'2000 took place on 1-5 May 2000 in Vilnius, Lithuania. It was organised by the Vilnius Gediminas Technical University, Institute of Mathematics and Informatics, Lithuania, and Lithuanian Computer Society. The workshop has been approved by the IEEE Communication Society for technical co-sponsorship.

The aim of the biannual Baltic Workshops on Databases and Information Systems is to provide a forum for the exchange ideas in the area of databases and information systems between the research communities of Baltic countries and the rest of the world. These workshops have become a real incentive of regional research and boost of international cooperation.

The idea to start the series of biannual Baltic workshops has been suggested by Janis Bubenko, jr. and Arne Solvberg. The first workshop was held in Trakai, Lithuania in 1994. Next workshops were held in Tallinn, Estonia in 1996 and in Riga, Latvia in 1998.

The international program committee selected for the BalticDB&IS'2000 39 research papers out of 60 submissions. All papers were reviewed in advance by three referees, as a rule, from different countries. After workshop the program committee selected 27 best papers to be published in this book.

Many people contributed to the organisation of the BalticDB&IS'2000. We would like to express our thanks to all authors, members of program committee, and additional referees for their efforts. We also would like to thank all institutions actively supporting the workshop, namely, Baltic Fund of VLDB Endowment, IEEE Communication Society, Vilnius University, Vytautas Magnus University, Kaunas University of Technology, Klaipeda University, and Law Academy of Lithuania.

Special thanks to the members of the organising committee R. Kacianauskas (Vilnius Gediminas Technical University), O. Vasilecas (Vilnius Gediminas Technical University), Audrone Lupeikiene (Institute of Mathematics and Informatics, Lithuania), Dale Dzemydiene (Institute of Mathematics and Informatics, Lithuania), Saulius Maskeliunas (Institute of Mathematics and Informatics, Lithuania), Juris Borzovs (Riga Information Technology Institute), Ahto Kalja (Institute of Cybernetics, Estonia), and Algirdas Pakstas (University of Sunderland). And last but not least we thank the members of advising committee Janis Bubenko, jr. (Royal Institute of Technology and Stockholm University) and Arne Solvberg (The Norwegian University of Science and Technology).

The following trademarks have been used in this book:

Jasmine™, a trademark of Computer Associate International, Inc.,

GemStone™, a trademark of Gemstone Systems, Inc.,

Windows NT , DCOM™, COM+™, ODBC™, OLE DB™, Microsoft SQL Server™, trademarks of Microsoft Corporation,

Informix Dynamic Server™,trademarks of Informix Corporation,

DB2 , a trademark of International Business Machines Corporation,

O2™, a trademark of O2 Technology, Inc.,

ObjectStore™, a trademark of Object Design, Inc.,

CORBA , Unified Modeling Language™, UML™, IDL™, ORB™, trademarks of Object Management Group Inc.,

Oracle , SQL*Net ‚ trademarks of Oracle Corporation,

Rational Rose , trademark of Rational Rose, Inc.,

Java , a trademark of Sun Microsystems, Inc.,

SONY , a trademark of Sony Corporation.

May 2000   Janis Barzdins
                                                             Albertas Caplinskas

Workshop Committee

Program Committee

Program Chairperson:
Albertas Caplinskas   Institute of Mathematics and Informatics (Lithuania)

Program Committee Members:

Janis Barzdins	University of Latvia (Latvia)
Alfs Berztiss	University of Pittsburgh (USA)
Janis Bicevskis	University of Latvia (Latvia)
Raimundas Ciegis	Vilnius Gediminas Technical University and Institute of Mathematics and Informatics (Lithuania)
Vytautas Cyras	Vilnius University (Lithuania)
Klaus R. Dittrich	University of Zurich (Switzerland)
Hans-Dieter Ehrich	Technishe Universität Braunschweig (Germany)
Remigijus Gustas	University of Karlstad (Sweden)
Janis Grundspenkis	Riga Technical University (Latvia)
Hele-Mai Haav	Institute of Cybernetics and Concordia International University (Estonia)
Jean-Luc Hainaut	University of Namur (Belgium)
Juhani Iivari	University of Oulu (Finland)
Leonid Kalinichenko	Institute for Problems of Informatics, Russian Academy of Science (Russia)
Audris Kalnins	University of Latvia (Latvia)
Pericles Loucopoulos	University of Science and Technology in Manchester (UK)
Kalle Lyytinen	University of Jyvaskyla (Finland)
Mihail Matskin	Norwegian University of Science and Technology (Norway)
Julie A. McCann	City University (UK)
Jorgen Fischer Nilsson	Technical University of Denmark (Denmark)
Algirdas Pakstas	University of Sunderland (UK)
Bronius Paradauskas	Kaunas University of Technology (Lithuania)
Jaan Penjam	Institute of Cybernetics and Tallinn Technical University (Estonia)
Jaanus Poial	Tartu University (Estonia)
Henrikas Pranevicius	Kaunas University of Technology (Lithuania)
Ivan Ryant	Intax s.r.o. (Czech Republic)
Keng Siau	University of Nebraska-Lincoln (USA)
Kazimierz Subieta	Institute of Computer Science, Polish Academy of Science (Poland)
Eugenijus Telesius	Vytautas Magnus University (Lithuania)
Jaak Tepandi	Tallinn Technical University (Estonia)
Janis Tenteris	Riga Technical University (Latvia)
Bernhard Thalheim	Brandenburg Technical University at Cottbus (Germany)
Kal Toth	University of Victoria (Canada)
Enn Tyugu	Royal Institute of Technology (Sweden)
Aphrodite Tsalgatidou	University of Athens (Greece)

Benkt Wangler	Stockholm University (Sweden)
Naoki Yonezaki	Tokyo Institute of Technology (Japan)
Edmundas Zavadskas	Vilnius Gediminas Technical University (Lithuania)

Additional Referees

Per Backlund	Skövde University (Sweden)
Andreas Behm	University of Zurich (Switzerland)
Eleni Berki	University of Sheffield (UK)
Rimas Butleris	Kaunas University of Technology (Lithuania)
Torben Braüner	Roskilde University (Denmark)
Janis Bubenko, jr.	Royal Institute of Technology and Stockholm University (Sweden)
Gintautas Dzemyda	Institute of Mathematics and Informatics (Lithuania)
Silke Eckstein	Technishe Universität Braunschweig (Germany)
Thomas Feyer	Brandenburgischen Technishe Universität Cottbus (Germany)
Hans Fritschi	University of Zurich (Switzerland)
Stella Gatziu	University of Zurich (Switzerland)
Åsa Grehag	Skövde University (Sweden)
Saulius Gudas	Kaunas University of Technology (Lithuania)
Ingi Jonasson	Skövde University (Sweden)
Panos Kardasis	The University of Science and Technology in Manchester (UK)
Lina Nemuraite	Kaunas University of Technology (Lithuania)
Karl Neumann	Technishe Universität Braunschweig (Germany)
Boris Novikov	University of St. Petersburg(Russia)
Anne Persson	Skövde University (Sweden)
Sobah Petersen	NCR Metis Solutions (Norway)
Vytautas Pilkauskas	Kaunas University of Technology (Lithuania)
Ralf Pinger	Technishe Universität Braunschweig (Germany)
Aida Pliuskeviciene	Institute of Mathematics and Informatics (Lithuania)
Denis Reilly	The University of Science and Technology in Manchester (UK)
Martin Schönhoff	University of Zurich (Switzerland)
Nikolay Skvortsov	Institute for Problems of Informatics, Russian Academy of Science (Russia)
Eva Söderström	Skövde University (Sweden)
Janis Stirna	Stockholm University (Sweden)
Bronius Tamulynas	Kaunas University of Technology (Lithuania)
Laimutis Telksnys	Institute of Mathematics and Informatics (Lithuania)
Olegas Vasilecas	Vilnius Gediminas Technical University(Lithuania)
Athanasios Vavouras	University of Zurich (Switzerland)

Advisory Committee

Janis Bubenko, jr.	Royal Institute of Technology and Stockholm University (Sweden)
Arne Solvberg	Norwegian Institute of Technology (Norway)

Part 1: Foundations of Databases

Object Views and Query Modification

Kazimierz Subieta and Jacek Plodzien

Polish-Japanese Institute of Information Technology &
Institute of Computer Science PAS, Warsaw, Poland
E-mail: {subieta, jpl} @ ipipan.waw.pl

Abstract

We attempt to widen the scope in which object views are typically set, following the paradigms of programming languages rather than traditional database concepts, such as relational/object algebras or calculi. A well-known environment stack is used as a semantic basis for definitions of query operators. In this setting naming, scoping and binding are central issues and a virtual (non-materialised) database view is a stored function. A function output is a structure built upon atomic values, references and names. Such functions perfectly simulate virtual objects and virtual classes. The approach can be coupled with the query modification technique based on macro-substitution. It significantly reduces performance problems related to processing views. The approach is relevant to object query languages such as OQL.

Keywords: object-oriented database, query language, stack-based approach, view, query modification.

1. Introduction

A view defines virtual data that are derived from stored data and are compliant to the assumed data model. Thus, views can be queried (and sometimes updated) similarly to stored data, by generic query and data manipulation facilities. Object-oriented views are considered very important for current and future database technologies due to the following potential qualities:

- *Customisation, conceptualisation, encapsulation.* The user works with a part of a database that is relevant to his/her area of interest in a way that is convenient for everyday processing routines and concepts.
- *Security, privacy, and autonomy.* Views restrict possible accesses only to a relevant part of a database. In federated databases this restriction supports the autonomy of local databases.
- *Interoperability, heterogeneity, schema integration, legacy applications.* Views enable integration of heterogeneous databases, allowing understanding and processing foreign, legacy or remote databases according to a common, unified schema.
- *Data independence, schema evolution.* Views enable the user to change physical and logical database organisation without affecting already written applications.

Still, object views present a hard problem. The mentioned above qualities are actually wishes. Currently, no commercial OODBMS implements views. There are some prototypes, e.g. a prototype for O2™ [8]. There are many other proposals (mostly theoretical), but in general the understanding of object-oriented views (virtual, transparent for the users) is low. In contrast to the relational era, there is no agreement which data model is adequate for object query languages (a basis for view definitions). There are various ideas: the ODMG object model [3], the SQL3 object

3

J. Barzdins and A. Caplinskas (eds.), Databases and Information Systems, 3–14.
© 2001 *Kluwer Academic Publishers.*

model, several approaches to formal semantics of OQL, nested relations (NF^2), object algebras, F-logic, comprehensions, monoid calculus, and others.

In our opinion these approaches have limitations, especially concerning the current trend of integrating querying and programming. Moreover, neglecting optimisation of queries invoking views may cause many approaches impracticable. We attempt to widen the scope in which object query languages are typically set, following the paradigms of programming languages rather than traditional database concepts, such as relational/object algebras, calculi and logic. The approach is relevant to ODMG OQL [2,3] and is able to explain some of its semantic inconsistencies [7, 11].

Assuming queries are programming languages' expressions, the concept of programming languages that is analogous to database views is a *functional procedure* (a *function*, for short) which can return a collection. The generality of views requires several features inherent to our approach:

- Renaming attributes in virtual objects (as SQL does);
- Views which hide some attributes of corresponding stored objects;
- Defining views through other views; recursive views;
- Defining virtual attributes and virtual links;
- Views in which virtual objects combine two or more stored objects;
- Updateable views;
- Clean integration of notions such as types, classes, encapsulation, inheritance, methods, etc.

Relational views can be efficiently processed by the query modification technique [9]. In comparison to view materialisation (calculating views in advance) query modification offers much better total performance. In our approach query modification means that a function declaration is treated as a macro-definition. Similar capabilities are introduced in the ODMG 2.0 standard as the "define" clause of OQL, which is essentially a macro-definition. Such an approach to views is limited, see [7]. There is also a proposal concerning views in the emerging SQL3 standard; however due to the size (ca. 1100 pages) and extreme eclecticism there are doubts if the idea is consistent, reasonable and implementable. Considering database views as functions is more systematic and opens many new possibilities: views defined by complex algorithms, stateful (capability-augmenting) views, views with parameters, recursive views, higher-order views, etc.

The rest of the paper is organised as follows. In Section 2 we formalise object data structures. In Section 3 we introduce the concept of environment stack and explain its role in the semantics of query languages. In Section 4 we present SBQL, a formalised OQL-like query language. In Section 5 we introduce functions that are to be object views. In Section 6 we discuss query modification and optimisation methods related to the idea. Section 7 concludes.

2. An Abstract Object-Oriented Store Model

Object-oriented data models are complex and introduce a lot of notions. The question how to formalise them is not trivial, because the formalisation must be simple formally and simultaneously must cover (at least potentially) all critical concepts of object databases. Some trade-off is presented in [12][1]. To eliminate secondary features of data structures the unification of records, tuples, arrays and all bulk structures is assumed. All these concepts are collections of elements, and in our model we abstract from their differences. Three sets are used to model objects:

- I – the set of internal identifiers,
- N – the set of external data names,
- V – the set of atomic values (integers, strings, blobs, etc.).

---

[1] To make the paper self-contained we repeat some definitions from [4,5,6,12] in sections 2, 3 and 4.

Each object has an *internal identifier* (OID; the identifiers are not printable); *external name* (to access the object from a source program), and *content* (which can be a value, a link, or a set of objects). Let $i, i_1, i_2 \in I, n \in N, v \in V$. Objects are modelled as the following triples:

- Atomic objects as $<i, n, v>$,
- Link objects as $<i_1, n, i_2>$,
- Complex objects as $<i, n, T>$, where T denotes a set of objects.

The definition is recursive and allows us to create complex objects with an arbitrary number of hierarchy levels. Relationships (references, pointer links) are modelled through link objects. To model collections (bags) we do not assume uniqueness of external names on any level of data hierarchy. Our model covers NF^2 data structures as a particular case. *Object store* is formed as a structure of objects (sub-objects, etc.), identifiers of *root objects* (starting points for querying), and constraints (uniqueness of OIDs, referential integrities, etc). Other features of object models (classes, inheritance, encapsulation, methods, etc.) require extensions of the presented model; see [11, 12]. For simplicity we omit them. We also abstract from strong typing issues.

In Fig.1 we present an example database with the following schema in (a bit extended) UML:

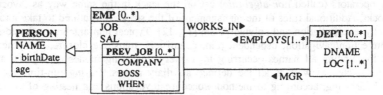

Figure 1. Database schema

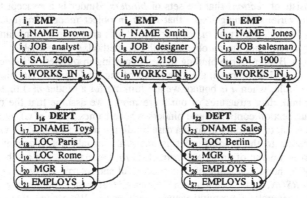

Figure 2. Tiny database according to the schema from Fig.1

The schema defines two collections of complex objects, *DEPT* and *EMP*, and an abstract class *PERSON*, having attribute *NAME*, a private attribute *birthDate*, and a method *age*. *EMP* has a collection of complex sub-objects *PREV_JOB* (previous jobs), and *DEPT* has a collection of atomic sub-objects *LOC* (location). An object/property name is followed by its cardinality unless it is [1..1]. Fig.2 presents a tiny database built upon the schema presented in Fig.1. The database will be used in detailed examples. Objects *EMP* and *DEPT* are the root objects in the database.

3. The Environment Stack, Scoping and Binding

In programming languages the environment stack (ES) accomplishes the abstraction principle, which allows the programmer to consider the currently written piece of code to be independent of the context of its possible use. ES is responsible for the scope control and binding names. (ES should not be confused with another concept, known as *execution stack* or *query result stack*.) ES is managed according to procedure calls and program blocks. A new section of volatile objects (so-called *activation record*) is pushed onto the stack when a procedure/block is started, and the section is popped when the procedure/block is terminated. The section for a procedure invocation contains volatile variables (objects) that are declared within this procedure, actual procedure's parameters, a return address, and sometimes other data. Binding follows the "search from the top" rule. The last added section is the first visited during the binding, and objects from some sections remain invisible for the binding (for so-called *lexical scoping*). In real languages ES exists in two shapes: as a static (compilation-time) stack, and as a dynamic (run-time) stack. In this paper we abstract from these two stack forms assuming for simplicity that binding is entirely dynamic.

The stack-based semantics of object query languages is explained in [12]. The idea is that some query operators (called *non-algebraic*) act on the stack in the same way as invocations of program blocks. Additional rules of the management of the stack are required to take into account class hierarchy, encapsulation and polymorphism [11, 12]. Typical non-algebraic operators include selection, projection/navigation, dependent join, quantifiers, transitive closure, and others. ES is responsible for binding all names occurring in a query, including names of objects, attributes, methods, views, etc., as well as all the defined auxiliary names. During run-time the stack is growing and shrinking, according to method/procedure invocations and nesting of non-algebraic operators in queries. A particular name occurring in a query is bound to a database/program entity in the proper stack section. In this way the stack accomplishes *scope rules*.

The stack consists of *sections* that are sets of *binders*. Binder is a concept that allows us to explain and describe various naming issues that occur in object models and query/programming languages. Formally, a binder is a pair (n, x), where $n \in N$ is an external name, and x is any query output; in particular, a reference (to an object, attribute, method, view, variable, etc.). Such a pair will be written as $n(x)$. Binders serve binding names occurring in queries. If binder $n(x)$ is present on ES and we want to bind the name n, then the result of the binding is x. The binding follows the "search from the top" rule: when n is bound, we are looking for a binder $n(x)$ that is closest to the stack top. To cover bulk data structures of our store model we assume that the binding is multi-valued: if the relevant section contains more binders whose names are n: $n(x_1)$, $n(x_2)$, $n(x_3)$,..., then all of them form the result of binding. In such a case binding n returns bag$\{x_1, x_2, x_3,...\}$.

Some modification to the binding rules is necessary to take into account inheritance and substitutability. If n_1 is a name of an object from class n_1, the class n_1 has a sub-class n_2, and ES contains a binder $n_2(x)$, then the binding of n_1 is successful and returns x. For instance, if we would like to bind name *PERSON*, and ES contains the binder $EMP(i_6)$, then the binding is successful and returns i_6. This rule is generalised for multi-valued bindings too. We assume that typing constraints disallow the use of attributes specific for *EMP*, when the binding concerns *PERSON*.

At the beginning of a user session ES consists of a single section containing binders to all root database objects. Fig.3a presents the initial ES state for the tiny database from Fig.2. The stack is growing (and then shrinking) according to nesting of non-algebraic operators, Fig.3b. The final state is the same as the initial state (if no side effect in the query).

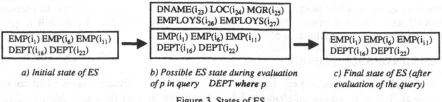

a) *Initial state of ES*

b) *Possible ES state during evaluation of p in query DEPT where p*

c) *Final state of ES (after evaluation of the query)*

Figure 3. States of ES

Fig.3 presents a simplified situation. General object-oriented data structures and complex query/programs may create complex states of ES. In Fig.4 we present a state which concerns binding name X in the predicate of some query selecting *EMP* objects. X can be the name of an *EMP* attribute, the name of a method from the *EMP* class, the name of a method from the *PERSON* class, the name of a database object, the name of a view, etc. X is to be bound to a proper entity of the entire environment, following the order determined by arrows.

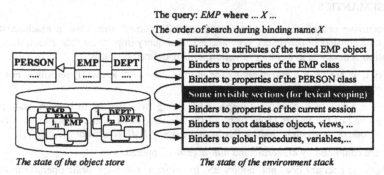

Figure 4. More complex state of ES

4. Formalised Query Language SBQL

SBQL (*Stack-Based Query Language*) is a formalised language in the spirit of OQL. All basic constructs of OQL have direct counterparts in SBQL. SBQL is implemented in Loqis [10].

4.1 SBQL SYNTAX

- A single name or a single literal is a query. For instance, *EMP, JOB, SAL, x, y,* "Smith", 2, 2500, etc. are (atomic) queries.
- If q is a query, and σ is a unary operator (for instance: sum, count, distinct, sin, sqrt, ...), then $\sigma(q)$ is a query. The operator defining a new name is a unary operator too (parameterised by a name); we use for it the traditional syntax q **as** n (where $n \in N$).
- If q_1 and q_2 are queries, and θ is a binary operator (for instance: **where**, (dot), |, +, =, <, **and**, **union**, ...), then $q_1 \theta q_2$ is a query. Quantifiers are considered binary operators too, but we apply to them the traditional prefix forms: $\forall q_1(q_2)$ and $\exists q_1(q_2)$.
- Except for typing constraints we assume full orthogonality of operators. For example, *DEPT, LOC, DNAME,* "Toys" are atomic queries, from which we can build complex ones, such as:
- (*DEPT* **where** (*DNAME* = "Toys")).*LOC*
- SQL equivalent: **select** *LOC* **from** *DEPT* **where** *DNAME* = "Toys". In contrast to SQL and OQL, SBQL queries have a very nice and unusual property: they can be perfectly decomposed

into subqueries, down to atomic ones, connected by unary or binary operators. In particular, *DNAME* and *LOC* are queries of their own rights. This is due to the fact that all SBQL queries are evaluated *relatively* to the state of ES; see Fig.3.

4.2 RESULTS OF SBQL QUERIES

An SBQL query (subquery) can return a value of any type, including atomic and complex (nested) ones. The result can be an element of $V \cup I$, a binder $n(x)$ where $n \in N$ and x is a query result, a row (tuple) of query results, or a bag of type-compatible query results. The definition is recursive and covers multi-level hierarchies of (named) values and references. If we abstract from ordered collections, then the definition conceptually covers *literals* defined by ODMG [3]. For example, an SBQL query can return the following structure:

bag{ row{ 2, *DNAME*(i_{23}), *empl*(bag{ row{n("*Smith*"), $s(i_9)$}, row{n("*Jones*"), $s(i_{14})$} }) } }

4.3 SBQL SEMANTICS

The recursive procedure *eval* maps a syntactically correct query and a machine state to a result. The state consists of the object store and ES. If a query implies no side effect, then the state after evaluation is the same as before evaluation. *eval* is defined by cases:

- For query l, where l is a literal denoting the atomic value $v \in V$, *eval*(l) returns v. For instance, query 2 returns the value 2.

- For query n, where $n \in N$, *eval*(n) inspects ES going from the top to bottom, and returns the result as a bag of the values taken from all the binders named n occurring in the first section containing one or more such binders. For instance query *EMP* returns bag{i_1, i_6, i_{11}}.

- Queries are combined by *algebraic* and *non-algebraic* operators.

An algebraic operator does not modify ES. In contrast, a non-algebraic operator modifies ES. Algebraic operators include numerical comparisons and operators, string comparisons, boolean **and, or, not**, aggregate functions, set, bag and sequence operators, Cartesian product (denoted here by comma), etc. Definitions of algebraic operators are rather obvious so we skip them. Some operators implicitly call the dereferencing operator; for example, in query   *SAL* > 1000   the comparison > calls dereferencing, which changes the reference returned by *SAL* into a value.

A construct q **as** n is an algebraic operator too. The operator makes binders through assigning name n to each element returned by q. For instance, if query *DEPT* returns bag{i_{16}, i_{22}}, then   *DEPT* **as** d returns bag{$d(i_{16})$, $d(i_{22})$}. Together with scoping and binding rules (explained in the following chapter) this operator becomes a surprisingly powerful facility, covering all cases of auxiliary naming in OQL-like languages, including iterator variables, variables bound by quantifiers, structure field labels, renaming attributes in views, etc.

4.4 NON-ALGEBRAIC OPERATORS

If $q_1\theta q_2$ involves a non-algebraic operator θ, then q_2 is evaluated in the context determined by q_1. Non-algebraic operators do not follow the basic property of algebraic expressions, which assume independent evaluation of operators' arguments. The reader may be surprised hearing that operators such as selection, projection and join are "non-algebraic", but our model is very different from the relational algebra (and incomparably more powerful). Unlike the algebra, our operators are not indexed by informal or semi-formal meta-language expressions. We are persistent in the idea that each name in a query precisely follows the same scoping-binding discipline.

If θ is a non-algebraic operator, then $q_1\theta q_2$ is evaluated as follows. For each element r of the bag returned by q_1 the subquery q_2 is evaluated. Before the evaluation ES is augmented by a section (sections) determined by r. After the evaluation the stack is popped to the previous state. A partial result is a combination of r and the bag returned by q_2. The final result is a combination of partial results; the combination depends on θ. The new stack section is formed in the following way:

- If r contains an object identifier, then the section contains binders to all internal properties of the object. For example, for i_{22} in r the section will contain the set of binders $\{DNAME(i_{23})$, $LOC(i_{24})$, $MGR(i_{25})$, $EMPLOYS(i_{26})$, $EMPLOYS(i_{27})\}$, see Fig.2 and 3. Additionally, the stack is augmented by sections containing binders to internal properties of its classes, as shown in Fig.4.
- If r contains an identifier of a link object, then the new stack section contains the binder to the object the link points to, e.g. for i_{10} it is $DEPT(i_{22})$.
- If r contains a binder, then it is copied (without changes) to the section.
- Constants and identifiers of atomic objects are ignored.
- The section is a union of all binders that are induced by elements of r.

This semantics is the uniform basis for the definition of several non-algebraic operators:

- **Selection:** q_1 where q_2, where q_1 is any query, and q_2 is a boolean-valued query. If for a particular r returned by the query q_1 the query q_2 returns $TRUE$, then r is an element of the final result bag; otherwise it is skipped.
- **Projection, navigation, generalised path expressions:** $q_1.q_2$. The result bag is the union of bags returned by q_2 for each r returned by q_1.
- **Dependent join:** $q_1 \mid q_2$. A partial result for a particular r returned by q_1 is a bag obtained by a concatenation of r with each row returned by q_2 for this r. The final result is the union of the partial results.
- **Quantifiers:** $\forall q_1(q_2)$ and $\exists q_1(q_2)$, where q_1 is any query, and q_2 is a boolean-valued query. For $\forall$ the final result is $FALSE$, if q_2 returns $FALSE$ for at least one r returned by q_1; otherwise the final result is $TRUE$. For $\exists$ we apply a dual definition.

SBQL can be considered a formalised version of OQL. For instance, the OQL query (*get managers' names, their department names, and number of their subordinates*):

> select $e.NAME$, $d.DNAME$, count(select x from $d.EMPLOYS$ as x)
> from EMP as e, $e.WORKS\_IN$ as d where $e.JOB$ = "manager"

has the following 1:1 equivalent SBQL version:

> $((((EMP$ as $e) \mid (((e.WORKS\_IN).\ DEPT)$ as $d))$ where $((e.JOB)$ = "manager"))) .
> $(((e.NAME),\ (d.DNAME)),\ count((((d.EMPLOYS).\ EMP)$ as $x).x))$

Here we have consciously written a lot of parentheses to show that all used SBQL operators are binary or unary. SBQL precedence rules allow us to skip majority of parentheses.

4.5 THE CLOSURE PROPERTY

The closure property was a basic assumption of relational query languages. According to it, an input to a query consists of relations, and an output from a query is a relation too. Many authors consider the closure property a *sine qua non* condition for nesting queries and to build an efficient theory of query languages and views. The whole issue, however, is not so clear:

- Some queries, e.g. select $avg(SAL)$ from EMP, return numbers rather than relations. Hence, the closure property should be extended to numbers (and perhaps other atomic types).
- A stored relation can be updated, while a query output cannot be. Hence, there is a fundamental semantic difference between "input" and "output" relations.
- A stored relation must be named, while a relation produced by a query is unnamed.

- Attributes of stored relations must be named, while attributes of relations produced by queries need not be (or attribute names are derived in some contrived way).
- A stored relation has no duplicate tuples, while an output of SQL queries can contain them.
- A stored relation is unordered, while the output from SQL queries can be ordered.

Obviously the closure property is questionable for SQL. In object query languages the closure property leads to new doubts. By the analogy to the relational model we have to assume that the input for queries is a set of collections of objects, and the output is a collection of objects too. Such an assumption ignores the fact that some queries return collections of values (literals, in ODMG terms) rather than collections of objects. The presented above naming issues (e.g. names of objects returned by queries) lead to difficulties too.

Moreover, there is a question concerning identifiers of objects returned by queries. If one assigns unique identifiers to such objects, then queries will become non-deterministic functions: each query execution (acting on the same collections of objects) will return a different result. To cope with this anomaly the authors of [1] propose to introduce an equivalence of query results modulo identifiers assigned to output objects. This idea introduces additional complexity to the formal model and still, does not explain all doubts that we have presented.

As a consequence of the closure property several authors propose to subdivide queries into "object preserving" (i.e. retaining original identifiers of stored objects) and "object generating" (i.e. producing objects with new identifiers). The question arises whether designers of query languages have to provide special syntax to distinguish these cases; at least, OQL does not provide it. We also note that in OQL the closure property has resulted in a very doubtful construct [2]; namely OQL queries can create new objects (they can update a database state).

In our opinion for object-oriented query languages such a naive formulation of the closure property is a conceptual and semantic nonsense. We propose another formulation. As shown, binding a name in SBQL returns references, hence in fact query operators act on *object identifiers* rather than on *objects*. Query operators make it possible to return complex hierarchical structures built upon references, atomic values and names. The closure property concerns such structures. This approach to semantics of object query languages follows the semantics of programming languages' expressions (see C++ and Java), it is fully consistent and makes no room for anomalies or subdividing queries into "object preserving" and "object generating".

5. Views as Stored Functions

In previous sections we have prepared the semantic basis for defining object-oriented views, which are essentially first-class (stored in a database) functions. They can return a bulk output (a collection). In Loqis a function can be defined as follows (we omit typing):

function *RichEmp*
  begin return *EMP* **where** *SAL* > 2000 **end**;

Such a function can be called in queries. For instance (*get names of rich designers*):

(*RichEmp* **where** *JOB* = "*designer*"). *NAME*

The query is executed as follows. First, the name *RichEmp* is bound and the function is invoked; thus a new section storing parameters and a local environment of this function is pushed onto ES. In this case the section contains a return address only. Then, the body of this function is executed. It consists of a single query referring to a database. The query is evaluated, and (c.f. Fig.2) will return bag$\{i_1, i_6\}$, containing OIDs of *Brown* and *Smith* objects. This bag is also returned as an output from the function. Then the function is terminated, and the ES section implied by the function invocation is popped. Next, the result returned by *RichEmp* is processed by the **where** operator having on the right side the predicate *JOB* = "*designer*". According to the previously defined semantics, it returns bag$\{i_6\}$. The result is processed by the dot operator, which has on its right side the query *NAME*. The evaluation will return bag$\{i_7\}$, as expected.

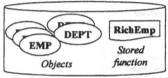 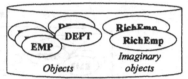

a) *The database seen by the view definer*   b) *The database seen by a view user*

Figure 5. Two points of view on the database content

The function named *RichEmp* simulates imaginary objects named *RichEmp*. Assuming the function will be stored in the database (on its top level), from the position of the view definer the situation is as presented in Fig.5a. The user perceives the database content as presented in Fig.5b. The imaginary *RichEmp* objects adopt the semantics of *EMP* objects. The user can use all attributes, methods and links defined for *EMP* objects, for instance (*is it true that all rich employees are over 50 and work in a department located in Rome?*):

$\forall RichEmp$ **as** r ($r.age > 50$ **and** *"Rome"* $\in r.WORKS\_IN.DEPT.LOC$)

The stack-based semantics makes no restriction in calling functions from inside of functions, i.e. to define a view through other views. Loqis makes it possible to define arbitrary stored functions (i.e. views), including functions with parameters (being arbitrary queries), with local objects, recursive, with side effects, and of higher-order (functions with parameters being functions). For example, the *WellPaid* function has a parameter *JobPar* and a local variable a:

```
function WellPaid( JobPar )
  begin
    real a := avg(EMP.SAL);
    return EMP where JOB = JobPar and SAL > 2*a;
  end;
```

Get companies where well-paid clerks used to work previously:

WellPaid(*"clerk"*)*.PREV_JOB.COMPANY*

Although the "algorithm" of computing the *WellPaid* function is indeed very simple, in general there are no limits on the complexity of an algorithm. Such general views can be useful when the mapping between stored and imaginary objects is complex; e.g. for resolving schematic discrepancies in heterogeneous database federations, for developing mediators, for semi-structured databases, for mappings between XML files and databases, etc.

5.1 VIEWS DEFINED BY JOINS

Similarly to the previous cases we can define views that stick two or more objects. For example, the function below defines imaginary objects *RichEmpRome*, which for rich employees from departments located in *Rome* contain the union of *EMP* and *DEPT* attributes:

```
function RichEmpRome
  begin return RichEmp | (WORKS_IN.DEPT where "Rome" ∈ LOC) end;
```

The function returns a bag of pairs of OIDs row$\{i_{EMP}, i_{DEPT}\}$ (for example, row$\{i_1, i_{16}\}$) simulating imaginary objects *RichEmpRome*. The query *RichEmpRome.(NAME, age, DNAME)* returns triples such as row$\{i_2, 45, i_{17}\}$, where 45 is calculated by the *age* method.

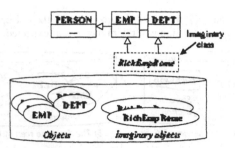

Figure 6. Imaginary class and imaginary objects

After inserting this function to the database the situation is as presented in Fig.6. The function defines imaginary objects *RichEmpRome* and virtually extends the class diagram by the imaginary class *RichEmpRome*, which inherits both from *EMP* and *DEPT* classes.

5.2 RESTRICTING, RENAMING AND ADDING ATTRIBUTES

In SBQL renaming view attributes does not require special syntactic and semantic features (unlike SQL). This fact is very important for the simplicity of the query modification algorithm. To this end we can apply the **as** operator. For example, the *RichEmpDept* view joins *EMP* and *DEPT* for employees earning over 2000; the view contains *NAME* renamed to *FirstName*, *DNAME* renamed to *Employer*, and *PrevJobsNbr*, which is the number of his/her previous jobs:

> **function** *RichEmpDept*
>   **begin**
>   **return** ((*EMP* **where** *SAL* > 2000) | (*WORKS_IN.DEPT*)).
>   (*NAME* **as** *FirstName*, *DNAME* **as** *Employer*, count(*PREV_JOB*) **as** *PrevJobsNbr*)
>   **end**;

Then, for instance, the user can ask the following query (*get the first name and the number of previous jobs for rich employees working in the Sales department*):

> (*RichEmpDept* **where** *Employer* = "*Sales*").(*FirstName*, *PrevJobsNbr*)

It is possible to combine identifiers of objects with newly defined attributes, for instance:

> **function** *RichEmpDname*
>   **begin**
>   **return** (*EMP* **where** *SAL*>2000) | ((*WORKS_IN.DEPT.DNAME*) **as** *Employer*)
>   **end**;

The function returns pairs row{i_{EMP}, *Employer*(i_{DNAME})}. Because such a pair contains the OID of an *EMP* object, thus the user can use all properties of *EMP* and *PERSON* classes, for instance (*get average age of rich Toys employees*):

> avg((*RichEmpDname* **where** *Employer* = "*Toys*").age)

Imaginary objects *RichEmpDname* form an imaginary class *RichEmpDname*, which can be considered a subclass of the *EMP* class with the additional attribute *Employer*.

5.3 VIRTUAL ATTRIBUTES AND VIRTUAL LINKS

So far we have presented functions stored at the same level as database objects. Hence, imaginary objects are considered database objects. Such functions can also be inserted into a class definition. In such a case they work as virtual attributes or virtual links. In the object-oriented literature they are called functional methods. Below we present an example.

Insert the virtual *NetSal* attribute into the *EMP* class; the net salary is calculated according to the formula *SAL* * (0.8 + 0.001 * *age*):

    function *NetSal* **begin return** *SAL* * (0.8 + 0.001 * *age*) **end**;

The function body refers directly to *SAL* and *age*, because it is executed in the environment of an *EMP* object, as shown in Fig.4. In object-oriented languages such names are usually preceded by pseudo-variables *self* or *this*. This is not required in our model (though not forbidden either). For example, we can ask now the following query (*get names of departments employing employees with the net salary lower than 70% of the average net salary*):

    distinct((*EMP* **where** *NetSal* < 0.7 * avg(*EMP.NetSal*)).*WORKS_IN.DEPT.DNAME*)

We can also define virtual links by inserting into a class definition a function returning references to objects. Unfortunately, current OODBMS-s do not store classes and methods as (persistent, dynamic) properties of a database, thus the described possibilities concern some future.

5.4 UPDATABLE VIEWS

The model that we have defined is already prepared for view updating. Because our views return references (to objects, attributes, links, etc.) we can use them as l-values in updating statements, for example (*increase by 100 the salary of all rich Rome employees*):

    RichEmpRome.(*SAL* := *SAL* + 100);

In SQL: **update** *RichEmpRome* set *SAL* = *SAL* + 100. However, such a straightforward approach implies undesirable effects. Correct translation and restriction of view updates is still a problem. The stack-based approach and considering views as stored functions enable deep investigations into correct translation of updates for powerful object views. The idea consists in defining (together with a view) additional procedures/methods, which overload generic updating operations acting on the view. Our results will be described in next papers.

6. Query Modification

Functions, which we have introduced as view definitions, have usually the following properties: they act on global data only (they do not introduce own local objects), they have no parameters, and they are dynamically bound. Such functions are semantically equivalent to macro-definitions. On the other hand, we have constructed our model in such a way that textual combination of queries with the *return* clause of such functions does not violate syntax/semantics/scoping. In effect, our query modification algorithm is extremely simple (in contrast to QUEL and SQL, where non-orthogonal syntax and underspecified semantics make algorithms complex and obscure). In our model this feature is already defined. We illustrate it by an example. Consider the query:

    (*RichEmpDept* **where** *Employer* = "*Sales*").*FirstName*

After textual substitution of *RichEmpDept* with the body of this function we obtain:

    ((((*EMP* **where** *SAL*>2000) | (*WORKS_IN.DEPT*)).
    (*NAME* **as** *FirstName*, *DNAME* **as** *Employer*, count(*PREV_JOB*) **as** *PrevJobsNbr*))
    where *Employer* = "*Sales*"). *FirstName*

We observe that the auxiliary name *PrevJobsNbr* is defined, but not used. Hence count(*PREV_JOB*) **as** *PrevJobsNbr*   forms a dead part, which can be removed. Similarly, the subquery (predicate) *Employer* = *"Sales"* can be factored outside the loops implied by the second **where** operator and the second dot operator (i.e. the selection is pushed before projection and join). In general, after query modification several rewriting rules can be applied (see [4,5,6]), in particular:

- Removing dead parts of queries;
- Factoring subqueries outside loops implied by non-algebraic operators, e.g. pushing selections before joins;
- Changing joins into less expensive dots;
- Removing auxiliary name definitions.

The result of these rewriting rules is the following:

((*EMP* **where** *SAL*>2000) | (*WORKS_IN.DEPT* **where** *DNAME* = *"Sales"*)).*NAME*

In many cases query modification opens the possibility to use indices, fast join algorithms and other access support structures and methods.

7. Conclusion

We have investigated object views and the application of the query modification technique to object views. It makes it possible to avoid severe performance penalty due to processing views. We have explained the method through the stack-based approach, a formal model of integrated query/programming languages for object bases. In this setting views are stored functions, and query modification is reduced to macro-substitution. We have shown that in comparison to other approaches our method makes it possible to define much more powerful views. We have also shown that queries resulted from query modification can be efficiently optimised by rewriting rules. Stored functions modelling views are already implemented in the Loqis prototype. Currently we extend this implementation, in particular, towards query modification and optimisation.

References

1. Abiteboul, S., Hull, R., Vianu, V. *Foundations of Databases*. Addison-Wesley, 1995.
2. Cluet, S. Designing OQL: allowing objects to be queried. *Information Systems*, 23(5), pp. 279-305, 1998.
3. ODMG Team. *The Object Database Standard ODMG, Release 2.0*. R.G.G. Cattel (ed.), Morgan Kaufmann, 1997.
4. Plodzien, J., Subieta, K. *Optimization of Object-Oriented Queries by Factoring Out Independent Subqueries*. Institute of Computer Science PAS, *Report 889*, Warsaw, 1999.
5. Plodzien, J., Kraken, A. Object query optimization in the stack-based approach. *Proceedings of ADBIS Conference*, Springer LNCS, **1691**, pp. 303-316, 1999.
6. Plodzien, J. *Optimization Methods in Object Query Languages*. PhD Thesis, Institute of Computer Science Polish Academy of Sciences, Warsaw, 2000.
7. Rupp, S. *A Critique of Release 2.0 of ODMG-93 Standard*. http://gameboy.gia.rwth-aachen.de/odmgbugs.
8. dos Santos, C. S. Design and implementation of object-oriented views. *Proceedings of DEXA Conference*, Springer LNCS, **978**, pp. 91-102, 1995.
9. Stonebraker, M. Implementation of integrity constraints and views by query modification. *Proceedings of SIGMOD Conference*, 1975.
10. Subieta, K. LOQIS: the object-oriented database programming system. *Proceedings of East/West Database Workshop*, Springer LNCS, **504**, pp. 403-421, 1991.
11. Subieta, K. Object-Oriented Standards: Can ODMG OQL be extended to a programming language? In *Cooperative Databases and Applications, World Scientific*, pp. 459-468, 1997.
12. Subieta, K., Kambayashi, Y., Leszczylowski, J. Procedures in object-oriented query languages. *Proceedings of VLDB Conference*, pp. 182-193, 1995.

On Materialising Object–Oriented Views[*]

Robert Wrembel

Poznań University of Technology, Institute of Computing Science
Piotrowo 3A, 60-965 Poznań, Poland
Robert.Wrembel@cs.put.poznan.pl

Abstract

The materialisation of views is an important technique for increasing efficiency in distributed database systems as well as in data warehousing systems. A lot of work has been done in the area of materialised relational views, while, to the best of our knowledge, much less work has been done to support object–oriented views materialisation and maintenance. In this paper we propose an approach to defining materialised object–oriented views. In our model an object–oriented view is defined as a view schema of an arbitrary complex structure and behaviour, composed of view classes. Each view class is derived from base classes by an OQL–like command. A view schema can be explicitly materialised, meaning that all the instances of view classes in this schema become persistent. Objects materialised in a view schema have to be consistent with their base objects. In order to maintain consistency between materialised view objects and objects in a database, we propose additional data structures that represent mappings between base and view classes as well as between their instances.

Keywords: object–oriented database, object–oriented view, view schema, view materialisation, maintenance of materialised views.

1. Introduction

Views in database systems are important mechanisms which provide among others: logical data independence, simplification of a database schema, shorthand for queries, and which are used for hiding data and implementing security policies. In distributed systems and in data warehousing systems views are used as means for the integration of data coming from remote sources as well as means for the materialisation of data in order to: (1) speed up access to information and (2) speed up the execution of complex analytical queries cf. [9, 16].

Contemporary database systems used in such areas as: CAD, CAM, CASE, GIS, CSCW, multimedia, and expert systems must support data models allowing to model objects of a complex structure and behaviour. This requirement can not be fulfilled by relational databases that are suitable for storing and processing simple data (mainly strings and numbers). For this reason, object–oriented databases (in central and distributed architectures) are used more and more frequently for modelling, storing, and processing data of complex structure (e.g. program codes, diagrams, and video sequences). In these database systems, object–oriented views are used for the same purposes as in traditional relational systems. However, while constructing object–oriented views we face open research problems concerning: (1) the design of such views that would be able to control data visibility, logical data independence, and would reflect the complexity of data, (2) techniques of object–oriented views materialisation, in order to increase systems efficiency, and (3)

---

[*] This work is supported by the grant No. 8T11C01018 from the State Committee for Scientific Research (KBN), Poland.

15

J. Barzdins and A. Caplinskas (eds.), Databases and Information Systems, 15–28.

the maintenance algorithms of such materialised views.

Several approaches to object–oriented views were proposed in scientific publications (reviews can be found in [15, 21]). However, none of them supports all the features of an object–oriented view detailed above. Consequently, the existing approaches can be applied only to a limited range of problems. As it concerns materialised object–oriented views, only few approaches exist. However, the main problem of maintaining consistency between source and materialised data in a view has been partially covered only in [12, 13].

In [22] we have defined a formal model of an object–oriented database with materialised views. In our model an *object–oriented view* is defined as a *view schema* that is composed of view classes. Each *view class* is derived from one or more base classes, i.e. classes in a database schema, called *base schema*. View classes in a view schema are connected by inheritance and aggregation relationships. The structure, behaviour, and the set of instances of a view class are defined by an OQL–like command. Several view schemas can be created from the same base schema. In order to check whether a given view schema is defined correctly we proposed the three following consistency criteria: (1) completeness with respect to types used to define view classes, called *structural closure*, (2) completeness with respect to methods calls and types used in methods, called *behavioural closure*, and (3) *inheritance hierarchy correctness* [24].

In this paper, however, we concentrate on the issues concerning: (1) the materialisation of object–oriented views with respect to the structure of objects and (2) the consistency maintenance of such views. Each view schema can be explicitly materialised, meaning that the instances of the underlying view classes become persistent. In order to maintain consistency between materialised views and a database we propose additional data structures that represent mappings between classes in a database schema and view classes in different view schemas, as well as between the instances of these classes. These structures are used to propagate updates performed on base objects only to these view objects that are really affected by the updates.

This paper is organised as follows: section 2 discusses related approaches to object–oriented views with respect to their materialisation and maintenance. Section 3 outlines our concept of views, whereas section 4 deals with the materialisation of view schemas and the maintenance of their consistency. Section 5 summarises the paper and points out the subjects for future work.

2. Related Work

Several approaches to object–oriented views were proposed in scientific publications (see [15, 21] for an overview). In the majority of these approaches a view is defined as a *virtual class* derived from one or more classes [20, 10, 1, 19, 5, 14, 2, 18, 6, 11]. The approaches of *MultiView* [17] and *eXoT/C* [7] consider a view as a more complex structure, i.e. a schema. In *MultiView* a view is defined as a portion of a database schema containing virtual as well as base classes. In *eXoT/C* a view, called *external schema*, is composed of derived classes only but the *eXoT/C* views can reference base classes in domains of attributes and method calls.

When views are used in a distributed environment or in data warehousing it may be desirable to materialise their contents for the reason of efficiency, rather than compute them on demand. Materialising data requires mechanisms that will propagate modifications of a database to materialised views. A lot of work has been done to maintain relational materialised views, where efficiency is achieved by using *incremental propagation* (refer to [9, 16] for an overview). While, to the best of our knowledge, much less work has been done to support object–oriented views materialisation [14, 8] and maintenance [12, 13].

The approach of [14] allows to materialise view classes and proposes the materialisation procedure, but does not consider views maintenance. Furthermore, the materialisation procedure is not described in detail. In [8] an arbitrary portion of a source database schema can be replicated (together with associated class instances) into a materialised view, called replica. The system automatically generates a replica schema that is closed, minimal, and well formed. However, it does not keep consistency between a database and replicas. The *MultiView* system [12, 13] supports incremental view maintenance. But the system materialises only pointers to base objects, and therefore it is not suitable neither for distributed databases nor for data warehousing systems, where integrated data should be stored/materialised locally for the reason of efficiency, rather than accessed remotely.

3. The Concept of Object–Oriented View Schemas

In our work we draw on the model of an object–oriented database, presented in [3], which we extended by the following concepts supporting object–oriented views, their materialisation and maintenance: (1) view class, (2) view object, (3) view schema, (4) mappings between database schema and views, and (5) mappings between objects in a database and those in views.

An *object–oriented view* is defined as a *view schema* of an arbitrary complex structure and behaviour. A view schema is composed of view classes. Each *view class* is derived from one or more *base classes*, i.e. classes in a database schema, called *base schema*. A view class is derived by an OQL–like command. View classes in a view schema are connected by inheritance and aggregation relationships. Several view schemas can be created from the same base schema.

In our approach a view schema has to be totally separated from its base schema, i.e. we neither allow to reference base classes from a view schema nor call from a view schema the methods defined in a base schema. The reason for this separation is that a view schema composed of both view classes and base classes or a view schema that uses methods defined in a base schema has two serious drawbacks. Firstly, such a view schema does not provide a strong mechanism for hiding data, as a user can navigate through aggregation links to base schema and further following these links read large parts of base objects. Secondly, a view schema does not provide full logical data independence because there is no separation between external schema (i.e. view) and logical schema (cf. [22]).

Several view schemas may be defined in one database and each of them is uniquely identified by its name. A view schema is derived in the four following steps: (1) the creation of a new empty view schema, (2) the derivation of view classes and their integration in the view schema, (3) the rewriting of methods in the context of a view schema elements, and (4) the consistency checking of a view schema (the detail information on view schema creation can be found in [23, 24]). In order to create a new view schema the following command is used:

create view schema vs_name;

Example 1. Let us consider a base schema composed of five classes: *RAM_Chip*, *RAM_Slot*, *Processor*, *Disk_Controller*, and *Main_Board* (cf. figure 1). Class *Main_Board* is composed of *Processor*, *Disk_Controller*, and *RAM_Slot*. *RAM_Slot* is a tuple of two collections (attributes *bank0* and *bank1*) with the domain of *RAM_Chip*. Each collection has two elements. All classes have methods computing the consumption of energy by each component.

From this schema two view schemas were derived, namely *VS1* and *VS2*. The former is composed of three view classes: *V_MB_Intel_CPU*, *V_Processor*, and *V_RAM_Slot*, whereas the latter is composed of only one view class *V_MB_Cyrix_CPU*.

View class *V_RAM_Slot* was derived from two base classes *RAM_Slot* and *RAM_Chip*. *V_RAM_Slot* merges information from its base classes, i.e. it takes some attributes from *RAM_Slot* as well as from *RAM_Chip*. Therefore, two derivation links connect this view class with its base classes.

View class *V_Processor* was derived from base class *Processor*. *V_MB_Intel_CPU* was derived from two base classes, namely *Main_Board* and *Disk_Controller*, with the predicate allowing to access only these main boards that use Intel processors, i.e. *cpu.type='Intel'*. *V_MB_Intel_CPU* merges information from its both base classes, i.e. it takes some attributes from *Main_Board* as well as from *Disk_Controller*. Therefore, two derivation links connect *V_MB_Intel_CPU* with base classes *Main_Board* and *Disk_Controller*. View class *V_MB_Intel_CPU* is additionally composed of *V_Processor* and *V_RAM_Slot*.

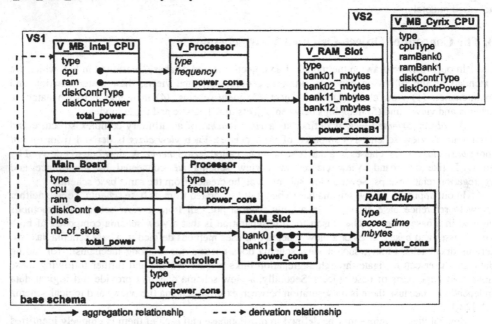

Figure 1. The example of a database schema and view schemas

The second view schema (*VS2*) is composed of only one view class *V_MB_Cyrix_CPU* that merges information from all classes in the base schema and it was derived with the predicate *cpu.type='Cyrix'*.

A view class is derived and placed in a selected view schema by the following OQL–like command:

```
create view class vc_name
[structure
        (tuple of (attribute₁:type, ..., attributeₙ:type) |
        set of (type) |
        array of [type] ) ]
[behaviour (method₁, ..., methodₙ)] | [no method]
[augment behaviour (methodⱼ:type, ..., methodⱼ:type)]
[superclass of cl_name]
[subclass of cl_name]
with
    {(populating query (object-oriented query)) |
     (conversion function cf_name)}
[persistence root pr_name]
in view schema vs_name;
```

The structure of a view class is inferred from the *select* clause of the *with populating query* clause, by default. Otherwise the structure has to be defined explicitly using the *structure* clause. A view class can have one of the three structures: either tuple or set or array (keywords *tuple of*, *set of*, *array of*, respectively).

None of the methods originally defined in a base class is added to a view class by default (*no method* clause is the default one). A database designer can include in a view class the methods selected from the base class, by placing their names in the *behaviour* clause (optional). As in our approach a view schema is separated from a database schema, included methods need redefinition so that these methods reference view classes rather than base classes (see [23] for details). The behaviour of a view class can be augmented by adding new methods. To this end, the signatures of new methods are placed in the *augment behaviour* clause (optional). The implementations of included methods as well as new methods are added to view classes by command *alter view class* (omitted here due to space limitations).

A view class can be made explicitly a super– or subclass of another view class. For this purpose, we use the *superclass of* and *subclass of* clauses, respectively. Omitting these clauses results in placing a view class as a subclass of the *ViewObject* class that is the root of inheritance hierarchy in a view schema.

Clause *with populating query*, apart from allowing to define the structure of a view class, is used also to define the set of instances of a view class. However, in case of a view class that performs complex restructuring of base data, e.g. merges/joins data coming from several base classes, the only way to populate such a view class with objects might be to define a conversion function that converts base objects to the new structure. In order to point out this function, clause *conversion function* is used, where *cf_name* is the name of the conversion function. A conversion function is implemented by a database designer. Implementation of a conversion function is added to a view class definition by using command *alter view class*.

The object–oriented query and conversion functions operate on roots of persistence attached to base classes. The *root of persistence* is a schema element that attributes persistence to objects. An object becomes persistent only when: (1) it is explicitly attached to the root of persistence or (2) it is referenced by another persistent object (cf. [4]), otherwise an object is temporary. This policy has two main advantages: (1) different instances of a given class may be temporary or persistent and (2) objects persistence is independent of a class definition. Optional clause *persistence root* defines the root of persistence for storing the instances of a view class when the class is materialised (see section 4).

4. View Schema Materialisation

4.1 BASIC CONCEPT

Instances of a view class are called *view objects*. View objects provided by a view schema are not persistent by default and they are recomputed each time the application (query) addresses this schema. A given view schema can be explicitly materialised, meaning that: (1) the instances of these view classes that have attached the roots of persistence become persistent and (2) the instances referenced by other persistent instances also become persistent. In order to materialise a view schema the following command is used:

materialise view schema vs_name;

In our approach we use the object generating semantics of all view classes, i.e. the instances of each view class are newly created objects and each view object is assigned new *view object identifier – vOid*. This policy is required when performing complex restructuring of base objects in a view class. Furthermore, object generation is suitable for materialising instances of view classes.

A view class can be a *component* of a *composite* view class. For example, *V_Processor* is the component of *V_MB_Intel_CPU*. A component view class that does not have the root of persistence attached to it (created without clause **persistence root**) is called *dependent component* and a view class that has an attached root of persistence (created with clause **persistence root**) is called *independent component*. Similarly, the instances of materialised dependent view class are called *dependent component view objects*, whereas the instances of materialised independent view class are called *independent component view objects*. Dependent component object can exist only when it is the part of a composite object, whereas independent component object can exist without any composite object.

Example 2. As an example let us consider the following command creating view class *V_Processor*.

```
create view class V_Processor
behaviour (power_cons:number)
with populating query
    (select p.type, p.frequency from p in RP_Processors where p.type='Intel')
persistence root VRP_Processors
in view schema VS1;
```

View class *V_Processor* is an independent component class whose instances are stored in the root of persistence *VRP_Processors*. This view class is populated by an OQL query returning all the Intel's instances of *Processor*. The instances of base class *Processor* are stored in the root of persistence *RP_Processors*.

4.2 ADDITIONAL DATA STRUCTURES

In order to propagate changes from base objects to their materialised counterparts in view schemas two additional data structures have to be maintained by the system. These structures, which are described below, are called *Class Mapping Structure* and *Object Mapping Structure*.

4.2.1 Class Mapping Structure

When view classes are derived from a given base class *C*, the system maintains links, called *derivation links*, between *C* and all view classes that were derived from it. The structure used to store derivation links is called *Class Mapping Structure*. It is used while:
- creating the instances of a view class (cf. section 4.3);
- propagating changes from base to materialised view objects (cf. section 4.4).

Class Mapping Structure (shortly *CMS*) is defined as the set of tuples having four fields. The first field stores the name of a base class *C*, the second field stores the array of attribute names of *C* that are used in the definition of view class *V*. The third field stores the name of view class *V* derived from *C* and the fourth field stores the array of attribute names used in *V*. This way *CMS* provides the mapping between not only base and view classes but also between base and view class attribute names. The name of each view class is proceeded with the view schema name in which this view class was placed.

In order to find mappings between base class *C* and view class *V* created from it, *CMS* is examined by the system function *CMS_Get_View_Class*. This function expects two input arguments. The first one is the name of a base class, whereas the second one is the name of a view schema. *CMS_Get_View_Class* returns the name of a view class created in an indicated view schema, from indicated base class *C* or *null* when no mapping is found.

Example 3. After the derivation of view class *V_Processor* (in view schema *VS1*) from *Processor* (cf. figure 1) the *CMS* has one record:

```
(Processor, [type, frequency], VS1.V_Processor, [type, frequency])
```

While the derivation of view class *V_MB_Intel_CPU* from base classes *Disk_Controller* and *Main_Board* results in two further records in **CMS**:

```
(Disk_Contorller, [type, power], VS1.V_MB_Intel_CPU,
     [diskContrType, diskContrPower])

(Main_Board, [type, cpu, ram, diskContr.type, diskContr.power],
     VS1.V_MB_Intel_CPU, [type, cpu, ram, diskContrType, diskContrPower])
```

as two base classes, i.e. *Main_Board* and *Disk_Controller*, are used to define *V_MB_Intel_CPU*. The aggregation relationships between *Main_Board* and *Disk_Controller* were replaced in a view class *V_MB_Intel_CPU* with two attributes *diskContrType* and *diskContrPower* and this is also reflected in the **CMS**.

CMS is used to check whether an update to the value of a base object needs propagation to materialised view objects. An update to the value of attribute *a* of the instance of base class *C* needs propagation if there exists at least one such a view class derived from *C* that uses attribute *a* as the source of values of its own attribute. In other words, an update needs propagation to the instances of a view class if the **CMS** contains the mapping record between *a* and an attribute of a view class. Otherwise the propagation is not performed. This checking is done by the function *Check_Attribute_Mapping* with the signature presented below.

```
Check_Attribute_Mapping (C : string, a : string, V : string) return boolean
```

The function takes three following arguments: the name of a base class (*C*), the name of attribute (*a*) of a base class, and the name of a view class (*V*). *Check_Attribute_Mapping* returns *true* if attribute a_i of base class C_i is mapped in view class V_i. Otherwise it returns *false*.

Updates are propagated from the instances of a base class to materialised view objects by using a conversion function (cf. section 4.3 and 4.4).

Example 4. Let us assume that there exist several instances of base class *Main_Board*. These instance are identified by object identifiers: mb_1, mb_2, ... mb_n. Let us further assume that some of these instances were materialised in view class *V_MB_Intel_CPU*. After updating the value of attribute *cpu* of base objects, the system examines the *Class Mapping Structure* in order to find such a view class derived from *Main_Board*, that maps *cpu* to its own attribute. There is only one such a view class in our example (cf. figure 1), namely *V_MB_Intel_CPU*. Updates are propagated to the materialised instances of this view class. On the contrary, when the value of attribute *bios* is updated, the propagation is not performed as no view class uses this attribute, i.e. there is no mapping of *bios* in **CMS**.

Updates of base object o_i should be propagated only to those view objects that were created from o_i. Therefore, one important issue that must be solved is the identification of these materialised view objects that are affected by the update of o_i. To this end the *Object Mapping Structure* is used.

4.2.2 Object Mapping Structure

Object Mapping Structure (**OMS** for short) provides the mapping between a base object and all view objects created from it. The **OMS** is created and maintained by the system for each base class C_i. All view classes derived from C_i also have access to **OMS**. This structure is organised as the set of tuples where the first field stores base object identifier (*oid*) and the second field stores the set of all view object identifiers (*vOid*) created from this base object.

The system examines the content of a given *Object Mapping Structure* while:
- checking whether a component view object has already been created from a given base

object, during the process of creating a view composite object (see section 4.3);
- propagating changes from base to view objects (see section 4.4).

In order to find mappings between base object o_i and all view objects created from it, **OMS** is examined by the system function *OMS_Get_View_Object*. This function expects two input arguments. The first one is the identifier of a base object, whereas the second one is the view schema name. *OMS_Get_View_Object* returns a view object identifier created in an indicated view schema from indicated base object or *null* when no mapping is found.

OMS can also be used while propagating updates of view objects back to base objects, however, in this paper we do not consider view updates and their propagation to base objects.

Example 5. As an example let us consider the fragment of the base schema and the view schema from figure 1, where only the relevant classes, roots of persistence, and objects are shown. Base class *Main_Board* has attached the root of persistence *RP_Main_Boards* that stores objects identified by mb_1, mb_2, and mb_3. Similarly, the instances of *Disk_Controller* and *Processor* are stored in roots *RP_Controllers* and *RP_Processors*, respectively (cf. figure 2).

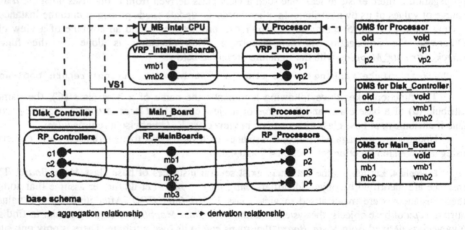

Figure 2. Base and view class objects and the corresponding *Object Mapping Structures*

View class *V_Processor* was derived from *Processor*. The former has two materialised instances, namely objects identified by vp_1 and vp_2, stored in the root of persistence *VRP_Processors*. View object vp_1 was created from p_1 and vp_2 was created from p_2. This information is stored in *Object Mapping Structure*, called *OMS for Processor* (cf. figure 3). View class *V_MB_Intel_CPU* merges information from two base classes, namely *Disk_Controller* and *Main_Board*. This view class has two instances, identified by vmb_1 and vmb_2, stored in the root of persistence *VRP_IntelMainBoards*. The value of vmb_1 comes from two base objects c_1 and mb_1, whereas the value of vmb_2 comes from c_2 and mb_2. Therefore, *OMS for Disk_Contorller* contains mapping from c_1 to vmb_1 and *OMS for Main_Board* contains mapping from mb_1 to vmb_1 (similarly for c_2 and mb_2). Base objects that do not have their counterparts in view objects do not appear in any of the *Object Mapping Structure*.

4.3 THE CREATION OF VIEW OBJECTS

The creation of the instances of a view class will be further called *view class instantiation*. View objects are created starting from these component view classes that are the leaves of aggregation hierarchy and that are defined by using the **with populating query** clause. All the instances of a view class V_i defined with this clause are returned by a query and appropriate object mapping structures of base classes of V_i are filled with mapping records. Whereas the instances of the view class that was defined by using the **with conversion function** clause are created only when appropriate composite objects are created that own the component objects.

4.3.1 Conversion function

A view class allows also to perform the restructuring of objects from a database, e.g. a view class can merge (join) several base classes. In such a case, a simple select command defining the structure, behaviour, and the set of view objects may not be sufficient. To perform advanced restructuring of base objects in a view class, a database designer uses clauses **structure**, **augment structure**, **augment behaviour**, and **with conversion function** (cf. section 3). The only way to instantiate such a view class might be to define a conversion function that creates view objects by restructuring base objects. A conversion function is defined by a database designer and it is associated with a view class. A conversion function is also used while propagating updates from base objects to view objects.

Example 6. Let us consider two commands presented below that create view classes *V_RAM_Slot* and *V_MB_Intel_CPU*.

a)
```
create view class V_RAM_Slot
structure tuple of
      [type:string,
      slot1_mbytes:number,
      slot2_mbytes:number,
      slot3_mbytes:number,
      slot4_mbytes:number,
      power:number]
with conversion function
      CF_V_RAM_Slot
in view schema VS1;
```

b)
```
create view class V_MB_Intel_CPU
structure tuple of
      [type:string,
      cpu:V_Processor,
      ram:V_RAM_Slot,
      diskContrType:string,
      diskContrPower:number]
augment behaviour
      (total_power:number)
with conversion function
      CF_V_MB_Intel_CPU
persistence root VRP_IntelMainBoards
in view schema VS1;
```

Conversion function *CF_V_RAM_Slot* transforms each composite instance of *RAM_Slot*, that is composed of the instances of *RAM_Chip* (cf. figure 1), into an object of structure *V_RAM_Slot*. *V_RAM_Slot* is a dependent component view class whose instances can exist only in the context of the instance of *V_MB_Intel_CPU*. There is no need to represent in a view class all the instances of *RAM_Slot* and only those *V_RAM_Slot* objects are created that belong to these main boards that use Intel processors. The instances of *V_RAM_Slot* become persistent while referenced by persistent instances of *V_MB_Intel_CPU*.

The relevant fragment of the pseudo–code of conversion function *CF_V_RAM_Slot* is presented below. This conversion function takes three arguments. The first one is a base object identifier (*ram* of type *RAM_Slot*), i.e. the instance of *RAM_Slot* from which a view object will be created. The second argument is a flag indicating whether a new view object is to be created from a given base object or whether updates of a given base object are to be propagated to an appropriate view object. The third argument is the name of a view schema (*VS* of type string) in which a view class was placed. *CF_V_RAM_Slot* returns the identifier of a newly created *V_RAM_Slot* instance. The conversion function is invoked from the conversion function creating a composite object, i.e. the instance of *V_MB_Intel_CPU*.

```
CF_V_RAM_Slot (ram : RAM_Slot, flag : string, VS : string)
                return vram : V_RAM_Slot
{
  vram : V_RAM_Slot;
  if flag='creating' then
                          /* if the instantiation of V_RAM_Slot is required */
  {
    vram : create new instance of V_RAM_Slot in view schema VS;
    vram.type:=ram.bank0[1].type;
    vram.bank01_mbytes:=ram.bank0[1].mbytes;
    vram.bank02_mbytes:=ram.bank0[2].mbytes;
    vram.bank11_mbytes:=ram.bank1[1].mbytes;
    vram.bank12_mbytes:=ram.bank1[2].mbytes;
    return (vram);
  }
  if flag='propagating' then ...
                          /* if the propagation of updates is required */
}
```

Due to space limitations the propagation part of a conversion function is omitted.

The creation of a composite view object is more complicated as it needs the look up to the *Object Mapping Structure* in order to find out whether a component view object has already been created. Let us consider a composite base object identified by oid_1, that is composed of another independent component object, identified by oid_{11} (cf. figure 3). Let us assume further that the view object identified by $vOid_{11}$ was created from oid_{11}. When a composite view object is created from oid_1 it has to be composed of $vOid_{11}$ because oid_1 is originally composed of oid_{11}, from which in turn $vOid_{11}$ was created. To find the mapping between oid_{11} and $vOid_{11}$ the appropriate *Object Mapping Structure* is examined by the function *OMS_Get_View_Object*.

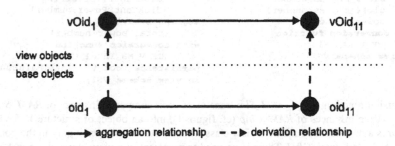

Figure 3. Mappings between base and view composite objects

Example 7. As an example illustrating the creation of a composite view object and the usage of function *OMS_Get_View_Object* let us consider the command creating view class *V_MB_Intel_CPU*, presented in example 6b. The instances of base class *Main_Board* are transformed to the structure of view class *V_MB_Intel_CPU* by conversion function *CF_V_MB_Intel_CPU*. This conversion function takes three arguments. The first one is a base object identifier (*mb* of type *Main_Board*), i.e. the instance of *Main_Board* from which a view object will be created. The second one is a flag indicating whether a new view object is to be created or whether updates are to be propagated to an appropriate view object. The third argument is the name of a view schema (*VS* of type string) in which a view class was placed. *CF_V_MB_Intel_CPU* returns the identifier of a newly created *V_MB_Intel_CPU* instance. The relevant fragment of the conversion function is presented below.

```
CF_V_MB_Intel_CPU (mb : Main_Board, flag : string, VS : string)
                  return vmb : V_MB_Intel_CPU
{
  vmb : V_MB_Intel_CPU;
  if flag='creating' then
  {
    vmb := create new instance of V_MB_Intel_CPU in view schema VS;
    vmb.type := mb.type;
     /* find the instance of V_Processor that was created
        from the processor pointed by mb.cpu */
    vmb.cpu := OMS_Get_View_Object(mb.cpu, VS);
     /* a call to the conversion function in order to create the instance
        of V_RAM_Slot in view schema VS*/
    vmb.ram := CF_V_RAM_Slot (mb.ram, 'creating', VS);
    vmb.diskContrType := mb.diskContr.type;
    vmb.diskContrPower := mb.diskContr.power;
    return (vmb);
  }
  else ... then ... /* if the propagation of updates takes place */
}
```

Let us assume that the instances of view class *V_Processor* have already been created and the *OMS for Processor* structure has been filled with the records presented in figure 2. When creating the instance of *V_MB_Intel_CPU* from base object mb_1 the system checks (using function *OMS_Get_View_Object*) whether an appropriate view instance of *V_Processor* was created. To this end it uses the *OMS for Processor* structure. As mb_1 is composed of p_1, the system checks which view object is mapped to p_1 – in our example it is vp_1. Next, vp_1 is referenced from view object vmb_1 created from mb_1.

The instances of a view schema are not persistent by default. As the result of issuing command **materialise view schema**, the instances of view classes belonging to the indicated view schema are made persistent, i.e. they are attached to appropriate roots of persistence (cf. section 4.1).

4.4 PROPAGATION OF UPDATES FROM BASE TO VIEW OBJECTS

View objects in a materialised view schema have to be kept up to date with their corresponding base objects. The framework that we developed allows to propagate updates to each view object immediately after the transaction updating the corresponding base object commits. Updates are propagated by the procedure *Propagate_Updates*, described below. It takes three input arguments. The first one (oid_{iCi} of type OID) is the identifier of an updated base object, the second one (C_i of type string) is the name of the base class whose instance was updated, and the third one (*attributes* of type set of string) is the set of attributes of C_i whose values were updated. This set can be empty in case when a base object is created or deleted.

```
Propagate_Updates (oid_{ici}: OID,
                   C_i : string,
                   attributes : set of string)
{
  vo_{ij} : OID;        // variable holding view object identifier
  V_i : string;         // variable holding view class name
  VS_i : string;        // variable holding view schema name
  a_i : string;         // variable holding attribute name
  prop_upd : boolean;   // flag indicating whether update propagation
                        // is required
  if created then       // if a new base object was created
```

```
{
   for each view schema VSᵢ do
   {
      /* get the name of a view class mapped to Cᵢ in view schema VSᵢ */
      Vᵢ := CMS_Get_View_Class (Ci, VSᵢ);
      /* create view object from oidᵢcᵢ using appropriate conversion function
         for view class Vᵢ in view schema VSᵢ */
      voᵢⱼ := CF_V_Vᵢ(oidᵢcᵢ, 'creating', VSᵢ);
      attach voᵢⱼ to the root of persistence of Vᵢ;
      insert into OMS for Cᵢ the mapping information between oidᵢcᵢ and voᵢⱼ;
   }
}
if deleted then   /* if a base object was deleted */
{
   for each view schema VSᵢ do
   {
      voᵢⱼ := OMS_Get_View_Object (oidᵢcᵢ, VSᵢ);
      delete voᵢⱼ;
      remove from OMS for Cᵢ the mapping information between oidᵢcᵢ and voᵢⱼ;
   }
}
if updated then   /* if a base object was updated */
{
   for each view schema VSᵢ do
   {
      prop_upd := false;
      for each aᵢ in attributes do
      {
         if Check_Attribute_Mapping(Cᵢ, aᵢ, CMS_Get_View_Class (Cᵢ, VSᵢ)) then
         /* if a mapping between attribute aᵢ (of base class Cᵢ) and an attribute
            of view class Vᵢ is found then updates need propagation */
         prop_upd := true;
      }
      if prop_upd then
      {
         voᵢⱼ := CF_V_Vᵢ(oidᵢcᵢ, 'propagating', VSᵢ);}
         /* propagate updates to the instance of view class Vᵢ in view schema VSᵢ
            by using conversion function */
      }
   }
}
```

5. Summary, Conclusions, and Future Work

In this paper we proposed a framework for object–oriented view materialisation and maintenance. In our approach a view schema can be materialised on demand. In order to maintain the consistency of materialised view objects we proposed two kinds of structures, namely *Class Mapping Structure* and *Object Mapping Structure*. These structures allow to propagate the updates of base objects only to these materialised view objects that are really affected by base objects modifications.

In our approach we have not dealt with view updates so far, because we are aiming at the application of our concept of view schemas for data integration in data warehousing systems, where view updates are rare. However, the propagation of updates from view to base objects would be feasible by:
   • using the information stored in *Object Mapping Structure* associated with a base class,

- extending the model of the view schemas so that backward update propagation functions could be defined for view classes by a view designer.

Our framework for materialised object–oriented views allows to maintain the consistency of different kinds of view classes defined by: selection of base objects that fulfil the criteria, projection of base class attributes, joining (merging) several base classes in a view class, and set operators. The framework has to be extended in order to allow the maintenance of aggregate view classes. The framework that we developed is suitable for implementing immediate propagation of updates from base to view objects, but it can be extended to support also on demand propagation. On demand propagation needs some additional structures containing among others the information about: changes made to base objects, already performed propagation, and propagation that need to be performed.

The propagation of changes from base to view objects requires look–ups to *Class* and *Object Mapping Structures*. Accessing them and searching for the information consume additional time, slowing down the propagation process. However, indexing techniques will be used to reduce the time of searching for information. The second element where the update propagation can be slowed down is the propagation function defined for a view class, so a view designer is responsible for defining an efficient conversion function.

The update of a base object has to be detected in order to start the propagation of this update to view objects. In order to detect the update immediately, a database system has to posses active capabilities, e.g. the mechanism of triggers. Otherwise, any modification of a base object has to be performed by an additional software layer (application), that will be responsible for detecting changes in base objects.

The most advanced approaches to object–oriented views are the following: *MultiView* [17, 12, 13] and [8]. Our approach differs from *MultiView* in the concept of view definition and materialisation. In *MultiView*, view classes are integrated into a base schema, whereas in our approach a view schema is totally separated from its base schema. Thanks to this separation we achieved two goals. Firstly, a view schema provides logical data independence and secondly, a view schema is suitable for controlling access to a database. Furthermore, view materialisation in *MutliView* results in the materialisation of pointers to base objects, whereas in our approach new objects are created as the instances of view classes. For this reason, the approach to object–oriented views that we developed is more suitable for application in distributed systems and in data warehousing systems. Our approach is similar to the one used in [8] as both allow to define a view as a separate schema of an arbitrary complex structure and behaviour. However, our approach considers also the maintenance of materialised views which is not the case of [8].

The issues that need further investigation are as follows:
- the extension of the proposed framework for view materialisation and maintenance by mechanisms allowing:
  - the consistency maintenance of aggregate views (defined using summaries, averages, etc.);
  - the support for on demand propagation;
  - the support for the materialisation of methods results and the maintenance of these materialised results;
- the implementation of our framework and the experimental evaluation of update propagation algorithms;
- the tuning of the propagation algorithm as well as *Class* and *Object Mapping Structure* in order to reduce time spent on accessing data stored in these structures.

References

1. Abiteboul, S., Bonner, A. Object and views. *Proceedings of the ACM SIGMOD Conference on Management of Data*, 1991, pp. 238-247.
2. Agrawal, R., DeMichiel, L. G. Type derivation using the projection operation. *Proceedings of Advances in Database Technology (EDBT'94)*, 1994, pp. 7-14.
3. Abiteboul, S., Hull, R., Vianu, V. *Foundation of Databases*. Addison–Wesley Publishing Company, 1995.
4. Bancillon, F., Delobel, C., Kannellakis, P. (eds.). *Building an Object–Oriented Database System – The Story of O2*. Morgan Kaufmann Pub., 1992.
5. Bertino, E. A view mechanism for object-oriented databases. *Proceedings of Advances in Database Technology (EDBT'92)*, 1992, pp. 136-151.
6. Busse, R., Fankhauser, P., Neuhold, E. J. Federated schemata in ODMG. *Proceedings of Second Int. East/West Database Workshop*, Workshops in Computing, 1995, pp. 330-352.
7. Dobrovnik, M., Eder, J. Logical data independence and modularity through views in OODBMS. *Proceedings of Engineering Systems Design and Analysis Conference*, 1996.
8. Dobrovnik, M., Eder, J. Partial replication of object–oriented databases. *Proceedings of Second East-European Conference on Advances in Databases and Information Systems – ADBIS'98*. Poland, 1998, LNCS, **1475**, pp. 260-271.
9. Gupta, A., Mumick, I. S. Maintenance of materialized views: problems, techniques, and applications. *Data Engineering Bulletin*, **18**(2), 1995, pp. 3-18.
10. Heiler, S., Zdonik, S. Object views: extending the vision. *Proceedings of Int. Conf. on Data Engineering*, 1990, pp. 86-93.
11. Kim, W., Kelley, W. On view support in object-oriented database systems. In W. Kim (ed.), *Modern Database Systems, The Object Model, Interoperability, and Beyond*, Addison–Wesley Publishing Company, 1995, pp. 108-126.
12. Kuno, H. A., Rundensteiner, E. Materialised object-oriented views in MultiView. *Proceedings of the ACM Research Issues in Data Engineering Workshop*, 1995.
13. Kuno, H. A., Rundensteiner, E. Using object-oriented principles to optimize update propagation to materialised views. *Proceedings of Int. Conf. on Data Engineering*, 1996, pp. 310-317.
14. Liu, K. W., Spooner, D. Object-oriented database views for supporting multidisciplinary concurrent engineering. *Proceedings of Int. Conf. on Data Engineering*, 1993, pp. 19-25.
15. Motschnig–Pitrik, R. Requirements and comparison of view mechanisms for object-oriented databases. *Information Systems*, **21**(3), 1996, pp. 229-252.
16. Roussopoulos, N. Materialized views and data warehouses. *SIGMOD Record*, **27**(1), 1998, pp. 21-26.
17. Rundensteiner, E. MultiView: a methodology for supporting multiple view schemata in object-oriented databases. *Proceedings of VLDB*, 1992, pp. 187-198.
18. dos Santos, C. S., Delobel, C., Abiteboul, S. Virtual schemas and bases. *Proceedings of Advances in Database Technology (EDBT'94)*, 1994, pp. 335-354.
19. Scholl, M. H., Laasch, C., Tresch, M. Updatable views in object-oriented databases. *Proceedings of Int. Conf. Deductive and Object–Oriented Databases*, 1991, LNCS, **566**, pp. 189-207.
20. Tanaka, K., Yoshikawa, M., Ishihara, K. Schema virtualization in object–oriented databases. *Proceedings of Int. Conf. on Data Engineering*, 1988, pp. 23-30.
21. Wrembel, R. Object–oriented views: virtues and limitations. *Proceedings of the 13th International Symposium on Computer and Information Sciences – ISCIS'98*, Turkey, 1998, pp. 228-235.
22. Wrembel, R. On a formal model of an object–oriented database with views supporting data materialisation. *Proceedings (of short papers) of Third East-European Conference on Advances in Databases and Information Systems - ADBIS'99*, Slovenia, 1999, pp. 109-116.
23. Wrembel, R. *Deriving Consistent View Schemas in an Object–Oriented Database* (extended version). Research report, Poznan (Poland) University of Technology, Institute of Computing Science, No. RA–007/99.
24. Wrembel, R. Deriving consistent view schemas in an object-oriented database. *Proceedings of the 14th International Symposium on Computer and Information Sciences – ISCIS'99*, Turkey, 1999, pp. 803-810.

Indexing on Multivalued Attributes:
Partial-Order Trees vs. Bitmaps

Krzysztof Goczyla

Technical University of Gdańsk, Department of Applied Informatics,
G. Narutowicza 11/12, PL-80952 Gdańsk, Poland
E-mail: kris@pg.gda.pl

Abstract

The paper presents two methods of indexing on attributes whose values are sets of primitive values. Attributes of such types are common in object-oriented and object-relational database systems and go beyond the first-normal form paradigm of relational data model. The paper introduces the concept of set-index and presents adequate index structures. The first index structure is based on a partial-order tree that is a tree derived from a partial-order relation imposed on sets with inclusion operator. For this index organisation, evaluating set predicates consists in traversal a multiway tree in a systematic fashion. The second structure is based on an array of bitmaps. For this structure, set predicates can be evaluated by retrieving appropriate rows from an array of bitmaps, depending on the index variant. Two variants of the latter structure are proposed: with fixed-sized rows and with variable-size rows. The index structures have been analysed and compared in context of time and space efficiency, flexibility in dynamic environments and other factors important for performing set predicates referring to whole sets.

Keywords: indexing, multivalued attributes, set predicates, query processing.

1. Introduction

In the paper we discuss the problem of indexing on multivalued attributes. The multivalued data types are an important feature of object-oriented and object-relational data models [18], as they remarkably extend the power of expression of the data model and allow for modelling complex structures without necessity of unnatural normalisation. Here we focus on the type **set**: values of the indexed attribute are sets of primitive values. We also assume that indexed collections contain objects identified by unique object identifiers (OIDs). The OID for an object also specifies the physical location of the object, either directly (like in O_2 or ObjectStore OODBMSs), or indirectly, through an additional mapping *OID→Address* (like in Gemstone, Jasmine or Itasca). The mapping of OIDs into physical addresses of objects is not discussed here; we simply assume that knowing the object identifier is enough to find the object. An excellent discussion of OID structures and their influence on different aspects of a database system can be found in [3].

The motivation for investigating the problem of indexing on sets is a uniformity in handling different data types in object-oriented databases: there should exist possibility to efficiently perform queries that address a set attribute using predicates referring to the whole value of the attribute rather than its primitive elements. This may be useful also in performing joins on relations (in object-relational systems) or on collections of objects (in object-oriented systems) with join conditions that use set comparisons. To accomplish this efficiently, we propose to employ index structures suitable for optimising evaluation of set predicates. The indices should be able to optimise execution of queries that involve the following predicates (postulated in papers on object-

29

J. Barzdins and A. Caplinskas (eds.), Databases and Information Systems, 29–42.
© 2001 *Kluwer Academic Publishers.*

oriented paradigm in databases, e.g. [1, 2, 15], and included into the recent ODMG object data model [4]): **is-equal**, **is-subset**, **is-superset**, and the like.

Previous work on performing set predicates in queries concentrated mainly on signatures ([10, 11]) applied to set-valued attributes. The approach presented here basically differs from the signature-based approach in several important aspects. Firstly, in our approach there are no *false drops*, which means that we do not retrieve objects that do not satisfy the query condition. Secondly, during evaluation of a query, we do not have to retrieve the objects at all; we retrieve only the OIDs of the objects that satisfy the query. Thirdly, our approach is independent of representation of sets, because we do not make any set comparisons. This is very important feature, because comparing sets is potentially a costly process.

The organisation of the paper is as follows: In the next section we present and illustrate the concept of indexing on sets. In Section 3 we describe the partial-order tree as an index structure. Different variations of the structure has been already presented before ([6, 7, 8, 9]). Here we make a concise overview of the structure, pointing out those features of the structure that is of significance for the rest of the presentation. The main contribution of this paper is Section 4, where we propose and analyse different bitmap structures for indexing on sets, and Section 5, where we make a comprehensive comparison of different index structures in the context of indexing on sets.

2. Indexing on Sets

Assume that we have a questionnaire for persons that apply for a job. One field on the form is for foreign languages that a person speaks. Obviously, a value of this field is a set of languages, say, a set of strings. After gathering the forms we create a collection (named Persons, see below) of objects of class Person (the syntax is close to Object Query Language of O_2, [16]):

```
class Person
  name: string,
  languages: set(string)
end;
name Persons: set(Person);
```

In order to find proper persons for positions in our company, we would like to query the collection Persons against values of the attribute languages, which are sets. For instance:

Q1. "Find all persons who know at least English and French":
```
select x
  from x in Persons
  where x.languages is-superset ("English","French");
```

Q2. "Find all persons who know French or German or Spanish, but nothing else" (e.g. we do not want them to be able to read our confidential documents in any other language!):
```
select x
  from x in Persons
  where x.languages is-subset ("French","German","Spanish");
```

Q3. "Find all persons who know French and Spanish, but nothing else":
```
select x
  from x in Persons
  where x. languages is-equal ("French","Spanish");
```

In the queries Q1-Q3 we used exemplary set predicates: **is-equal**, **is-subset** and **is-superset**. One can think of other useful predicates acting on set values, e.g.: **is-proper-subset**, **is-proper-**

superset, is-non-empty-subset (as a matter of fact, such predicate would be more appropriate for Q2), **is-non-full-superset, is-k-subset** ("Find all persons who know at least k languages from the following ones: ..."), **is-l-superset** ("Find all persons who know at most l languages and at least the following ones: ..."), **is-k-l-subsuperset** (the combination of the latter two), etc.

One possibility of indexing on set attributes is a B+ tree with the primitive elements as the index keys. The lowest level of such an index is a list of pairs $(e_i, <O_i>)$, where e_i is the i-th primitive value, and $<O_i>$ is the list of OIDs of those objects from the indexed collection that have e_i in the value of the multivalued attribute. In this way, each object appears in the index as many times as many elements its value of the attribute contains. Such an index (referred to as *element-index*, in short: *e-index*) is presented in Fig. 1.

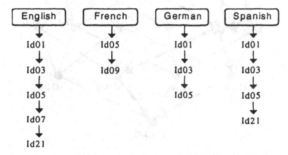

Figure 1. An example of an element index

Different variants of an e-index have been implemented in some object management systems, ([12], [14], [19]). However, in these systems an e-index is used only to optimise queries that use the **in** predicate (a special case if **is-superset** predicate). For instance, the query below could be optimised by means of an e-index:

Q4.　"Find all persons who speak German":

```
select x
   from x in Persons
   where "German" in x.languages;
```

Q4 may be rewritten in the following way:

```
select x
   from x in Persons
   where x.languages is-superset ("German");
```

In general, the e-index structure is not adequate for optimisation of set predicates. Performing the set predicates by means of an e-index requires time-consuming set-theory operations to be performed on lists of OIDs that, in addition, must be kept ordered to make the operations feasible ([8]). Below we present two index structures that are able to perform the set predicates in a natural way. In these indices (called *set-indices*, or *s-indices*), index keys are sets of primitive values rather than single primitive values.

3. The S-Index Based on a Partial-Order Tree

The *partial-order tree* of degree n (denotation: $PO^{(n)}+$) is a tree that is a subgraph of a Hasse diagram for the partially ordered set $\langle X, \subseteq \rangle$, where X is a powerset of $\{1, ..., n\}$, and $\subseteq$ is the set inclusion operator. The $PO^{(n)}+$ tree is created from the full Hasse diagram for $\langle X, \subseteq \rangle$ (depicted in Figure 2 below for $n = 4$) by eliminating some arcs, so that there is only one path from the root node to any other node. (A precise definition of $PO^{(n)}+$ can be found in [8].)

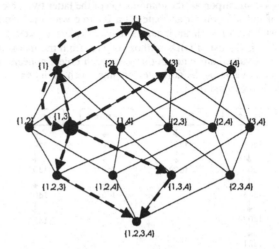

Figure 2. The idea of performing set predicates in a Hasse diagram, $n=4$

Figure 2 presents the idea of performing basic set predicates by an index with a structure of a Hasse diagram ($n = 4$). Assume that to each node of the diagram there is attached a list of OIDs of those objects, for which the value of the indexed set attribute is equal to the set associated with the node. Performing an **is-equal** predicate is accomplished by the access to the appropriate node of the diagram and retrieving the list of OIDs attached to this node. Performing an **is-superset** predicate requires moving down the diagram, starting from the node associated with the right-hand side operand of **is-superset**, and concatenating the corresponding lists of OIDs. Similarly, performing an **is-subset** predicate requires moving up the diagram, starting from the same node, and concatenating appropriate lists of OIDs (in Fig. 2, the rounded arrows correspond to **is-equal** $\{1,3\}$, the arrows pointing upwards—to **is-subset** $\{1,3\}$, and the arrows pointing downwards—to **is-superset** $\{1,3\}$).

For the purpose of indexing on set attributes, the Hasse diagram is redundant—it has too many arcs. Indeed, note that in a full Hasse diagram in general there are many paths for performing **is-subset** and **is-superset** predicates (in Fig. 2 there are two paths for **is-subset** and two paths for **is-superset**). We can eliminate majority of arcs from the Hasse diagram so that each node (except the root) has exactly one arc pointing to it. After this process we obtain a tree called the partial-order tree. The method of traversing the index graph must be appropriately modified (except for **is-equal**), because not all paths are now available. In our algorithms we employed the depth-first (i.e. lexicographical) fashion of traversal. Figure 3 illustrates an index based on the partial-order tree and the sequence of nodes visited for performing the following predicates: **is-subset** $\{1,3,4\}$ and **is-superset** $\{2,3\}$. The numbers in the shaded boxes correspond to the sequence of visiting the nodes. Note that for the **is-superset** predicate, lists of OIDs attached to some nodes should be ignored. In our example these nodes are: $\{\ \}$, $\{1\}$, $\{1,2\}$ and $\{2\}$; they are pointed to by solid arrows. The traversal for **is-equal** is not shown in Figure 3, because the sequence of visiting nodes is the same as in the Hasse diagram (in Figure 2).

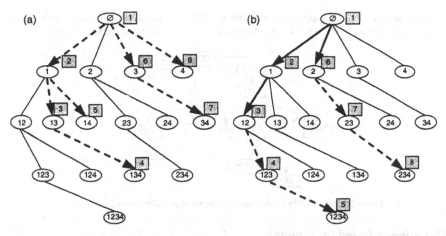

Figure 3. Traversal of a $PO^{(4)}+$ during evaluation of set predicates: (a) **is-subset** {1,3,4}, (b) **is-superset** {2,3}

To construct an *s-index*, we additionally need to define a one-to-one mapping of primitive values into integers. Such a mapping we call a *directory* of the index. In the figure below we assume the following index directory: "English" → 1, "French" → 2, "German" → 3, "Spanish" → 4.

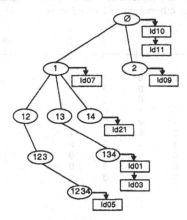

Figure 4. An exemplary s-index that is a non-full partial-order tree

The partial-order tree is a dynamic structure: it allows for increase of its degree n in a smooth way. It is due to the fact, that for any $n \geq 0$ $PO^{(n)}+$ is a subgraph of $PO^{(n+1)}+$. So, if a new primitive value appears (e.g. "Russian", to be mapped in the directory into integer 5), we do not have to reorganise the index; it is enough to add appropriate pointers to some nodes (the detailed procedure of growing a $PO^{(n)}+$ tree is given in [8]). It is a very useful feature when we do not know a priori the cardinality of the primitive domain or when this cardinality is large. In the opposite situation, when we know the cardinality and it is small, we can exploit a static version of the partial-order tree (denoted by $PO^{(n)}$). In the static partial-order tree we reduce the number of nodes by assigning two sets to each node: the set resulting from the corresponding Hasse diagram (a *key* of the node) and its complement (an *anti-key*). Consequently, two lists of OIDs can be attached to each node. Figure 5 below depicts an s-index based on $PO^{(4)}$ tree for the same collection of objects as before.

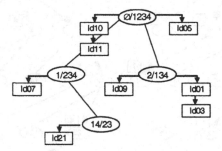

Figure 5. An exemplary s-index based on the static partial-order tree ($n = 4$)

4. The S-Index Based on Bitmaps

In this section we will show how to exploit bitmaps for indexing on sets. Bitmap indices are used in some relational databases and data warehouses ([13], [17]). A relational bitmap index is an array of bitmaps. A bitmap for the value v_i of an attribute A of relation R is a table whose elements are bits, each bit corresponding to one tuple of R. The k-th bit of the table is 1 if the attribute A of the k-th tuple of R has the value v_i, otherwise it is 0 (see Fig. 6.).

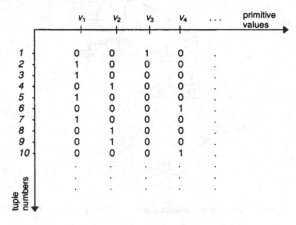

Figure 6. A relational bitmap index

To be used in object-oriented databases, the bitmap index structure must be modified to reflect the fact, that an object in the database is not identified by its position in a group of objects (like a tuple is identified by its consecutive number within a relation), but by its unique identifier. The integers that compose the domain of object identifiers do not form a continuous sequence nor show any regularity at all, so the "tuple numbers" dimension of the bitmap index must be modified appropriately. With each row of the array we can associate a list of OIDs of those objects for which the value of A corresponds to the row. In this way we replace the "tuple numbers" dimension with the "lists of OIDs" dimension. Figure 7 depicts such an object-oriented bitmap index that could correspond to the relational bitmap index from Fig. 6 (the tuples 1 through 10 have been replaced with objects Id01 through Id10).

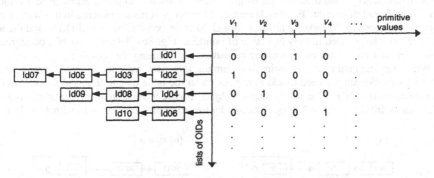

Figure 7. A bitmap index in an OO database

Let us assume that A is a set attribute of objects in the indexed collection of objects. To build an s-index on A, it is enough to alleviate the restriction that there exists only one 1 in a row of the array. We can put into a row any number of 1s, according to the cardinality of the set that is the value of A. The following two figures depict two variants of an s-index based on bitmaps. Different possible variants of the s-index originate from the fact that in a bitmap index in an object-oriented database we can choose an order of bit patterns in the rows of the index array. We can also decide whether to include all possible bit patterns or only those that represent set values existing in the indexed collection.

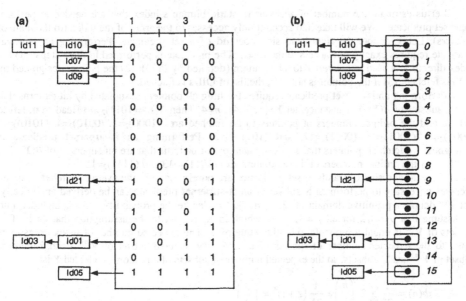

Figure 8. A static bitmap s-index of degree $n = 4$; (a) before, and (b) after reduction

Figure 8 presents a variant that we call a *static* bitmap s-index. In this index the number of rows in the array is equal to 2^n, where n is the cardinality of the primitive domain. The order of bit patterns in the array is imposed by the natural order of binary numbers represented by the bit patterns, read from left to right (Fig. 8a). Note that if the bit patterns are ordered in this way, they do not have to be stored in the index at all. It is enough to store pointers to lists of OIDs, and the array of the index can be reduced to only one table of pointers (Fig. 8b). The position of a pointer in the table uniquely determines the corresponding bit pattern representing the set value.

When the cardinality of the primitive domain increases by one, a static bitmap s-index doubles its size. We simply need to add new pointers to the table of pointers, and make one of the pointers point to the OID of the newly inserted object. Figure 9 illustrates the process of growing a bitmap s-index from degree $n_1=2$ to $n_2=3$, caused by insertion of the object Id15 with $A = \{1, 3\}$.

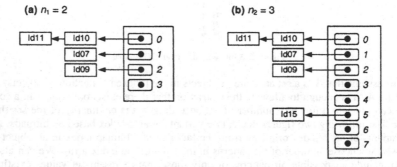

Figure 9. Growing a static bitmap s-index from (a) degree $n_1=2$ to (b) degree $n_2=3$

Let us estimate the number of accesses to static bitmap s-index that are needed to perform basic set predicates. We will take into account only accesses to the array of the index (to the table of pointers). Let Y denote the right-hand side operand of a set predicate. Performing an **is-equal** predicate requires exactly one access to the index. The predicate is performed in three steps: (1) the index directory is used to convert Y to a bit pattern (denoted by $B(Y)$); (2) the pointer designated by $B(Y)$ is fetched; (3) if the pointer is not null, the list of OIDs is fetched.

Performing an **is-subset** predicate requires fetching all pointers designated by bit patterns that are bit subsets of $B(Y)$. For instance, let $Y=\{1, 3, 4\}$, $n=4$. Then $B(Y)=(1011)_2=13$ (read from left to right!), and the ordinal numbers of pointers to be fetched are: $(1000)_2=1$, $(0010)_2=4$, $(1010)_2=5$, $(0001)_2=8$, $(1001)_2=9$, $(0011)_2=12$, and $(1011)_2=13$. Performing an **is-superset** predicate is analogous: we fetch all pointers that are designated by bit patterns that are bit supersets of $B(Y)$. For $Y=\{1, 3, 4\}$ the ordinal numbers of these pointers are: $(1011)_2=13$ and $(1111)_2=15$.

If right-hand side operands of set predicates are purely random, the average number of index accesses necessary to perform an **is-subset** or an **is-superset** predicate can be derived analytically. Let $V^{(n)}$ denote a primitive domain $\{1, 2, ..., n\}$. Let p_j denote the probability that j is included into Y. Assume that $p_j = 1/2$ for all $j = 1, ..., n$, which is equivalent to the assumption that each of 2^n subsets of $V^{(n)}$ is equally probable to be the value of Y. The expected number of index accesses is equal to the expected number of subsets of a randomly selected subset of $V^{(n)}$. Each k-element subset of $V^{(n)}$ has 2^k subsets, so the expected number of subsets of a randomly selected Y is:

$$Sub(n) = \frac{1}{2^n}\sum_{k=0}^{n} 2^k \binom{n}{k} = \frac{1}{2^n}(2+1)^n = \left(\frac{3}{2}\right)^n \qquad (1)$$

Analogously, the expected number of index accesses required to perform an **is-superset** predicate is equal to the expected number of supersets of a randomly selected subset of $V^{(n)}$. Each k-element subset of $V^{(n)}$ has 2^{n-k} supersets, so the expected number of supersets of a randomly selected Y is:

$$Super(n) = \frac{1}{2^n} \sum_{k=0}^{n} 2^{n-k} \binom{n}{k} = \frac{1}{2^n} (1+2)^n = \left(\frac{3}{2}\right)^n \qquad (2)$$

Thus, the fraction of rows in a static s-index to be fetched during performing a set predicate (which in fact is the *selectivity* of a predicate) in a purely random environment can be expected to be $(1/2^n)$ for **is-equal**, and $(3/4)^n$ for **is-subset** and **is-superset**. Due to paging, the number of real disk accesses may be considerably lower than that given by (1) or (2), as there is a non-zero probability that the page already cached in main memory contains the next pointer needed.

Let P is the size of a pointer, I is the size of object identifier, and M is the cardinality of the indexed collection. The size of a static s-index of degree n is equal to

$$S_S(n, M) = 2^n \cdot P + M \cdot I \qquad (3)$$

Note that the first component is the size of the array and it does not depend on the cardinality of the indexed collection. So, regardless of this cardinality, the size of an index may easily become prohibitive, even for moderate n. For instance, for $n = 20$ (which is small in real-life applications) and $P=4B$, the array of the index occupies 4MB, which may be tolerable. However, if $n = 30$ (which is still quite small), this size grows to 4GB, which is rather large. The exponentially growing size of the index limits its practical application to relatively small values of n, not much exceeding 20.

In the dynamic variant of a bitmap s-index, only rows that have lists of OIDs associated with them are present in the array. Thus, the number of rows in the array is equal to the number of different values of A in the indexed collection of objects, and never exceeds 2^n nor M. Figure 10 depicts a dynamic variant of the static s-index from Fig. 8.

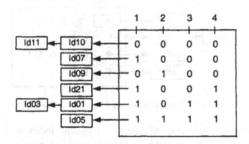

Figure 10. A sorted dynamic bitmap s-index of degree $n = 4$

The order of rows in the array can be arbitrary. In a static environment with no insertion we can build the index in such a way that the rows are sorted by their binary values (as in Fig. 10). In an environment with insertions, a row being inserted would be appended to the end of the index array, and the resulting order of rows would be determined by the order in which objects with new values of A were inserted into the indexed collection. At the insertion, a new bitmap may be added to the array, if necessary (i.e. if the degree of the index grows). This new bitmap has exactly one 1: at the row being appended. It may happen that more than one bitmap has to be added at one insertion. For instance, if the objects are inserted into our exemplary indexed collection in the following order: Id09, Id11, Id01, Id07, Id10, a dynamic s-index will grow in the way depicted in Fig. 11.

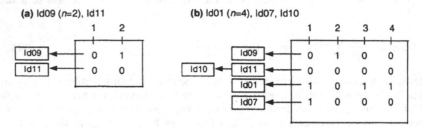

Figure 11. Growing an unsorted dynamic bitmap s-index from (a) $n=2$ to (b) $n=4$

Note, that upon insertion of Id01 with $A = \{1, 3, 4\}$, two bitmaps have been added: number 3 and number 4, with 1s at the row just appended (Fig. 11b). It may seem that if A were $\{1, 4\}$, the bitmap number 3 would have all 0s. Recall however that the directory of the index is used for mapping primitive values into consecutive integers. In the above case, if the current degree of the index is 2, the set $\{1, 4\}$ never appears—it would be reduced to the set $\{1, 3\}$.

Adding a new bitmap to a bitmap index may be a costly process. Instead, in each row of the index array we can keep the *row degree*: an integer indicating the position of the rightmost 1 in the bit pattern. The row degree can be treated as the *effective length* of the row. The size of the index may be reduced in this way. Because the records of the index array become of varying size, the index processing is more complicated. However, if we assume no specific order of bit patterns in the index, performing set predicates involves sequential scanning the index array, so the variable-sized records cause no additional problem. Figure 12 depicts this variant of a dynamic bitmap s-index. The sequence of insertions is the same as in Fig. 11. The degrees of rows are circled.

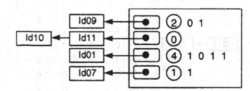

Figure 12. A dynamic bitmap s-index with row degrees

Let us estimate $S_D(n, M)$, the expected size of a dynamic index of degree n with fixed-sized rows. Let $R_D(n, M)$ denote the expected number of rows in the index array.

$$S_D(n, M) = R_D(n, M) \cdot (P + n/8) + M \cdot I \qquad (4)$$

$$R_D(n, M) \leq \min(2^n, M) \qquad (5)$$

If values of the multivalued attribute A are purely random, $R_D(n)$ can be estimated more precisely. Let q_j denote the probability that the attribute A for a randomly selected object contains j, and assume that $q_j = 1/2$ for all $j = 1, ..., n$. As before, it is equivalent to the assumption that each of 2^n subsets of $V^{(n)}$ is equally probable to be the value of A. Probability that a given bit pattern is not present in the index array is:

$$Q(n,M) = \left(1 - 2^{-n}\right)^M \qquad (6)$$

Hence,

$$R_D(n, M) = 2^n - 2^n \cdot Q(n, M) = 2^n \left(1 - \left(1 - 2^{-n}\right)^M\right) \qquad (7)$$

Let us closer analyse the expected fraction of all rows that appear in the index array. This fraction (called the *usage* of the index, denotation: u) equals to $1 - Q(n,M)$, hence, $R_D(n,M) = u \cdot 2^n$. Normally, both 2^n and M are large, so we can approximate (6) by a power of e in the following way:

$$Q(n,M) = \left(1 - 2^{-n}\right)^{2^n \left(M \cdot 2^{-n}\right)} \cong e^{-\left(M \cdot 2^{-n}\right)} = e^{-m} \qquad (8)$$

So, the usage can be estimated by $1 - e^{-m}$, where $m = M/2^n$ represents how many times the number of objects in the indexed collection is greater than the maximum number of rows in the index array. For instance, for $m = 1$ the usage is about 0.63; for $m = 3$ the usage is 0.95, etc. For $k \geq 3$ the number of rows in a dynamic index becomes practically the same as for a static index. In this case it does not pay off to use a dynamic index; it is better to create and use a static index. However, this situation is possible only if n is relatively small. Assume that n is big (say, 30), so that keeping a static variant of the index is not feasible, and that $m < 1$ (which is normal for such n). In this case, the usage will be small: for $m = 0.5$ an estimate of the usage is 0.39; for $m = 0.25$ it is 0.22; for $m = 0.01$ it is 0.01 etc. For very small m the usage can be estimated by m, because in the random environment practically all lists of OIDs have only one element.

The situation changes, if the distribution of q_j is not uniform. In our example, in the sets of foreign languages our applicants can speak some languages (say, English and German) are more frequent, while others (say, Turkish and Chinese) are rare. Also, cardinalities of 1, 2 or 3 foreign languages are obviously much more probable than 10. Therefore, the probability distribution for values of A is not uniform and some sets are much more probable than others. In consequence, lists of OIDs in a dynamic s-index tend to be longer than 1, even for $m \ll 1$, which may considerably decrease the usage (and the size) of the index. Now, we analyse, how much space we can gain using the variant of the dynamic s-index with row degrees. In a random environment, the expected number of bits in a bit pattern in the index array, $L(n)$, is:

$$L(n) = \frac{1}{2^n} \sum_{k=1}^{n} k \cdot 2^{k-1} = (n-1) + 2^{-n} \cong n - 1 \qquad (9)$$

So, the expected gain in the length of a row in the array is insignificant. Because we have to include the row degrees in the array, an s-index with variable-sized rows is, on average, bigger than a corresponding s-index with fixed-sized rows. In an environment that is not purely random, the size if an s-index with row degrees may depend on the order in which new objects are inserted, and on the mapping of primitive values into integers. This effect is shown in Figure 13. The primitive domain contains the following values: a, b, c, d, e. Objects are inserted in the following order of As: {a}, {b}, {c}, {d}, {e}, {d, e}, {c, e}, {c, d, e}. The array of rows in Fig. 13a corresponds to the following mapping: a $\rightarrow$ 1, b $\rightarrow$ 2, c $\rightarrow$ 3, d $\rightarrow$ 4, e $\rightarrow$ 5. This mapping (referred to as the *natural mapping*) results directly from the order of insertions. The size of resulting array is 30 bits. If we used another, non-natural mapping: e $\rightarrow$ 1, d $\rightarrow$ 2, c $\rightarrow$ 3, b $\rightarrow$ 4, a $\rightarrow$ 5, the size would be 23 (Fig. 13b). Also, if the order of insertion is different: {e}, {d}, {d, e}, {c}, {c, e}, {c, d, e}, {b}, {a}, the latter mapping becomes the natural one, and the size of array is again 23 (Fig. 13c).

If the index is sorted and has fixed-sized rows, we can employ binary search throughout the array. To perform an **is-equal** predicate, on the average $\log_2 R_D(n, M)$ accesses are needed. From (1) and (2) we obtain, that the expected numbers of accesses needed to perform an **is-subset** or **is-superset** predicate are $(3/2)^n \cdot \log_2 R_D(n, M)$. If the usage of the index is close to 1, then $\log_2 R_D(n, M) \cong n$ and these numbers are close to n and $(3/2)^n \cdot n$, respectively. If the usage of the index is close to 0 and the distribution of values of A is uniform, then $\log_2 R_D(n, M) \cong \log_2 M$ and the numbers of accesses should be adjusted accordingly to $\log_2 M$ and $(3/2)^n \cdot \log_2 M$. If the distribution is non-uniform, the figures can be much less.

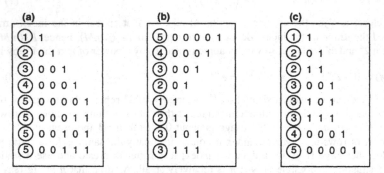

Figure 13. Different s-index arrays for the same values of A

It may easily turn out that performing an **is-subset** or an **is superset** predicate by sequentially scanning the whole index array requires less accesses than performing it by binary search. The sequential scan will cost less than the binary search, if

$$R_D(n, M)/\log_2 R_D(n, M) < (3/2)^n \tag{10}$$

This inequality can hold for practical values of n and M. For instance, if the number of rows in the index is 2^{20} (about 1 million), then (10) holds already for $n \geq 27$. This means that for index degrees exceeding 26 and for any collection of objects of cardinality not exceeding 1 million, the sequential scan outperforms the binary search. This is true regardless of the distribution of values of A (a non-uniform distribution can only decrease $R_D(n, M)$, and the left-hand side of (10)).

Performing **is-equal** by means of an unsorted bitmap s-index with fixed-sized or any (sorted or unsorted) bitmap s-index with variable-sized rows involves sequentially scanning the index array until the appropriate bit pattern is found. This on average requires accessing a half of the array rows, i.e. $R_D(n, M)/2$ accesses (which is much greater than $\log_2 R_D(n, M)$). Performing **is-subset** and **is-superset** costs twice as much, because the whole array must be scanned in search for any matching bit patterns.

5. A Comparison of S-Index Structures

In this section we compare the index structures presented in this paper in the context of time and space performance. The comparison summarises the formula and qualitative reasoning from Section 3 and Section 4.

5.1 STATIC INDICES

If the degree of an index, n, is known in advance and is not big, we can use static variants of a partial order-tree index (Fig. 5) and bitmap index (Fig. 8b). The space occupied by an index array of a bitmap index is given by the first component of (3), i.e. $2^n \cdot P$. The space occupied by a PO tree depends on the usage of the index, because the number of nodes in the tree is close to $u \cdot 2^{n-1}$ (for simplicity, we neglect the possibility of presence of nodes with no lists of OIDs). Each node contains two pointers to lists of OIDs and a number of pointers representing the tree arcs. The total number of arcs is close to the total number of nodes in the tree. Let the size of pointers of both kinds is the same: P. Then, the size of the $PO^{(n)}$ tree approximates to $u \cdot 2^{n-1} \cdot 3P = (3/2) \cdot u \cdot 2^n \cdot P$. So, a relation between the sizes depends on the index usage: if the usage is small (less than 2/3), *PO* tree occupies less space than a corresponding bitmap index. As it was pointed before, for small n, in real-life situations (for large databases) m is much greater than 1 and the usage is close to 1, so in that case a bitmap is smaller than a tree.

The time efficiency of both structures strongly depends on the set predicate to be performed. For **is-equal**, a bitmap s-index requires exactly one access to the index, while in a *PO* tree s-index we must traverse the path from the root to the appropriate node (if exists). This path will not be longer than $\lfloor n/2 \rfloor + 1$. For **is-subset** (or **is-superset**), a bitmap s-index requires, on average, $(3/2)^n$ accesses (see (1) or (2)). In a *PO* tree, this number in general will be less, as we will not try to access the nodes that do not exist. However, if the usage is close to 1, the number of nodes accessed will be close to that for the corresponding bitmap index.

To summarise, for small index usage the *PO* tree seems to outperform the bitmap both in time and space. However, for static indices, where degrees are small, the usage is likely to be close to 1 and a bitmap is a preferable solution (unless the distribution of A is very non-uniform).

5.2 DYNAMIC INDICES

If the degree of the index, n, is big, we use a dynamic variant of a partial order-tree index (Fig. 3) and a dynamic bitmap index without or with row degrees (Fig. 10 or Fig. 12). The space occupied by the index array of a bitmap index without row degrees is given by the first component of (4), i.e. $u \cdot 2^n \cdot (P+n/8)$. The space occupied by a *PO+* tree is close to $u \cdot 2^n$. Now, each node contains one pointer to lists of OIDs and pointers representing tree arcs. The size of a $PO^{(n)}+$ tree approximates to $u \cdot 2^n \cdot 2P$. So, the tree will be smaller than the bitmap array if $P < n/8$. If we use 16-bit pointers, then the threshold value of n is $n_0 = 128$; for 32-bit pointers $n_0 = 256$.

In the end of Section 4 we have shown that keeping a dynamic bitmap sorted is unnecessary complication, and in an environment with insertion may be not feasible. Therefore, performing an **is-equal** and **is-subset** (or **is-superset**) predicate requires on average, respectively, $u \cdot 2^{n-1}$ and $u \cdot 2^n$ accesses to the index. In a *PO+* tree, to perform an **is-equal** predicate, we traverse a path that is not longer than $n+1$, which normally is much smaller than $u \cdot 2^{n-1}$. To perform an **is-subset** (or **is-superset**) predicate, we visit practically only those nodes that satisfy the predicate. From the analysis leading to the formulas (1) and (2) we deduced, that if both A and Y are purely random, the expected selectivity of any of these predicates is $(3/4)^n$. Hence, performing a predicate will require $(3/4)^n \cdot u \cdot 2^n$ accesses. The fraction $(3/4)^n$ decreases rapidly with n: already for $n > 15$ it is less than 0.01. So, the time of performing any set predicate by means of a *PO+* tree will be a small fraction of the time needed when using a bitmap.

The estimations made above do not change much, if we use a dynamic bitmap index with row degrees. So we can summarise that in a dynamic environment with large index degree an s-index based on a *PO+* tree structure outperforms a bitmap s-index structure both in time and space efficiency. The cost to be paid for that is more complicated implementation of *PO+* trees.

6. Conclusions

In the paper we have proposed two totally different index structures, suitable for indexing on set attributes: a partial-order tree and a array of bitmaps. These structures allow for efficiently performing set predicates that refer to whole sets values rather than to single primitive values. The analysis has shown that in dynamic environments, with large index degrees, the tree structure promises better performance that the bitmap structure. In static environment, with small index degrees and high index usage, a bitmap may be a better solution. However, some further investigation would be useful to verify these conclusions against real implementations. This investigation should certainly involve some carefully designed simulation experiments, because performance of the index structures depends on distributions of set values, which is hard to analyse mathematically if distributions are non-uniform. It would be also interesting to compare the structures presented here with the aforementioned signature-based approach, e.g. in performing index joins using s-indices against nested-loop or hash joins using signatures.

There are also some possibilities to refine and extend the index structures presented here. One problem is that of paging. For *PO* trees a paging algorithm is needed that would take into account the assumed lexicographical order of tree traversal. For bitmap indices, one can think about putting the bitmap rows into pages of a B+ tree, which could result in considerable performance gain for some set predicates. This is however complicated by the fact that dynamic bitmap s-index has variable-length rows, which causes difficulties with tree balancing (however, some results from [5] seem to be adequate to alleviate this problem). Another challenging problem is to find the optimal mapping of primitive values into integers to minimise the size of an s-index, which is desirable regardless of method of paging applied.

References

1. Bertino, E., Martino, L. *Object-Oriented Database Systems. Concepts and Architectures.* Addison-Wesley, 1993.

2. Bertino, E., Foscoli, P. Index organisations for object-oriented database systems. *IEEE Trans. on Knowledge and Data Engineering*, 2(7), 1995, pp. 193-209.

3. Cattell, R. G. G. *Object Data Management - Object-Oriented and Extended Relational Database Systems. Revised Edition*, Addison-Wesley, 1994.

4. Cattell, R. G. G., Barry, D. G. (eds.). *The Object Data Standard: ODMG 3.0.* Morgan Kaufmann Pub. Inc., 2000.

5. Faloutsos, Ch., Jagadish, H. V. On B-tree indices for skewed distributions. *Proc. 18th VLDB Conference*, Vancouver (Canada), 1992.

6. Goczyla, K. The partial-order tree: a new structure for indexing on complex attributes in object-oriented databases, *Proc. 23rd Euromicro Conference*, IEEE Computer Society, Budapest, Hungary, 1997, pp. 47-54.

7. Goczyla, K. Extendible partial-order tree: a dynamic structure for indexing on multivalued attributes. *Proc. of the 20th International Conference on Information Technology Interfaces*, Pula, Croatia, 1998, pp. 317-322.

8. Goczyla, K. *Methods of Indexing in Object-Oriented Databases*. Technical University of Gdańsk, Technical Notes 565, 1998, pp. 3-134 (in Polish).

9. Goczyla, K. Indexing on multivalued attributes using partial-order trees. *Proc. of Short Papers, 3rd European Conference ADBIS'99*, Maribor, Slovenia, 1999, pp. 16-23.

10. Helmer, S., Moerkotte, G. Evaluation of main memory join algorithms for joins with subset join predicates. *Proc. of the 23rd VLDB Conference*, Athens, Greece, 1997, pp. 386-395.

11. Ishikawa, Y., Kitigawa, H. Ohho, N. Evaluation of signature files as set access facilities in OODBS. *Proc. of the ACM SIGMOD '93*, Washington D.C., USA, 1993, pp. 247-256.

12. Ishikawa, H., Yamane, Y., Izumida, Y., Kawato, N. An object-oriented database system Jasmine: implementation, application, and extension. *IEEE Trans. on Knowledge and Data Engineering*, 2(8), 1996, pp. 285-303.

13. Johnson, T. Performance measurement of compressed bitmap indices. *Proc. of the 25th VLDB Conference*, Edinburgh, Scotland, 1999, pp. 278-289.

14. Kim, W., Kim, K.-C., Dale, A. Indexing techniques for object-oriented databases. W. Kim and F. H. Lochovsky, (eds.). *Object-Oriented Concepts, Databases, and Applications*, Addison Wesley, 1989, pp. 371-394.

15. Kim, W. *Introduction to Object-Oriented Databases*. The MIT Press, Cambridge, 1990.

16. *ODMG OQL User Manual.* O$_2$ Technology, Versailles, France, 1998.

17. O'Neil, P., Quass, D. Improved query performance with variant indices. *Proc. of the ACM SIGMOD'97*, Tucson, USA, 1997, pp. 38-49.

18. Stonebraker, M., Brown, P. *Object-Relational DBMSs. Tracking the Next Great Wave.* Morgan Kaufmann Pub, Inc., 1999.

19. *The O$_2$ System Administration Guide, Release 5.0. Chapter 5: Index.* O$_2$ Technology, Versailles, France, 1998.

Part 2: Knowledge Management, Data Mining, and Data Warehousing

Knowledge Management, Metadata and Information Systems: An RDF-Compliant Version of the NKRL Language

Gian Piero Zarri

CNRS – 44, rue de l'Amiral Mouchez - 75014 Paris - France
zarri@ivry.cnrs.fr

Abstract

We describe the data structures proper to NKRL (Narrative Knowledge Representation Language), a language expressly designed for representing, in a standardised way (*metadata*), the semantic content (the 'meaning') of complex multimedia documents. For example, it is now used in the CONCERTO European Esprit project to encode the conceptual annotations that will be added to Web documents in order to facilitate their 'intelligent' retrieval, processing, displaying, etc. A new, XML/RDF-compliant version of NKRL implemented in Java, has been realised in the framework of this project.

Keywords: knowledge representation, intelligent indexing, metadata, NKRL, XML/RDF.

1. Introduction

It is today widely admitted that an effective retrieval of information from large bodies of multimedia documents requires, among other things, a characterisation (*indexing*) of such documents in terms of some metadata. The term *metadata*, i.e., data about data, denotes, in general, any piece of knowledge that can be used in order to represent information about the structure and the content of a (usually huge) collection of data. A relevant metadata function consists then in superimposing some sort of conceptual organisation over the unstructured information space characteristic of the Web, in order to facilitate the intelligent retrieval of the original documents. Querying or retrieving various types of digital media is executed directly at the metadata level.

Among the classes of metadata proposed by the scientific literature, only *content-specific metadata* "reflect the semantics of the media object in a given context" and provide a sufficient degree of generality [1]. Unfortunately, a veritable access by semantic content is particularly difficult to achieve, especially for non-textual material (images, video, audio). In those cases, content-based access is often supported by the use of simple keywords, or of features more related with the physical structure of multimedia documents (such as colour, shape, texture, etc.) than to their true semantic content. In order to overcome the limitations of such approaches, *conceptual annotations* have been introduced for describing in some depth the context of digital objects [4, 3]. However, the current approaches, often based on the use of simple ontologies in a description logic style, have several limitations in terms of description of complex semantic contents — see, e.g., the description of complex events [12].

To get over these problems, we have implemented an approach for building up conceptual annotations for multimedia documents that is based on a *two-step* annotation process [8]:

- In the first step, we annotate any interesting multimedia document with a simple Natural Language (NL) caption in the form of a short text, representing a general, neutral description of the content of the document. In the case of textual objects, the interesting parts of the text, or the

45

J. Barzdins and A. Caplinskas (eds.), Databases and Information Systems, 45–56.

text itself, could represent the NL caption. This approach corresponds to the typical process of annotating a paper document, by underlying the interesting parts or writing down remarks and personal opinions. In the case of other media documents, the NL caption may represent the semantic content of the document and additional observations associated with it.

• During the second phase, annotations represented by NL captions are (semi-automatically) converted [8] into the final conceptual annotations, represented in NKRL (*Narrative Knowledge Representation Language*) [9, 10] terms. In NKRL, the metaknowledge associated with a document consists not only in a set of concepts and instances of concepts (individuals) but also in a structured set of more complex structures (occurrences) obtained through the instantiations of general classes of events called *templates*, see the next Sections.

Note that this twofold annotation process guarantees a high level of flexibility in querying. First of all, it provides a general solution for the mixed media access. This means that a single metadata query can retrieve information from data that pertain to different media since the same mechanism is used to represent their content. Moreover, the first step of the annotation process is quite useful to support a similarity-based indexing: by associating similar captions to different documents we make them 'similar' with respect to the content and, therefore, to the retrieval.

This paper focuses, Sections 2 and 3, on a description of the main data structures of NKRL, proposed here as a high-level device to implement true semantic-based, content-oriented metadata structures. Note that NKRL is already been used, in similar contexts, in European projects like Nomos (Esprit P5330), Cobalt (LRE P61011), and WebLearning (GALILEO Actions). It is now employed in the new CONCERTO (Esprit P29159) and EUFORBIA (IAP P2104) projects to produce conceptual annotations according to the two-step process mentioned above. A new version of NKRL, implemented in Java and XML/RDF compliant, has been realised in the CONCERTO's framework, where RDF (*Resource Description* Format) [7, 2] is used for the internal representation of NKRL. A description of some problems encountered when translating into RDF the NKRL data structures, and of the solutions adopted in this context, Section 4, will conclude the paper.

2. The Structural Design of NKRL

NKRL is organised according to a two-layer approach. The lower layer consists of a set of general representation tools that are structured into several integrated components, four in our case, i.e., the definitional, enumerative, descriptive and factual components.

The definitional component of NKRL supplies the tools for representing the important notions (*concepts*) of a given domain; in NKRL, a concept is, therefore, a definitional data structure associated with a symbolic label like `physical_entity, human_being, city_`, etc. These definitional structures are, substantially, frame-like structures; moreover, all the NKRL concepts are inserted into a generalisation/specialisation (tangled) hierarchy that, for historical reasons, is called H_CLASS(es), and which corresponds well to the usual ontologies of terms.

A fundamental assumption about the organisation of H_CLASS concerns the differentiation between 'notions which can be instantiated directly into enumerable specimens', like 'chair' (a physical object) and 'notions which cannot be instantiated directly into specimens', like 'gold' (a substance). The two high-level branches of H_CLASS stem, therefore, from two concepts labelled as `sortal_concepts` and `non_sortal_concepts`, see Figure 5. The specialisations of the former, like `chair_, city_` or `european_city`, can have direct instances (`chair_27, paris_`), whereas the specialisations of the latter, like `gold_`, or `colour_`, can admit further specialisations, see `white_gold` or `red_`, but do not have direct instances.

The enumerative component of NKRL concerns then the formal representation of the instances (`lucy_, taxi_53, paris_`) of the sortal concepts of H_CLASS. In NKRL, their formal representations take the name of *individuals*. Throughout this paper, we will use the italic type style to represent a `concept_`, the roman style to represent an `individual_`.

The 'events' proper to a given domain — i.e., the dynamic processes describing the interactions among the concepts and individuals that play a role in the contest of these events — are represented by making use of the descriptive and factual tools.

The descriptive component concerns the tools used to produce the formal representations (*predicative templates*) of general classes of narrative events, like 'moving a generic object', 'formulate a need', 'be present somewhere'. In contrast to the dyadic structures used for concepts and individuals, templates are characterised by a complex threefold format connecting together the *symbolic name* of the template, a *predicate* and its *arguments*. The arguments are, in turn, linked with the predicate by a set of named relations, the *roles*. If we denote then with L_i the generic symbolic label identifying a given template, with P_j the predicate used in the template, with R_k the generic role and with a_k the corresponding argument, the NKRL data structures for the templates will have the following general format:

$$(L_i (P_j (R_1 a_1) (R_2 a_2) ... (R_n a_n))) .$$

See the examples in subsection 3.1. Presently, the predicates pertain to the set {BEHAVE, EXIST, EXPERIENCE, MOVE, OWN, PRODUCE, RECEIVE}, and the roles to the set {SUBJ(ect), OBJ(ect), SOURCE, BEN(e)F(iciary), MODAL(ity), TOPIC, CONTEXT}. Templates are structured into an inheritance hierarchy, H_TEMP(lates), which corresponds, therefore, to a taxonomy (ontology) of events.

The instances (predicative occurrences) of the predicative templates, i.e., the representation of single, specific events like "Tomorrow, I will move the wardrobe" or "Lucy was looking for a taxi" are, eventually, in the domain of the last component, the factual one.

The upper layer of NKRL consists of two parts. The first is a *catalogue* describing the formal characteristics and the modalities of use of a set of well formed, 'basic' templates (like 'moving a generic object' mentioned above), belonging to the H_TEMP hierarchy and permanently associated with the language. Presently, the basic templates are about 200, pertaining mainly to a (very broad) socio-economico-political context where the main characters are human beings or social bodies. By means of proper specialisation operations it is then possible to obtain from the basic templates the derived templates that could be needed to implement a particular application. The second part of the layer is given by the general concepts (general notions) that belong to the upper level of H_CLASS, such as `sortal_concepts`, `non_sortal_concepts`, `physical_entity`, `modality_`, `event_`, etc., see again Figure 5. They are, as the basic templates, invariable.

3. A Survey of Some Important NKRL Data Structures

3.1 DESCRIPTIVE AND FACTUAL COMPONENTS

Figure 1 reproduces the NKRL 'external' representation of a simple conceptual annotation like "Three nice girls are lying on the beach", that could be associated with a WWW image.

The predicative occurrence `c1` (factual component), instance of a basic template, brings along the main features of the event to be represented. EXIST is a predicate, SUBJ(ect) and MODAL(ity) are roles. In the structured argument (*expansion*) introduced by the SUBJ role, `girl_1` is an individual (an instance of a concept); `nice_` and `cardinality_` are concepts, as the argument, `lying_position`, introduced by MODAL. A *location attribute* (a list that contains here the individual `beach_1`) is linked with an argument, here, the SUBJ argument, by a colon, ':'.

The *attributive operator*, SPECIF(ication), is one of the NKRL operators used to build up expansions, see [9] (and Section 4 below). The SPECIF lists, with syntax (SPECIF e_1 p_1 ... p_n), are used to represent some of the properties which can be asserted about the first element e_1, concept or individual, of the list — i.e., in c1, the properties associated with girl_1 are nice_ and (cardinality...), the property associated with cardinality_ is '3'.

The non-empty HasMember slot in the data structure explicitly associated with the individual girl_1 (enumerative component), instance of an NKRL concept (girl_), makes it clear that this individual is referring in reality to several instances of girl_ (plural situation). In Figure 1, we have supposed that the three girls were, *a priori*, not sufficiently important *per se* in the context of the caption to justify their explicit representation as specific individuals, i.e., girl_1, girl_2, girl_3. Note that, if not expressly required by the characteristics of the application, a basic NKRL principle suggests that we should try to avoid any unnecessary proliferation of individuals.

```
c1)     EXIST SUBJ   (SPECIF girl_1 nice_ (SPECIF cardinality_ 3)): (beach_1)
            MODAL   lying_position

    [ girl_1
        InstanceOf :   girl_
        HasMember  :   3 ]
```

Figure 1. Annotation of a WWW image represented according to the NKRL syntax

A conceptual annotation like that of Figure 1 can be used for posing queries in the style of: "Find all pictures of multiple, recumbent girls", with all the possible, even very different, variants; the queries must be expressed in NKRL terms giving then rise to data structures called *search patterns*. Search patterns are NKRL data structures that represent the general framework of information to be searched for, by filtering or unification, within an annotation (metadata) repository, see also Figure 2 below and, for the technical details, [11].

We reproduce in Figure 2 the coding of an information (e.g., a textual narrative fragment) like: "On June 12, 1997, John was admitted to hospital" (upper part of the Figure). This occurrence can be successfully unified with a search pattern (lower part of the Figure) as: "Was John at the hospital in July/August 1997?" (in the absence of explicit, negative evidence, a given situation is assumed to persist within the immediate temporal environment of the originating event, see [10]).

```
c2)     EXIST SUBJ  john_: (hospital_1)
            [ begin ]
            date-1: (2-june-97)
            date-2:

(?w  IS-PRED-OCCURRENCE
        :predicate  EXIST
        :SUBJ       john_
        (1-july-1997, 31-august-1997))
```

Figure 2. NKRL coding of temporal information, and a simple example of search pattern

From Figure 2 (upper part), we see that temporal information in NKRL is represented through two *temporal attributes*, date-1 and date-2. They define the time interval in which a predicative occurrence (i.e., the 'meaning' represented by the occurrence) 'holds'. In c2, this interval is reduced to a point on the time axis, as indicated by the single value, the timestamp 2-july-93, associated with the temporal attribute date-1; this point represents the 'beginning of an event' because of the presence of begin (a *temporal modulator*). The temporal attribute date-1 is then represented 'in subsequence' (category of dating); see [10] for the full details. The two timestamps of the search pattern in the lower part of Figure 2 constitute the *search interval* to be used to limit the search for unification to the slice of time that it is considered appropriate to explore. Search patterns form the basic tools used in NKRL to set up complex search and inference procedures; examples of high-level inferences characteristic of the NKRL approach are the *transformation rules*, see [11].

As a further example of factual structures we give now, Figure 3, an NKRL interpretation of the sentence: "We have to make orange juice" that, according to Hwang and Schubert [5], exemplifies several interesting semantic phenomena. A sentence like this could be included in an audio document. To translate then the general idea of "acting to obtain a given result", we use:

- A predicative occurrence (c3 in Figure 3), instance of a basic template pertaining to the BEHAVE branch of the template hierarchy (H_TEMP), and corresponding to the general meaning of 'focusing on a result'. This occurrence is used to express the 'acting' component, i.e., it allows us to identify the SUBJ of the action, the temporal co-ordinates, possibly the MODAL(ity) or the instigator (SOURCE), etc.
- A second predicative occurrence, c4 in Figure 3, with a different NKRL predicate and which is used to express the 'intended result' component. This second occurrence, which happens 'in the future', is marked as hypothetical, i.e., it is always characterised by the presence of an *uncertainty validity attribute*, code '*'.
- A *binding occurrence*, c5, linking together the previous predicative occurrences and labelled with GOAL, an operator pertaining to the taxonomy of causality of NKRL, see [10]. Binding structures — i.e., lists where the elements are symbolic labels, c3 and c4 in Figure 3 — are second-order structures used to represent the logico-semantic links that can exist between (predicative) templates or occurrences.

```
c3) BEHAVE SUBJ (SPECIF human_being (SPECIF cardinality_ several_))
               [oblig, ment]
               date1:  observed date
               date2:

*c4)   PRODUCE SUBJ  (SPECIF human_being (SPECIF cardinality_ several_))
               OBJ   (SPECIF orange_juice (SPECIF amount_))
               date1: observed date + i
               date2:

c5) (GOAL   c3   c4)
```

Figure 3. Representation in NKRL of 'wishes and intentions'

The general schema for representing the 'focusing on an intended result' domain in NKRL is then:

```
cα)    BEHAVE  SUBJ  <human_being_or_social_body>
*cβ)   <predicative_occurrence>, with any syntax
cγ)    (GOAL cα cβ)
```

In Figure 3, oblig and ment are *modulators*, see [9]. ment(al) pertains to the *modality modulators*. oblig(atory) suggests that 'someone is obliged to do or to endure something, e.g., by authority', and pertains to the *deontic modulators* series. Other modulators are the *temporal modulators*, begin, end and obs(erve), see Figure 2 and, again, [10]. In the constructions for expressing 'focus on ...', the absence of the ment(al) modulator in the BEHAVE occurrence means that the SUBJ(ect) of BEHAVE takes some concrete initiative (acts explicitly) in order to fulfil the result; if ment(al) is present, as in Figure 3, no concrete action is undertaken, and the 'result' reflects only the wishes and desires of the SUBJ(ect).

Figure 4 represents a tiny fragment of the H_TEMP hierarchy. This includes the template 2.31 at the origin of occurrence c2 of Figure 2.

```
name: Exist:BePresent
father: Exist:
position in H_TEMP: 2.3 ; NL description: 'Be Present Somewhere'

        EXIST        SUBJ         var1: (var2)
                     [OBJ         var3: (var4)]
                     [SOURCE      var5: [(var6)]]
                     !(BENF)
                     [MODAL       var7]
                     [TOPIC       var8]
                     [CONTEXT     var9]
                     { [ modulators ], ≠abs }

        var1  =  var3 = var5 = <human_being_or_social_body>
        var7  =  <action_name>
        var8  ≠  <property_>
        var9  =  <event_> | <action_name>
        var2, var4, var6 =  <physical_location>


name: Exist:BePresentAutonomously
father: Exist:BePresent
position: 2.31 ; NL description: 'Be Present in an Autonomous Way'

        EXIST        SUBJ         var1: (var2)
                     !(OBJ)
                     [SOURCE      var3: [(var4)]]
                     !(BENF)
                     [MODAL       var5]
                     [TOPIC       var6]
                     [CONTEXT     var7]
                     { [ modulators ], ≠abs }

        var1  =  var3  = <human_being_or_social_body>
        var5  =  <action_name>
        var6  ≠  <property_>
        var7  =  <event_> | <action_name>
        var2, var4  =<physical_location>


name: BePresentWithSomeone
father: Exist:BePresent
position: 2.32  ; NL description: 'Be Present Somewhere with Someone'

        EXIST        SUBJ         var1: (var2)
                     OBJ          var3: (var4)
                     [SOURCE      var5: [(var6)]]
                     !(BENF)
                     [MODAL       var7]
                     [TOPIC       var8]
                     [CONTEXT     var9]
                     { [ modulators ], ≠abs }

        var1  =  var3 = var5 = <human_being_or_social_body>
        var7  =  <action_name>
        var8  ≠  <property_>
        var9  =  <event_> | <action_name>
        var2, var4, var6 =  <physical_location>
        var2  =  var4
```

Figure 4. A tiny fragment of the H_TEMP hierarchy of templates

In the three templates of Figure 4, optional roles and fillers are in square brackets; 'forbidden' roles are indicated by a '!' code. The variables, $(var_1 \ldots var_n)$, that appear in the templates are replaced by concepts (definitional component) or individuals (enumerative component) according to the associated constraints; constraints are expressed in general under the form of associations of high-level concepts of H_CLASS. Note that the difference between the 2.31 and 2.32 templates consists in the presence or not of the OBJ(ect) role, forbidden in 2.31 and mandatory in 2.32. If OBJ is present, the template takes the specific meaning of 'stay with someone'.

3.2 DEFINITIONAL AND ENUMERATIVE COMPONENTS

Figure 5 gives a simplified representation of the upper level of H_CLASS (hierarchy of concepts, definitional component). From this figure, we can note that *substance_* and *colour_* are regarded in NKRL as examples of non-sortal concepts, see [9].

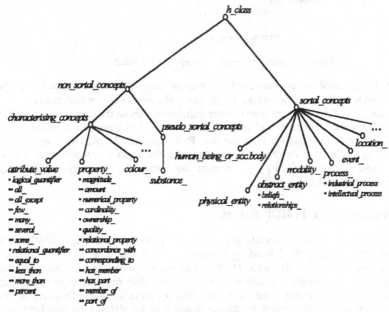

Figure 5. An abridged view of the 'upper level' of H_CLASS

Coming now to the data structures used for concepts and individuals, see also Figure 1 above, they are essentially frame-based structures and their design is relatively traditional. These structures are composed of an OID (object identifier), and of a set of characteristic features (slots). Three different types of slots are used, 'relations', 'attributes', and 'procedures'; a general schema for concepts or individuals is then represented in Figure 6.

The slots of the 'relation' type are used to represent the relationships of an NKRL entity, concept or individual, to other entities. For the time being, NKRL provides for eight general system-defined relationships. They are IsA, and the inverse HasSpecialisation, InstanceOf, and the inverse HasInstance, MemberOf (HasMember) and PartOf (HasPart). We can note that a concept or an individual cannot make use of the totality of the eight relations. The relation IsA, and the inverse HasSpecialisation, is reserved to concepts. HasInstance can only be associated with a concept; InstanceOf with an individual (i.e., the concepts and their instances, the individuals, are linked by the InstanceOf and HasInstance relations). MemberOf (HasMember) and

PartOf (HasPart) can only be used to link concepts with concepts or instances with instances, but not concepts with instances.

```
{ OID
[ Relation
      (IsA | InstanceOf :
      HasSpecialisation | HasInstance :
      MemberOf :
      HasMember :
      PartOf :
      HasPart : )
  Attribute
      (Attribute₁ :
            …
      Attributeₙ : )
  Procedure
      (Procedure₁ :
            …
      Procedureₙ : ) ] }
```

Figure 6. A general schema for concepts and individuals

The slots of the 'attribute' type are used to represent some characteristic, intrinsic properties of a concept/individual, like, e.g., the ColourOf property of a sortal concept like *chair_*.

Finally, the 'procedure' slots are used to store information about the dynamic characterisation of (particularly important) concepts and individuals: we can find there the description of their typical behaviour, the instructions for their use, etc. Procedures can be pieces of procedural code implemented using ordinary tools like demons. However, the main characteristic of the NKRL procedures consists in the possibility of implementing them in a declarative style using the descriptive component templates, see [9].

4. Implementing NKRL in RDF Format

RDF (*Resource Description Format*), see [7, 2], is a proposal for defining WWW metadata that is developed by a specific W3C Working Group (W3C = *World Wide Web Consortium*). The model, implemented in XML (*eXtensible Markup Language*), makes use of Directed Labelled Graphs (DLGs) where the nodes, that represent any possible Web resource (documents, parts of documents, collections of documents etc.) are described by using attributes that give the named properties of the resources. The values of the attributes may be text strings, numbers, or other resources.

The first, general problem we had to solve for the implementation of the XML/RDF-compliant version of NKRL has concerned the very different nature of the RDF and NKRL data structures. The first are *dyadic*, i.e., the main RDF data structure can be assimilated to a triple where two resources are linked by a binary conceptual relation under the form of a property. We have seen on the contrary, in Section 2, that the basic building block of the NKRL descriptive and factual structures is a complex *threefold* relationship associating a symbolic label, a predicate, one or more roles and the corresponding fillers (arguments of the predicate). To assure then the conversion into RDF format, the first move was that of representing the NKRL data structures as intertwined dyadic 'tables', see Figure 7 that describes the RDF-compliant, general structure of an NKRL template. For simplicity's sake, this figure does not take into account the hierarchical relations between templates or the relationships between templates and occurrences.

More specific problems have concerned the (still limited) choice of knowledge representation tools that are presently associated with RDF. To give only an example, let us consider the solutions that, making use of the *containers* — RDF tools for describing collections of resources, see [7] — we have adopted in order to reproduce the semantics of the so-called *AECS sublanguage* [9] of NKRL. The AECS operators are used to build up expansions (structured arguments) like those included in Figures 1 and 3 above.

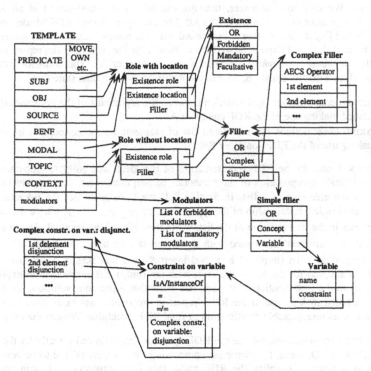

Figure 7. General structure of an NKRL template according to a 'dyadic' view

AECS includes four operators, the disjunctive operator (ALTERNative = A), the distributive operator (ENUMeration = E), the collective operator (COORDination = C), and the attributive operator (SPECIFication = S). The semantics of SPECIF has already been explained in Section 3.1 above; the semantics of ALTERN is self-evident. The difference between COORD and ENUM consists in the fact that, in a COORD expansion list, all the elements of the expansion take part (necessarily) together in the particular relationship with the predicate defined by the associated role. As an example, we can imagine a situation similar to that described in Figure 2 above, where John and Peter have been admitted *together* to hospital: the SUBJ of EXIST would be, in this case: (COORD john_ peter_). In an ENUM list, each element satisfies the same relationship with the predicate, but they do this separately. RDF defines on the contrary three types of containers:

- 'Bag', an unordered list of resources or literals, used to declare that a property has multiple values and that no significance is associated with the order in which the values are given;
- 'Sequence', Seq, an ordered list of resources or literals, used to declare that a property has multiple values and that the order of these values is significant;

- 'Alternative', Alt, a list of resources or literals that represent alternative for the (single) value of a property.

Of these, only Alt presents a very precise coincidence with an AECS operator, obviously, ALTERN; moreover, we have at our disposal only *three* container constructions to represent *four* NKRL operators. We can note, however, that the use of a Bag construction is an acceptable approximation to represent the semantics of COORD. For example, in the "RDF Model and Syntax Specification" report [7], the use of Bag is associated with the representation of the sentence: "The committee of Fred, Wilma and Dino approved the relation". As the editors of the report say, "...the three committee members *as a whole* voted in a certain manner...". This situation corresponds certainly in NKRL to a COORD situation. As a first conclusion, we can then state that:

- The ALTERN constructions (a disjunction between the arguments of the constructed complex filler) are described making use of the RDF container Alt.
- The COORD constructions (an unordered list of elements of the conceptual hierarchy) are represented making use of the RDF container Bag.

With respect now to the RDF representation of the ENUM and SPECIF constructions, we make use of a 'liberal' interpretation of the semantics of Seq containers. Seq introduces an order relation between the elements of a list. In Section 3.1, we have seen that the operator SPECIF introduces a 'partial order' relationship of the type (SPECIF e_i p_1 ... p_n), where the element e_i necessarily appears in the first position of the list, while the order of the residual elements p_1 ... p_n (the 'properties' or 'attributes' associated with e_i) is, on the contrary, indifferent. We can then include these properties in an (implicit) Bag, and insert e_i and this Bag in a Seq list. The same solution has been adopted for the ENUM operator, with the (only) difference that an explicit enum identifier appears in the first position of the Seq list. Note that a previous solution, see [6], where ENUM was represented making use of the RDF 'repeated properties' has been abandoned because that it could lead to an unacceptable proliferation of final RDF structures. We can than say that:

- For the SPECIF constructions, we use the RDF operator Seq followed directly by the elements of the SPECIF list. Of these, the elements representing the 'properties' are to be considered as inserted into a Bag; to simplify the RDF code, this Bag construction is conceived as an 'implicit' one, and the Bag operator is not expressly mentioned.
- The ENUM constructions are coded by using a Seq container where the first element is the identifier enum.

As an example, let us consider, Figure 8, the RDF representation of occurrence c2 of Figure 2 where, for completeness' sake, we have assumed again that John *and Peter* have been admitted *together* (COORD) to hospital. In general, the RDF text associated with each predicative occurrence is composed by several tags, all nested inside the <CONCEPTUAL_ANNOTATION> tag and belonging to two different namespaces, rdf and ca. The first namespace describes the standard environment under which RDF tags have to be interpreted. The second namespace describes specific tags defined in the context of an application, in this case, the CONCERTO project. More precisely, the tag <ca:Template*i*> is used to denote that the predicative occurrence is an instance of the template identified by Template*i*. The other tags specify the various roles of the predicative occurrence, together with the associated value. For example, the tag <ca:subject> specifies the role SUBJ of c2. A tag for each additional information concerning a role is nested inside the role tag. Additional tags are used to represent temporal information and modulators used in the context of the considered predicative occurrence. The code li means 'list item', and it was chosen in RDF to be mnemonic with respect to the corresponding HTML term.

```
<?xml version="1.0" ?>
<!DOCTYPE DOCUMENTS SYSTEM "CA_RDF.dtd">
<CONCEPTUAL_ANNOTATION>
  <rdf:RDF xmlns:rdf="http://www.w3.org/1999/02/22-rdf-syntax-ns#"
  xmlns:rdf="http://www.w3.org/TR/1999/PR-rdf-schema-19990303#"
  xmlns:ca="">
    <rdf:Description about="occ3">
    <rdf:type resource="ca:Occurrence"/>
        <ca:instanceOf>Template2.31</ca:instanceOf>
        <ca:predicateName>Exist</ca:predicateName>
        <ca:subject rdf:ID="Subj2.31" rdf:parseType="Resource">
          <concerto:filler>
            <rdf:Bag>
              <rdf :li rdf:resource="#john_"/>
              <rdf :li rdf:resource="#peter_"/>
            </rdf:Bag>
          </concerto:filler>
        </ca:subject>
        <ca:listOfModulators>
            <rdf:Seq><rdf:li>begin</rdf:li></rdf:Seq>
        </ca:listOfModulators>
        <ca:date1>02/06/1997</ca:date1>
    </rdf:Description>
  </rdf:RDF>
</CONCEPTUAL_ANNOTATION>
```

Figure 8. The RDF format of a predicative occurrence

5. Conclusion

In this paper, we have described some of the main data structures proper to NKRL, a language expressly designed for representing, in a standardised way ('metadata'), the semantic content (the 'meaning') of multimedia documents. Our aim was to show that the use of this language could present some advantages, from the point of view of an in-depth content representation and semantic indexing of multimedia documents, with respect to the current metadata techniques. In particular, we would like to emphasise here two very important features of NKRL :

- Making use of a relatively simple, flexible and easily manageable formalism NKRL offers some interesting solutions to very hard problems concerning the 'practical' aspects of the knowledge representation endeavour. These include, e.g., the representation of implicit and explicit enunciative situations, of wishes, desires, and intentions (modals), of plural situations, of causality, and of other second order, intertwined constructions.
- A second, important characteristics of NKRL is represented by the fact that the catalogue of basic templates, see Section 2 above, can be considered as part and parcel of the definition of the language. This approach is particularly important for practical applications, and it implies, in particular, that: i) a system-builder does not have to create himself the structural knowledge needed to describe the events proper to a (sufficiently) large class of narrative texts and documents ; ii) it becomes easier to secure the reproduction or the sharing of previous results.

References

1. Boll, S., Klas, W., Sheth, A. Overview on using metadata to manage multimedia data. In A. Sheth, W. Klas. (eds.). *Multimedia Data Management - Using Metadata to Integrate and Apply Digital Media*, New York, McGraw Hill, 1998.

2. Brickley, D., Guha, R.V. (eds.). *Resource Description Framework (RDF) Schema Specification*, W3C, 1999. URL: http://www.w3.org/TR/WD-rdf-schema/.

3. Decker, S., Erdmann, M., Fensel, D., Studer, R. Ontobrocker: ontology based access to distributed and semi-structured information. In Meersman *et al.* (eds.). *Database Semantics: Semantic Issues in Multimedia Systems,* Dordrecht, Kluwer Academic Publishers, 1999.

4. Heflin, J., Hendler, J., Luke, S. Coping with changing ontologies in a distributed environment. In *Proceedings of the AAAI-99 Workshop on Ontology Management,* Menlo Park (CA), AAAI, 1999.

5. Hwang, C.H., Schubert, L.K. Meeting the interlocking needs of LF-computation, deindexing and inference: an organic approach to general NLU. In *Proceedings of the 13th IJCAI Conference,* San Francisco, Morgan Kaufmann, 1993.

6. Jacqmin, S., Zarri, G.P. *Preliminary Specifications of the Template Manager* (CONCERTO NRC-TR-4). Paris, CNRS, 1999.

7. Lassila, O., Swick, R.R. (eds.). *Resource Description Framework (RDF) Model and Syntax Specification.* W3C, 1999, URL: http://www.w3.org/TR/REC-rdf-syntax/.

8. McNaught, J., Black, W.J., Rinaldi, F., Bertino, E., Brasher, A., Deavin, D., Catania, B., Silvestri, D., Armani, B., Leo, P., Persidis, A., Semeraro, G., Esposito, F., Candela, V., Zarri, G.P., Gilardoni, L. Integrated document and knowledge management for the knowledge-based enterprise. In *Proceedings of the Practical Application of Knowledge Management Conference, PAKeM 2000,* Blackpool, The Practical Application Company, 2000.

9. Zarri, G.P. NKRL, a knowledge representation tool for encoding the 'meaning' of complex narrative texts. *Natural Language Engineering,* **3,** 1997, pp.231-253.

10. Zarri, G.P. Representation of temporal knowledge in events: the formalism, and its potential for legal narratives. *Information & Communications Technology Law,* **7,** 1998, pp. 213-241.

11. Zarri, G.P., Azzam, S. Building up and making use of corporate knowledge repositories. In E. Plaza, R. Benjamins (eds.), *Knowledge Acquisition, Modeling and Management, Proceedings of EKAW'97,* Berlin, Springer-Verlag, Berlin, 1997.

12. Zarri, G.P., Bertino, E., Black, W.J., Brasher, A., Catania, B., Deavin, D., Di Pace, L., Esposito, F., Leo, P., McNaught, J., Persidis, A., Rinaldi, F., Semeraro, G. CONCERTO, an environment for the 'intelligent' indexing, querying and retrieval of digital documents. In *Foundations of Intelligent Systems, Proceedings of ISMIS'99,* Berlin, Springer-Verlag, 1999.

Precise Enterprises and Imperfect Data

Panagiotis Chountas and Ilias Petrounias

Department of Computation, UMIST,
PO Box 88, Manchester M60 1QD, UK
E-mail: {chountap, ilias}@sna.co.umist.ac.uk

Abstract

One of the main uses of an information system is the representation and management of large amounts of indicative information from multiple sources describing the state of some enterprise. Most current information systems model enterprises that are crisp. A crisp enterprise is defined as one that is highly quantifiable; all relationships are fixed, and all attributes are atomic valued. The premises on which this paper is based are precise enterprises, where data are imperfect. In such cases information can be certain, imprecise or uncertain, temporal, or any possible combination of each two of them, depending on the application domain. Additionally, in domains where the information is perfect, all information sources are absolutely reliable and trustworthy. In more speculative domains, like diagnosis, information may be asserted relatively to some time intervals in which it is possibly defined and probably believed. In such domains different sources of information may be assigned different degrees of reliability. This paper is presenting a framework for the conceptual integration and uniform treatment of all these types of information.

Keywords: value imperfection, temporal imperfection, multiple information sources, consistency principle, conceptual modelling, nested relational databases.

1. Introduction

Imperfect information is the partial knowledge of the true value of the real world. It is an epistemic property caused by lack of information. Elements of the enterprise ontology, involved in information imperfection are:

- the might happen ability of things, or the tendency of things to occur,
- the concept of time,
- the information source or provider.

A database attempts to represent an abstract version of the enterprise reality; the level of it is determined by the expected applications. Work in this area is considering imperfect information arising from elements of the enterprise ontology but always in isolation form each other. This paper is suggesting that the elements involved in information imperfection are related and affecting each other and concepts at the specification level. More than one information provider might be describing the same fragment of information, expressing logical views about the same facts that are defined over the 3-dimensional space of *time, belief and reliability,* named as the *multidimensionality* of the source. Facts are expressing associations between objects but not in isolation, always in some form of relationship with each other.

The rest of the paper is organised as follows. Section 2 evaluates existing work dealing with imperfect information. Section 3 presents a framework for dealing with imprecise temporal information. Section 4 presents a formalism for capturing and representing temporal and value imperfection in a multisource environment, where each source is carrying a degree of reliability.

J. Barzdins and A. Caplinskas (eds.), Databases and Information Systems, 57–68.

Section 5 provides the mapping of the formalism to a nested relational database. Section 6 suggests a set of NF^2 algebraic operators. Section 7 points at work in progress.

2. Related Work

The main stream of researchers is dealing with either temporal or value imperfection. The difference between temporal and value imperfection can be characterised as that between "do not know what" and "do not know when" information. Approaches for representing temporal or value imperfection can be weighted or unweighted. Weights are normalised values in the range [0,1]. Weights are assigned to alternatives or possibilities of an imperfect value. For a possibility a weight deals with the might happen ability of the possibility to be the actual value. Unweighted imperfect information may be either restricted or unrestricted [7].

Other researchers are considering the existence of multiple conflicting sources accommodated in a database. All these are assuming that there are no intentional inconsistencies between different sources. It is assumed that the point of conflict is that two or more information sources provide different answers to the same query (extensional inconsistencies), provided that those sources do not have internal disharmonies (internal extensional inconsistencies).

This section evaluates approaches in the literature according to the following criteria: relevance to real world representation of concepts, power offered by the proposed model, minimality of concepts (formalisms should not contain overlapping concepts), formality in the representation to avoid ambiguities. In addition, it examines whether support for temporal uncertainty is offered by the models and whether uncertainty about both temporal and value aspects is supported. Finally, models are evaluated as to whether they offer support for multiple information sources.

2.1 POSSIBILISTIC OR FUZZY DATABASES

When considering uncertain information enterprises are considered as either precise or vague. In vague enterprises it is assumed that attribute values are not precise and are presented as linguistic terms. Early possibilistic approaches extended the relational model with the acceptance of fuzzy functional [11] and fuzzy multivalued dependencies [2]. Based on the definition of a fuzzy resemblance relation EQ(UAL) over domains of attributes, a set of inference rules for fuzzy functional and multivalued dependencies is proposed ([2, 11]). The main disadvantage of both is that they support only a limited number of possible associations between the elements of the application domain in order to keep the models in 1NF. Recently these ideas moved towards the support of similarity relations in a nested relational model for representing uncertain, complex data [18].

In the case of precise enterprises, information can be certain, uncertain or imprecise. The key notion is that while one value applies to the enterprise, the database extension may contain a set. The application of imprecise or uncertain information to the precise enterprise means that the value in the database is a possibility distribution. This is taken to show the limits of knowledge concerning the actual value and the significance of ordering. Other research has made attempts to identify whether the uncertainty property can be presented as part of ER diagrams [17]. This is influenced by approaches for treating uncertainty proposed by the AI community [13] and is trying to embody linguistic terms, as part of the ER formalism or as part of the relational theory.

2.2 PROBABILISTIC DATABASES

The key notion here is that while one value applies to the certain enterprise, the database extension may contain a set (probabilistic distributions). In that way value imperfection is accommodated. The field of probabilistic databases covers a wide spectrum of different approaches. Probabilistic weights are used to express that an attribute value can be a set of alternative data values ([1, 6]) or to express the likelihood that a tuple belongs to a relation. Other approaches [8] are using separate probabilistic weights to express the logic view that a tuple belongs to a relation and different probabilistic weights to express the intent that an attribute value may be a set of alternative data values.

There is a debate on whether an interval of probabilities or a single probability is better for expressing the tendency of things to occur ([8, 10]). There is also concern if events should be considered dependent or independent. However, uncertainty is treated only at the database level ignoring the specification level, leading to complex probabilistic reasoning with no knowledge of the primitive notions of the model that can produce imperfect information.

The main issue is if the model is in 1NF or in NF^2. It is argued in this paper that imperfection should firstly be considered at the conceptual level. If imperfection is not accommodated by conceptual modelling formalisms (i.e. ER diagrams, object role modelling approaches) then it cannot appear in the resulting databases (which are after all the result of a mapping from the conceptual schema).

2.3 TEMPORAL PROBABILISTIC DATABASES

While in reality a time interval applies to an event, in temporal probabilistic databases the database extension may contain a set of possible intervals.

In valid time indeterminacy [7] it is known that an event did in fact occur but is not known exactly when. The model is presented as an extension of the SQL data model. If a tuple k in relation R is timestamped with the interval $[t_1...t_2]$, then this is interpreted as tuple k holds at some point t in interval $[t_1...t_2]$. Query constructs are defined to specify belief (Correlation credibility) in the underlying data and their plausibility (Ordering Plausibility) in the relationships among the data. However, valid time indeterminacy is treated at the database level instead of arising from the conceptual level that states exactly which primitive notions may be involved in valid time indeterminacy.

A probabilistic temporal algebra is suggested in [4] for expressing information of the following type: tuple d is in relation R at some point of time in interval $[t_1, t_2]$ with probability between p1 and p2. A range of probability distributions is supported to allocate the probability measure over the set of time points of the interval. Different valid times related to a tuple may have different probability distributions in nature.

The main problem in ([4, 7]) is that if the type of the probability distribution is known then it is known beforehand that some time points in an interval have greater probability, thus a subinterval of the initial time interval is more probable. Therefore, there is a fact somewhere that makes our knowledge about the real world more explicit but it is not present in the conceptual schema or in the database. Temporal probabilistic databases are a natural extension of probabilistic databases. Imperfection of the information is treated only at the database level ignoring the specification level, leading to complex probabilistic reasoning with no explicit specification of concepts.

2.4 DATABASES WITH MULTIPLE INFORMATION SOURCES

The key notion here is the representation of a certain enterprise, where only one value applies, while the database extension may contain a set because of different conflicting sources. The IST approach [16] is using information source vectors to accommodate multiple conflicting sources and define the conditions under which a tuple is valid. Each attribute value in a tuple is associated with an information source vector to state whether an attribute value is valid, therefore certainty about certainty can be expressed. [14] assumes that data models can be mapped, resolving only existential inconstancies. Both approaches are ignoring intentional inconsistencies between different sources since both approaches are treating conflicting values at the database level ignoring the specification level. Furthermore, it is assumed that there are no internal extensional inconsistencies. Both are modelling the certain world. Models are trying to resolve information coming from different sources, which are conflicting.

3. Considerations for a Dynamic Conceptual Model

In any enterprise environment of multiple information sources it is undeniable that more than one sources describe the same portion of the enterprise world differently. The conceptual model is acting as a gateway between different sources, permitting different sources to express information in a single and highly abstract level, the level of concepts (metamodel level).

The approach followed here is based on a type of object role modelling formalism [15]. A fact is a true logical proposition about the modelled world. Each fact instance is a semantically irreducible proposition in the real world about one or more entity instances. Irreducible means that the fact cannot be split into facts involving fewer entities without loss of information. A dynamic database environment is presenting certain or plausible information about the past and present of the modelled world. Therefore, there is a need to express imperfect information as a part of the fact formalism and to identify the impact of the time and belief dimension on it, before proceeding with database considerations:

- If a fact is related to the belief dimension, with a degree of belief less than one it is simply declared that an association between objects possibly stands in the enterprise world (value imperfection).
- If a fact is linked with the time dimension, it is simply declared that a certain association between objects is valid for a certain time period. However, if the time dimension is associated with the belief dimension it is simply declared that a certain fact is possibly defined over that period (temporal imperfection). In most of the research proposals only value or temporal imperfection can be expressed. This paper suggests that both kinds of imperfection (value and temporal) can be represented in a database environment.
- If a fact is associated with the belief dimension and the time that a fact is defined over (valid time according to the temporal database literature [7]) is also allied to the belief dimension, then both value and temporal imperfection can be expressed. Expressing temporal and value imperfection simultaneously, permits the representation of statements arising from everyday enterprise activities.
- In cases of either value or temporal imperfection the belief dimension is affected by the reliability of the source. The reliability of the source is expressing the humans' concern about the identity and trustiness of the source that is responsible for a particular piece of information.

4. The Temporal Multisource Belief Model (TMBM)

The basic items that one wishes to reason about are objects in terms of the roles that they play within a domain [15]. In general a fact type is composed of the arguments shown in Figure 1, where n is the arity of the fact type. The way that one can refer to specific entities is through reference labels.

If the modelled world is certain then the label value is a single value. The time interval Δt that a fact instance is defined over has an explicit duration since both ends of the interval are unambiguously defined in the time line. If the modelled world is imperfect then a label value may be a possible multiset of values (π_Label Type) [3]. Each member (value) of the possible multiset is an alternative value with an indicative belief. The time interval that a fact is defined over, is an alternative from a multiple set of time intervals, with an indicative belief. In either the certain or imperfect modelled world the reliability of the source is forming the conclusive belief for the timestamped fact. A graphical representation of the concepts is shown in Figure 2. Fact types can be of any degree [15]. For example, (Figure 3) in a ternary fact type, there will be three entity types involved with three different roles. The relationship between two entity types of the ternary fact can be regarded as an entity type itself (objectified fact type).

$$F = \{\,\{\,\{\,<E_1, L_1, R_1>,\ldots, <E_n, L_n, R_n>\,\},\{\,\Delta t \leq\ T\}\,\},\, m\,\}$$

where :
F is a fact type consisting of k fact instances
T is the time interval that an irreducible fact type is defined in the real world.
E_i is the ith entity type playing a role in the fact type
L_i is the label type (referencing E_i)
R_i is the ith role of the fact type

Δt is the time interval that an irreducible fact instance is defined in the real world

m is the reliability of the source that circulates a particular fact type. The reliability of

the source is a domain independent variable.

Figure 1. Fact types

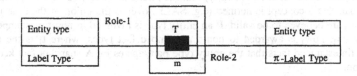

Figure 2. Graphical notation of a fact type

In Figure 3, the entity types (E) are (Supplier, Product, Location) and the corresponding reference labels are (Supplier-Name, π (Product–Name), City-Name). Supplier-Name and City-Name are deterministic label types. Product-Name is a stochastic label type (π). The meaning of a stochastic label type is that a label value can take a possible (π) set of values and each member of the set is an alternative value with an indicative belief (probability, (p)). Based on the possibility/ probability consistency principle [12] a connection between the measure of randomness (p) or observation and compatibility (π) can be achieved. In this way a fact is presenting information that is observed and testified by one or more information sources therefore a set of alternatives is defined with p > 0 and π = 1. A fact may also represent information that is compatible with its domain, p = 0 and 0 < π < 1 based on some specified or unspecified criterion. However, the information source cannot testify these values, but does not have any reason to reject them. In that way information that is more elementary and less context dependent can be represented.

Any instance of the (SALE-LOCATION) in Figure 3 must exist during the period (or at the same period) that the corresponding SALE fact type exists. The following relationship between T and T_1 must exist: (T_1 during T) or (T_1 same as T). A time period is defined as a temporal constraint over a linear hierarchy of time units, denoted H_r. H_r is a finite collection of distinct time units, with linear order among those units. For instance H_1 = day $\subseteq$ month$\subseteq$ year, H_2 = minute$\subseteq$hour$\subseteq$ day$\subseteq$ month $\subseteq$year are all linear hierarchies of time units defined over the Gregorian Calendar. A time point in a linear hierarchy is simply an instantiation of each time unit in H_r. A calendar r consists of a linear hierarchy H_r of time units and a validity predicate that specifies a non empty set, of time points. In that way an application may assume the existence of an arbitrary but fixed calendar.

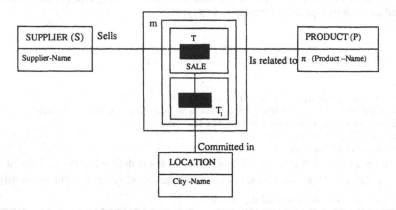

Figure 3. Uncertain timestamped fact

In case of temporal imperfection, the time interval over which a fact instance is valid, is accompanied by an indicative belief (probability) that the relationship between T and T_1 still holds. The validity lifespan that a concept is defined (e.g. SALE) over is the union of the time intervals that 'sale' instances are believed to be valid. If an entity type is involved in non-timestamped facts, the interval [now - t_1, now] is awarded to non-timestamped fact types, where t_1 is the smallest granularity of all timestamped facts that the entity type participates in. A snapshot fact keeps only current information.

The reliability of a provider or source (m), (Figure 3) is acting as a creditor of trust towards facts expressed by this particular source and is associated with an instantaneous event e. The event supplies the system with the reliability of the source. The time point (t_e) in the time line associated with the particular event is recorded. The interval [t_e, now] is the valid period that the reliability measure is defined for a particular source. The 'now' upper bound, will updated to t_{e1}, when t_{e1} is the time point another instantaneous event e_1 is triggered and subsequently modifies the reliability measure of the source.

5. Mapping to a Nested Relational Model

The 1NF relational model is simple and mathematically tractable but not rich enough to model complex objects. In order to represent complex objects hierarchical structures are used instead of flat tables [5]. A relation schema R is recursively defined as:

i.   If {$A_1, ..., A_n$}$\subseteq$U and $A_1...A_n$ are atomic valued attributes then R={$A_1,..., A_n$} is a relation schema.

ii.   If {$A_1, ..., A_n$}$\subseteq$U and $A_1...A_n$ are atomic valued attributes and $R_1,...,R_n$ are relation schemas then R=($A_1,...,A_n,R_1....R_n$) is a relation schema .

The atomic valued attributes $A_1,...,A_n$ are called zero order attributes. $R_1,...,R_n$ are called relation-valued attributes or high order attributes.

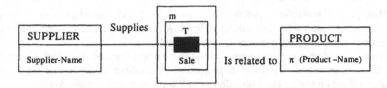

Figure 4. The Sale fact type

Consider fact type Sale in Figure 4. Supplier-Name is an atomic value attribute. π(Product – Name) declares that a single label value can be a possible (π) set of values and each member of the set is an alternative value with an indicative belief (probability, (p)). Product is a relation schema or a high order attribute. The time interval $\Delta t \subset T$ that a fact instance is defined over may be explicitly known or may be a set of possible time intervals (π) where each interval is accompanied by an indicative belief. T is represented by a high order attribute. Another separate relation represents the information source and its reliability (0< M≤1). M affects only the probability measure. In Figure 5, a sample population for the fact type Sale is presented. In it two kinds of value imperfection found in the real world can be modelled: the possible ($\pi=1$) and probable ($0<p≤1$) or the possible ($0<\pi<1$) and unexpected, improbable (p=0). In Figure 6 Sale is presented as a hierarchical structure. A node can be either an atomic value attribute or a relation.

Timestamped Fact Type Sale				Valid Time	
Multisource Fact Type Sale				Δt / (p)	Source
Supplier-Name	π(Product-Name)				
	Name / Probability(p)	Source	Possibility		
	Water / 0.5	Ivi			
	Wine / 0.2	John	1		
	Oil / 0.3	Minerva		[10/06/99,15/08/99] / 0.6	Ivi, John
				[10/07/99,15/10/99]/ 0.4	Minerva
Amber Smith					
	Cigarettes / 0	Paul	0.5		

Figure 5. Multisource timestamped fact type Sale

6. A Recursive NF² Algebra

A set of relational operators (Select, Project, Cartesian product and Join) is presented with the emphasis on processing queries which include join operations in the nested relational model. Operators are recursively defined so that each operator can be applied to subrelations at all levels.

Selection (σ): For all nodes ∈ node S where $S_a \neq S_b$, if node S_a is a child of an ancestor of a node S_b, then S_a, S_b are called selection comparable nodes ($S_a \xrightarrow{\sigma} S_b$).

For example, in figure 6 (Valid Time$(R_1)^\sigma \rightarrow$Supplier–Name) and (Valid Time$(R_1)^\sigma \rightarrow \pi$(Product –Name)) are selection comparable notes. Since there is a path between

π(Product–Name) and Valid Time (R_1) then (R_1) is also comparable to Name/Probability (p). However Valid Δt/(p), Supplier–Name are not selection comparable nodes. Selection conditions are comparisons between attributes and constants and may include also membership operators.

Projection (π'): A projection operation is a way of accessing attribute values or relation schemas from the outermost level to the innermost level. A projection can be defined as a nesting of multiple projections in the attribute domains of a relation schema.

Many project operators have been proposed in the context of nested relational models [9] but existing projection operators deal only with projection of attribute values based on a selection condition that is defined on the attribute domain (e.g. π'(Supplier Name = 'John Smith')).

For all nodes $\in$ node (S) if two nodes are selection comparable notes then the projection operator is defined. In figure 6 (Supplier Name $\xrightarrow{\pi'}$ π(Product–Name), (π(Product–Name)$\xrightarrow{\pi'}$Possibility) are selection comparable notes. In this case the project operator is defined as an ordered sequence of zero level attributes and relation valued attributes (section 5).

Projection operators can be either simple or complex. A simple projection involves a one level vertical or horizontal path (e.g. Supplier-Name$\xrightarrow{\pi'}$ π(Product–Name)). In this example, for a Supplier-Name instance the whole relation valued attribute π(Product–Name) is derived.

A complex projection involves the derivation of values through paths in the tree hierarchy (e.g. Supplier Name$\xrightarrow{\pi'}$ SP (Source Identity/reliability). Duplicates are not eliminated in the case that the values of the timestamps are different or the conclusive beliefs are different.

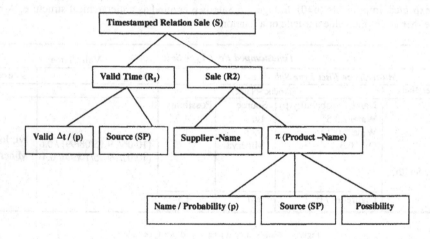

Figure 6. Nested schema tree for value and temporal imperfection

Cartesian Product ($\times^\varepsilon$): The idea behind the extended Cartesian product is to combine relations with common high order attributes not only at the top level but also at the subschema level. Let R be the relational relation schema and T be the schema tree of R, the path $P_r = (M_1...M_k)$ is a join-path of R if M_1 is a child of root (T) and M_k is a non-leaf node of T.

Path expressions describe routes along the composition hierarchy and expressions describe links between attribute domains. They flatten any nested relation structure in one way – no need to break paths in the schema into several expressions and apply a fold up operator to each one. The idea is to combine to high order relational attributes not only at the top level but also at the subschema level. The definition of the Cartesian Product does not have any major practical value, since it is clearly a mathematical operation. However, it underlines the theoretical framework for defining the P Join operator.

P Join ($^{\rho}\times$): The same attribute names in two join relations may appear in multiple subtrees. The P join can be extended with multiple path joins, which exploit the more general situation. In Figure 5 only the information sources, are stated and not they reliability. The way that the reliability measure is changing throughout time has been discussed in section 4. Assuming that the following relation describes the information source (Figure 7), a P Join can be used to relate the reliability (m) of the source and the belief expressed for the value or temporal part of a fact instance.

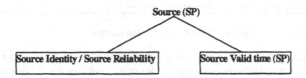

Figure 7. Relation SP for the Information provider

The source attribute presented by the Source relation (SP) in Figure 7, is evident in two relational subschemes R_1, R_2 of Figure 6. A join path between R_1, R_2 and SP can be defined. Subrelation R_1 is expressing the time dimension of the fact type sale. In defining the path join between the relation SP and R_1 the following relationship must exist: Valid time $(SP_i) \cap$ Valid time $(Rt_i) \neq \varnothing$ (1).

If and only if (1) is true then a path join between R_2 and SP can be defined. Otherwise, it is accepted that a source can be temporally imperfect. If the time that an event occurred is not known (no matter if it is known to what extent an event did occur), the provided information is still incomplete.

Maybe P Join ($m^{\rho}\times$): A maybe P Join is defined as an extension of the P-Join and is also an extended natural join. With the maybe P Join attribute values defined using a probability can encapsulate the belief of the source and express the conclusive belief in a single complex value, thus forming higher level attributes with complex data types. The conclusive belief for a possible value is defined as the product of reliability and probability measure $C_p=(p \times m)$. The same applies when two probabilities have to be joined $(p_1 \times p_2)$. When elements of different possibility distributions are joined then the min $(\pi_1...\pi_n)$ possibility is the common one. If n sources are expressing the same belief (p) for an attribute value, having different degrees of reliability (m) then the conclusive belief (C_p) of the attribute value is defined by the following formula:

$$C_p = \min (m_1 \times p, m_2 \times p... m_n \times p) \qquad (2)$$

The time interval that the conclusive belief is defined is the intersection of the time intervals that the sources $(SP_1...SP_n)$ are defined. $\Delta t_{Cp} = \Delta t_1 SP_1 \cap \Delta t_2 SP_2 \cap .... \cap \Delta t_n SP_n$ (3)
It should be stated that (1) must be always true.

Figure 8 presents relation $(Sm^{\rho} \times SP)$ after applying the Maybe P Join. Relation S is from figures 5 and 6. Relation SP is from figure 7.

Union ($\cup$): Union compatibility in the fact formalism (section 4), means that two relations are union compatible if and only if they have the same arity or degree and their corresponding attributes are based on the same domain. Attribute names may not be the same. Attributes may be zero level or (e.g. supplier Name) or relation value attributes π(Product–Name). If two relations are not union compatible the project operator can be used to identify the union compatible attributes of the relation. The defined projection operator is a way of accessing attribute values or relation schemas from the outermost level to the innermost level, thus projecting zero or high order attributes at different levels in the nested schema tree.

		$((\Delta t / C_{p1}),\quad (\Delta t\ C_{p1},\ \text{Source Identity}))$
Supplier-Name	π (Product-Name)	
	$(((\text{Name } /C\ p),(\Delta tCp,\text{Source Identity}))\text{Possibility})$	

Figure 8. S m^p×SP maybe P Join example

In Figure 8 projecting the source identity from the outermost level, the sources supplying the possible set of times that the fact sale occurred are known. Applying the project operator in the π(Product–Name), a relation-valued attribute will result in defining the sources that give the possibility that a fact instance is defined. Applying the union operator the total population of sources involved in either value or temporal imperfection, or both are derived. Instances of a timestamped fact with the same entity instances involved are considered different if the values of the timestamps are different or the conclusive beliefs are different.

Intersection ($\cap$): The intersection operation is defined in analogy with the union operator. Relations must be union compatible. Similarly as in the case of the union operator the project can be applied to guarantee union compatible zero level or relation value attributes. In figure 8 projecting the source identity from the outermost level, and intersecting them with the source identity after applying the project operator in the π(Product–Name), the members from the population of sources that are involved in both temporal and value imperfection are derived.

Difference (–): The difference operation accepts as inputs two zero level or relation value attributes and returns instances that it will be members of the population of the first operand that are not members of the population of the second operand. The definition is based on the intuition that two attributes (zero level, relation valued) r, s represents information that two different actors (sources) have about the same world then r–s should represent the information about the real world that r has and s does not

7. Conclusions

A single conceptual framework has been proposed for treating either value or temporal information imperfection. A conceptual model describes the real world and descriptions at the database level must be defined according to the conceptual model that states the static and dynamic elements of an application domain that may generate imperfect information. Certainty about certainty can be expressed. Extensional inconsistencies between different sources can be represented and queried.

A relational algebra that integrates both value and temporal imperfection is also proposed. This can pave the way towards a recursive SQL. An important point is that of integrity constraints. What does it mean for a database state to satisfy an integrity constraint, when in fact information reflects a set of possible states, together with an associated probability distribution? A major research issue is that of supporting probabilistic aggregate functions. This is needed to support queries of the form find the 'X' most probable events that occurred during the time interval $[t_1, t_2]$, or find the 'X' most probable events recurring in the temporal element $\{[t_1, t_2],\ldots, [t_k, t_n]\}$.

Definite Temporal Information is presented by the proposed conceptual and algebraic formalism. However if one considers other applications like scheduling, diagnosis, one may find that information is indefinite.

Indefinite temporal information is conceptually captured and algebraically extracted. The use of probability intervals may suit better applications where marginal errors in the probability distribution are needed.

Quite often another kind of information is required in applications (e.g. the board of directors of a company will meet every Friday, starting from today, 25/02/00).

Infinite temporal information can not be algebraically captured or extracted from our model. This will require the algebraic extension of the model.

This can be achieved with the use of linear equations to describe the lower and upper bound of a time interval, and linear constraints to limit the time window and achieve an intervalic and finite time representation. Time intervals may still be related with probability intervals, thus presenting infinite temporal uncertain information.

References

1. Barbará, D., Garcia-Molina, H., Porter, D. The management of probabilistic data. *IEEE Transactions on Knowledge and Data Engineering*, 4(5), 1992.

2. Bhattacharjcee, T., Mazumdar, A. *Axiomatisation of Fuzzy Multivalued Dependencies in a Fuzzy Relational Data Model*. Elsevier, Fuzzy Sets and Systems, 1996.

3. Chountas, P., Petrounias I. Representing and querying multiple information sources in a single database environment. *Proceedings of 12th International Conference on Software & Systems Engineering and Applications (ICSSEA'99)*, Paris, December, 1999.

4. Dekhtyar, A., Ross, R., Subrahmanian, V. S. *TATA Probabilistic Temporal Databases, I: Algebra*. Department of Computer Science, University of Maryland, USA, 1999.

5. Delgado, M., Moral, S. On the concept of possibility-probability consistency in fuzzy sets for intelligent systems. In D. Dubois, H. Prade, and R. Yager, (eds), *Readings in Fuzzy Sets for Intelligent Systems*, Morgan Kaufman Publishers, 1993, pp 247-250.

6. Dey, D., Sarkar, S. A probabilistic relational model and algebra. *ACM Transactions on Database Systems*, 21(3), 1996.

7. Dyreson, C. E., Snodgrass, R. T. Support valid-time indeterminacy. *ACM Transactions on Database Systems*, 23(1), 1998, pp. 1-57.

8. Fuhr, N., Rölleke, T. *A Probabilistic NF2 Relational Algebra for Imprecision in Databases*. Technical Report, University of Dortmund, 1995.

9. Golby, L. A recursive algebra and query optimisation for nested relations. *Proceedings of ACM SIGMOD International Conference on Management of Data*, 1989.

10. Lakshmanan, L. V. S., Leone, N., Ross, R., Subrahmanian, V. S. *ProbView: A Flexible Probabilistic Database System*. Technical Report, Department of Computer Science, Concordia University, 1997.

11. Li Dey, Liu Dongbo. *A Fuzzy Prolog*. Database System Research Studies, John Wiley, 1988.

12. Liu, H. C., Ramamohanarao, K. Algebraic equivalences among nested relational expressions. *Proceedings of ACM Conference on Information and Knowledge Management (CIKM)*, 1994.

13. Mamdani, E. H. On the classification of uncertainty techniques in relation to the application needs. In A. Motro, P. Smets, (eds), *Uncertainty Management in Information Systems: from Needs to Solutions*, Kluwer Academic 1997, pp. 397-408.

14. Motro, A. *A Formal Framework for Integrating Inconsistent Answers from Multiple Information Sources*. Technical Report ISSE-TR-93-106, Department of Information and Software Systems Engineering, George Mason University, 1993.

15. Petrounias, I. A conceptual development framework for temporal information systems. *Proceedings of Conceptual Modelling - ER '97, 16th International Conference on Conceptual Modelling*, Los Angeles, California, USA, November 1997.

16. Sadri, F., Alagar, V. S., Said, J. N. Semantics of an extended relational model for managing uncertain information. *Proceedings of ACM Conference on Information and Knowledge Management (CIKM)*, 1995.

17. Vandenberghe, R., van Gyseghem, N., van Schooten, A., de Caluwe, R. Integrating fuzziness in database models. In P. Bosc, J. Kacprzyk, (eds), *Fuzziness in Database Management Systems*, Physica-Verlag, 1995, pp. 71-114.

18. Yazici, A., Soyal, A., Buckles, B., Petry, F. Uncertainty in a nested relational database model. *Journal of Data and Knowledge Engineering*, **30**, 1999, pp. 275-302.

Statistical Quality Control of Warehouse Data

Holger Hinrichs

Oldenburg Research and Development Institute
for Computer Science Tools and Systems (OFFIS),
Escherweg 2, 26121 Oldenburg, Germany
holger.hinrichs@offis.de

Abstract

The increasing popularity of data warehouse systems reflects the rising requirement to make strategic use of data integrated from heterogeneous sources. While the research subject of schema integration has been extensively discussed for many years, data integration has been neglected up to the recent past. Data integration often reveals deficiencies of data quality, e. g. inconsistency, redundancy, and incompleteness. Up to now, there are hardly any mellow methods for data quality control. In this paper, we propose an adaptation of statistical process control (SPC), a technique well–established in manufacturing for several decades, to the data quality field. After reviewing basic concepts of SPC, we introduce an appropriate SPC–oriented algorithm for data quality control. By means of several scenarios, we demonstrate the applicability of our approach. Finally, we integrate our concepts into a system architecture for data quality management.

Keywords: data quality, data warehousing, statistical process control.

1. Introduction

The increasing popularity of data warehouse systems [3] reflects the rising requirement to make strategic use of data integrated from heterogeneous sources. Heterogeneity of sources results from incompatible hardware platforms and software environments, diverse data models, schematic conflicts, and finally data conflicts [6]. The latter comprise contradictory data values resulting from defective or subjective acquisition or temporal variance (obsolescence) of data. While platform and schematic conflicts need to be solved once per source, the resolution of data conflicts represents a permanent task in the operation of a data warehouse system.

The topic of data conflicts is closely related to the topic of (data) quality, generally defined as "fitness for use" [5]. Data quality is a multidimensional concept which can be described by a hierarchy of (partially interrelated) *data quality dimensions* (see Fig. 1). Deficiencies of data quality often remain undetected until data integration. If data do not suffice given quality requirements, their use may lead to wrong decisions with serious consequences ("garbage in, garbage out"). Consequently, some kind of data quality control is necessary. The importance of data quality for organisational success has been underestimated for a long time. Gradually, however, organisations become aware of the fact that data quality assurance requires a comprehensive support by suitable software systems [7].

In our work, we concentrate on data conflicts and data integration. We assume that schema integration [14] has already been done and that there is one global database schema (which is assumed to be implemented within a temporary data store called *staging area* [8]) where data from different sources are being stored temporarily. These data possibly still contain data deficiencies like inconsistencies, redundancy, and incompleteness. Before they can be transferred into a data warehouse, they

69

J. Barzdins and A. Caplinskas (eds.), Databases and Information Systems, 69–84.

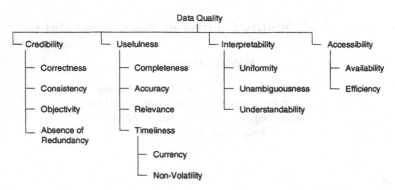

Figure 1. Dimensions of data quality

have to undergo a quality control, comparable to quality control in manufacturing. The placement of our work within the scope of a data warehouse system is depicted in Fig. 2. Although data quality control at the staging area of a data warehouse system is an important issue, it is essential not to neglect the root of data quality problems, i. e. data acquisition, taking place at the data sources.

Unfortunately, there is a profound lack of methods for data quality control. In order to control data quality, it is necessary to measure the degree of fulfilment of pre–defined quality requirements and to establish means to improve quality. In manufacturing, quality control of products has become a matter of course. Statistical methods play a prominent role in this context, e. g. design of experiments (DoE), sampling inspections [12], and statistical process control (SPC) [19], to name just a few. In recent literature, there is a broad acceptance that information can be viewed as a sort of (immaterial) product [18], called *information product*. An information product is being formed out of raw data (cf. raw materials) by applying some kind of information processing. This analogy enables us to transfer concepts of quality control in manufacturing to information technology. However, it must not be neglected that there are some specific characteristics of information products, e. g. no consumption, no wearout, replicatability, low storage costs, and context sensitivity.

In this paper, we propose an adaptation of SPC to the data quality field. The paper is organised as follows: Section 2 describes basic concepts of SPC. In Sect. 3, we show how these concepts can be applied to information technology by introducing an appropriate SPC–oriented algorithm and presenting several application scenarios. In Sect. 4, we integrate our concepts into a system architecture for data quality management. An overview of future work is given in Sect. 5.

2. Statistical Process Control

The basic ideas of statistical process control (SPC) were developed by W. A. Shewhart in the 1920s [15]. During the 1930s and 1940s, SPC was extensively implemented in manufacturing. SPC assumes that the environment of a manufacturing process is never constant, but is undergoing variations permanently. For this reason, values of a quality attribute (e. g. length or toughness) of a product will always fluctuate around the desired value. The causes of these variations can be classified into two categories [11]:

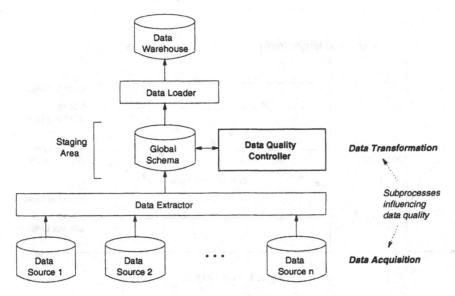

Figure 2. Data integration process in data warehousing

- *Common causes* are inherent to the process. They can be influenced (especially minimised) only by changing the process itself, e. g. by introducing a novel manufacturing method.

- *Special causes* are not inherent to the process. They appear when controllable process parameters change over time, e. g. the inner temperature of a cutting machine or the concentration of a chemical substance. Special causes result in a shift of the process mean and in an increased process variation, which in turn increases the number of defective products.

Special causes have to be eliminated in order to make the process stable and thus put it under statistical control. Stability of a process is a basic premise if reasonable statements about the process are to be made, especially predictions of its future performance. Stability can be judged by analysing the past and present performance of the process. SPC concentrates on the elimination of special causes in order to improve process quality (and thus product quality).

Once control is established, future performance of a process is predictable. The next step is to decide whether the predicted quality level is acceptable or not. This decision depends on (user specific) quality requirements which have to be defined in advance.

The main instrument of SPC are so–called *quality control charts* (QCC). QCCs are used to document statistical parameters of a manufacturing process as they change over time, e. g. arithmetic mean or standard deviation, assessed by means of statistical samples X. If a priori defined limits of these parameters are exceeded during the ongoing process, regulating interferences are made. These limits comprise lower and upper (action) control limits (LCL, UCL) and (optionally) lower and upper warning limits (LWL, UWL). Figure 3 shows an example QCC from the nail manufacturing domain.

In literature, many different types of QCCs have been proposed [19]. They can be classified into QCCs without memory (only the current sample is considered in analysis, so–called Shewhart

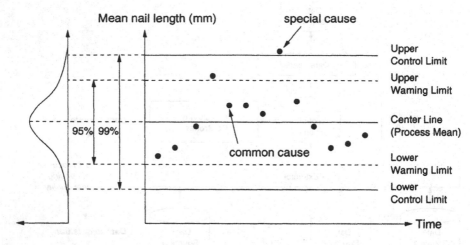

Figure 3. A typical QCC

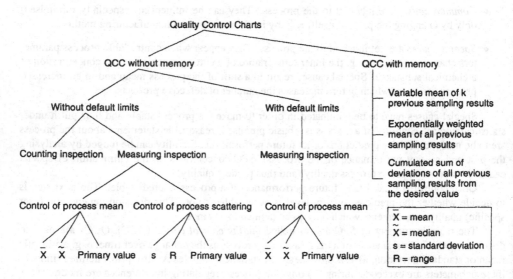

Figure 4. Overview of QCC types

charts) and QCCs with memory (previous samples are also taken into account). Orthogonally, QCCs can be categorised by several other criteria (see Fig. 4). In Sect. 3.3, we will pick up some of these QCC types and introduce them in some more detail.

SPC using QCCs is made up of three phases [19]:

1. *Process Analysis*

   In this preparatory phase, statistical parameters of the process have to be assessed, resulting in an appropriate model of distribution.

   Important parameters comprise the estimated process mean μ, the standard deviation σ, and the defect rate p, each computed of a sample $X = \{x_1, ..., x_m\}$:

$$\mu = \frac{1}{m} \sum_{i=1}^{m} x_i \tag{1}$$

$$\sigma = \sqrt{\frac{1}{m} \sum_{i=1}^{m} (x_i - \mu)^2} \tag{2}$$

$$p = \frac{M}{m} \tag{3}$$

   with M = number of defective products in the sample X.

2. *Design*

   During this phase, a QCC type is selected (see Fig. 4), and the sample size n (potentially different from the sample size m of the analysis phase) as well as the sampling interval Δt are specified (empirically). Furthermore, action control limits (LCL, UCL) and perhaps warning limits (LWL, UWL) are designated.

   Setting up the lower and upper limits is a difficult task: If they are too close, they may be exceeded by variations of common causes. If they are too far apart, regulating actions will not be taken although necessary. In the case of $\overline{X}$–charts (control of process mean), so–called 3σ limits resp. 2σ limits are commonly used to define the lower and upper action control resp. warning limits, where σ is the (estimated) standard deviation of the process (see above):

$$LCL = \mu - 3\sigma \tag{4}$$

$$UCL = \mu + 3\sigma \tag{5}$$

$$LWL = \mu - 2\sigma \tag{6}$$

$$UWL = \mu + 2\sigma \tag{7}$$

   [10] describes several variants of these formulae which are tailored to specific environments.

3. *Controlling*

   This operational phase of SPC includes the subtasks of keeping the QCC up to date at runtime and regulate the process, if necessary.

   At each time interval Δt, a sample of size n is drawn. The sample is then condensed to a statistical parameter value $g(x)$ (typically mean or standard deviation) and recorded on the QCC. Depending on the sampling result, one of three measures can be taken:

- If $LWL < g(x) < UWL$, no action is taken.
- If $LCL < g(x) \leq LWL \lor UWL \leq g(x) < UCL$, special attention is necessary, e. g. by increasing the sampling rate or drawing an additional sample. If this sample shows an equally bad or even worse result, an interference should be made.
- If $g(x) \leq LCL \lor UCL \leq g(x)$, the process is out of statistical control. Consequently, a regulating interference is inevitable.

Beyond these basic measures, there are some pragmatic rules of thumb that can be used as indicators of special process variations. Prominent examples are *zone tests* like "2 consecutive or 2 out of 3 consecutive points beyond either 2σ limit" and *trend tests* like "7 consecutive points ascending or descending" [11].

3. Adaptation of SPC to the Data Quality Context

The idea of using SPC methods for data quality control was already mentioned in [11]. The author introduces a particular measurement protocol called *data tracking*. Although it includes some interesting aspects, we do not believe that data tracking can be successful in practice because it suffers from some basic drawbacks. Before we describe our own approach to SPC–based data quality control, we briefly sketch the data tracking concept.

3.1 DATA TRACKING

[11] correctly states that it is not reasonable to draw *independent* samples (as common in manufacturing) at different checkpoints of an information producing process, because semantic data defects, i. e. incorrect data, can only be detected by a comparison with the real world, which usually is not practicable or even possible. To solve this problem, the author suggests to make use of the redundancy of data, indicating the reappearance of data within several subsequent processes that manipulate them. [11] introduces the term "information chain", meaning the concatenation of these processes. In the following, for reasons of accuracy, we will use the term *information processing process chain (IPPC)* instead of "information chain".

In data tracking, the redundancy of data with respect to an IPPC is – allegedly – used to measure the rate of data defects by tracking data along their way through the IPPC. It is important to understand that data tracking does *not* measure the quality of data, but rather the quality of IPPCs, i. e. software processes. The data which move through an IPPC are just a means to an end.

The essence of data tracking is described by the following key steps [11]:

1. Take a random sample of records entering the IPPC and label each sampled record for later identification.

2. Track sampled records as they progress through the IPPC until they finally enter some sort of data sink, e. g. a data warehouse. Log the contents of the tracked records at predefined checkpoints of the IPPC.

3. Identify defects produced by the IPPC.

4. At appropriate intervals, summarise the progress of sampled records and analyse the results by SPC methods. If necessary, re–establish control and suggest process improvements.

The third step is particularly questionable. No means are given by which defects can be detected. The author simply states that so–called "spurious operational changes" possibly occur which introduce incorrect values, but he does not give any hints *how* to mark off this type of changes from other types of changes, especially intended data transformations.

Spurious changes are being analysed at the fourth step. [11] suggests – among others – the following analysis instruments:

- Plots of the "number of changes per record" against time.

- Flow charts of percentages of spuriously changed attributes between processes.

- Pareto charts [9] of proportions of spurious changes in each attribute.

- Pareto charts of proportions of inconsistencies between redundant databases.

- $\overline{X}$–charts (controlling process mean) and s–charts (controlling process scattering) of process cycle times.

We will now point out our main objections against the data tracking approach:

- The basic assumption of data tracking does not stand real–world requirements. Redundancy alone does not help at all to detect data defects. Instead, it is inevitable to take domain knowledge into account.

- Only inconsistencies between (redundant) databases are considered, whereas inconsistencies within records or between records of the same database are neglected.

- No means to identify spurious changes are provided. The author simply assumes that they *are* detected somehow.

- The number of changes per record does not say anything about the quality of an IPPC and thus about the quality of data.

- Measurement of process cycle times, i. e. time efficiency of software, is rather an issue of software engineering than of data quality control.

Altogether, we do not believe that data tracking is a feasible technique for data quality control. Nevertheless, we think that SPC methods are well suited for the data quality context. In the following section, we present our own concept of SPC–based data quality control.

3.2 A NEW APPROACH TO SPC–BASED DATA QUALITY CONTROL

Our approach to SPC–based data quality control is significantly different from data tracking in the following point: Although we also track records on their way through an IPPC, we do not simply log changes of values, but concentrate on data quality dimensions instead (cf. Fig. 1). A sample of records is analysed at different checkpoints of the IPPC, making use of dedicated (possibly domain–dependent) measuring methods for each dimension. This analysis results in a vector of quality values. The dimensionality of the vector equals the number of quality dimensions considered. This is called a *dimension specific tracking* of samples. (Alternatively, the single quality values of a record could be merged to one overall quality value, e. g. by computing a weighted sum, which is then being tracked along the IPPC.) We take the following quality dimensions into consideration, since we believe they are the ones to be measured and influenced most easily:

- Consistency

- Absence of redundancy

- Completeness

- Accuracy

- Timeliness (including currency and non–volatility)

- Interpretability (including uniformity, unambiguousness, and understandability)

Due to some deviating characteristics of information products compared to physical products (see Sect. 1), SPC in information processing must be inherently different from SPC in manufacturing in the following aspects:

- Since data quality checks are usually done within milliseconds or even less, even very large sampling sizes (up to 100%) can be handled without significant loss of efficiency. Real–time applications are an exception to this rule (see Sect. 3.4).

- Since the matter being tracked is data quality, an upper control limit is usually not necessary when using $\overline{X}$– or $\tilde{X}$–charts (controlling the quality mean and median, respectively). (Data quality cannot be *too high*.) There is an exception to this rule as well: Confidential data (e. g. personal data in a cancer registry) may have to be made anonymous by decreasing their accuracy or completeness on purpose, e. g. by generalising a person's local area code resp. leaving out the address.

If we intend to adapt statistical process control methods to the data quality field, we have to identify which processes must be taken into account. In data warehousing, the subprocesses "data acquisition" and "data transformation" may influence data quality, as illustrated in Fig. 2.

As in manufacturing, attribute values of information products are subject to permanent variation. This variation can be due to one of the following reasons [13]:

- *Common causes*

    If data acquisition is done manually, there will always be some subjective influence, also called *subjective bias*. For example, different physicians will code the diagnosis of a disease in a slightly different way. This influence should be minimised by strict guidelines, but it probably cannot be eliminated completely. In a broader sense, variations resulting from different automatic acquisition methods (e. g. mercury thermometer vs. alcohol thermometer) can also be viewed as some kind of subjectivity. With regard to SPC, we impute such variations to common causes.

- *Special causes*

    Input deficiencies subsume inconsistent, inaccurate, omitted, obsolete, redundant, and inadequately represented values. They correspond to the data quality dimensions listed above and are imputed to special causes in the sense of SPC.

We intend to use SPC to detect input deficiencies. In our opinion, the employment of SPC in information processing is not possible as a stand–alone method. Instead, it has to be based on dimension specific metrics and measuring algorithms, as described in the following section.

3.3 AN ALGORITHM FOR SPC–BASED DATA QUALITY CONTROL

Our approach to SPC–based data quality control comprises the following steps, reflecting the three SPC phases known from Sect. 2:

1. *Process Analysis*

   (a) Select data quality dimensions $d_1, ..., d_k$ to be considered (e. g. d_1 = consistency, d_2 = accuracy, d_3 = completeness, etc.).

   (b) Specify a list $C = c_1 \rightarrow ... \rightarrow c_{max}$ of IPPC checkpoints to be considered.

   (c) Draw a sample $X = \{x_1, ..., x_m\}$ of data objects at each of the previously defined IPPC checkpoints. (For reasons of clarity, we will omit the additional index for the checkpoint in the following formulae, writing e. g. q_{ij} instead of q_{ijc} meaning the quality value of sample element x_i along dimension d_j at IPPC checkpoint c.) A *data object* is a unit of data whose quality is to be checked. Depending on the application, two levels of granularity can be distinguished:

$$granularity(x_i) = \begin{cases} \text{a single database record} \\ \text{a set of database records} \end{cases} \tag{8}$$

   In data warehousing, the IPPC should comprise those subprocesses of data integration that influence data quality, i. e. data acquisition (at the sources) and data transformation (at the staging area), as shown in Fig. 2.

   (d) Compute an $(m \times k)$–dimensional *quality matrix* q at each checkpoint, whereby k is the number of quality dimensions considered and each coordinate q_{ij} represents a quality value of data object x_i along dimension d_j:

$$q = \begin{pmatrix} q_{11} & q_{21} & \cdots & q_{m1} \\ q_{12} & q_{22} & \cdots & q_{m2} \\ \cdots & \cdots & \cdots & \cdots \\ q_{1k} & q_{2k} & \cdots & q_{mk} \end{pmatrix} \tag{9}$$

   The quality values q_{ij} are determined by measuring x_i along dimension d_j by means of a dimension specific measuring function f_j (potentially domain specific, e. g. checking the plausibility of medical information, and granularity specific, e. g. determining the degree of redundancy within an arbitrary set of database records):

$$q_{ij} = f_j(x_i) \tag{10}$$

   (e) Compute k–dimensional vectors μ and σ of mean and standard deviation values of sample X along quality dimensions $d_1, ..., d_k$:

$$\mu = \begin{pmatrix} \mu_1 \\ \mu_2 \\ ... \\ \mu_k \end{pmatrix} \tag{11}$$

with $\mu_j = \frac{1}{m} \sum_{i=1}^{m} q_{ij}$ $(j = 1, ..., k)$.

$$\sigma = \begin{pmatrix} \sigma_1 \\ \sigma_2 \\ ... \\ \sigma_k \end{pmatrix} \tag{12}$$

with $\sigma_j = \sqrt{\frac{1}{m} \sum_{i=1}^{m} (q_{ij} - \mu_j)^2}$ $(j = 1, ..., k)$.

2. *Design*

(a) Specify the sample size n and the sampling rate r (both domain–dependent). r can be either a temporal value (e. g. 10 samples per minute) or a quantifying value (e. g. 1 sample per 1.000 records). At the staging area of a data warehouse system, for example, n and r should be set subject to the update dynamics of data resp. to the number of records extracted at once in consequence of the implemented extraction strategy (periodical, query–driven, event–driven, or immediate) [17].

(b) Specify the QCC type choosing an $\overline{X}$–chart to control the quality level and an s–chart to control the quality scattering. (Other QCC types like $\widetilde{X}$–charts (median control) or R–charts (range control) have not been considered yet.)

(c) In case of an $\overline{X}$–chart, specify lower control and warning limits for each quality dimension d_j (remember upper limits are not necessary). These limits are domain–dependent, so we just give an example of typical values (cf. Sect. 2):

$$LCL_j = \mu_j - 3\sigma_j \tag{13}$$
$$LWL_j = \mu_j - 2\sigma_j \tag{14}$$

In case of an s–chart, specify the upper control and warning limits for each quality dimension d_j (lower limits are not necessary because scattering cannot be too low). Again, these limits are domain–dependent. If, for example, standard deviation obeys a χ^2 distribution with $n - 1$ degrees of freedom, the limits should be specified as follows, using the tabulated 0.99 resp. 0.95 percentiles appendant to the above χ^2 distribution [12]:

$$UCL_j = \sqrt{\frac{\chi^2_{n-1;0.99}}{n-1}} \sigma_j \tag{15}$$
$$UWL_j = \sqrt{\frac{\chi^2_{n-1;0.95}}{n-1}} \sigma_j \tag{16}$$

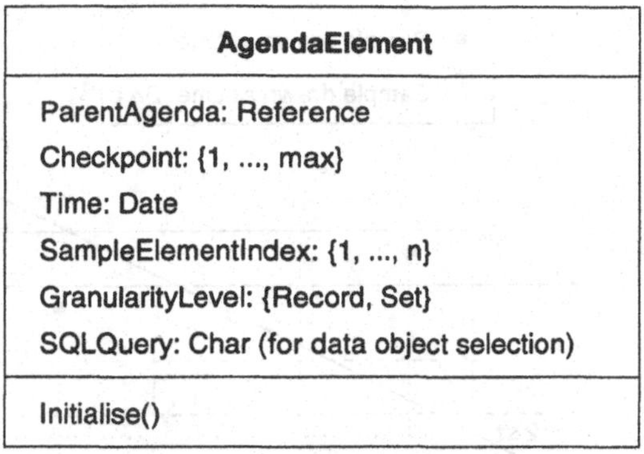

AgendaElement
ParentAgenda: Reference Checkpoint: {1, ..., max} Time: Date SampleElementIndex: {1, ..., n} GranularityLevel: {Record, Set} SQLQuery: Char (for data object selection)
Initialise()

Figure 5. Internal structure of an agenda element (UML notation)

3. Controlling

(a) At time t (derived from r), activate the first checkpoint of the IPPC ($c := c_1$).

Ideally, this first checkpoint should be positioned after the first data entry step at a data source. In practice, however, data sources and staging area typically operate in remote environments. Consequently, it is not possible to concatenate source subprocesses and staging subprocesses to one single IPPC. Instead, they have to be split up into two separate IPPCs.

(b) Draw a sample $X_c = \{x_{c1}, ..., x_{cn}\}$ of data objects at checkpoint c.

(c) Label the elements of X_c by storing all relevant information in a special container structure called *agenda*:

$$agenda.insert(X_c) \tag{17}$$

The internal structure of an agenda element is illustrated in Fig. 5.

(d) Compute the quality matrix q_c of data objects at checkpoint c as described above.

(e) Compute a k–dimensional vector $g(X_c)$ by calculating the mean or standard deviation vector (dependent on QCC design) of the sample X_c as described above.

(f) Record $g(X_c)$ on the QCC (see Fig. 6 for an example).

(g) Subject to the following conditions, take an appropriate measure:

If $\exists j \in \{1, ..., k\} : g_j(X_c) \leq LCL_j$ (in case of an $\overline{X}$–chart) resp. $\exists j \in \{1, ..., k\} : g_j(X_c) \geq UCL_j$ (in case of an s–chart), initiate a correcting interference into the process. The kind of interference depends on the respective domain. If the instability is detected at the staging area of a data warehouse system, for example, the data source that delivered the defective data should be informed immediately.

If $\exists j \in \{1, ..., k\} : LCL_j < g_j(X_c) \leq LWL_j$ ($\overline{X}$–chart) resp. $\exists j \in \{1, ..., k\} : UWL_j > g_j(X_c) \geq UWL_j$ (s–chart), continue at step 3b (i. e. draw a new sample at the same checkpoint, infinite loops should be prohibited by appropriate abort criteria).

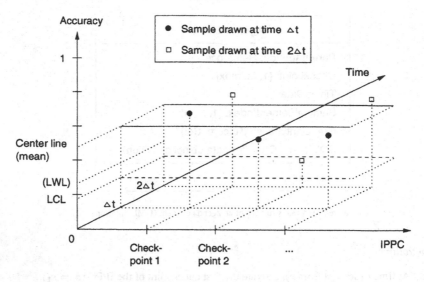

Figure 6. Example of a 3–dimensional $\overline{X}$–chart

If $\forall j \in \{1, ..., k\} : g_j(X_c) > LWL_j$ ($\overline{X}$–chart) resp. $\forall j \in \{1, ..., k\} : g_j(X_c) < UWL_j$ (s–chart), then – in case of $c = c_i$ $(1 \leq i < max)$ – activate the next checkpoint ($c := c_{i+1}$) and continue at step 3b. In case of $c = c_{max}$, continue at step 3a and thus start a new pass.

In contrast to conventional SPC, our approach is inherently multidimensional, particularly in two ways:

- Instead of a single process parameter, a number of (possibly interrelated) parameters are controlled at the same time, namely data quality along k different dimensions.

- Data quality is controlled both over time and along various checkpoints of an IPPC.

Altogether, we are concerned with $(k + 2)$–dimensional QCCs (time, IPPC, plus k quality dimensions). Obviously, in case of $k > 1$ it gets difficult to use the classical (i. e. graphical) QCC notation. But this is a minor problem, since our algorithm can be automated easily, and it is nothing special for a computer to manage a $(k + 2)$–dimensional data structure. Figure 6 shows the special case of a 3–dimensional $\overline{X}$–chart, controlling only one quality dimension (accuracy, exemplarily). The lower warning line is not depicted for reasons of clarity.

The fact that both time and IPPC checkpoints are considered implies that our algorithm can be parallelised, provided that suitable hardware is available: While sample X is being controlled at checkpoint c_i, a previously drawn sample Y that already passed c_i can be controlled at checkpoint c_{i+1}. The number of simultaneous control processes thus correlates with the number of checkpoints of the IPPC.

3.4 APPLICATION SCENARIOS

In this section, we present three scenarios to which our approach is applicable. The scenarios focus at different subprocesses of the data integration process depicted in Fig. 2, namely data acquisition (automatic and manual) and data transformation.

3.4.1 Satellite Data (Subprocess "Automatic Data Acquisition")

Imagine a satellite in outer space continuously collecting data (e. g. weather information) via a measuring instrument on board. Normally, recorded data values will always lie within certain ranges (generally spoken: within a union of disjoint intervals) and have a certain accuracy. From time to time, for reasons of machine wearout or external circumstances, the measuring instrument possibly starts to deliver inconsistent, incomplete, or inaccurate data. This decline of data quality, originating from special causes in the sense of SPC, has to be detected as soon as possible. A correcting interference into the process is necessary in order to reestablish a state of stability. This can be done by readjusting the measuring instrument automatically or – in case of more serious damage – by informing ground control.

Since satellites typically record data continuously, it might be too time–consuming to check each and every data value. Therefore, statistical methods like SPC seem to be predestined for data quality control in such real–time environments.

3.4.2 Cancer Registry Data (Subprocess "Manual Data Acquisition")

Epidemiological cancer registries perform a population–based registration of cancer cases in order to analyse temporal and spatial trends, to identify risk groups and factors, etc. [4]. These tasks can only be fulfilled with a complete and valid collection of cancer cases. This requires integration of data from different, heterogeneous sources. Usually, data integration is rendered more difficult by a number of data conflicts which have to be solved. Notifications on cancer cases typically contain information of varying quality and different representations; one often has to deal with redundant, incomplete, invalid, or inconsistent data. Each cancer case is to be stored in the registry only once, even if it is transmitted several times by different organisations (physicians, hospitals, pathologies, etc.). Several notifications referring the same patient or tumour have to be condensed to *one* explorable database record. The resulting record should contain the most reliable or most specific values of the single notifications.

Particularly critical with regard to data quality issues in cancer registries is manual data acquisition, since data entry clerks often...

- operate on legacy software lacking appropriate input checks, resulting in invalid, inaccurate, or missing values, inconsistencies, and representational conflicts,

- add a subjective bias to data,

- use obsolete coding schemes, and

- enter cancer cases already known to the registry, introducing unintentional redundancy.

SPC can be used to detect process variations originating from one of the causes mentioned above. In contrast to the satellite scenario, this should be a long–term observation, keeping track of the evolution of data quality over months or even years. It should be done specifically for each data source to be able to identify sources delivering data of constantly low or decreasing data quality.

3.4.3 Metadata for Data Cleansing (Subprocess "Data Transformation")

In the course of data integration into a data warehouse, some kind of data cleansing is inevitable. As there are various cleansing algorithms available [16], it is not easy to decide which of them to use in which combination. Furthermore, quality dimensions may be interrelated, so it is especially important to take an overall view at all quality dimensions under consideration. Both synergistic and competing relationships are possible, e. g. increasing consistency will usually also increase correctness while increasing timeliness may decrease accuracy.

Altogether, empirical knowledge about which algorithms work best can be very useful. SPC helps to build up this knowledge by tracking metadata about data quality along the cleansing process.

4. Integration into a Data Quality Management System

A software system responsible for data quality control in an organisation is called a *data quality management system (DQMS)* [2]. Since SPC – as we have shown in this paper – is suitable to facilitate data quality control, it should be explicitly supported by a DQMS. Figure 7 shows the architecture of such a DQMS. The data whose quality is to be assured are temporarily stored at a special location which can be viewed as the staging area of a data warehouse system. A loader is responsible for transferring quality assured data from the temporary store to a data warehouse.

The single phases of a data quality management (DQM) process (planning, measurement, analysis, and improvement of quality) are reflected by corresponding software modules. The cooperation of these modules is managed by a DQM controller interacting with the user via a graphical user interface. The DQMS provides a variety of data cleansing methods comprising data migration as well as data scrubbing and data auditing [1]. Each quality management module accesses metadata by means of a central repository. The DQMS provides a high degree of automation, as manual interferences are reduced to system configuration, specification of quality requirements, and solving data conflicts that cannot be handled automatically.

Since our SPC approach rests upon "conventional" quality measurement methods, the corresponding software module, called *SPC engine*, is situated on top of the measurement module. Besides, it accesses the metadata repository and the temporary data store. According to the main phases of SPC, there are the following submodules within the SPC engine:

- A *process analyser* which helps to select quality dimensions, data objects, and checkpoints to be considered and calculate basic parameters like mean and standard deviation.

- A *QCC designer* which provides means to specify a QCC type, define sample size and sampling rate, and finally calculate control and warning limits.

- An *IPPC controller* which keeps the QCC up to date, triggering interferences if necessary, according to the algorithm described in Sect. 3.3.

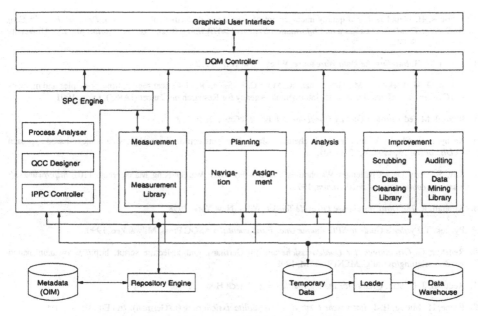

Figure 7. Architecture of a DQMS supporting SPC

5. Conclusions

In this paper, we reviewed the concepts of statistical process control (SPC) and proposed an adaptation of these concepts to the data quality field. We then evaluated the data tracking approach of [11], concluding with the insight that it does not fit practice needs. Next, we developed a new approach to SPC–based data quality control and presented three different scenarios to which it could be applied. Finally, we integrated our concepts into a data quality management system.

Future work will include:

- Refinement of our SPC process model, amongst other things by integrating additional QCC types like $\tilde{X}$–charts and R–charts and by defining abort criteria in case of quality values exceeding warning limits.

- Prototypical implementation of the SPC engine.

- Evaluation of our concepts and implementation by means of an epidemiological cancer registry.

References

1. Chaudhuri, S., Dayal, U. An overview of data warehousing and OLAP technology. *ACM SIGMOD Record*, **26**(1), 1995, pp. 65–74.

2. Hinrichs, H. Metadata–based quality management of warehouse data. In K. Richta, (ed.), *Proc. of the 19th Conf. on Current Trends in Databases and Information Systems (DATASEM), Brno, Czech Republic*, Masaryk University, 1999, pp. 239–248.

3. Inmon, W. H. *Building the Data Warehouse*. Wiley, New York, 1992.

4. Jensen, O. M., Parkin, D. M., MacLennan, R., Muir, C. S., Skeet, R. G. Cancer registration: principles and methods. *IARC Scientific Publications No. 95*, International Agency for Research on Cancer (IARC), Lyon, 1991.

5. Juran, J. M. (ed.) *Juran's Quality Handbook*. 5th Ed., McGraw–Hill, 1999.

6. Kashyap, V., Sheth, A. Semantic and schematic similarities between database objects: a context–based approach. *VLDB Journal*, 5, 1996, pp. 276–304.

7. Kay, E. Dirty Data Challenges Warehouses. DWS – For Data Warehousing Management (10), *http://www.softwaremag.com/data_whs/dw10intr.htm*, 1997.

8. Kimball, R. *The Data Warehouse Lifecycle Toolkit*. Wiley, New York, 1998.

9. Pyzdek, T. *Pyzdek's Guide to SPC Volume One: Fundamentals*. ASQC Press, Milwaukee, 1990.

10. Redeker, G. *Grundlagen der Qualitaetssicherung* (in German). Online lecture script, http:// www.iq.uni-hannover.de/vorlesung/qs1/allg/_MENUE.HTM, 1998.

11. Redman, T. C. *Data Quality for the Information Age*. Artech House, 1996.

12. Rinne, H., Mittag, H.-J. *Statistische Methoden der Qualitaetssicherung* (in German). 2nd Ed., Hanser, 1991.

13. Sachtleber, M. *Eine generische Bibliothek von Datenqualitaetsmessverfahren fuer Data Warehouses* (in German). Diploma thesis, University of Oldenburg, Germany, 1999.

14. Sheth, A. P., Larson, J. A. Federated database systems for managing distributed, heterogeneous, and autonomous databases. *ACM Computing Surveys*, **22**(3), 1990, pp. 183–236.

15. Shewhart, W. A. *Economic Control of Quality of Manufactured Product*. D. Van Nostrand, New York, 1931.

16. Vality Technology Inc. *http://www.vality.com*, 2000.

17. Vavouras, A., Gatziu, S., Dittrich, K. R. The SIRIUS approach for refreshing data warehouses incrementally. *Proc. of the GI Conf. BTW'99, Freiburg, Germany*, Springer, 1999, pp. 80–86.

18. Wang, R. Y. Total data quality management. *Communications of the ACM*, **41**(2), 1998, pp. 58–65.

19. Wheeler, D., Chambers, D. *Understanding Statistical Process Control*. 2nd Ed., SPC Press, 1992.

Data Mining within DBMS Functionality

Maciej Zakrzewicz

Poznan University of Technology, Poland
mzakrz@cs.put.poznan.pl

Abstract

Data mining slowly evolves from simple discovery of frequent patterns and regularities in large data sets toward interactive, user-oriented, on-demand decision supporting. Since data to be mined is usually located in a database, there is a promising idea of integrating data mining methods into database management systems (DBMS). In this paper we present the results of developing our research prototype for DBMS-integrated data mining. We focus on two main contributions: query language for data mining and constraints-driven algorithm for association rules discovery.

Keywords: data mining algorithms, data mining architectures.

1. Introduction

Data mining, also referred to as database mining or knowledge discovery in databases (KDD), is a new research area that aims at the discovery of useful information from large datasets. Data mining uses statistical analysis and inference to extract interesting trends and events, create useful reports, support decision making etc. It exploits the massive amounts of data to achieve business, operational or scientific goals. One of the most promising data mining applications is affinity analysis, which provides a user with the knowledge about item co-occurrences in item sets. The most common representation of item co-occurrences are association rules.

The problem of association rules discovery is an interesting subfield of data mining. By an association rule, that holds in a database of item sets (e.g. big-store transactions), we mean a formula of the form $X \rightarrow Y$, where X and Y are two sets of items. We refer to the left hand side of the rule as the *body* and to the right hand side as the *head*. Additionally, each rule has two associated measures of statistical significance and strength: *support* and *confidence*. The support is the joint probability to find X and Y in the same items group. The rule confidence is the conditional probability to find in the item group Y having found X.

A number of association rules discovery algorithms has been proposed. Most of them discover rules that have support and confidence greater than given minimum values, however, the data mining process is more interactive and more iterative in nature. It requires not only high-performance and rapid-response algorithms, but also the environmental support that assists users in data selection, rule generation and rule filtering.

In this paper we present the architecture of our research prototype, called RD2, which extends DBMS functionality toward on-demand association rules discovery. The prototype implements our improved algorithm for association rules discovery and provides a user with an SQL-like query language which is used to control the algorithm. The paper illustrates the need and the solution for integrating data mining methods with core DBMS functions.

85

J. Barzdins and A. Caplinskas (eds.), Databases and Information Systems, 85–96.

1.1 BASIC DEFINITIONS

Let $L=\{l_1, l_2, ..., l_m\}$ be a set of literals, called items. Let a non-empty set of items T be called an *itemset*. Let D be a set of variable length itemsets, where each itemset $T \subseteq L$. We say that an itemset T *supports* an item $x \in L$ if x is in T. We say that an itemset T *supports* an itemset $X \subseteq L$ if T supports every item in the set X.

An *association rule* is an implication of the form $X \rightarrow Y$, where $X \subset L$, $Y \subset L$, $X \cap Y = \varnothing$. Each rule has associated measures of its statistical significance and strength, called *support* and *confidence*. The support of the rule $X \rightarrow Y$ in the set D is:

$$support(X \rightarrow Y, D) = \frac{\left|\{T \in D \mid T \text{ supports } X \cup Y\}\right|}{|D|}$$

In other words, the rule $X \rightarrow Y$ holds in the set D with support s if $(100*s)\%$ of itemsets in D support $X \cup Y$. The confidence of the rule $X \rightarrow Y$ in the set D is:

$$confidence(X \rightarrow Y, D) = \frac{\left|\{T \in D \mid T \text{ supports } X \cup Y\}\right|}{\left|\{T \in D \mid T \text{ supports } X\}\right|}$$

In other words, the rule $X \rightarrow Y$ has confidence c if $(100*c)\%$ of itemsets in D that support X also support Y.

Example. Consider a supermarket with a large collection of products. When a customer buys a set of products, the whole purchase is stored in a database and referred to as a transaction having a unique identifier, date, and a customer code. Each transaction contains the set of purchased products together with their quantity and price. An example of the database of customer transactions is depicted below. The attribute *trans_id* represents the transaction identifier, *cust_id* - the customer code, *product* - the purchased product, *qty* - the quantity and *price* - the price.

trans_id	cust_id	product	date	Qty	Price
1	908723	soda_03	02/22/98	6	0.20
1	908723	potato_chips_12	02/22/98	3	0.99
2	032112	beer_10	02/22/98	4	0.49
2	032112	potato_chips_12	02/22/98	1	0.99
2	032112	diapers_b01	02/22/98	1	1.49
3	504725	soda_03	02/23/98	10	0.20
4	002671	soda_03	02/24/98	6	0.20
4	002671	beer_10	02/24/98	2	0.49
4	002671	potato_chips_12	02/24/98	4	0.99
5	078938	beer_10	02/24/98	2	0.49
5	078938	potato_chips_12	02/24/98	4	0.99
5	078938	diapers_b01	02/24/98	10	1.49

The strongest association rules that can be found in the example database are listed below:

beer_10 → potato_chips_12	support=0.60	confidence=1.00
potato_chips_12 → beer_10	support=0.60	confidence=0.75
beer_10 ∧ diapers_b01 → potato_chips_12	support=0.40	confidence=1.00
diapers_b01 ∧ potato_chips_12 → beer_10	support=0.40	confidence=1.00
diapers_b01 → beer_10 ∧ potato_chips_12	support=0.40	confidence=1.00
diapers_b01 → beer_10	support=0.40	confidence=1.00
diapers_b01 → potato_chips_12	support=0.40	confidence=1.00
beer_10 ∧ potato_chips_12 → diapers_b01	support=0.40	confidence=0.67
beer_10 → diapers_b01 ∧ potato_chips_12	support=0.40	confidence=0.67
beer_10 → diapers_b01	support=0.40	confidence=0.67
soda_03 → potato_chips_12	support=0.40	confidence=0.67
potato_chips_12 → beer_10 ∧ diapers_b01	support=0.40	confidence=0.50
potato_chips_12 → diapers_b01	support=0.40	confidence=0.50
potato_chips_12 → soda_03	support=0.40	confidence=0.50

For example, the association rule `"beer_10 → potato_chips_12 (support=0.60, confidence=1.00)"` states that every time the product *beer_10* is purchased, the product *potato_chips_12* is purchased too and that this pattern occurs in 60 percent of all transactions. Knowing that 60 percent of customers who buy a certain brand of beer also buy a certain brand of potato chips can help the retailer determine appropriate promotional displays, optimal use of shelf space, and effective sales strategies. As a result of doing this type of association rules discovery, the retailer might decide not to discount potato chips whenever the beer is on sale, as doing so would needlessly reduce profits.

1.2 BASIC ALGORITHM FOR ASSOCIATION RULES DISCOVERY

The first algorithm for association rules discovery was presented in the paper of Agrawal, Imielinski and Swami [1]. The algorithm discovered all association rules whose support and confidence were greater than some user specified minimum values. In [6], an algorithm called *SETM* was proposed to solve this problem using relational operators. In [3], two new algorithms called *Apriori* and *AprioriTID* were proposed. These algorithms achieved significant improvements over the previous algorithms and became the core of many new ones [11, 5, 10, 12, 13, 4].

The algorithm called *Apriori* discovers in a given database all association rules with support and confidence above some minimum values. We assume that items in each itemset are kept sorted in their lexicographic order. In this algorithm, the problem of association rules discovery is decomposed into two subproblems:

1. Iteratively find all possible itemsets that have support greater or equal to a given minimum support value (*minsup*). Itemsets satisfying the above constraint are called *large* itemsets, and all others are *small* itemsets. The first pass of the algorithm counts item occurrences to determine the large 1-itemsets (each 1-itemset contains exactly one item). In each of the next passes, the large itemsets L_{k-1} found in the (k-1)th pass are used to generate the candidate itemsets C_k, using *apriori-gen* function described below. Then, the database is scanned and the support of candidates in C_k is counted. The output of the first phase of the *Apriori* algorithm consists of a set of k-itemsets (k=1, 2, ...), that have support greater or equal to a given minimum support value. Figure 1 presents a formal description of this part of the algorithm.

2. Use the large itemsets to generate the desired rules. For each large itemset *l*, find all non-empty subsets *a* of *l*. For each subset *a*, output a rule of the form $a \rightarrow (l - a)$ if *support(l)/support(a)* is greater or equal to a given minimum confidence value (*minconf*). Notice, that if a rule $a \rightarrow (l - a)$ has the confidence value less than *minconf*, then any rule $b \rightarrow (l - b)$, where $b \subset a$, also has the confidence values less than *minconf*. Thus, the rule generation begins with the empty head that is being expanded unless the confidence value falls below *minconf*.

```
L₁ = {large 1-itemsets};
for ( k = 2; Lₖ₋₁ ≠ 0; k++) do begin
    Cₖ = apriori_gen (Lₖ₋₁ );
    forall transactions t ∈ D do begin
            Cₜ = subset (Cₖ , t);
            forall candidates c ∈ Cₜ  do
                    c.count ++;
    end
    Lₖ = { c ∈ Cₖ | c.count ≥ minsup};
    end
Answer = ∪ₖ  Lₖ;
```

Figure 1. Large itemset generation phase of Apriori algorithm

In the algorithm *Apriori*, candidate itemsets C_k are generated from previously found large itemsets L_{k-1}, using the *apriori-gen* function. The *apriori-gen* function works in two steps: 1. join step and 2. prune step. First, in the join step, large itemsets from L_{k-1} are joined with other large itemsets from L_{k-1} in the following SQL-like manner:

```
insert into Ck
select p.item1, p.item2, ..., p.itemk-1, q.itemk-1
from Lk-1 p, Lk-1 q
where p.item1 = q.item1
  and p.item2 = q.item2
  ...
  and p.itemk-2 = q.itemk-2
  and p.itemk-1 < q.itemk-1;
```

Next, in the prune step, each itemset $c \in C_k$ such that some (k-1)-subset of c is not in L_{k-1} is deleted:

```
forall itemsets c∈Ck do
  forall (k-1)-subsets s of c do
    if (s ∉ Lk-1) then delete c from Ck;
```

The set of candidate k-itemsets C_k is then returned as a result of the function *apriori-gen*.

2. RD2 System Architecture

RD2 is our prototype extension to *Oracle DBMS* which implements association rules discovery methods. From a user's point of view, *RD2* is a transparent layer, located on top of *Oracle DBMS*, extending *SQL* language with a set of new statements and functions, which can be used to discover association rules in database tables. From a programmer's point of view, *RD2* delivers a universal *API* (Application Programmer Interface), which can be used to build data mining applications.

A user, or an application, specifies data mining problems in the form of declarative queries, similar to those in *SQL*. The queries are processed by *RD2* and the association rules satisfying given constraints are discovered and presented to the user. The user can analyse the rules or store them in the same database for future retrieval.

The general architecture of *RD2* is given in Figure 2. The user application sends the queries via the *RD2* network layer, using *TCP/IP* protocol. The queries are parsed by the extended *SQL* parser, and then either processed by a data mining algorithm or sent directly to the *DBMS* for further processing. Finally, the discovered association rules are returned to the user.

RD2 core modules are located on the machine running the *DBMS*. It results in fast database access, without the need to transfer large data volumes through networks.

We have also developed a user tool for ad-hoc rule queries execution. The tool window is presented in Figure 3 – the user specifies the rule query from keyboard and watch the resulting association rules on the screen.

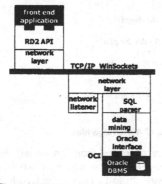

Figure 2. RD2 internal architecture

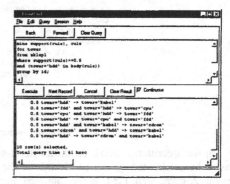

Figure 3. The user tool for ad-hoc rule queries

2.1 SQL LANGUAGE EXTENSION

We have proposed the extension of industry-standard SQL language to handle data mining, called *MineSQL*. In *MineSQL*, users express their specific problems by means of rule queries. The rule queries are processed by a data mining engine, which generates demanded rules from the given relational database. Sets of discovered rules are then returned to the users.

The main difference between industry-standard *SQL* language and the *MineSQL* language is the addition of the *MINE* statement, which is used to extract rules from database tables. The *MINE* statement can also be used as a query or subquery in another statement (e.g. *SELECT, INSERT*). The general syntax of the *MINE* statement is defined as follows:

```
MINE rule_expr [,...]
[FOR {data_expr [USING tax_name][,...]| *}]
[TO {data_expr [USING tax_name][,...]| *}]
FROM table [, table] ...
[WHERE    {data_condition|rule_condition}
[(AND|OR){data_condition|rule_condition}]
   ... ]
[GROUP BY data_expr [, data_expr]... [HAVING condition]]
[ORDER BY rule_expr [(ASC|DESC)][,...]]
```

The *MINE* statement produces a set of rules or rule expressions. It defines the structure of rules: the body is defined as a subset of attribute expressions in the *FOR* clause, the head is defined as a subset of attribute expressions in the *TO* clause. The *AS* keyword can specify a taxonomy (conceptual hierarchy) used in generalising item values. The clause *FROM* specifies which tables or views to explore. The selection constraints for both table data and rules extracted are specified in the *WHERE* section. The *MINE* statement inspects table records grouped by attributes indicated in the *GROUP BY* clause: records belonging to a group are characterised by the same value of the grouping attribute. The result rules may be sorted by the *ORDER BY* expressions in ascending or descending order. We also support user-defined discretisation of attribute values by means of stored database procedures.

Rule expressions used in the *MINE* statement are combinations of rules, constants and rule functions. The *MineSQL* language supports a wide collection of rule functions. The rule functions operate on rules. The most commonly used rule functions are:
- `support(r)` - returns the support value of the rule r,
- `confidence(r)` - returns the confidence value of the rule r,
- `body(r)` - returns the rule r body,
- `head(r)` - returns the rule r head,
- `bodylen(r)` - returns the number of rule r body elements,
- `headlen(r)` - returns the number of rule r head elements,
- `rulelen(r)` - returns the number of rule r body and head elements.

The *MineSQL* language also allows *IN* and *NOT IN* set operators to be used on a rule, rule body and rule head items. For two sets of items A and B, the expression A IN B is true if: $A \neq \varnothing$ and $A \subseteq B$.

To illustrate the *MINE* statement, let us consider the following example.

Example. Assume that a user looks for all association rules about products of today's big-store transactions such that: the body of the rule contains the element *product='milk'* or *product='butter'*, the confidence of the rule is at least 10%, the support is at least 20% and the head of the rule contains only one element. Additionally, the user would like to explore only this year's transactions.

The query specified above is represented in MineSQL as follows:

```
mine rule, support(rule)
for product
from shoppings P
where ('product=''milk''' in body(rule)
       or 'product=''butter''' in body(rule))
   and confidence(rule) > 0.1
   and support(rule) > 0.2
   and headlen(rule)=1
   and p.date >= '01.01.97'
group by transaction_id
order by support(rule)
```

Let us assume that the customer's purchase table *Shoppings* is organised as follows:

```
TRANS_ID CUST PRODUCT DATE     PRICE QUANT
-------- ---- ------- -------- ----- -----
1        101  BREAD   17/02/97 0.75  1
1        101  MILK    17/02/97 0.40  2
2        100  BUTTER  17/02/97 1.80  1
2        100  BREAD   17/02/97 0.75  3
2        100  MILK    17/02/97 0.40  1
3        105  BUTTER  28/12/96 1.80  1
4        100  WINE    20/12/96 9.90  1
4        100  MILK    20/12/96 0.40  2
4        100  PAPER   20/12/96 2.50  1
```

Then the result of the query is:

```
RULE                                               SUPPORT(RULE)
-------------------------------------------------- -------------
PRODUCT='MILK'->PRODUCT='BREAD'                    1.00
PRODUCT='BUTTER'->PRODUCT='BREAD'                  0.50
PRODUCT='BUTTER'->PRODUCT='MILK'                   0.50
PRODUCT='BUTTER' & PRODUCT='MILK'->PRODUCT='BREAD' 0.50
PRODUCT='BREAD' & PRODUCT='BUTTER'->PRODUCT='MILK' 0.50
```

3. Constraints-Driven Algorithm for Association Rules Discovery

In this Section, our constraints-driven algorithm for on-demand mining of association rules is presented. It is built as an extension of the basic *Apriori* algorithm. However, it introduces the general techniques that can be applied to a wide variety of association rules mining algorithms.

The key idea of the constraints-driven algorithm is following. User expresses the rule query using MineSQL language. The rule query contains selection constraints that should be satisfied by extracted rules. These constraints are then converted into *an external selection formula*, which is a logical combination of binary functions, representing simple selection conditions. In the next step, the external selection formula is transformed into an *internal selection formula*, which is directly applied in rule generation phase. For each conjunction of the internal selection formula, a set of rules is generated.

The algorithm reduces the processing time as well as temporary storage requirements by:

- filtering out input item groups that contain unnecessary items (such constraints are called *dataset filtering constraints*), e.g. if only rules involving an item x in the body are of interest, then it is sufficient to process only those record groups that contain x,
- not accepting the candidate itemsets that do not satisfy the extended constraints (not only the minimum support constraint), called *itemset preaccepting constraints*, e.g. if rules of length d are of interest, then it is unnecessary to accept candidates that are longer than d,
- pruning the itemsets accepted in the previous iteration of the algorithm (*itemset accepting constraints*). We can prune only those itemsets that will not be needed to determine rules'

confidence factors. For example, if only rules involving an item x are of interest, then we can prune all itemsets that do not contain x, on the condition that they will not be needed to determine other rules' confidence,

- controlling the rules generation process - pruning the rules that do not satisfy the extended constraints, called *rules accepting constraints*, e.g. if only rules containing x in the body are of interest, then it is unnecessary to continue generating rules that do not contain x in the body (remember that the rule head can only expand in a rule generation process).

3.1 SELECTION CONSTRAINTS

We first introduce some definitions necessary to define the algorithm.

Definition. External selection predicate σ(class, value) is a binary function that evaluates to 1 if the condition described by *class* is satisfied by a *value*. The *value* is a constant of integer, real, character or set type.

We consider the following external selection predicate types:
- support predicates, concerning the number of data groups that support a rule:

    $\sigma(SG, \alpha) = 1$, if: support(rule) =< α

    $\sigma(SL, \alpha) = 1$, if: α =< support(rule)
- confidence predicates, concerning the measure of rule's strength:

    $\sigma(CG, \alpha) = 1$, if: confidence(rule)=< α

    $\sigma(CL, \alpha) = 1$, if: α =<confidence(rule)
- contents predicates, concerning restrictions on items that can appear in a rule:

    $\sigma(IH, A) = 1$, if: A IN head(rule)

    $\sigma(IB, A) = 1$, if: A IN body(rule)

    $\sigma(IR, A) = 1$, if: A IN rule

    $\sigma(EB, A) = 1$, if: body(rule) = A

    $\sigma(EH, A) = 1$, if: head(rule) = A

    $\sigma(ER, A) = 1$, if: rule = A

    $\sigma(BI, A) = 1$, if: body(rule) IN A

    $\sigma(HI, A) = 1$, if: head(rule) IN A

    $\sigma(RI, A) = 1$, if: rule IN A

    $\sigma(NIH, A) = 1$, if: A NOT IN head(rule)

    $\sigma(NIB, A) = 1$, if: A NOT IN body(rule)

    $\sigma(NIR, A) = 1$, if: A NOT IN rule

    $\sigma(NEH, A) = 1$, if: head(rule) <> A

    $\sigma(NEB, A) = 1$, if: body(rule) <>A

    $\sigma(NER, A) = 1$, if: rule <> A

    $\sigma(HNI, A) = 1$, if: head(rule) NOT IN A

    $\sigma(BNI, A) = 1$, if: body(rule) NOT IN A

    $\sigma(RNI, A) = 1$, if: rule NOT IN A
- cardinality predicates, concerning the length of the rule, of the body or of the head:

    $\sigma(RLL, \alpha) = 1$, if: α < rulelen(rule)

    $\sigma(BLL, \alpha) = 1$, if: α < bodylen(rule)

    $\sigma(HLL, \alpha) = 1$, if: α < headlen(rule)

    $\sigma(RLS, \alpha) = 1$, if: rulelen(rule) < α

    $\sigma(BLS, \alpha) = 1$, if: bodylen(rule) < α

    $\sigma(HLS, \alpha) = 1$, if: headlen(rule) < α

- complex predicates, as none of the above:
  $\sigma(\text{CPX}, C) = 1$, if condition C is satisfied

Definition. External selection formula E is a logical combination of external selection predicates, involving the connectives: $\wedge, \vee, (,)$.

Example. For the following *WHERE* clause of the *MINE* statement:

```
WHERE support(rule) > 0.8
  AND confidence(rule) > 0.5
  AND 'product=''bread''' in body(rule)
  AND 'product=''butter''' in body(rule)
```

the external selection formula is the following:

```
E =    σ(SG, 0.8) ∧ σ(CG, 0.5) ∧ σ(IB, "product='bread'") ∧
       σ(IB, "product='butter'")
```

Definition. Internal selection predicate γ(class, subclass, value) is a binary function that evaluates to 1 if the condition described by *subclass* is satisfied by a *value*. The *value* is a constant of integer, real, character or set type. The *class* determines the verification point in the data mining algorithm.

We consider the following internal selection predicate types:
- dataset filtering predicates (DF), for filtering input item groups that contain unnecessary items:
  $\gamma(\text{DF}, \text{FI}, A) = 1$, for all groups that contain all items of A,
  $\gamma(\text{DF}, \text{PI}, A) = 1$, for all groups that contain at least one item of A,
  $\gamma(\text{DF}, \text{L}, \alpha) = 1$, for all groups that contain more than α items,
- itemset preaccepting predicates (IP), for pruning the candidate itemsets:
  $\gamma(\text{IP}, \text{ILS}, \alpha) = 1$, for all itemsets that have less than α items,
  $\gamma(\text{IP}, \text{SG}, \alpha) = 1$, for all itemsets that have support greater or equal to α
- itemset accepting predicates (IF), for pruning the itemsets pre-accepted in the previous iteration of the algorithm:
  $\gamma(\text{IA}, \text{SL}, \alpha) = 1$, for all itemsets that have support less than α,
  $\gamma(\text{IA}, \text{FI}, A) = 1$, for all itemsets that contains all items of A,
  $\gamma(\text{IA}, \text{PI}, A) = 1$, for all itemsets that contain at least one item of A,
  $\gamma(\text{IA}, \text{ILL}, \alpha) = 1$, for all itemsets that have more than α items,
- rules accepting predicates (RP), for pruning the rules during rules generation step:
  $\gamma(\text{RA}, \text{HLS}, \alpha) = 1$, for all rules whose head has less than α items,
  $\gamma(\text{RA}, \text{BLL}, \alpha) = 1$, for all rules whose body has more than α items,
  $\gamma(\text{RA}, \text{CG}, \alpha) = 1$, for all rules that have confidence greater or equal to α,
  $\gamma(\text{RA}, \text{FIB}, A) = 1$, for all rules whose body contains all items of A,
  $\gamma(\text{RA}, \text{PIB}, A) = 1$, for all rules whose body contains at least one item of A,
  $\gamma(\text{RA}, \text{NFI}, A) = 1$, for all rules whose head does not contain all items of A,
  $\gamma(\text{RA}, \text{NPIH}, A) = 1$, for all rules whose head does not contain any item of A,
- rules filtering predicates (RF), for the final pruning of the rules:
  $\gamma(\text{RF}, \text{CPX}, C) = 1$, if condition C is satisfied

In the above definitions, by *filtering* we mean 'not taking into account' and by *pruning* - 'removing from memory'.

Definition. Internal selection formula I is a disjunctive normal form of combination of internal selection predicates (disjunction of conjunctions), involving the connectives: $\wedge, \vee$.

Example. As we will explain it later, the internal representation of the external selection formula E from the previous example:

```
E =    σ(SG, 0.8) ∧ σ(CG, 0.5) ∧ σ(IB, "product='bread'") ∧
       σ(IB, "product='butter'")
```

is the following:

```
I =    γ(IP, SG, 0.8, itemset) ∧ γ(RA, CG, 0.5, rule) ∧
       γ(DF, FI, 'bread', itemset) ∧ γ(RA, FIB, 'bread', rule) ∧
       γ(IA, FI, 'bread', itemset) ∧ γ(RP, FI, 'bread', itemset) ∧
       γ(DF, FI, 'butter', itemset) ∧ γ(RP, FI, 'butter', itemset) ∧
       γ(RF, CPX, 'body(rule) contains 'butter'', rule)
```

As it was mentioned before, an external selection formula E is transformed into an internal selection formula I. The transformation is done according to the transformation table T, given in Figure 4. The structure of the transformation table T is the following. Each row k corresponds to an external selection predicate and each column l corresponds to as internal selection predicate. The sign '+' on a crossing (k, l) means that the external selection predicate k is replaced with the internal selection predicate l. If more than one internal selection predicate corresponds to an external selection predicate, then the external selection predicate is replaced with a conjunction of those internal selection predicates.

internal / external	DF,FI	DF,PI	DF,IL	IP,ILS	IP,SG	IP,FI	IA,ILL	IA,SL	IA,FI	RP,FI	RP,PI	RP,RL	RP,RS	RA,PI	RA,HS	RA,BL	RA,CG	RA,FIB	RA,PIB	RA,NFIH	RA,NPIH	RA,HI	RF,CPX
SG					+																		
SL																							+
CG																	+						
CL																							+
IH	+									+													+
IB	+								+	+								+					+
IR	+																						+
EB	+								+	+								+					+
EH	+									+													+
BI		+									+								+				+
HI		+									+												+
NIH																				+			+
NIB																							+
NIR				+																			
NEH																				+			+
NEB																							+
HNI																					+		+
BNI																							+
HS															+								
BS																							+
RS			+									+											
HL		+									+												+
BL		+									+					+							
RL		+									+												
CPX																							+

Figure 4. Transformation table

3.2 ALGORITHM

Constraints-driven algorithm for mining association rules satisfying given selection constraints is presented below.

Input: A set of database relations r_1, r_2, ..., r_n, containing item sets, data and rule selection conditions expressed in SQL-like language, minimum confidence value for generated rules - *minconf,*
Output: The set of demanded association rules.
Method:

1. Express the given selection constraints in the form of *external selection formula E*
2. Transform *E* into *internal selection formula I*
3. *forall* conjunctions *i* of *I do*
4. $result(i) = \varnothing$
5. $C_1 = \{$all 1-itemsets from item sets satisfying all *DF* predicates of *i*$\}$;
6. $A_1 = \{c \in C_1 \mid c$ satisfies all *IP* predicates of *i*$\}$;
7.   *for* ($k = 2$; $A_{k-1} \neq 0$; $k++$) *do begin*
8. $C_k = $ apriori_gen $(A_{k-1}$);
9.   *forall* candidates $c \in C_k$ *do*
10.   *forall* item sets satisfying all *DF* predicates of *i do*
11.   *if* contains (t, c) *then* c.support $++$;
12. $A_k = \{ c \in C_k \mid c$ satisfies all *IP* predicates of *i*$\}$;
13. $L_{k-1} = \{ a \in A_{k-1} \mid a$ satisfies all *IA* predicates of *i*$\}$;
14.   *end*
15. $L_k = \{ a \in A_k \mid a$ satisfies all *IA* predicates of *i*$\}$;
16.   compute
17.   *for* ($m = 2$; $m <= k$; $m++$) *do*
18.   *forall* itemsets $S \in L_m$ *do*
19.   *if* S satisfies all IA predicates of *i then* genrule(S, $\varnothing$);
20. *end*

procedure genrule (*body, head*)
begin
  forall item $\in$ *body do*
    if item > maxitem(*head*) *then*
      begin
        newbody = *body* - *item;*
        newhead = *head* + *item;*
        if (*newbody→newhead*) satisfies all RF predicates od *i then*
          return (*newbody→newhead*);
        if (*newbody→newhead*) satisfies all RA predicates od *i then*
          genrule (*newbody, newhead*);
      end;
end;

The most important points of the algorithm are the following. In the lines (5) and (10) we filter out those item groups that contain unnecessary items (verifying *dataset filtering constraints*). In (6) and (12) the candidate pre-accepting is done - candidates that do not satisfy *itemset preaccepting constraints* are pruned. In the lines (13) and (15) we prune the unnecessary itemsets of the ones accepted in the previous iteration (according to *itemset accepting constraints*).

The procedure *genrule* receives an accepted itemset and generates all possible body-head combinations. The generation always starts with an empty head and then expands the head recursively with the succeeding body elements. The rules satisfying *rule filtering constraints* are returned. The generation process can be stopped (not continued) if a rule that do not satisfy *rule accepting constraints* is built.

3.3 EXPERIMENTAL RESULTS

To assess the performance of the implemented algorithm, we performed several experiments on PC Pentium 150MHz, with 128 MB of main memory, running *Windows NT*. We used a synthetic database, created by *GEN* generator from *QUEST* project [2]. Several parameters affect the distribution of the synthetic data. These parameters are shown in Table 1 (see [2] for details).

Table 1. Synthetic data parameters

parameter	value
n_{trans}	number of item sets, 50,000
n_{items}	number of different items, 2000
t_{len}	average items per set, 5
n_{pats}	number of patterns, 500 and 10000
patlen	average length of maximal pattern, 4
corr	correlation between patterns, 0.25

Table 2. Experimental *MineSQL* statements

label	statement
A	``` MINE rule IN item FROM data_table WHERE support(rule)>=0.0033 ```
B	``` MINE rule IN item FROM data_table WHERE support(rule)>=0.0033 AND body(rule) CONTAINS 10 ```
C	``` MINE rule IN item FROM data_table WHERE support(rule)>=0.0033 AND length(rule)>=4 ```
D	``` MINE rule IN item FROM data_table WHERE support(rule)>=0.0033 AND length(rule)<=2 ```
E	``` MINE rule IN item FROM data_table WHERE support(rule)>=0.0033 AND body(rule)='10 & 20' AND head(rule)='30 & 40' ```

In the scope of our experiment, we compared the performance of different rule queries. The queries were expressed in *MineSQL* language (Table 2). Figure 5 illustrates execution times of the example rule queries.

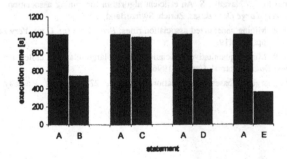

Figure 5. Execution times of example experimental statements

The rule query *A* does not use any advanced features of our constraints-driven algorithm – it plays the role of a reference here. Its execution time presents the capabilities of the original Apriori algorithm. The statements *B, C, D, E* are optimised using additional steps in our algorithm.

4. Conclusions and Future Work

In this paper we have presented the architecture of our prototype DBMS – Data Mining integration. The new SQL-like language for data mining from relational databases, called *MineSQL*, has been presented together with the constraints-driven algorithm used to process its rule queries.

Our future research directions are oriented toward database sequences (ordered sets) processing. We plan to extend *MineSQL* in order to allow sequence processing and frequent subsequence discovery and to develop a similar constraint-driven algorithm for processing new *MineSQL* constructs.

References

1. Agrawal, R., Imielinski, T., Swami, A. Mining association rules between sets of items in large databases. *Proc. ACM SIGMOD*, Washington DC, USA, May 1993, pp. 207-216.

2. Agrawal, R., Mehta, M., Shafer, J., Srikant, R., Arning, A., Bollinger, T. The Quest Data Mining System. *Proc. of the 2nd International Conference on Knowledge Discovery in Databases and Data Mining*, Portland, Oregon, 1996.

3. Agrawal, R., Srikant, R. Fast algorithms for mining association rules. *Proc. 20th Int. Conf. Very Large Data Bases*, Santiago, Chile, 1994, pp. 478-499.

4. Cheung, D. W., Han, J., Ng, V., Wong, C. Y. Maintenance of discovered association rules in large databases: an incremental updating technique. *Proc. Int. Conf. Dana Eng.*, New Orleans, USA, February 1996.

5. Han, J., Fu, Y. Discovery of multiple-level association rules from large databases. *Proc. 21th Int. Conf. Very Large Data Bases*, pp. 420-431, Zurich, Switzerland, Sept. 1995.

6. Houtsma, M., Swami, A. *Set-Oriented Mining of Association Rules*. Research Report RJ 9567, IBM Almaden Research Center, San Jose, California, USA, October 1993.

7. Manilla, H., Toivonen, H., Inkeri Verkamo, A. Efficient algorithms for discovering association rules. *Proc. AAAI Workshop Knowledge Discovery in Databases*, 1994.

8. Morzy, T., Zakrzewicz, M. *Constraints-Driven Algorithm for Mining Association Rules on Demand*. Technical Report RA-004/97, Poznań University of Technology, 1997.

9. Morzy, T., Zakrzewicz, M. SQL-like language for database mining. *1st Int. Conference on Advances in Databases and Information Systems*, St. Petersburg, 1997, pp. 311-317.

10. Savasere, A., Omiecinski, E., Navathe, S. An efficient algorithm for mining association rules in large databases. *Proc. 21th Int. Conf. Very Large Data Bases*, Zurich, Switzerland, 1995.

11. Srikant, R., Agrawal, R. Mining generalized association rules. *Proc. 21th Int. Conf. Very Large Data Bases*Zurich, Switzerland, Sept. 1995. pp. 407-419.

12. Srikant, R., Agrawal, R. Mining quantitative association rules in large relational tables. *Proc. 1996 ACM SIGMOD Int. Conf. Management Data*, Montreal, Canada, 1996, pp. 1-12.

13. Toivonen, H. Sampling large databases for association rules. *Proc. 22nd Int. Conf.*, Bombay, India, 1996.

Parameterised Patterns for Conceptual Modelling of Data Warehouses

Olaf Herden

Oldenburg Research and Development Institute
for Computer Science Tools and Systems (OFFIS),
Escherweg 2, 26121 Oldenburg, Germany
olaf.herden@offis.de

Abstract

Conceptual multidimensional modelling of data warehouses can be improved by using patterns, e. g. the time of modelling can be reduced and modelling errors can be avoided. This paper focuses on offering better support to users by providing a concept for the definition and administration of patterns. These patterns can be parameterised and their configuration is done in an interactive dialogue.

Keywords: data warehousing, conceptual modelling, patterns.

1. Introduction

In recent years, data warehouses (DWs) caused a lively interest in research and practice. A DW is a very large database offering an integrated view to data being important for decision support. These data are integrated from operational systems of an organisation and often supplemented by data from external sources. Typically, these data are modelled multi-dimensionally. The most important characteristic of the multidimensional model is dividing data into facts (also called measures or quantifying data) and dimensions (also called qualifying data). To provide data on a suitable level of granularity hierarchies are built on the dimensions. The combination of facts and dimensions is often called (hyper)cube. Figure 1 explains these terms by means of an example.

Since operational and strategic decisions made on the basis of data warehouses are very important for an organisation a comprehensible methodology for designing data warehouses is necessary. Within the scope of our research project ODAWA (OFFIS Tools For Data Warehousing) [15] we are developing such a methodology. It is based on the approach of three–level–modelling well–known from building OLTP (Online Transaction Processing) databases. Moreover, we are distinguishing between language and (graphical) representation on the conceptual level and we want to offer continuous tool support for every phase of development. Figure 2 summarises our framework.

For the conceptual level we have developed a multidimensional language, called MML (Multidimensional Modelling Language) [13, 14]. MML is an object–oriented language and therefore provides a good basis for flexible, implementation independent modelling. Furthermore, MML meets the needs of conceptual multidimensional models like e. g. sophisticated dimensional structures and enables schema evolution. A fraction of the MML–class diagram being relevant later on in this paper is depicted in Figure 3.

With the MML as basis different front end tools can be used. Exemplarily, we have developed ₘUML. ₘUML is an extension of UML (Unified Modelling Language) [19, 20], using stereotypes

97

J. Barzdins and A. Caplinskas. (eds.), Databases and Information Systems, 97–108.

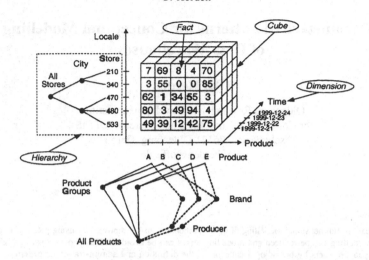

Figure 1. The multidimensional data model

and tagged values as mechanisms of extensibility. Its implementation (see Figure 4) has been done as an extension of the commercial CASE tool Rational Rose [18]. The MML is implemented as a class library in C++.

In the last decade patterns became a topic of interest in the field of software engineering. Unfortunately, 'there exists no standardisation of the term design pattern in the realm of object–oriented software development' [17]. In the context of this paper patterns are characterised in a very general way as generic structures won by experience of modelling in the past. They can be of different sizes, e. g. whole reference models for a branch of industry or only part of a model. Moreover, patterns can be abstract (describing the structure of a model) or concrete (describing one special model) and they can have parameters and configuration steps describing in which way and order the parameters are used. By using approved patterns modelling errors can be avoided and the time of modelling can be reduced. In consequence of these reasons using patterns can implicate economical benefits like increasing productivity, increasing quality of software, reducing time–to–market, and reducing cost of software. Patterns can be classified by the following orthogonal characteristics:

- Level
  Patterns can be defined on different levels, e. g. organisation patterns or pieces of software.

- Magnitude
  Patterns can be of different sizes, e. g. whole schemas (reference models for branches of industry or contexts) or simply part of a schema.

- Concreteness
  Patterns can describe a concrete object or can be more abstract describing only its structure.

- Parameterizability
  Patterns can either be fixed or they can have parameters determining their concrete extension.

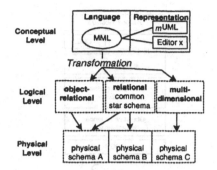

Figure 2. Three–level modelling

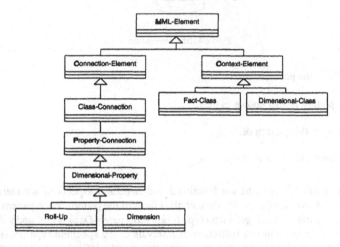

Figure 3. Fraction of MML–class diagram

Since MML is an object–oriented language and patterns are a powerful aspect in object–oriented soft-ware engineering we have applied patterns to our approach of conceptual data warehouse modelling. The remainder of the paper is organised as follows: in section 2 we enrich our framework for conceptual multidimensional modelling by adding the possibility to define, administrate and use parameterised patterns. The pattern language PL is introduced and demonstrated by examples in sec-tion 3. After reflecting related work, the paper finishes with a conclusion.

2. Parameterised Patterns for Conceptual Multidimensional Modelling

2.1 PATTERN MODEL

The model for parameterised patterns to support multidimensional modelling is depicted in Figure 5 (all associations without multiplicities in the diagram are many–to–many).

The most important class *Pattern* is described by the following attributes:

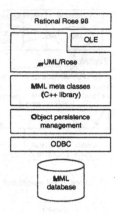

Figure 4. Implementation

- *Name:* name of the pattern.

- *Synonyms:* pattern is also known as these.

- *Purpose:* why is this pattern defined.

- *Examples:* contexts of use of the pattern.

While these attributes describe the functional and structural aspects of a pattern the classes *Parameter, Step* and *MML–Script* specify the technical facet of the pattern. Each pattern has got a list of parameters. Each parameter has got a data type (class *Parameter–Data–Type*) and a domain (class *Parameter–Domain*). A domain is a collection of intervals of the specified type (class *Parameter–Domain–Part*). The model considers the data types string and cardinal and arrays of these basic types. Beside the standard operations (e. g. addition on cardinals or concatenation on strings) for arrays of cardinal there are defined the functions *max* and *min* returning the maximal resp. minimal entry of the array.

For specifying the configuration process of a pattern an ordered list of steps is assigned to each pattern. The association between the classes *Parameter* and *Step* defines which parameter can be determined by the user at which step. Instantiating a pattern is traversing these steps in the defined order. After the last step of this configuration process the MML–Script associated to the pattern is executed with the chosen parameters. A MML–Script is a sequence of statements. Statements can be either simple constructor calls or assignments to variables or they can be more complex in form of while–loops or if–then–else–constructs. Both last–named statements use expressions over the parameters as arguments. When the execution of a MML–script ends all created objects are made implicitly persistent in the MML–repository.

For better handling of large sets of patterns the model offers the following:

- It is possible to organise sets of patterns in libraries (class *Pattern–Library* and association to *Pattern*).

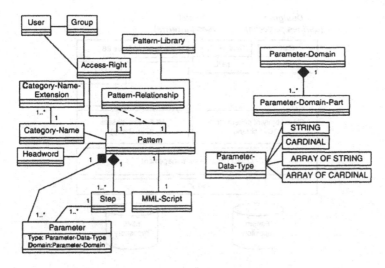

Figure 5. Model for parameterised patterns

- The self–referencing association *Pattern–Relationship* contains pairs of patterns and describes their similarities and differences in verbal form. There are three kinds of relationships between two patterns: simple relationship, part–of and specialisation.

- The classes *Pattern–Category* and *Pattern–Category–Extension* enable the classification of patterns according to the classification given in the introduction. Moreover, this classification schema can be extended by the user by defining new categories respectively adding extensions to any category.

- Assigning *headwords* to patterns is similar to categorising but the designer has all the freedom possible because entries can be free text and are not limited to any categories. By using headwords the user can build a subject catalogue on the patterns.

It is also possible to create users (class *User*), combine them to groups (class *Group*) and restrict their access to selected patterns only (class *Access–Right*). In case of conflict the rule *lex specialis ante lex generalis* is in force, e. g. more special rights to a user overlies the rights of his group.

2.2 IMPLEMENTATION

In this section our architecture depicted in Figure 4 is extended by the model introduced in the previous section. This extended architecture is depicted in Figure 6. We distinguish between two kinds of users: a designer who defines the patterns and a modeller who defines multidimensional schemas by using the patterns. Both of them can communicate with the system via a GUI or a script language. Analogous to distinguishing users we differentiate between DPL (designer's pattern language) and MPL (modeller's pattern language). Both languages use a class library realizing the model from the previous section. The object persistence management layer and the database driver can be reused. The patterns are stored in a repository persistently. The pattern and MML repositories can coincide on the physical level.

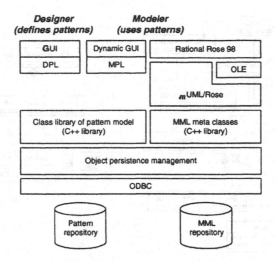

Figure 6. Environment for pattern use

3. Pattern Language PL

The pattern language PL is composed of the DPL for the pattern designer and the MPL for the modeller.

3.1 DESIGNER'S PATTERN LANGUAGE

DPL provides the following statements:

- CREATE, UPDATE and DELETE PATTERN <pattern> for creating and manipulating patterns.

- CREATE USER, DELETE USER, ADD <user> TO GROUP <group> and GRANT/REVOKE <access–right> ON <pattern> TO <user> | <group> for user and right administration.

- CREATE LIBRARY <library> and ADD <pattern> TO LIBRARY <library> for organising patterns in libraries.

- CREATE CATEGORY <category>, INSERT <extension> INTO CATEGORY <category> and ASSIGN <category>.<extension> TO <pattern> for handling the classification of patterns within the schema of categories.

- ASSIGN HEADWORD <headword> TO <pattern> for handling classifications of patterns with free text.

With the CREATE PATTERN–statement as the most complex one the designer can create new patterns. The following example should demonstrate its use:

CREATE PATTERN 'Multiple Hierarchies'
SYNONYMS 'Simple Hierarchy with many roll–up paths'
PURPOSE 'A typical dimensional structure able in many cases'
EXAMPLES 'Hierarchy of products in a sales cube; rolled up by product groups and brands'
PARAMETERS (
('Name of the dimension',Dim-Name,STRING),
('Number of hierarchies',N,CARDINAL,[1..100]),
('Number of levels in hierarchy I',M[I], ARRAY OF CARDINAL,[1..100],I=[1..N]),
('Name of level I in hierarchy J', Lev-Name[I][J],ARRAY OF STRING, I=[1..max(M)],J=[1..N]),
('Name of top–level',Top-Lev-Name,STRING),
('Fact to connect',Fac-Name,STRING))
STEPS(
(1,'Defining name of dimension','What is the name of the new dimension?',Dim–Name),
(2,'Defining number of hierarchies','How many hierarchies should be defined?',N),
(3,'Defining number of levels','How many levels does hierarchy $M[I]$ have?',M[I]),
(4,'Naming the levels','What is the name of level I in hierarchy J?',Lev–Name[I][J]),
(5,'Naming the top-level','What is the name of top-level',Top-Lev-Name),
(6,'Defining corresponding fact','To which fact will the dimension be connected ?',Fac-Name)),
MML-Script <Path-Of-File>;

In this example a pattern called 'Multiple Hierarchy' is defined. The clauses SYNONYMS, PURPOSE and EXAMPLES are descriptions of the pattern. With these attributes the designer characterises the pattern and later the modeller identifies the patterns appropriate for his use by means of these descriptions. Thus these attributes serve as a communication interface between designer and modeller. After the keyword PARAMETERS the parameters of the pattern are listed: their name, data type, domain of the parameter and in case of arrays the range of the index variables.

The components of each step are sequence number, name, dialogue question to the modeller and the parameter to be determined in this step. A dialogue question can contain parameters. They are included by '$'. The MML–script clause references a file. In our example the MML–script is defined as follows:

```
Dimensional-Class(Dim-Name);
Dimension(Fac-Name,Dim-Name,Dim-Name);
I=1;
while (I¡=N)
  J=2;
  while (J¡=M[I]+1)
    Dimensional-Class(Lev-Name[I][J-1]);
    if J=2 then
      Roll-Up(Dim-Name,Lev-Name[I][J-1],Lev-Name[I][J-1]);
    else
      Roll-Up(Lev-Name[I][J-2],Lev-Name[I][J-1],Lev-Name[I][J-1]);
    end
    J=J+1;
  end;
  I=I+1;
end;
```

In the first two lines the root of the dimension is defined and connected to the fact. The outer while–loop runs over the different hierarchies and the inner one over the levels of each hierarchy. For every level a dimensional class is created. To get a connection between these classes a roll–up path is created.

To provide more ergonomy, on top of DPL a GUI (graphical user interface) should be realised. Figure 7 shows the specification of a screen for manipulating a pattern definition.

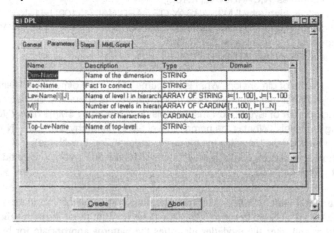

Figure 7. Designer's GUI for manipulating patterns

3.2 MODELLER'S PATTERN LANGUAGE

The most important statement of MPL is INSTANTIATE PATTERN. In the script language the parameters must be indicated, e. g.

INSTANTIATE PATTERN'Multiple Hierarchies'
PARAMETERS ((Dim-Name='Product'),
                (N=2),
                (M[1]=1,M[2]=2),
                (Lev-Name[1][1]='Product Groups'),
                (Lev-Name[2][1]='Brand'),
                (Lev-Name[2][2]='Producer'),
                (Top-Lev-Name='All Products'),
                (Fac-Name='Sales'));

Much more user–friendly is configurating a pattern with the GUI of MPL. This GUI is dynamically in the way that the dialogue windows are created during the process of instantiation by using the parameters and the configuration logic defined by the steps in the CREATE PATTERN statement. The process of instantiation of our example with the dynamic GUI is shown in Figure 8.

After executing the INSTANTIATE PATTERN–statement or finishing the GUI–dialogue the MML–script of the pattern *Multiple Hierarchy* is executed with the desired parameters and finally all

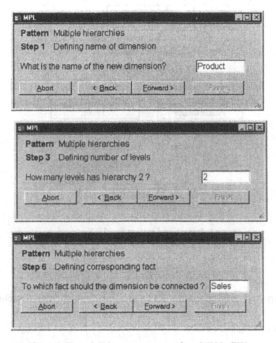

Figure 8. Part of dialogue sequence of modeller's GUI

instantiated objects are made persistent in the repository.

The modeller can observe the result after refreshing in Rational Rose. Individual modifications and additions are possible. The result of our example can be viewed in Figure 9 in notation of the ₘUML. The result is a multiple hierarchy on dimension 'Product' depicted in the example in Figure 1.

3.3 BROWSING THE PATTERN LIBRARY

In this subsection browsing large pattern libraries is illustrated. After determining his search criteria the user should be presented a result like that one depicted in Figure 10. In the right part the search criteria are repeated and the resulting patterns are listed. If the user selects one of it this pattern and its relationships to other patterns are represented in the left part. Furthermore, the transitive closure of pattern relationships is shown. In this manner the modeller can explore the collection of patterns. By dragging the mouse pointer over a pattern additional information about this pattern should be displayed.

4. Related Work

In the area of data warehouses some approaches for conceptual multidimensional modelling have been developed, namely MERM (*Multidimensional E/R Model*) [21], ADAPT (*Application Design for Analytical Processing Technologies*) [3] and DFM (*Dimensional Fact Model*) [12]. But they

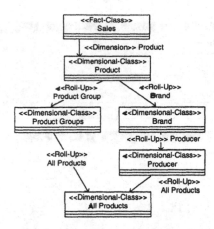

Figure 9. Instantiated pattern in ₘUML–notation

have some deficits:

- No adequate expressiveness, especially for modelling sophisticated dimensional structures.

- No compatibility among each other.

- No support by tools.

- No strict distinction between design levels.

On the other hand some commercial tools for designing DWs are available but they are most often proprietary. Hence conceptual modelling is often left out in practice or the conceptual and logical levels coincide, e. g. applying Kimball's dimensional modelling [16].
Patterns have their origin in architecture: the aim to build high–quality homes and to make urban planning with reusing patterns was described in [1] and [2]. With the emergence of object–oriented design of software and object–oriented programming languages in the late eighties and early nineties patterns also became relevant in this field [5]. In [11] a team of authors called 'Gang of Four' published a collection of patterns and leveraged the idea in the community. Since then patterns have been used for many different domains ranging from organisations and processes to teaching and software architecture. Another approach in the area of patterns is made by [4]. In opposite to the 'Gang of Four' the authors wanted to provide a system of patterns instead of just a pattern catalog. This aim should be reached by having an unified description of patterns, by describing relationships between patterns, by classifying patterns and last but not least by providing search strategies to support the user in finding the right pattern. As a conclusion we can say that at present the software community is using patterns largely for software architecture, design and software development processes.
Important references concerning relevant topics about patterns are [6, 7, 8, 9, 10, 22].
The idea of designing parameterised patterns by an interactive dialogue with the user can also be found in [23].

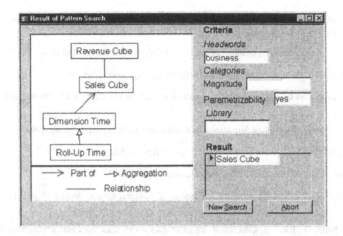

Figure 10. Result of pattern search

5. Conclusions

In this paper we have suggested a concept for using parameterised patterns to support conceptual multidimensional modelling. After giving a brief introduction we proposed a model for parameterised patterns. Then we showed how our current architecture can be extended by implementing this model. Afterwards, we distinguished between two kinds of the users: designers (who are defining patterns) and modellers (who are using patterns to create multidimensional schemas). For both groups we have introduced both a script language and a GUI.

As future tasks we want to do the following:

- evaluating our approach in a real world project,

- constructing libraries of patterns,

- defining patterns by a graphical editor,

- supporting the modeler in the way that he can trace his work graphically when using the dynamic GUI,

- expanding the library by so–called anti–patterns which describe a bad solution from the past.

References

1. Alexander, C., Ishikawa, S.,Silverstein, M. *A Pattern Language: Towns, Buildings, Construction*. Oxford University Press, 1977.

2. Alexander, C. *Timeless Way of Building*. Oxford University Press, 1979.

3. Bulos, D. A new dimension. *Database Programming & Design*, 6, 1996, pp. 33–37.

4. Buschmann, F., Meunier, R., Rohnert, H., Sommerlad, P., Stal, M. *Pattern-Oriented Software Architecture. A System of Patterns*. John Wiley and Sons Ltd., 1996.

5. Coad, P. Object–oriented patterns. *Communications of the ACM*, 9(35), 1992, pp. 152–159.

6. Coad, P. *Object Models: Patterns, Strategies and Applications*. Englewood Cliffs, 1995.

7. Coplien, J.O. A generative development–process pattern language. In J.O. Coplien, D. Schmidt, (eds.), *Reading MA*, 1995, pp. 183–237.

8. Coplien, J.O. *Homepage Jim Coplien*. http://www.bell-labs.com/people/cope/index.html, 1999.

9. Coplien, J.O., Schmidt, D.C. *Pattern Languages of Program Design*. Addison Wesley, 1995.

10. Fowler, M. *Analysis Patterns, Reusable Object Models*. Menlo Park, 1997.

11. Gamma, E., Helm, R., Johnson, R., Vlissides, J. *Elements of Reusable Object-Oriented Software*. Addison-Wesley, 1995.

12. Golfarelli, M., Maio, D., Rizzi, S. Conceptual design of data warehouses from E/R schemes. In *Proc. of Hawaii International Conference On System Sciences*, Maui, Hawaii, 1998.

13. Harren, A., Herden, O. Conceptual modeling of data warehouses. In *Proc. of Demonstrations and Posters E/R99*, Paris, France, 1999, pp. 17–18.

14. Harren, A., Herden, O. MML und „UML – Sprache und Werkzeug zur Unterstuetzung des konzeptionellen Data Warehouse–Designs (In German). In *Proceedings DMDW99*, Magdeburg, Germany, 1999, pp. 57–67.

15. Herden, O. *ODAWA Homepage*. http://odawa.offis.uni-oldenburg.de, 1999.

16. Kimball, R. *The Data Warehouse Toolkit*. John Wiley and Sons, Inc., 1996.

17. Pree, W. *Design Patterns for Object-Oriented Software Development*. Addison Wesley, 1995.

18. Rational Software Corporation. *Rational Rose 98*. http://www.rational.com/rose, 1998.

19. Rational Software Corporation. *The Unified Modeling Language, Version 1.1*, http://www.rational.com/uml, 1998.

20. Rational Software Corporation and UML Partners. *UML Summary. Version 1.1*, Object Management Group, OMG Document ad/97-08-03, 1997.

21. Sapia, C., Blaschka, M., Hfling, G., Dinter, B. Extending the E/R model for the multidimensional paradigm. In *Proc. International Workshop on Data Warehouse and Data Mining*, 1998.

22. Vlissides, J.M., Coplien, J.O., Kerth, N.L. *Pattern Languages of Program Design 2*. Addison Wesley, 1996.

23. Wohed, P. Tool support for reuse of analysis pattern: a conceptual modeling wizard for the booking domain. In *Proc. of Demonstrations and Posters E/R99*, Paris, France, 1999, pp. 15–16.

Part 3: Distributed Information Systems, Mobile Computing, and Agents

Agent-Oriented Analysis and Design
of Organisational Information Systems

Gerd Wagner

http://www.inf.fu-berlin.de/~wagnerg
Institut für Informatik, Freie Universität Berlin
Takustr. 9, D-14195 Berlin, Germany
E-mail: gw@inf.fu-berlin.de

Abstract

In this preliminary report, we propose an agent-oriented approach to the design of organisational information systems, called *Agent-Object-Relationship (AOR)* modelling, where an entity is either an object, an
agent, an event, an action, a claim, or a commitment, and where special relationships between agent classes
and event, action, claim and commitment types supplement the fundamental association, composition and
specialisation relationship types of Entity-Relationship modelling. In this approach, an organisation is
viewed as a complex *institutional agent* defining the rights and duties of its sub-agents that act on behalf
of it, and being involved in a number of interactions with external agents. An organisational information
system, then, is viewed as an artificial agent possessing a global view of the organisation and interacting
both with sub-agents and with external agents. We argue that AOR modelling offers a research perspective
to integrate the static, dynamic and deontic aspects of an organisational information system.

Keywords: objects, agents, events, commitments, information modelling.

1. Introduction

In order to capture more semantics of the dynamic aspects of information systems, such as the
events and actions related to the ongoing business processes of an enterprise, it is necessary to make
an ontological distinction between active and passive entities, that is, between *agents* and *objects*. In
particular, the semantics of *business transactions* can only be captured if the specific business agents
associated with the involved events and actions are explicitly represented in the information system
in addition to passive business objects.

Our work is inspired by the *Agent-Oriented Programming (AOP)* proposal of [10]. AOP is an
extension of object-oriented programming. The two main points of AOP are:

1. While the state of an object has no generic structure, the state of an agent has a 'mentalistic'
   structure: it consists of *mental components* such as beliefs and commitments.

2. While messages in object-oriented programming are coded in an application-specific ad-hoc
   manner, a message in AOP is coded as a 'speech act' according to a standard *agent communication language* that is application-independent.

We attempt to show that the intuitions underlying AOP have an even greater potential for information
systems engineering than for general software engineering.

J. Barzdins and A. Caplinskas (eds.), Databases and Information Systems, 111–124.
© 2001 *Kluwer Academic Publishers.*

After discussing the basic features of agents and discussing the 'agentification' of information systems in Section 1, the conceptual modelling method of *Agent-Object-Relationship (AOR)* modelling is presented in Section 2. Finally, in Section 3, the algorithmic transformation of an AOR model into a database schema is briefly sketched.

1.1   TABLES AND OBJECTS

Current information system concepts and technologies are largely based on the Entity-Relationship (ER) meta-model of [1] and the Relational Database (RDB) model of [2]. Driven both by the inherent shortcomings of relational databases and the success of the object-oriented programming paradigm, concepts and techniques from object-oriented programming are now increasingly applied in the area of information systems. However, there is no single generally acknowledged model of object-orientation, and object-oriented programming differs from object-oriented information systems engineering. In the former, everything is viewed as an object, from GUI push buttons to entire server programs, while in the latter, typical examples of objects are customers, bank accounts and other 'business objects'. Concerning database systems, the most important object-oriented features are object IDs, object references, abstract data types (including user-defined base types), object-valued attributes, and subtables.

While ER modelling has always been object-oriented to some degree, through its support of inheritance and complex-valued attributes, the RDB model is going to be conservatively extended to the *Object-Relational* Database (ORDB) model as exemplified by a number of research prototypes and commercial systems, and as expressed by the new SQL-99 standard.[1]

Current information system technologies do not support the concept of an agent: no matter if the customers of an enterprise are represented in a RDB table or in an object table of an ORDB, they are not explicitly represented and treated as agents but rather as objects in the same way as items or bank accounts.

1.2   AGENTS

The agent metaphor subsumes both natural and artificial systems. A formal agent concept for the purpose of representing agents in information systems may abstract away from many of the higher-level cognitive aspects of agents. It only needs to capture those aspects that are relevant for tracking and evaluating the events and interactions of interest. In an enterprise information system, for instance, only events and interactions associated with business processes are of interest.

There are several approaches to defining agents, only two of them being relevant for our purposes:

1. The *software engineering* approach emphasises the significance of application-independent high-level **agent-to-agent communication** as a basis for general software interoperability. E.g., in [4], the following definition of agents is proposed: *An entity is a software agent if and only if it communicates correctly in an agent communication language.*

2. The *mentalistic* approach, based on the knowledge representation paradigm of AI, points out that the state of an agent consists of **mental components** such as beliefs, perceptions, memory,

---

[1]See [11] for a discussion of ORDBs from the SQL programming perspective, and [14] for a theoretical presentation of the ORDB model.

commitments, expectations, goals and intentions, and its behaviour is the result of the concurrent operation of its perception (or event handling) system, its knowledge system (comprising an update and an inference operation), and its action system (responsible for epistemic, communicative and physical actions and reactions). E.g., in the approach of [10], *an agent is an entity whose state is viewed as consisting of mental components such as beliefs, capabilities, choices, and commitments.*[2]

According to our ontological distinction between agents and objects, only agents can perceive events, perform actions, communicate, or make commitments. Objects are passive entities with no such capacities.

This contrasts with the language used in the literature on object-oriented programming, where objects 'communicate' or 'interact' with each other by sending 'messages'. Notice that this corresponds only to a very low-level sense of communication and interaction. In fact, sending a 'message' in the sense of OO programming corresponds rather to a remote procedure call, and not to a communication act (or *speech act*): while an OO message has no generic structure at all, a speech act message has the form $m(c)$ where m is the message type (expressing the 'illocutionary force'), and c is the message content (typically a list of argument terms).

Conceptually, it is therefore not justified to model customers and suppliers as 'business objects' in the same way as bank accounts and software engineering objects (such as GUI push buttons). Object-orientation does not capture communication and interaction in the high-level sense of business processes. This is also confirmed by the complete lack of any notion of commitments in object-orientation.

Our view is shared by Jacobson [6] who remarks (p.36) that "it is bizarre to apply the way of thinking that governs computer systems to business processes".

1.3 INFORMATION SYSTEMS AS AGENTS

The following definition of [5] summarises the most important features of agency: *Intelligent agents continuously perform three functions: perception of dynamic conditions in the environment; action to affect conditions in the environment; and reasoning to interpret perceptions, solve problems, draw inferences, and determine actions.*

In the case of an agentified information system,

1. *'perception of dynamic conditions in the environment'* refers to incoming messages representing communication events (such as receiving a request for a sales quotation or an acknowledgement of a sales order) and environment events (such as receiving a payment);

2. *'action to affect conditions in the environment'* refers to communication acts of the agentified IS (such as acknowledging a sales order) and to physical acts (such as delivering goods or making a payment);

3. finally, *'reasoning to interpret perceptions, solve problems, draw inferences, and determine actions'* refers to things like the proper processing of incoming messages, the computational

---

[2]Another choice of basic mental components is proposed in the *BDI* approach of [9]: *beliefs, desires,* and *intentions.* Notice that in both lists of basic mental state components, two important components are missing: *perceptions,* e.g. in the form of incoming messages representing communication and environment events, and *memory* of past events and actions. In fact, although perceptions are temporally not as stable as beliefs, they form the basis of reactive behaviour, and are therefore more fundamental than many other mental components such as desires and intentions.

inference of correct answers to queries, and the determination of proper actions (such as locking all sales orders of a customer whose credibility is in question or issuing an alert when the fulfilment of a commitment is overdue).

An information system may be explicitly designed as an agent by

1. treating its information items as its *beliefs* or *knowledge*;[3]

2. adding further mental components such as *perceptions* (in the form of incoming messages), *memory*, and *commitments*;

3. providing support for agent-to-agent communication on the basis of a standard agent communication language.

In order to agentify an information system, its schema has to be partitioned: in addition to the tables representing the current state of affairs that form its beliefs, special tables are needed for representing its memory (about past events and actions) and its commitments and claims. For querying the perception state by processing incoming messages a built-in data structure (such as an *event queue*) has to be added. Finally, the *reaction patterns* representing the reactive and communicative behaviour of the information system have to be specified, e.g. by means of *reaction rules*. Depending on a triggering event type and possibly on a mental condition (involving beliefs, memory, commitments and claims), a reaction pattern specifies an action and an associated mental effect that may lead to updates of belief, commitment and claim tables. In this way, an information system turns into a *knowledge-perception-memory-commitment (KPMC) agent*.

2.   Agent-Object-Relationship Modelling

In this section we propose a new modelling paradigm: the agent-object-relationship (AOR) meta-model for modelling agent-oriented information systems. As in ER modelling, the purpose is to provide a generic methodology for IS design. In the same way as an ER model can be effectively transformed into a relational or object-relational database schema, an AOR model should be transformable into a corresponding database schema.[4] We sketch such a transformation briefly in the next section.

ER modelling does not account for the dynamic aspects of information and knowledge processing systems. These aspects are related to notions like communication, interaction, events, activities and processes. For capturing semantic aspects related to the dynamics of information systems, it is necessary to distinguish between *agents* and passive *objects*. While both objects and agents are represented in the system, only agents *interact* with it, and the possible interactions may have to be represented in the system as well.

UML, the current object-oriented modelling standard, does not support the concept of an agent as a first class citizen. In UML, agents are only considered as 'actors' that are involved in 'use cases'

---

[3]Unlike in philosophy, it does not make sense to distinguish between knowledge and beliefs in the design and engineering of agent systems where both terms simply refer to the information that is available to the agent under construction. We will interchangeably use these terms without making any reference or commitment to philosophical theories.

[4]Notice that this implies that the elements of the AOR meta-model must have a formal semantics. We will show in a future paper that the logical and operational model of *knowledge- and perception-based agents* of [13] provides the basis of such a formal semantics for the AOR meta-model.

but remain external to the system model. Both the customers and the suppliers of a company would have to be modelled as UML objects in the same way as currencies and bank accounts. UML treats the dynamic aspects of an application system by providing a multitude of process modelling diagrams largely unrelated with each other and with the ER (or object class) diagram of the system.

Since interaction takes place in a social context, deontic concepts such as commitments and claims with respect to external agents, and rights and duties with respect to internal agents, are essential for understanding and controlling coherent interaction. Neither ER modelling nor UML provide any means to account for the deontic aspects of an information system.

In AOR modelling, an entity is either an event, an action, a claim, a commitment, an agent, or an object. Only agents can communicate, perceive, act, make commitments and satisfy claims. Objects do not communicate, cannot perceive anything, are unable to act, and do not have any commitments or claims. Being entities, agents and objects of the same type share a number of attributes representing their properties or characteristics. So, in AOR modelling, there are the same notions as in ER modelling (such as entity types, relationship types, attributes, etc.). Notice that it is a matter of choice whether to represent active entities as agents or as objects. The concept of an agent extends that of an object. If the agent-specific properties do not matter, one may simply ignore them and treat an agent like an ordinary object. For instance, if the business-to-supplier interaction does not have to be explicitly modelled in an enterprise information system, suppliers may be simply represented as objects in the same way as items and bank accounts.

While ER modelling and UML support the design of *object-oriented* information systems realized with the help of relational and object-relational database technology, AOR modelling allows the high-level design of *agent-oriented* information systems.

2.1   AN ER MODELLING EXAMPLE

We restate the ontological principles of ER modelling:

1. An information system has to represent information about **entities** that occur in the **universe of discourse** associated with its application domain, and that can be uniquely identified and distinguished from other entities.

2. Entities have **properties** and participate in **relationships** with other entities.

3. In order to represent entities in an information system, they are classified by means of **entity types**.

4. Each entity type defines a list of (stored and virtual) **attributes** that are used to represent the relevant properties of the entities associated with it.

5. Together, the values of all attributes of an entity form the **state** of it.

6. In order to represent ordinary domain relationships (**associations**) between entities, they are classified by means of **relationship types**.

7. There are two designated relationships between entity types that are independent of the application domain: **specialisation** (subclass) and **composition** (component class).

A subclass is visualised as a rectangle within its superclass. A *component* class is visualised as a rectangle with dotted lines drawn within the superior class it belongs to.[5]

We now present an ER modelling example in order to compare it with the corresponding AOR model in the next section.

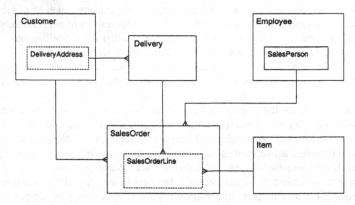

Figure 1. An ER diagram about sales orders

In the ER diagram of Figure 1, there are eight entity types: Item, SalesOrder, SalesOrderLine, Delivery, Customer, DeliveryAddress, Employee, and SalesPerson. A *SalesOrderLine* is a component of a *SalesOrder* and involved in many-to-one relationships with *Item* and with *Delivery* entities. *SalesPerson* is a subclass of *Employee*. Both *Customer* and *SalesPerson* stand in a one-to-many relationship with *SalesOrder*. There is no distinction between passive and active entities (i.e. between objects and agents). Also, there is no distinction between a basic entity type like *Item* and an event type like *Delivery*. An ER diagram captures only the state schema of an information system. It does not model any dynamic or deontic aspect.

2.2 ONTOLOGICAL FOUNDATIONS OF AOR MODELLING

In [16], it is convincingly argued that an enterprise modelling approach should be based on clear ontological principles explaining and justifying the vocabulary employed independently of any specific implementation technique. In laying out the ontological foundations of a modelling method, one may consider both the concepts and terminologies established in the practice of developing and using information technologies and the theories of traditional and contemporary philosophy. In traditional philosophy, however, ontology was mainly an issue of theological and metaphysical speculation, while for the purpose of enterprise and information system modelling, ontology is a purely pragmatic issue.

AOR modelling adds to the above principles of ER modelling the following ones:

1. Different entities may belong to different epistemic categories. There are **agents, events, actions, commitments, claims,** and **objects**.

---

[5]Recall that a component cannot exist independently of the whole. If the whole ceases to exist, all of its components also cease to exist.

2. Some of these modelling concepts are **indexical**: actions of other agents are viewed as events, and commitments of other agents are viewed as claims against them.

3. There are six designated relationships in which specifically agents, but not objects, participate: only agents PERCEIVE environment events, RECEIVE and SEND messages, DO physical actions, ARE-COMMITTED-TOWARDS and HAVE-CLAIMS-AGAINST other agents.

4. **Communication** is viewed as asynchronous point-to-point message passing.

5. An organisation is viewed as an **institutional agent** that consists of a certain number of (institutional, artificial and human) *sub-agents* acting on behalf of it.

6. Each **sub-agent** has certain *rights* and *duties*.

7. A **duty** refers to some type of commitment to be fulfilled, claim to be monitored, or event to be reacted to on behalf of the organisation.

8. A **right** refers to an action type such that the sub-agent is permitted to perform actions of that type on behalf of the organisation.

2.3 OBJECT CLASSES

Objects, such as sales orders or items, are visualised as rectangles essentially in the same way like entities in ER diagrams, or classes in UML class diagrams. They may participate in association or in composition relationships with other objects and with agents.

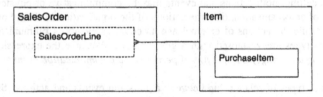

Figure 2. *SalesOrderLine* is a component class of the object class *SalesOrder*. *Item* participates in a one-to-many relationship with *SalesOrderLine*. *PurchaseItem* is a subclass of *Item*

Multiplicity of relationships can be specified like in UML (by means of declarations such as 0..1 or 1..*), but for visual clarity, we use the simpler crows feet notation in this paper.

2.4 AGENT CLASSES

We may distinguish between artificial agents, human agents and institutional agents. An organisation is an example of an institutional agent. Examples of human agent classes are Person, Employee, Customer, Student, Nurse, or Patient. In certain application domains, there may be also artificial agent classes, such as software agents (e.g., involved in electronic commerce transactions) or robots.

An agent class is visualised as a rectangle with rounded corners. In order to distinguish sub-agents from external agents, they are visualised by such a rectangle with a dotted line (like *Employee* in Figure 3).

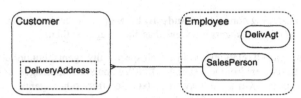

Figure 3. *Customer* is an external agent class, while *Employee* is an internal agent class

Agent classes may be defined as subclasses of other agent classes, thus inheriting all of their attributes (and 'methods'). For instance, in Figure 3, *SalesPerson* and *DeliveryAgent* are subclasses of *Employee*. An agent may have sub-agents. For instance, organisational units, viewed as institutional agent classes, may have sub-agent classes visualised as sub-agent rectangles drawn within the organisational unit rectangle.

An agent class may also have object component classes. For instance, *DeliveryAddress* is a component class of *Customer*.

Agents may be related to other entities by means of ordinary domain relationships as in ER modelling. In addition to the designated relationship types *specialisation* and *composition* of ER/OO modelling, there are 12 further designated relationship types relating agents with events, actions and commitments. They are discussed below.

2.5   ACTIONS AND EVENTS

In AOR modelling, both actions and events may be communicative or physical. Recall that, in the perspective of an organisation, only the actions of the organisation itself and of its sub-agents count as actions, while the actions of external agents count as events. Communication event and communication act types are visualised with a grey shadow. We take the expressions *receiving a message* and *sending a message* as synonyms of *perceiving a communication event* and *performing a communication act*.

There are four types of relationship between agents and events and actions: SENDS and RECEIVES are relationship types that relate agents with communication acts and events, while DOES and PERCEIVES are relationship types that relate agents with physical actions and environment events. These special relationship types are designated with particular arrow types as in Figure 4.

2.6   COMMITMENTS AND CLAIMS

In the subjective perspective of an organisation, commitments are commitments towards other agents, while commitments of other agents are viewed as *claims* against them. A commitment towards another agent (such as a commitment towards a customer to deliver an item) is coupled with the associated action (such as a *deliverItem* action). It is visualised as a rectangle with a dotted line on top of the associated action rectangle as in Figure 5.

A claim against another agent (such as a claim against a customer to pay an invoice) is coupled with the associated event (such as a *payInvoice* event). It is visualised as a rectangle with a dotted line on top of the associated event rectangle as in Figure 6.

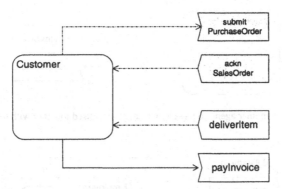

Figure 4. An enterprise RECEIVES submitPurchaseOrder messages from customers, SENDS back acknSalesOrder messages, DOES deliverItem actions, and PERCEIVES payInvoice events

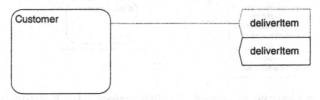

Figure 5. A commitment towards another agent (to deliver an item) is visualised together with the associated action (of carrying out the delivery)

2.7 RIGHTS AND DUTIES OF SUB-AGENTS

An organisation, as an institutional agent, consists of a number of (institutional, artificial and human) sub-agents acting on behalf of it. Each sub-agent, by virtue of its *position* and the *roles* associated with it, has certain *rights* and *duties*. In AOR modelling, a duty refers to certain organisational commitments whose fulfilment is delegated to a sub-agent, or to certain events that a sub-agent has to monitor and possibly react to, while a right refers to an action type such that the sub-agent is permitted to perform corresponding actions. The duty (say, of a DeliveryAgent) to fulfill a certain commitment (e.g., to deliver an item to a customer) is visualised by means of a dotted line between the (*DeliveryAgent*) agent class and the (*deliverItem*) commitment type. The responsibility to respond to a communication event is visualised by means of a DUTY-TO-RESPOND relationship connection between the communication event type and the responsible sub-agent class, while the responsibility to react to an environment event is visualised by means of a DUTY-TO-REACT relationship connection between the environment event type and the responsible sub-agent class. Likewise, the right to perform certain actions is visualised by means of a RIGHT-TO-DO relationship connection between the sub-agent class and the action type.

Like in standard deontic logic, the DUTY-TO-FULFILL some kind of commitment implies the RIGHT-TO-DO the corresponding type of action.

An example of an AOR diagram is given in Figure 8. In comparison with Figure 1, *Customer* and *Employee* are now considered agent classes, such that *SalesPerson*, *DelivAgt* and *Clerk*

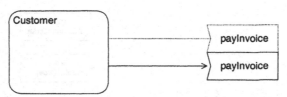

Figure 6. A claim against another agent (to pay an invoice) is visualised together with the associated event (of making the payment)

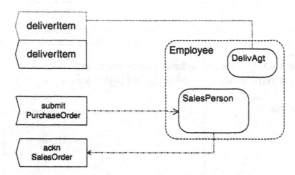

Figure 7. The DUTY-TO-RESPOND to a submitPurchaseOrder message and the RIGHT-TO-SEND an acknSalesOrder message of salespersons, and the DUTY-TO-FULFILL deliverItem commitments of delivery agents

are subclasses of *Employee*. The entity type *Delivery* has turned into the action type *deliverItem* and the associated commitment type. The interaction frame between the organisation and the agent class *Customer* comprises the commitment/action table pair *deliverItem*, the claim/event table pair *payInvoice*, the communication event type *submitPurchaseOrder*, and the communication act type *acknSalesOrder*.

2.8   INTERACTION FRAMES

An *interaction frame* defines the possible, and records the past, interactions between an organisation and an agent class. It consists of the six kinds of tables visualised in the AOR diagram of Figure 8 in between the customer and the employee rectangle:

1. Event log tables for recording **communication events** created by those communication acts of other agents that may take place within the interaction frame.

2. Action log tables for recording those **communication acts** (of the IS or of other sub-agents) that take place within the interaction frame.

3. Claim tables for recording the relevant **claims** against other agents.

4. Event log tables for recording **environment events** which may indicate the fulfilment of corresponding claims.

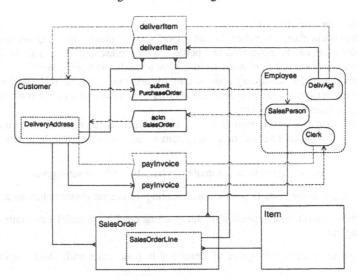

Figure 8. An Agent-Object-Relationship diagram

5. Commitment tables for recording the organisation's **commitments towards other agents**.

6. Action log tables for recording **physical actions** which may be performed in order to fulfill corresponding commitments or in response to other actions of the interaction frame.

3. Transforming an AOR Model into a Database Schema

We briefly sketch the transformation of an AOR model into an object-relational (SQL-99) database schema. A more elaborate account of this transformation can be found in [15].

Object classes and association relationship types are transformed like in the standard implementation of ER models (that is, object classes and many-to-many associations are implemented as separate tables, one-to-many and one-to-one associations are represented as additional reference columns in the participating object tables). A component class is transformed into a corresponding complex-valued attribute of the super-ordinate class it belongs to. Subclasses are represented by means of the SQL-99 subtable construct.

A communication event type (or incoming message type) is transformed into a special table schema with three additional implicit columns for the ID of the sender, the ID of the sub-agent who is the addressee, and the time instant at which the message has arrived. Likewise, a communication act type (or outgoing message type) is transformed into a special table schema with three additional implicit columns for the ID of the sub-agent who has sent the message, the ID of the external agent who is the addressee, and the time instant at which the message has been sent.

A commitment (or claim) type is transformed into a table with the same base schema as the action (or event) type it refers to but with different implicit columns: the first additional column represents the ID of the agent towards whom the commitment (or against whom the claim) holds, and the second additional column represents the temporal constraints for fulfilling the commitment (or for obtaining the benefits from the claim).

An external agent class is transformed into a special table schema including declarations of the actions and events that can be performed and perceived by representatives of that class, and of the commitments and claims that the organisation may have towards and against them.

An internal agent (or sub-agent) class is transformed into a special table schema including declarations of the events, commitments and claims that its representatives must react to, fulfill and monitor, and the actions they may perform.

The assignment of event, commitment and claim types as responsibilities to internal agent classes enables the organisational information system to play an active role in a number of basic business processes, such as to

1. define tasks to be performed in an automated fashion by artificial sub-agents;

2. maintain role-specific to-do-lists for communicating the current duties to human sub-agents;

3. remind the responsible sub-agents of an approaching deadline to fulfill a commitment towards another agent;

4. remind the responsible sub-agents of deadlines in connection with claims against external agents.

4.   Related Work

Agent-oriented modelling techniques are still in their infancy. The *Resource-Event-Agent (REA)* modelling framework of [8] can be regarded as an early predecessor of agent-oriented information systems modelling. It was proposed as a new approach to accounting systems that aims at reconciling the specialist accounting view of enterprise resource management with the more general views of other business areas. In accounting, special attention is paid to economic resources that are subject to financial and managerial accounting requirements. These resources are associated with increment and decrement events which are, in turn, associated with economic agents. While the REA framework suggests to distinguish between the entity categories of resources, events and agents, it does not provide any visual or formal modelling language that allows to map these conceptual distinctions. AOR modelling, by providing such visualisation and formal language constructs, seems to support the REA accounting framework very well.

In [19, 18], an agent-oriented modelling framework, called i^*, for early *requirements engineering* is proposed stressing the role of *dependencies* between agents. Since AOR modelling provides a technique for *designing* information systems, it may be a possible target language for transforming i^* models into it.

In [7], a methodology for the analysis and design of multi-agent systems based on object-oriented modelling principles is presented, requiring compliance with the particular paradigm of 'Belief-Desire-Intention (BDI)' agents proposed in [9]. More general approaches to agent-oriented software engineering, considering issues such as agent roles, rights and duties, contracts and communication protocols, are proposed in [3, 17]. A conceptual framework for agent-oriented workflow modelling based on agent roles and the communication protocols, qualifications, and rights and duties associated with them, is proposed in [20]. In the business-rules-centered approach to the modelling of agent-oriented information systems of [12], software agents are used to represent "functional business units/actors and also external units/actors like customers or suppliers". The business case of a car rental company is used to demonstrate the agent-based implementation of business rules.

5. Conclusion

Similar to 'object', the term 'agent' denotes an abstraction that leads to more natural and more modular software concepts. It helps to capture more semantics about natural and artificial systems an organisational information system has to represent and to deal with. We have presented an agent-oriented approach to information modelling that allows an integrated treatment of the static, dynamic and deontic aspects of these systems, and thus offers a methodology that is semantically richer than many other meta-models.

References

1. Chen, P. The entity-relationship model – toward a unified view of data. *ACM Transactions on Database Systems*, 1(1), 1976, pp. 9–36.

2. Codd, E. F. A relational model of data for large shared data banks. *Communications of the ACM*, 13(6), 1970.

3. Elammari, M. and Lalonde, W. An agent-oriented methodology: High-level and intermediate models. In G. Wagner and E. Yu, (eds.), *Proc. of the 1st Int. Workshop. on Agent-Oriented Information Systems*, 1999.

4. Genesereth, M. R. and Ketchpel, S. P. Software agents. *Communication of the ACM*, 37(7), 1994, pp. 48–53.

5. Hayes-Roth, B. An architecture for adaptive intelligent systems. *Artificial Intelligence*, 72, 1995, pp. 329–365.

6. Jacobson, I. *The Object Advantage*. Addison-Wesley, Workingham, England, 1994.

7. Kinny, D., Georgeff, M., and Rao, A. A methodology and modeling technique for systems of BDI agents. In W. Van de Velde and J.W. Perram, (eds.), *Agents Breaking Away*, *Lecture Notes in Artificial Intelligence*, **1038**, Springer-Verlag, 1996, pp. 56–71.

8. McCarthy, W. E. The REA accounting model: A generalized framework for accounting systems in a shared data environment. *The Accounting Review*, LVII(3), July 1982, pp. 554–578.

9. Rao, A. and Georgeff, M. Modeling rational agents within a BDI-architecture. In J. Allen, R. Fikes, and E. Sandewall, (eds.), *Proc. KR-91*, San Mateo (CA), Morgan Kaufmann, 1991.

10. Shoham, Y. Agent-oriented programming. *Artificial Intelligence*, **60**, 1993, pp. 51–92.

11. Stonebraker, M. and Moore, D. *Object-Relational DBMS*. Morgan Kaufmann Publishers, San Francisco, 1996.

12. Taveter, K. Business rules approach to the modeling, design and implementation of agent-oriented information systems. In G. Wagner and E. Yu, (eds.), *Proc. of the 1st Int. Workshop on Agent-Oriented Information Systems*, 1999.

13. Wagner, G. A logical and operational model of scalable knowledge- and perception-based agents. In W. Van de Velde and J.W. Perram, (eds.), *Agents Breaking Away*, of *Lecture Notes in Artificial Intelligence*, **1038**, Springer-Verlag, 1996, pp. 26–41.

14. Wagner, G. *Foundations of Knowledge Systems – with Applications to Databases and Agents, Advances in Database Systems*, 13, Kluwer Academic Publishers, 1998. http://www.inf.fu-berlin.de/~wagnerg/ks.html.

15. Wagner, G. Towards agent-oriented information systems. Technical report, Freie Universität Berlin, Institut für Informatik, 1999. See http://www.inf.fu-berlin.de/~wagnerg/AOIS.ps.

16. Wand, Y. and Woo, C. Ontology-based rules for object-oriented enterprise modeling. Technical Report 99-MIS-001, Faculty of Commerce and Business Administration, Univ. of British Columbia, 1999.

17. Wooldridge, M., Jennings, N. R., and Kinny, D. A methodology for agent-oriented analysis and design. In O. Etzioni, J. P. Müller, and J. M. Bradshaw, (eds.), *Proc. of the 3rd Int. Conf. on Autonomous Agents*, ACM Press, 1999, pp. 69–76.

18. Yu, E. and Mylopoulos, J. From E-R to 'A-R' – modeling strategic actor relationships for business process reengineering. *Int. J. of Intelligent and Cooperative Information Systems*, 4(2-3), 1995, pp. 125–144.

19. Yu, E. *Modeling Strategic Relationships for Process Reengineering*. PhD thesis, Computer Science Department, Univ. of Toronto, Toronto, Canada, 1995.

20. Yu, L. and Schmid, B. F. A conceptual framework for agent-oriented and role-based workflow modeling. In G. Wagner and E. Yu, (eds.), *Proc. of the 1st Int. Workshop. on Agent-Oriented Information Systems*, 1999.

Development of Distributed Systems with Java™ and CORBA™ Issues and Solutions

Adomas Svirskas

Computer Network Research Center, St. Cloud State University
St. Cloud, Minnesota, USA
E-mail: svirskas@stcloudstate.edu, adomas.svirskas@maf.vu.lt

Jurgita Sakalauskaite

Vilnius University, Faculty of Mathematics and Informatics
Vilnius, Lithuania
E-mail: jurgita.sakalauskaite@maf.vu.lt

Abstract

This paper summarises experience gained designing, developing, deploying and promoting distributed objects systems using Java™ platform, Common Object Request Broker Architecture (CORBA™) and the World Wide Web during more than 3 years. The main question to be answered is: "How to build distributed business information systems with reasonable costs and time to market?" Paper provides three contributions to the study of distributed object computing in practice. First, we outline generic system architecture, which is quite common for many applications, and identify some issues that are important in applications of this type. Second, we discuss our solutions, which proved to be reusable across several different projects. And third, we present analysis of our CORBA components and Java class libraries from the reusability point of view.

Keywords: distributed object systems, Internet, e-commerce, WWW, HTML, Java™ platform, CORBA™, multi-tier architecture, software component, business object, Java™ Servlets, XML.

1. Introduction

The component-based approach becomes the true standard of today's information systems development. This paradigm allows delivering more scalable, robust and adaptive systems by promoting software assembly from reusable parts. However, the component-oriented system design raises high demands for a lot of development techniques: components must be portable across different platforms at run time, interoperable with each other, customisable for the deployment, manageable - this list can be continued. In addition to the listed features of the components, the robust infrastructure for the component deployment, the efficient, service-rich middleware and powerful development tools are necessary. And last but not least – skilled software architects and developers. This approach is by no means simple for developers, yet it is the way to go - huge industry investments and success stories prove the power of the mentioned technologies.

The architectures of the distributed object systems evolved dramatically during the last decade. There is a long way from the first object request brokers (ORB) introduced 7-8 years ago and today's Web Application Servers powered by the object transaction monitors (OTM), integrated with industry best DBMS. Some of our solutions seem to be redundant today in the

125

J. Barzdins and A. Caplinskas (eds.), Databases and Information Systems, 125–138.

context of modern Application Server and, of course, our proprietary frameworks are gradually replaced by the standards-based commercial of the shelf software (COTS). However, even now, not every project has a budget, which allows purchasing of this expensive software. On the other hand, the highly praised "Their Majesty Application Server" not always keeps its promises, so our component development investment still pays dividends.

At the time we started our CORBA/Java development (1997), there was no Application Server, as we understand it now (object persistence, transaction support, connection pooling, etc.) on the market, nor was there the architecture like Enterprise Java Beans (EJB) in place. All we had was shaky Java JDK 1.1.3, the implementation of CORBA 2.0 from Visigenic (acquired by Borland later) and our experience of working with IBM's implementation of CORBA 1.x – System Object Model (SOM). And, of course, the strong commitment to the platform-neutral distributed object technology – the sad experience of the poorly portable software fuelled our desire to put Java's promises to work. Many of our solutions proved themselves over time either to be reused directly or as a foundation for the further development of the reusable parts. There were some projects, where the degree of reuse and customised assembly was really high and time to market pretty short.

This paper is organised as follows: Section 2 provides a short background about the general system architecture and the choice of technologies; Section 3 identifies some issues, which are common to multiple projects and application domains, and presents our reusable solutions in detail; Section 4 presents the results of our reusability analysis; and Section 5 provides concluding remarks.

2. Overall Background

We shall not spend much time explaining details of the particular distributed architectures – this information is widely available from a number of sources these days. It is more useful to outline the main principles of our architectural decisions and explain our choices of the implementation tools and techniques.

2.1 GENERAL ARCHITECTURE

A great deal of modern information systems are to be used in situations where Internet, intranet and extranet are used as a common infrastructure, when the intensity of the system load varies and the usage of the thin client is highly desirable. For example, one our project was IS for the mass-media business, which had to interact with its customers via the WWW, maintain business-to-business (B2B) relations with information suppliers and corporate consumers using the proprietary protocols and provide the back-office interfaces for the internal usage.

We have had to design and implement systems, which meet these requirements. Having recognised the need for flexibility, portability, scalability and the commitment to standards, we chose 3-tier architecture as a basis. This architecture provides a very clear separation of the functionality between logical tiers and, in our opinion, it is the best choice for the modern distributed information systems.

The architectural model shown in Figure 1 illustrates the typical usage of the different kinds of the software in each of logical tiers.

2.2 MIDDLEWARE CHOICES

One of the most important things in the development of the distributed system is to choose the proper type of middleware for interaction between the components of the system. In fact, several types of middleware are used simultaneously in many cases. This diversity is frequently caused by the need to optimise particular segment of interaction, comply with standards, meet security restrictions, ensure reliability, etc.

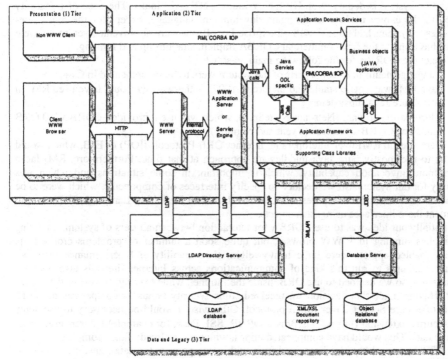

Figure 1. Typical 3-tier system architecture

There is quite a wide choice of different middleware tools: conversational middleware (proprietary application protocol on top of the transport layer API), remote procedure calls (RPC), distributed objects, message oriented middleware (MOM), database middleware, etc. Sometimes the usage of general-purpose middleware becomes standard-de-facto and a new type of middleware emerges – Hypertext Transfer Protocol (HTTP) or the so-called Web Middleware, for example. HTTP protocol itself is quite an ordinary application of TCP transport protocol – Sockets API, but the usage of it became so common to produce the concept of Web Middleware as such.

The following types of middleware will be discussed in this paper: Distributed Objects – CORBA and Remote Method Invocation (RMI), some CORBA services, HTTP, database middleware.

2.3 DISTRIBUTED OBJECTS

This type of middleware its the component oriented approach of the system design and development. There is no impedance mismatch between the object model of the system and its implementation – all the abstractions of the application domain entities and design artefacts map to the implementation entities quite straightforwardly.

We suppose that the advantages of this approach over other kinds of middleware are so obvious, that we do not need to advocate this paradigm further. Let's explain our preference to the certain type of ORB. We had the following options to consider: Java Remote Method Invocation (RMI) and CORBA 2.0 compliant ORB. Microsoft's DCOM was not among the candidates, since we needed the true platform-neutral solution for the very first of our Java projects (the system is deployed on HP-UX, Windows NT and Linux). The need of portability also led to the choice of Java as the main development language, except for the few places where legacy systems had no Java API. Enterprise Java Beans were not invented yet, so we were lucky to have one of the first commercial CORBA implementations up and running.

We chose CORBA for the following main reasons:

- Language neutrality - some parts of the system were to be implemented in C++;
- Java RMI was not so stable and mature in 1997 – otherwise we could have used RMI in some pure Java subsystems;
- Third-party software (Netscape SuiteSpot), which was used, provided CORBA 2.0 ORB and some CORBA services (Event and Naming).

There was no RMI over Interoperable Internet ORB Protocol (IIOP) or EJB, which would allow us to use mostly pure Java middleware approach at that time. Furthermore, RMI lacks asynchronous invocation capability, which is important in some situations and which was necessary for our system. So we decided to specify interfaces of components, which were to be used across different address spaces, via CORBA Interface Definition Language (IDL), and to implement these interfaces using Java objects.

Initially our idea was to use CORBA for interaction between all tiers of system, including Java applets running in WWW browser, but quite soon a number of problems cropped up. CORBA-enabled applets were quite heavyweight, their stability and performance were not adequate, attempts to run this kind of communications across Internet firewalls also revealed certain issues, so we decided to use ORB inside the intranet, while leaving the rest of the job for HTTP. Having made this decision we received some security bonus as compensation: HTTP support of Secure Socket Layer (SSL) protocol. Otherwise it would be necessary to use some ORB security extension (Inprise VisiBroker ORB™ SSL Pack, for example) for transmission of sensitive data. This would have complicated things, which were already fairly complex.

HTTP protocol has also been used from within components for data transfer to and from some legacy systems, which exposed data by means of authorised access to HTTP server. Automated interactions with Web-based administration interface of certain systems (to restart automatically Netscape Enterprise server after scheduled user registry and Access Control List (ACL) synchronisation session, for example) were also held via HTTP.

In some of our recent projects we chose RMI as an alternative to CORBA due to the following reasons: RMI is free of charge, it became more reliable and robust, EJB – emerging server-side component infrastructure is based on RMI. There also are ways of interoperability between RMI and CORBA via Java-to-IDL and RMI over IIOP. Some modern application servers (BEA WebLogic, for example) provide their own implementations of Sun JavaSoft RMI specification, which are more scalable and optimised.

The absence of pass-by-value mechanism in CORBA 2.0 made things inconvenient when it was necessary to pass parameters and return results in operations of CORBA components. This created some Java-CORBA object model impedance mismatch and required mapping from Java objects to CORBA IDL structures. Sometimes we used Java serialisation to pass flattened Java object as a parameter of CORBA object operation.

2.4   CORBA SERVICES

There were not so many commercially available CORBA services at the time we started to design and build our first CORBA/Java system. Another problem is that implementations of CORBA services are expensive and quite difficult to use. For these reasons we use only two services: Naming and Events. The usage of the Events service will be described later, when we shall present one of the particular design solutions.

2.5   JAVA™ PLATFORM

As it has been mentioned before, we made a decision to use Java in all possible places of implementation, to achieve maximum portability of system components via promised "write once, run anywhere" technology. We think that this decision was right – we have achieved our main goals and Java Platform itself took a big leap towards the stable and mature application development environment. Major software vendors also proved their commitment to Java technology. However, two or three years ago Java was not as mature as it is now and this caused much trouble, sometimes resulting in project delays. We can mention several reasons of this: first, the latency of 3rd party Java-based product supplies or the inadequate quality of products; second, the underestimation of the necessary development resources and their qualification; third, the rapidity of changes in Java technology area. Sometimes it was painful "write once, debug everywhere" experience.

2.6   DYNAMIC WEB CONTENT

The significant part of the user interface in our systems is Web-based. This requirement causes a strong need of tight integration between HTTP server and application services at the middle tier of the system, because the most part of the Web interface is to be generated dynamically on demand. This integration was not such a trivial issue, since there was no universal solution to the problem. Common Gateway Interface (CGI) is quite slow and very inelegant from the architectural point of view. It also poorly integrates with Java-based application services. Some proprietary solutions from different vendors like Server-Side Java Script (SSJS) or different HTTP Server APIs are not portable across different HTTP servers, yet suffer from the same integration problems. Scripting tools like Perl and Php3 do not scale well, and, in our opinion, scripting tools should be used sparingly.

Having tried some proprietary solutions (SSJS, namely) we experienced troubles due to poor integration, portability, and limited functionality. Server-side Java standard – Servlet specification and reference implementation issued by Sun Microsystems was just on time for us. This pure Java HTTP server extension has the following main advantages: it is portable across different HTTP servers (most HTTP servers provide means to integrate servlets); it is simple and easy to use; it has direct access to all the Java APIs, and, inherently, has no integration problems with the rest of the system. This choice proved to be a reliable and portable solution, and we have used it in different environments - from simple Servlet Runner available free of charge from Sun, to quite sophisticated products like IBM WebSphere Application Server.

3.   Common Issues and Reusable Solutions

In this section we shall discuss the most important issues, which are quite general to a number of distributed object-oriented applications, and present our solutions for these problems.

3.1   OBJECT PERSISTENCE FRAMEWORK

Perhaps one of the most important issues for a lot of applications is the external storage access. There are two main problem areas – the manipulation of the data, and the persistence of the run-time objects. These areas are often tightly coupled – tables in relational database are often used to store application entities and, on the other hand, some run-time entities are stored in a different kind of external storage - Lightweight Directory Access Protocol (LDAP) server, for example. Since there is a great deal of interaction with database, both for object persistence and data access, there is a need for the convenient persistence framework, abstract enough to be reusable independently of the particular application logic and the external storage type. This framework should provide interfaces to obtain the connection to the data store, add, update, search and retrieve persistent entities. Implementation of this interface should also be independent of changes in the database layout.

We designed persistence frameworks in Java and in CORBA and implemented them on top of JDBC - relational database middleware of choice for our applications. These frameworks are able to accommodate any storage-dependant implementation under single interface. Later we expanded the implementation of our framework by adding classes for an interaction with LDAP services and we have plans to implement access to the XML-based storage using the same interface.

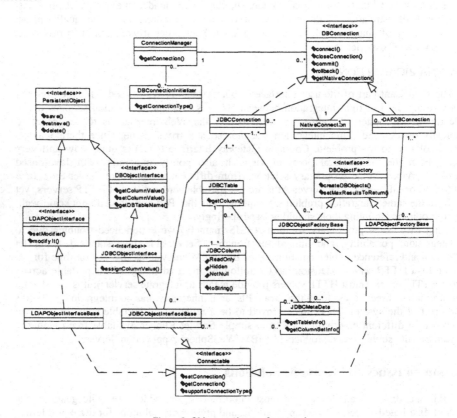

Figure 2. Object persistence framework

The usage of the relational database meta-data allowed us to develop implementation, which is independent of RDBMS table structure. The Factory pattern is used to obtain the results of the queries against the databases. The set of application objects is produced based on SQL or other type of (LDAP, for example) queries. There is also a possibility to specify a set of the so-called data sinks for a factory. We can define data sink as an object, which is able to consume and process a single data item from the query result set. Each sink class implements uniform interface and encapsulates the logic of the data item conversion to some alternative representation. Sink is supplied with the data transformation object, which is in charge of the actual further presentation of the data. Thus, an item of the query result set can be passed to the array of sinks and directed to different destinations, if necessary.

The main idea behind this factory/sink framework is to speed-up the delivery of the retrieved data to the destination. This is especially important when the number of items can be large and network transfer rate between the components is limited – in WWW based search/retrieve applications, for example. Having data sinks, which share the same interface, it is possible to use the pipelining techniques to retrieve data items and transfer objects simultaneously. This architecture proved itself to be very efficient for handling of bulky data retrieves and presentation, especially in WWW applications. The users of WWW based search/retrieval system were satisfied when the results of their queries started to appear on the browser screen sooner than all results of the query were processed.

Figure 2 shows part of UML class diagram of our persistence framework. We also use some connection pooling mechanism, which allows more efficient usage of database connections. Modern application servers provide connection pooling, but sometimes they are limited to specific database vendors, so our simple pooling technique can be useful even in that case.

3.2   DE-COUPLED PROCESSING OF DATABASE OPERATIONS

Another important persistence-related issue is where to concentrate the processing activities of database interactions, since they mostly are resource hungry. Sometimes it is highly desirable to have a possibility to relocate database processing to another physical machine(s) when workload grows.

DECOUPLED DATABASE OPERATIONS

DB operations components class diagram

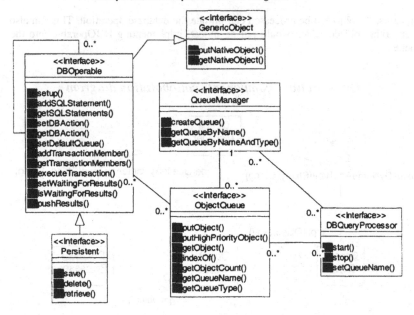

Figure 3. De-coupled database operations

We have designed the distributed framework based on the producer-consumer pattern, which uses queue-based mechanism to separate the producers and the consumers. The main aim is to encapsulate the processing of all forms of database operations – SELECT, UPDATE, DELETE statements, etc. Two essential parts of the implementation are:

- CORBA object implementing specific interface (DBOperable), which contains information needed for executing of the database operations – query or other SQL statement to be executed, what results are to be returned, etc.
- CORBA object (DBQueryProcessor), which has the connection to the database and can process objects implementing interface mentioned above.

The main goal is load balancing and the optimal usage of the system processing power – it is possible to plug additional machines running DB query processors, they would connect to Queue Manager, obtain ObjectQueue name and would participate in the query or, to be more exact, database operations processing activity. Upon completion of database operation, DB processor returns results to the client component via call-back interface.

We have designed and implemented a simple object queue framework with two different communication options:

- Communication via simple data structures – client just puts other objects or itself into a queue, and processor of database operations (DBProcessor) gets them from it. Object queue has a possibility to accept objects only of specific type, process objects with different priorities, etc. DBProcessor also can choose queue of specific type.
- Communication via encapsulated CORBA Event Service. DBProcessor objects register as pull consumers; some objects can register as push suppliers for the specific event channel. One queue can have multiple Event Service channels. The implementation of the queue encapsulates the creation of the channels, etc. and exposes comprehensive interface for the clients.

In both cases, the object to be processed can initiate the database operation. This can also be done by any other object, which would put an object, implementing DBOperable into the particular queue.

DB operations components collaboration diagram

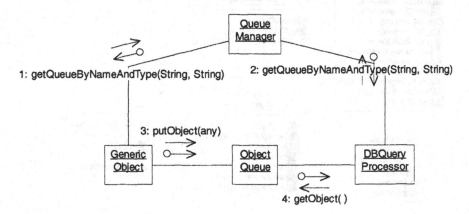

Figure 4. Communication using queues

3.3 SHARED OBJECT POOL

One of the questions, which frequently arises when the distributed systems for the multiple concurrent usage are designed, is how to reuse the objects instead of instantiating them repeatedly. We are talking about objects that share the same data and need to be accessed by multiple concurrent users. There is quite a simple solution using the pool of shared remote objects. The instance of remote object (for example, CORBA or RMI) resides where it was created – on the server side. When the client needs the specific object, it looks up in the pool for such an object. If there's no object with such properties, the new object is created, the implementation is left in the pool on the server side, and reference to that object is returned to the client. When some client is looking up for the particular object for the second time, there's no need to create another similar object. When the client invokes any method, which changes the state of a shared object, all clients using the same object can see these changes instantly – there is no need for refreshing of object set at the client side. Moreover, object pool can implement such features as periodical and asynchronous cleaning up of the objects that are not used by any client.

3.4 SEPARATION OF PRESENTATION AND CONTENTS USING TEMPLATES

The creation of the user interface components or data output results is often the area of activities of the WWW designers rather than the software developers. On the other hand, the content of the presentation is determined by the application, thus it is necessary to separate the presentation layout from its contents. This issue is especially important in WWW applications, where the layout is the most flexible and dynamic. We shall present our approach to this problem and outline some future steps and work in progress.

The simplest way to produce HTML output on the WWW server is to write HTML elements one by one to the output stream, producing contents for WWW client. This technique, however, is very poorly scalable, since it locks the layout of the document inside an application, making it impossible to change the presentation part without changing the processing part. Another approach is to mix scripting language and HTML, but since we decided to use pure Java implementation of HTTP server extension, this option was also inappropriate. We have designed and implemented a solution based on the usage of the templates. Each presentation element can have a template, which contains placeholders of the macro variable names and optionally special tags for the recursive data.

The administrators and the end-users can freely edit templates, provided that the placeholders and the other reserved constructs remain unchanged. Each visual entity (HTML page, for example) is represented at runtime by Java object, which is constructed by using particular template. These objects have methods for setting values of the macro variables, expansion of the template, writing expanded contents to the stream, etc. Two approaches are possible to the externalisation of the contents. When output element is relatively small, all the processing is performed in memory, then expanded contents is written to the output stream. However, when the template contains recursive constructs, the processing can take a lot of memory, so there is a possibility to specify output stream and make the so-called "shadow writing", i.e. to write portion of the formatted data to that output stream, when the data becomes available. This technique works well together with the data sinks discussed earlier, especially in WWW applications, where considerable amounts of output are being generated.

We are working towards using Extensible Markup Language (XML) for template specification and separating of the presentation layout via Extensible Stylesheet Language (XSL), to be compliant with the emerging industry standards and to use the advantages of XML parsers rather than implementing our own. XML will also allow us to create Document Type Definitions (DTD) for the contents validation, if need be. At the time we devised our template-based approach, XML was not as popular as it is now, there was a significantly smaller choice of XML parsers and other XML-related software.

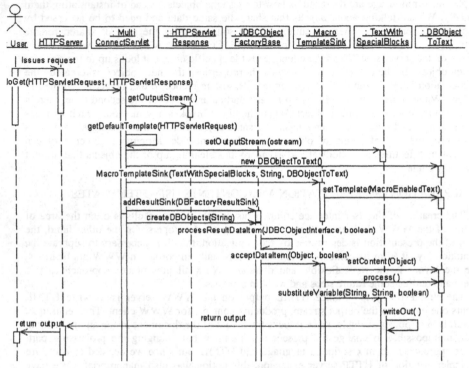

Figure 5. Example of usage of templates and data sinks with Servlets

4. Analysis of Created Software for Reusability

At first we would like to review all of our software code and to evaluate its reusability percentage in terms of lines of code (LOC) and number of Java source files (one source file - one public class in Java).

Table 1. Distribution of code according to reusability level

	LOC		Source files	
	Number	Percent	Number	Percent
Reusable	17755	24.88%	150	37.88%
Domain dependent	15891	22.27%	61	15.40%
Application dependent	37718	52.85%	185	46.72%
Total	71364	100%	396	100%

We shall sort out all implemented components and classes in three groups: *reusable* - context independent, can be used in any application, in any business domain, *domain dependent*

- can be used in any application for this business domain, reusable in domain context, *application dependent* - used only in particular applications, not reusable.

From these numbers we can see that reusable components (one Java source file corresponds to one class or component) are usually smaller in terms of LOC, they have lower degree of cohesion than application or domain dependent components. Now let us examine what part of total components is Java class libraries and what CORBA components.

Figure 6 shows the distribution of CORBA components and Java class libraries by source files. The percentage of CORBA in reusable components is not high - about 14 percents. The other part of reusable components is implemented as Java class libraries. One of the reasons for this is that usage of CORBA is not always required, sometimes Java is quite sufficient. If there is some reusable Java class, its CORBA wrapper, if needed, can be implemented at any time and at low cost. In addition, the latest developments like RMI-IIOP allow reusing Java components by CORBA clients, if necessary. CORBA components take greater part in domain-dependent components. They were developed for two projects from the same domain, where CORBA component framework was necessary. Application dependent components consist mainly of Java applications or quite independent application parts, and these applications only use domain dependent CORBA components, but are not CORBA components themselves.

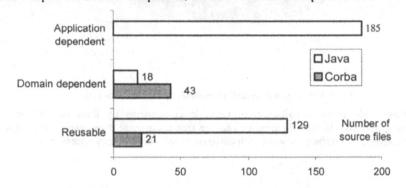

Figure 6. Reusability of Java and CORBA code by number of source files

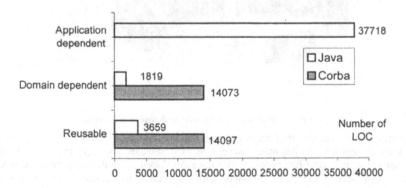

Figure 7. Reusability of Java and CORBA code by LOC

The difference between the diagram in Figure 6 and the one presented above is that CORBA components take much higher percent in lines of code. The main reason for this is that the implementation of CORBA component in Java, especially if that component takes a lower place in component inheritance hierarchy, consumes much more lines of the code. This happens because CORBA does not allow the inheritance of particular implementation, so CORBA component operations always must be overwritten, which is not necessary in Java class inheritance hierarchy.

Now, let us examine reusable components - what kind of components usually need to be implemented, what domains of standard Java API lack some functionality. Figure 8 shows the distribution of reusable components by source files in such domains like persistence, graphical user interface, network and input output, data models and collections, various handy utilities and generic classes (generic exceptions, objects, etc.).

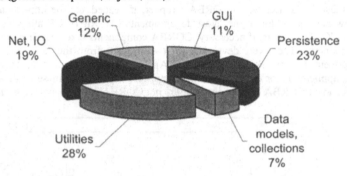

Figure 8. Distribution of reusable components by domain/source files

Figure 9 shows the distribution of reusable components by lines of code in the corresponding domains. In both figures we can see that persistence takes one of the greatest parts, thus convenient interface for work with database objects is obviously necessary.

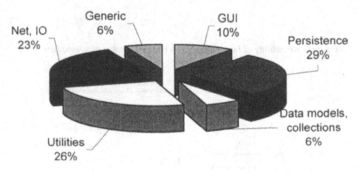

Figure 9. Distribution of reusable components by domain/lines of code

The third highest number is taken by network and input/output domain. Though Java was created to work in network and has many useful classes in standard packages java.net, java.io, there is a shortage of that kind functionality. We have developed reusable components to work with URL's, Java Servlet hierarchy (Servlets with connection to databases, to work with dynamic HTML templates, etc.).

Now let us evaluate reusable components according to the following reuse metrics: commonality (frequency of use across systems) and reuse threshold (minimum number of reuse for paying back). We shall try to examine sets of components according to the domains discussed earlier (GUI, persistence, etc.).

Table 2. Degree of reusability in different design domains

	Commonality	Reuse threshold
Persistence	100%	10 – 15
Network, I/O	80%	7 - 10
GUI	30%	2 - 3
Utilities	60%	4 - 6
Generic	80%	7 - 8
Data models	50%	4 - 6

As we can see, persistence related reusable components are most frequent. If there is no need for the relational database, then sometimes LDAP servers are necessary when working through LDAP protocol. Reusable components that encapsulate the main LDAP operations fall into the same Java persistence framework. Other frequent domains are network and generic. Note that the more frequent the usage of the component is, the more times it must be reused for paying back. It, of course, depends on the implementation and maintenance costs of component. Frequently used components need more careful implementation (to cover all inconveniences and create really good interface) and more intensive maintenance.

5. Conclusions

In this paper we summarise our experience in design and development of the distributed object systems. Generic system architecture, which proved to be successful in our projects, is described. Due to the limited space of this paper we were not able to discuss all of our reusable solutions, so we have chosen those, which we think, are the most important and successful, and hope that our experience can be useful. Of course, some solutions may be unnecessary if some more expensive application server software is used, however this is the lower-cost approach; high cost and sound promises of application server vendors also need proof that they deliver right functionality.

It is our opinion that distributed object technologies and Java platform is suitable for the development of the production-level information systems. There were quite hard times to develop working systems using Java, however it seems that it has changed for the better. Software industry is taking these technologies seriously, making the promise of the portability a reality.

References

1. Allen, P., Frost, S. An integrated component-based process. *Object Magazine*, February, 1998.
2. Ceponkus, A., Hoodbhoy, F. *Applied XML A Toolkit for Programmers.* Wiley, 1999.
3. Eastman, J. Building scalable CORBA distributed systems. *Object Magazine*, April, 1997.
4. Edwards, J. *3-Tier Client/Server at Work.* Wiley, 1997.
5. Glushko, R. J., Tenenbaum, J. M., and Meltzer, B. An XML framework for agent-based E-commerce. *Communications of the ACM*, 3(42), 1999, pp. 106-114.
6. Goldman, J., Rawles, P., and Mariga, J. *Client/Server Information Systems A Business-Oriented Approach.* Wiley, 1999.

7. Henning, M. Binding, migration, and scalability in CORBA. *Communications of the ACM*, **10**(41), 1998, pp. 62-71.

8. Kara, D. Next up... Java application servers. *Object Magazine*, March, 1998.

9. Morgenthal, J. P. The impact of Enterprise JavaBeans. *Object Magazine*, March, 1998.

10. Morghental, J. P. Enterprise application integration tutorial. *Presentations of OMG Enterprise Application Integration Workshop*, February 7-10, 2000, Orlando, FL, USA.

11. Object Management Group. *UML 1.1. Specification*. OMG document, 1998.

12. Ohnjec, V, Kranz, D. Developing distributed object systems. *Object Magazine*, February, 1998.

13. Orfali, R., Harkey, D., and Edwards, J. *Client/Server Programming with Java and CORBA*. Wiley, 1997.

14. Orfali, R., Harkey, D., and Edwards, J. *Instant CORBA*. Wiley, 1997.

15. Orfali, R., Harkey, D., and Edwards, J. *The Essential Distributed Objects Survival Guide*. Wiley, 1996.

16. Pyarali, I., Schmidt, D. C. An overview of the CORBA portable object adapter. *Standard View, ACM perspectives of standardization*, **1**(6), 1998, pp. 40-43.

17. Roman, E. *Mastering Enterprise JavaBeans and the Java 2 Platform*. Enterprise Edition, Wiley, 1999.

18. Schmidt, D. Evaluating architectures for multithreaded object request brokers. *Communications of the ACM*, **10**(41), 1998, pp. 54-60.

19. Stal, M. Worldwide CORBA: distributed objects and the net. *Object Magazine*, March, 1998.

20. Vinoski, S. New Features for CORBA 3.0. *Communications of the ACM*, **10**(41), 1998, pp. 44-52.

21. Wong, D., Paciorek, N. and Moore, D. Java-based mobile agents. *Communications of the ACM*, **3**(42), 1999, pp. 92-104.

Configured Replication for Mobile Applications *

Astrid Lubinski

Computer Science Dept.,
University of Rostock, Germany
E - mail: lubinski@informatik.uni-rostock.de

Andreas Heuer

Computer Science Dept.,
University of Rostock, Germany
E - mail: heuer@informatik.uni - rostock.de

Abstract

Replication is an essential utility in mobile environments. Mobile units not connected to fixed networks are left with their own data resources, which may or may not contain the necessary data. This paper describes benefits and problems using replication in mobile infrastructures. We compare different replication approaches for fixed and mobile systems. We show that traditional protocols are inadequate for the requirements of mobile environments, especially when accessing multimedia data.

The objectives of replication, high availability, permanent consistency, and low communication costs, are incompatible. Consequently, replication protocols must find suitable compromises. However, rather than creating a general approach for all possible mobile environments, we tailor suitable replication mechanisms for special mobile environments and data types. This approach allows for configured replication based on various environmental and data characteristics.

Keywords: mobile information systems, replication, integrity, adaptability.

1. Introduction

Portable computers and advances in wireless communication provide mobile processing like "outdoor" tasks. These kinds of tasks require determined applications on special whereabouts. Thus, mobile work is context - sensitive work with contexts describing environmental characteristics and the relationships between them. Applications and required data are *location dependent*, but their access must be *location transparent*. Context information comprehends further which people and objects in the environment stay. This includes differing views on data or an appropriate selection of applications for existing means and tools.

Supporting mobile work involves providing access to interesting, possibly multimedia data available just-in-time and on the scene, i.e., at the appropriate location, time, and device (where and when the data are used) based on user aims, preferences, knowledge, and skills. A predictive replication is necessary to fulfil this objective.

---

*This work is part of the Mobile Visualisation Project (MoVi) and has been supported by the German Research Association under contract Schu 887 / 3 - 2.

J. Barzdins and A. Caplinskas (eds.), Databases and Information Systems, 139–151.

But, users pay for mobility with restrictions of the mobile infrastructure limiting available volume and type of data and the data transfer. The consideration of restrictions first requires management of different information regarding the current infrastructure, mobile resources, connectivity, costs and duration of connections, and available bandwidths. Mobile work is characterised by infrequent and temporary short connections to the fixed network (low connectivity) and by a variety of access types (register data, queries).

Summarising, the *mobile context* covers:

- human factors, their tasks, roles, other persons;

- location (and changing location in time);

- hard and software (mobile site and network characteristics, equipment and tools);

- information, application characteristics (like media type, size).

Mobile users access data that are also accessed by other users or itself on different locations and devices, respectively. Because of rare, sporadic, and weak connections, a local copy must be maintained on the mobile device to avoid the establishment of an expensive connection and the remote accessing and transferring of data and to do any meaningful work with the mobile system. Such a copy increases availability, decreases answer time, and also improves fault-tolerance. Replication is a well-known concept in distributed database systems. The DBMS enforces consistency of replicas. Replication is a system-controlled copy of database fragments on different sites, so that each replica is an instantiation of a database fragment (In general, there are copies without having any original.).

The replicated data have to be kept consistent with the data on the stationary server. However, this consistency has to be ensured without frequent connections to the server - for cost reasons, among others. An apparently impossible endeavour?

Replication is one of the key problems of mobile information systems. An applicable handling of replication in this new computing paradigm needs new solutions not served by existing replication protocols, and is able to considerably improve the acceptance, efficiency, and transparency of mobile information systems.

Commercial database and information systems currently in use in mobile environments burden the user with maintaining the consistency of the replicated data. Prior to beginning mobile work, the user assembles the data to be used on the mobile device and transfers it from the server. The user subsequently adjusts parameters to specify which actions are possible on the particular data located either on the mobile client or on the server. The user has to rely upon the consistency of the data while working in a disconnected environment. If new or more current data is required, the user must independently connect to the server in order to transfer the data. When querying the mobile information system in a disconnected environment, the user has to assess the up-to-dateness and consistency of data without the system's help. Consistency checks are first possible when the data are transferred back to the server after finishing the mobile work. Any subsequent conflicts in consistency must be manually solved by the user.

In mobile application systems, ad hoc replication techniques prevail because the majority of these application systems are not supported by database technology (electronic mail systems according to the POP3 or IMAP protocol, e.g.). In these cases, only certain consistency checking mechanisms are feasible. Working with the application system in a mobile environment does not provide location transparency because the user notices differences between the stationary server and the mobile client.

In order to avoid restricted functionality, restricted up-to-dateness, and restricted consistency, replication techniques used in mobile environments need to meet the following requirements:

- High availability of data on the mobile device despite low costs and an acceptable consistency of data.

- Use of semantic context information about user, application, and data attributes, in order to perform meaningful consistency checking at low costs.

- Use of semantic context information for realising dynamic replication, that is transparent loading of information to be updated from the server on request (when querying the mobile system, e.g.).

In this paper, replication techniques are evaluated against the first two demands; the last one will be motivated. Additionally, a replication mechanism is introduced that can optimally "tailor" existing replication techniques to applications when appropriate information about the application is available.

This paper is organised into the following sections. In section 2, we provide an overview of replication protocols, their tasks, and how they work. We describe classical replication protocols and their types used for mobile environments. Since existing mobile replication strategies use little semantic information, in section 3 we outline information usable for configuring or tailoring a suitable approach. Section 4 concludes the paper.

2. Replication Protocols

The replication approach of commercial database systems described above can result in rolling back of mobile transactions. For example, a conflict arises if one of the fixed users modifies a *product price*, but the mobile user still sells the product at the previous price, unaware of the price alteration. While synchronous propagation of each modification to every replica-holding site avoids conflicts, it also increases the communication costs of distributed systems and requires protocols to enforce consistency mechanisms.

Replication protocols manage replicas in a replication scheme, i.e., database fragments in a fragmentation scheme are allocated to several sites on the network. Multiple allocation of a particular fragment creates replicas. Because the management of replicas is a database task, selection of one copy for access should be transparent for users and their transactions. Access is processed like access to a single (uncopied) datum. This transparency, together with the ensured serialisable execution of transactions, is called 1-copy-serialisability and results in one copy being selected for access. However, modifying access to one copy can lead to inconsistencies between replicas, which means replication protocols must incorporate modification propagation strategies, including strategies for network or site failures or disconnections, respectively.

2.1 MOBILE REPLICATION

Disconnections and limited resources are stringent mobile requirements that affect the consistency. We maintain that network partitioning, although an exception in traditional networks, is a normal mobile requirement. Furthermore, we distinguish between switching off a mobile device and interrupting the connection to model autonomous (disconnected) work with a mobile device. Every access must determine, besides the location of the replicas, whether replica-holding sites are reachable.

Additionally, mobile environments are characterised by their dynamics. Changing mobile resources, like available storage, may result in inappropriate replica sizes. Replicated data must be erased and the replication scheme has to alter. The availability is limited. Replicas can be adjusted to small mobile resources with the help of abstraction techniques. This makes modifications more complicate. Just as dynamic resources, the changing user location and environment, e.g., present

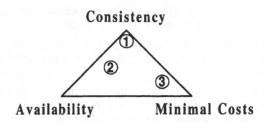

Figure 1. Replication objectives

persons, can alter tasks and hence, applications and data are treated. Finally, communication is an expensive factor in wireless networks belonging to monetary costs. Therefore, most disconnections, besides involuntary, are intended. Numerous connections cover cost overhead for connecting and disconnecting time before and after the data transfer, and small bandwidths prolong the transfer time. Subsequently, a user will strive for rare and short connections.

These characteristics of mobile environments deal with the three main objectives of replication. Replication seeks to provide *high availability* on mobile sites during disconnected phases, *consistency*, and *low communication costs*. These objectives can be organised as a triangle illustrating the impossibility of achieving the three objectives simultaneously. Achieving one objective requires making cuts in at least one of the two remaining objectives. For example, a user expects consistent data (see Fig.1, case 1). This can only be attained by reducing availability (less copies means less possible inconsistencies) and/or immediate modification propagation, which increase costs. If cost reduction is a primary concern and is achieved using infrequent and short connections, consistency and availability are not attainable (see Fig.1, case 3, e.g.).

The next subsections provide an overview of the types of replication protocols that exist for distributed systems and particularly for mobile environments. Replication strategies will be classified considering frequent disconnections.

2.2 REPLICATION PROTOCOLS FOR DISTRIBUTED SYSTEMS

This chapter outlines well known replication techniques for distributed systems (described for example, in [3]). First of all, we must distinguish between synchronised or non-synchronised replicas. Non-synchronised copies are non-germane in the database environment because they are only snapshots without replication control and management and are not kept up-to-date. Synchronising protocols can work optimistically or pessimistically.

Optimistic protocols enable parallel and disconnected access to more than one copy. Furthermore, disconnected work is possible. A necessary reintegration phase after isolated accesses should work as automatically as possible with the help of syntactic rules or be based on semantic knowledge about transactions to reduce reintegration transactions (transformation log method, data patch method). Because inconsistencies and update conflicts occur and remain until the reintegration, optimistic protocols are recommended only if

- there is a small likelihood of updates or,
- the insufficient correctness of data is tolerable.

In general, optimistic protocols are not feasible because application-specific knowledge is needed for reintegration rules.

On the other hand, *pessimistic* methods guarantee fast read accesses and permanently consistent data by propagating the performed updates in wired network environments. Transactions are complete after updating every copy. In case of a failure, this rule (ROWA -read one write all) is problematical because transactions are delayed while waiting for all sites. Therefore, in order to increase the availability of write operations, other pessimistic protocols were developed. In order to avoid imbalances of read and write availability, the *Write-all-Available* protocol was proposed. Non-available copies are updated after their reconnection based on a log file. The outstanding updates are copied to the reconnected data.

Primary protocols designate either one site or one copy to be the primary. Write transactions are complete when the primary is updated. Other copies are updated asynchronously. Write operations are not dependent on network partitioning or unavailable sites. Several *Voting* protocols form quorums to determine updates. Part of the quorum can be replica-holding sites or other sites, such as ghosts or witnesses. These protocols require intensive communication for co-ordination.

We subsequently compared protocols by using the objectives of the replication, high availability, permanent consistency, and low costs. Optimistic protocols permit high availability for a limited consistency and incur low communication costs. Pessimistic protocols enforce high consistency but at the expense of availability. Depending on the particular protocol, communication costs can range from low to high. Protocol classifications can also be distinguished by observing the type of update propagation, such as synchronous (like in ROWA) or asynchronous (like in optimistic strategies).

2.3 *TRADITIONAL* REPLICATION TECHNIQUES UNDER MOBILE CONDITIONS

Traditional replication techniques are inadequate if a disconnection occurs or the bandwidths are low. We have implemented a simulation system to compare the application of the *traditional* replication techniques under mobile conditions with slow transfer rates and disconnections (see appended figures 2, 3, 4, 5). The model consists of five sites. Three of them (nodes: 100, 200 and 300) build a fixed network and the remaining (nodes: 500 and 600) are connected wireless. The transfer rates of mobile links differ from the transfer rates of stationary network links. Each node stores a copy, which means that the database is fully replicated.

Each node initiates one read and one write transaction per simulation, chronologically. Mobile sites are disconnected after 400 time units for a period of 400 time units. Each simulation is run with a different transfer rate of the wireless link (x-axis). The y-axis represents the transaction time in time units. Two of the simulated replication techniques are presented in the appended diagrams, the primary site and the ROWA (read one write all) protocols. Node 100 represents the primary site, which is always up-to-date and propagates modifications asynchronously.

Read transactions of a ROWA strategy realise fast local accesses (Figure 2) and would be qualified for mobile environments. The primary site strategy implements a local read access, but locks the stationary primary for guaranteeing the consistency of the local copy. This strategy needs a wireless communication for every transaction increasing delay and communication costs (Figure 3). Low baudrates improve the delay rapidly because of periodical appearing disconnections for 400 time units.

Each write transaction of the ROWA strategy locks every node (Figure 4). This strategy makes the use of ROWA with wireless participating clients impossible. A write transaction on a primary site locks only the primary and the delays of all nodes start later than in the ROWA strategy (all update propagation are carried out asynchronously, see Figure 5).

The resulting diagrams clearly illustrate improving difficulties with smaller transfer rates. The restricted bandwidth leads to delays for the mobile nodes, as well as the stationary nodes. Fixed nodes even depend on mobile transactions due to their locking in case of mobile write accesses. Transactions of the fixed sites are delayed when mobile sites are disconnected or the bandwidths are low. Transaction delays for write transactions are unacceptable even for this simple scenario.

2.4 REPLICATION PROTOCOLS FOR MOBILE SYSTEMS

Customary replication protocols used for distributed systems with mobile participants show great limitations because of the previously discussed mobile characteristics. Therefore, there are many approaches to define special protocols for such an environment. Summarising the approaches, we state that there are the well known strategies extended with few mobility supporting mechanisms. Approaches offer a range of concepts from restricting the mobile work over lazy consistency to mobile work reserved.

In [2], authors attempted to solve replication problems in mobile environments with exiting replication techniques. They distinguished between updateable core copies for read- and write-access, read-only cached copies, and the directory to manage copies. Updating the directory implies a reorganisation of core copies for the disconnected case. The paper emphasised "that mobility does not introduce any fundamental new problems or algorithms for replicated data management". The authors recommended, beside a good fragmentation, not placing core copies on "low-bandwidth, limited power mobile sites". As a result of PDA's widespread acceptance, numerous applications have arise where users are working isolated but require more than cached copies. Their approach attains good values for replication objectives but with restrictions for mobile work.

Recent papers even focus on these problems. The user's work may not be restricted; however, inconsistencies should be managed carefully.

Many experiences with disconnected operations exist in context with the Coda File System [11]. File system approaches to manage cached copies usually apply an optimistic strategy ([4], Coda [11], Little Work [9], Ficus [7]). MIo-NFS [6] realises a pessimistic method with the help of tokens to permit write accesses. Ficus introduced an interesting Gossip-protocol to propagate updates between disconnected sites. Little Work requires more communication to avoid conflicts, which hinders mobile communications.

File system approaches handle whole files whereas database systems manage a finer granularity and are able to use data semantics. Replication management and enforcement of replication objectives are integral parts of the DBMS.

In [13], a mix of optimistic and pessimistic strategies is proposed. The application or the database system determines which copies are core or quasi copies, respectively. Quasi copies are consistent inside a cluster whereas core copies are consistent throughout the entire database. Weak operations on quasi copies result in inner-cluster consistency, strict operations (transactions) enforce database consistency. Conflicting operations between different combinations of weak or strict and read or write are described. Inter-cluster inconsistencies are temporarily possible. The reintegration (reconciliation) strategy for strict transactions is left open. The inner-cluster inconsistencies are bound by a number d of e.g., weak transactions or diverging data. The choice of such a definition is the task of the database system or the application. Semantic based inconsistency bounding seems to us to be more sufficient than an arbitrarily selected d.

While the availability of this approach in case of disconnections is high, consistency and costs depend on the r / w pattern of core copies.

Using a primary copy on a mobile disconnected site makes it impossible to update the other sites. In [2], authors proposed to "combine the primary copy strategy with frequent backups to a cached copy". Authors of [5] developed a primary copy strategy especially for this problem, the *Virtual Primary Copy*. The Home Base Node contains the virtual primary copy as representative for the disconnected primary copy (VPC). Consistency is endangered for mobile sites without connection, but the data are available. The costs are average on the base of connections to the mobile primary.

MAID [16] described the use of active database systems in mobile environments. Active rules are also used for replication. Local acceptance criteria control local access and facilitate the reintegration after disconnections. It recognises a strict-connected, a weak-connected, and a disconnected state. An additional update propagation path builds direct-communicating mobile sites (e.g., via infrared) forming a consistency cluster. Because of the access limitations, availability is average, while costs are low. In consistency clusters, only local consistency can be achieved.

[14] focused on this special aspect using peer-to-peer replication. The authors used an optimistic protocol.

Other replication approaches cope with network failures by changing the strategy. The ROWA strategy switches to a *Quorum Consensus* strategy, whereas only the bigger partition (with more sites) is able to perform write operations, which in general excludes the mobile site from write operations. Another strategy reduces the number of copies to one (primary) copy [15].

In [12], a "mixed mode replication is presented where pessimistically controlled replicas coexist with optimistically controlled ones". Operations are grouped into three sets of operations which: 1. cannot invalidate others, 2. be invalidated by others, or 3. are the set of all operations. The author used categories of past, present, future, and optimism. This approach improves the consistency of mobile copies.

A basic scenario, where the client reads a copy from data and the server writes data, is considered in [1]. Copies can reside on the mobile client, the mobile server, or their location servers. The authors distinguished between copies on which read and write operations are possible and cached copies, which are updated in case of a read access. When considering a copy and a cached copy, there are six different scenarios to place a copy. The propagation of updates (in the non cached type) coincides with the ROWA strategy. An important, but only briefly discussed aspect, is reviewing the r/w activity to determine where to place a copy. The reflected costs are costs for searching the current location server and base station. This point of interest diverges from today's replication studies, where occasional connections mainly establish replication.

3. Configuration of Suitable Protocols

We have shown, both pure optimistic and pure pessimistic strategies are inadequate for mobile environments. Whereas the first one causes inconsistencies and complex and perhaps expensive reintegration, the second one does not consider disconnections. Although it is not a new approach, we follow recent publications combining both strategies. Nevertheless, we are convinced that there is no approach, also no hybrid approach being able to cover all of the replication objectives. However, our tailored approach need not be related to specific cases or static environments. Rather, it can be adapted to dynamic contextual requirements defining the level of optimistic or pessimistic replication protocol.

We have discussed the impossibility of simultaneously achieving high availability, permanent consistency, and low costs. Therefore, our objective seeks a satisfactory level of availability and known consistency using infrequent and temporary short connections. We now present such a tailored approach using environmental semantics. In the first step, we determine the exploitable information, its assumptions and its limitations, and where it can be acquired. Then we show its application in building a dynamic, tailored replication.

3.1 EXPLOITABLE INFORMATION

We list the information with short descriptions and origination on the one hand and their employment and limitations, on the other hand. The information concerns the following layers: network, devices, data, applications, and user. System statistics, heuristics, context information, and user decisions are employed for determining and estimating the information. The information can be modelled or estimated in run time.

- *Network* connectivity: This includes knowledge about forthcoming switch-off of the device, just occurred switch-on, or user intended disconnections/connections. It is possible to prepare and subsequently treat these activities. Outlined below are the different scenarios for mobile sites

  - switched off

  - going to switch off

  - switched on and the link is

    1. disconnected: the mobile site has no connection to other sites;

    2. in d-c-transition (from disconnect to connect): the disconnection can be subsequently treated;

    3. connected: the work is related to the possibly restricted bandwidth;

    4. in c-d-transition (from connect to disconnect): the disconnection can be prepared.

The replication protocol uses information about connection/disconnection times like frequency and duration and average bandwidths to delay or enforce transfers for remote accesses, update propagation, or reintegration. Transactions are bundled to fully occupy bandwidths and reduce connection time. Moreover, d-c and c-d-transitions make it possible to alter the replication strategy, e.g., from a pessimistic strategy in the connected state to an optimistic strategy during the disconnected state. Short connections allow for direct contact to concurrent accessing users to arrange further strategies, such as the exchange of a r/w-token.

A c-d-transition can be used to prepare the disconnection and the transferring of data most likely to be accessed.

- *Site* resources: Site resources determine the size, and hence, the type of replicated data and the replicated metadata. The metadata include the replication (allocation) scheme, the transaction log for the reintegration, and the information discussed here used for replication tailoring.

- *Data* characteristics: The data layer provides data characteristics dealing with replication. This covers version numbers of the copies, the number of inconsistent data, the number of updates since last connection, the current kind of operation (read or write), and the time since last update or reintegration. This information is exploited to bound inconsistencies. Other data characteristics include alternative usable data. Alternatives (for example abstractions or data of differing media [8]) are necessary if expensive multimedia data are in contrast to the available site resources. Using resource saving alternatives results in differing replicas of one and the same data item on several sites!
Another interesting method to estimate consistency is to assign an expiration date to serve as an approximate range of validity. For example, we know a weather report in a newspaper is valid for up to three days, while a road map could be valid over a period of years.

- *Application* layer: An important and obvious criterion is the ratio of the number of reads to the number of writes. In order to minimise communication costs, local accesses are preferred. The replicas should be placed where they are used. [15] presented a technique for a dynamic allocation. The allocation adapts gradually, i.e., copies are moved to neighbouring sites based on the read/write-patterns. The implicit assumption is a relatively homogeneous access pattern. This technique is partially applicable for mobile environments, but results in increased communication overhead caused by access comparisons. [10] focused on optimising communication costs by allocating copies according to the r/w patterns. The copy was stored on the fixed site. An allocation to a mobile site then depends on read requests compared to the update rate. Communication costs were modelled by connection time and message-based. The allocation scheme is changing over time based on the last k requests. This is a pure pessimistic approach.
Read and write or write and write, respectively, on a particular data item are conflicting operations. Because of update propagation, writes are more expensive operations. Hence,

conflicting operations should be examined. With the help of data patch rules, write and write do not necessarily result in conflicting operations. E.g., salesmen enter addresses of new customers. These write operations are not in conflict.

Moreover, an interesting aspect is the frequency of appearing conflicts. In summary, the r/w-patterns decide the number of replicas as well as the site where copies are allocated. This decision is supported by homogeneous access patterns. Statistics concerning conflict frequencies for fine granular data provide the decision which data can be handled optimistically. The r/w ratio also can be used to decide about update propagation initiated by the updating site or its representative (like a primary) or in case of a read access. The last case saves communication costs by bundling infrequent updates.

Additional application information focuses on data requirements related to location and the mobile environment.

- *User* preferences: We argue for softening the replication transparency. The user should be informed about the consequences of infrequent connections and weak updates. Users must also be included in ranking the importance of replication objectives relating to particular data and in determining which replication strategy the replication protocol should follow.

3.2 TAILORING THE REPLICATION

Three steps lead to the configured replication:

1. set the importance of the three aims, consistency, availability, and minimal costs, perhaps with the help of a scale,

2. evaluate the available information about the network, device, application, data, and user,

3. model strategies depending on the available knowledge for all possible states (site and connection states).

In the first step, the application is placed into the triangle for the three replication objectives. The importance of one aim establishes a smaller importance of the two remaining aims. The importance determines the applicable strategies.

In the second point, all of the available data described above are collected or acquired, respectively. The more data that are available, the better the replication mechanism can be tailored.

In the third point, requirements meet available conditions. The following decisions can be made. The first step is selecting a replication strategy (optimistic, pessimistic, hybrid, changing) based on the selected objective. The strategy, application, and data characteristics decide the placing of data and metadata (like replication scheme). Data granularity is a factor that is applied to use hybrid techniques and affects the placing. Therefore, granularity design (fragmentation) is a priority task.

If the *availability* is restrictable, a pessimistic (maybe combined with an optimistic) strategy can be selected. The restriction on the number of copies or transactions on the copies also decreases the availability. An extreme reduction up to one copy endangers the entire replication concept. A suitable compromise must be found.

Optimistic strategies are usable if *consistency* is less important. This strategy is only usable if few and simple conflicts (see [12]) are expected or conflicts are avoided by restriction of accesses (see [13]). The above application and data characteristics can be used for optimising the strategy.

Hybrid strategies are introduced if *communication costs* can be extended. Extending the duration of connections makes voting strategies possible, but the connections are badly occupied. Increasing the frequency of connections allows bundling transactions, but increases management costs.

The three steps tailoring a suitable replication mechanism are applied once before starting mobile work or to refresh the strategy any time after using current statistical material.

3.3 EXAMPLES

To illustrate the tailoring approach, we apply our tailoring process to two short examples with differing requirements.

The first one is a tourist guide available on PDAs. The sight-seeing information is managed on a fixed server, and tourists require location dependent tourist information. Data consistency is not a priority, because the update rate is low and concerns primarily layout and size of the information, whereas communication costs have a high relevance. However, availability can be only somewhat reduced. In this scenario, it is possible to use a pure optimistic strategy. This is simply possible because of a low write rate. Mobile users, tourists, do not have any possibility to modify data, i.e., they have a read-only access to copies. Small communication costs assume short connections requiring connection-preparing operations. The location and the direction of tourists are known. Therefore, a c-d-transition is used to transfer most likely asked information about the local tourist's environment to mobile sites predictable. The bandwidth can be fully occupied and the number of connections are reduced. We keep the fully transparent replication apart from some information that has a restricted expiration date validating the tourist information (e.g., season dependent business hours).

The second example is a hospital environment. Many doctors and nurses treat numerous patients. The medical data of patients are of immediate significance. Therefore, consistency and availability are of major priority. Consequently, each doctor accesses their own copy, which is managed by a pessimistic method. Applying this to every patient's data, mobile device resources are insufficient. In order to eliminate this problem, we divide patient data into two sets a and b. Set a contains all data where every modification is relevant and will be propagated to all copies, e.g., with the ROWA strategy. The propagation must be performed immediately. Set b contains further patient data that are relevant only in special situations, particularly in a consultation context. This data can be updated in the case of an access, i.e., optimistically. The replication protocol should have the ability to provide data most likely to be accessed. For example, when a doctor on rounds requests data for a patient in one room, the data for other patients at the same location (e.g., same room or adjacent room) would be made available, if they have not been replicated before. Online accesses, instead of replication, are possible, but are dependent on network capacity. The replication scheme is very dynamic in such an environment, but a permanent data replication of patients in critical states of health is advisable. Dependent on data set (a or b), this application avails of optimistic and pessimistic strategies, whereas optimistic handling should be restricted to a defined number of operations.

The two examples show the wide range of mobile applications and a suitable application of the described framework resulting in two very different replication strategies.

4. Conclusion

Replication is an important mechanism in mobile environments. Customary replication protocols for distributed (database) systems are not up to the demands of mobile applications and mobile used data. The simulation illustrated the limitations. In general, neither the optimistic nor the pessimistic replication approach meets mobile requirements. For that reason, a pessimistic restricting optimistic (hybrid) strategy realises and supports a satisfactory degree of consistency and availability considering disconnections. Because data and applications change within a dynamic mobile environment, the replication protocol must also have sufficient flexibility to adjust. Hence, we described a framework using a variety of syntactic and semantic knowledge which would be very helpful to tailor a suitable replication strategy corresponding to the mobile environment, including its technical and infrastructural conditions, as well as user-forced regulations.

The simulation tool is not able to cover all of the semantic knowledge and would be too complex if it realises all varieties of possible decisions. Therefore, we are in the process of implementing a test system. Test data are emails managed in database systems for mobile users on stationary and mobile sites. The test environment consists of a database system on a PDA and on a stationary site. After a scenario description, an extension of the IMAP-4 protocol follows. Besides usual mail clients, an implemented mail client realises the desired replication strategies.

A tailoring approach may require more management overhead, but it also uses information stored for other purposes.

Furthermore, we emphasise softening the replication transparency for applications and users in order to inform them about possible inconsistencies, waiting periods or necessary communications, and cost effects of forced consistency.

References

1. Badrinath, B. R. and Imielinski, T. Replication and mobility. In *2nd IEEE WS on Management of Replicated Data*, 1992.

2. Barbara, D. and Garcia-Molina, H. Replicated data management in mobile environments: anything new under the sun? In *IFIP Conference on Applications in Parallel and Distributed Computing*, 1994.

3. Beuter, T. and Dadam, P. Prinzipien der Replikationskontrolle in verteilten Datenbanksystemen. *Informatik Forschung und Entwicklung*, (11), 1996, pp. 203-212.

4. Duchamp, D. and Tait, C. T. An interface to support lazy replicated file service. In *2nd WS on Management of Replicated Data*, 1993.

5. Faiz, M., Zaslavsky, A., and Srinivasan, B. Revising strategies for mobile computing environments. In *ECOOP'95 WS on Mobility and Replication*, 1995.

6. Guedes, V. and Moura, F. Replica control in MIo-NFS. In *ECOOP'95 WS on Mobility and Replication, Aarhus*, 1995.

7. Heidemann, J. S., Page, T. W., Guy, R. G., and Popek, G. J. Primarily disconnected operation: experiences with Ficus. In *2nd WS on the Management of Replicated Data*, Los Alamitos, 1992.

8. Heuer, A. and Lubinski, A. Data reduction - an adaptation technique for mobile environments. In *Interactive Applications of mobile Computing (IMC'98)*, 1998.

9. Honeyman, P. and Huston, L. B. Communications and consistency in mobile file systems. *IEEE Personal Communications*, 6(2), 1995, pp. 44-48.

10. Huang, Y., Sistla, P., and Wolfson, O. Data replication for mobile computers. In *ACMSIGMOD Conference*, Minneapolis, 1994.

11. Kistler, J. J. and Silberschatz, M. Disconnected operation in the coda file system. *ACM Transactions on Comp. Syst.*, 10(1), 1992, pp. 3-25.

12. Kottmann, D. A. Serializing operations into the past and future: a paradigm for disconnected operations on replicated objects. In *ECOOP'95 WS on Mobility and Replication*, 1995.

13. Pitoura, E. A replication schema to support weak connectivity in mobile systems. In *7th Int. Conference on Database and Expert Systems Applications (DEXA'96)*, 1996.

14. Ratner, D. H., Reiher, P. L., Popek, G. J., and Guy, R. G. Peer replication with selective control. In *Interactive Conference on Mobile Data Access*, 1999.

15. Wolfson, O., Jajodia, S., and Huang, Y. An adaptive data replication algorithm. *ACM Transactions in Database Systems*, 22(2), 1997, pp. 255-313.

16. Zukunft, O. *Integration mobiler und aktiver Datenbankmechanismen als Basis für die ortsgebundene Vorgangsbearbeitung*. PhD thesis, University of Oldenburg, 1997.

Appendix

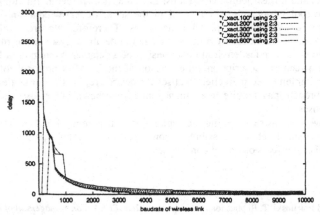

Figure 2. Read Transactions - ROWA

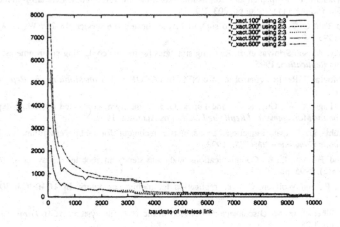

Figure 3. Read Transactions - Primary Site

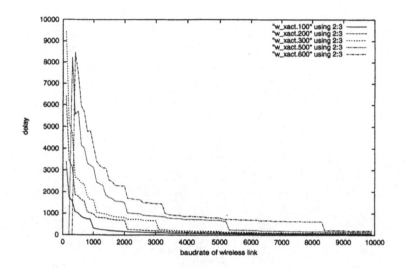

Figure 4. Write Transactions - ROWA

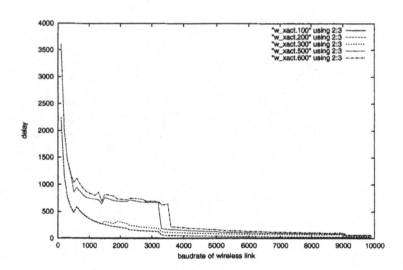

Figure 5. Write Transactions - Primary Site

Part 4: Network-based Information Systems

An Infrastructure for an Electronic Market of Scientific Literature

Michael Christoffel, Jens Nimis, Bethina Schmitt, Peter C. Lockemann

Fakultät für Informatik, Universität Karlsruhe, Karlsruhe, Germany
{christof, nimis, schmitt, lockeman}@ira.uka.de

Sebastian Pulkowski

University Library, Universität Karlsruhe, Karlsruhe, Germany
pulkowsk@ira.uka.de

Abstract

The success of the Internet has brought a large quantity of providers offering search and delivery services for scientific literature. We observe the development of an information market, where the value of a piece of information is determined by the law of supply and demand. This situation raises questions as to the future of university libraries. The objective of this paper is to find answers to these problems and to develop an architecture for the integration of information services in the field of scientific literature under the premise of an open, heterogeneous and dynamic market. With the UniCats system, we provide an integration architecture that supports all, customers, providers, and the traditional library. Technical basis is the UniCats environment, a framework for communicating UniCats agents. The most important agent types are trader, wrapper and user agent.

Keywords: information market, digital libraries, service integration, electronic commerce infrastructure.

1. Introduction

Information has become one of the most important goods in the modern society. Consequently, accessing and providing information has become an important and lucrative business. This trade with information underlies the same rules as the trade with traditional goods, and we observe the development of an information market, which is dominated by factors like cost, price, consumer value, ease of access, delivery times, and the quality of the information. This development does not stop in front of scientific literature supply. Even traditional institutions like university libraries cannot ignore this market and are going to loose their monopoly of assisting university members to find the required information. They have to face the new situation and support their academic clientele with new services.

One change that undergoes traditional marketplaces also emerges in the information market: the pure delivery of a good is only a small part of what customers demand. It is the whole range of accompanying services that determine the value of this good.

In the scientific and university area, scientists and students depend on the supply with information and on worldwide information exchange. Due to the success of the Internet and the World Wide Web, scientists and students have electronic access to a large quantity of providers offering information services all over the world. Searching, ordering, and, often, delivery can be done without leaving the work desk. Traditional libraries and bookstores are supplemented by new services: Internet bookstores, bibliographic databases that offer a huge amount of references and documents, technical report servers, publishing houses that market their books and journals on their own, delivery services that send documents by fax or by e-mail, and electronic journals.

Just because the information is now available electronically does not mean that the providers offer their services for free. Scientific literature continues to command a price, but now the players

155

J. Barzdins and A. Caplinskas (eds.), Databases and Information Systems, 155–165.

have become more numerous and competition more pronounced. Just consider that even public and university libraries will be forced to charge for their services as public funds dry up.

Price has to have a counterpart in value. Unfortunately, the new market is not transparent. But what are the obstacles to transparency?

For one, the customer (the scientist, the student) faces a sheer multitude of services and is unable to find the services that fit best for his/her special request. Even if he/she knows the addresses of some providers by chance, he/she will have no fast and objective criterion to assess and to compare their services.

Second, each information provider offers its own user interface. That means, for every contacted information provider, the customer has to learn how to deal with it. Different languages is only one problem. The customer has to be able to cope with differences in input forms and result fields in the provider's Web site as well as differences in navigating through a complex tree of Web pages while submitting a request. Likewise, differences occur in the result formats. Nor is there a simple learning process possible because in a typical scenario, the customer contacts several sources just to find documents of interest, and afterwards several sources to find where he/she may obtain these documents. In doing so the customer will expend time and money, both often to an unnecessary extent.

Of particular concern to us is the future of university libraries. Our aim is to make university libraries fit for the new world of the information marketplace, by suggesting innovative services so that they are able to compete with other libraries and information providers all over the world.

In this paper, we present a framework that helps providers, customers and libraries to overcome the problems arising from the new market situation so they can gain the whole benefit from the information era. In particular, this framework will give assistance to

- providers so that they have an easy way to take part of the market and to become known to the customers;
- customers so that they have one uniform and adaptable user interface for the combined access to those services that are appropriate for his/her request;
- libraries so that offer value-added services by integrating existing services and offering new information brokerage services.

Therefore, we will continue as follows: In the next section, we introduce the UniCats project and outline our basic solution. Section 3 and 4 present the technical aspects of the framework, with section 3 concentrating on the communication infrastructure and section 4 on the principle structure of our system components. In section 5, we introduce the basic components of our framework. Section 6 examines related projects. Section 7 concludes this paper.

2. The UniCats Project

Our work, the UniCats project[1] [2] is part of a nationwide German initiative in digital libraries. Its main idea is to contribute solutions to the aforementioned problems, not by adding yet another service but by integrating existing services under a common interface. UniCats is a joint project of the Institute for Program Structures and Data Organisation and the university library at the Universität Karlsruhe.

Assistance services will be provided by (at least) three different kinds of intermediaries:

- *wrappers* that establish the interface towards the different providers;
- *user agents* that establish the interface towards the customer;
- *traders* that bring together supply and demand.

---

[1] The UniCats project is funded by the German Research Foundation (DFG) as a part of the strategic research initiative "Distributed Processing and Exchange of Digital Documents (V^3D^2)".

In terms of the problem statement above, providers are given assistance by traders and wrappers, and customers by user agents. The new value-added services that let libraries compete in this new world come from providing the service platform for the university campus as well as supplying prototypical user agents, specialised traders and, in some cases, even wrappers.

We developed a suitable service infrastructure, the *UniCats environment*. It consists of a platform for independent and communicative software components, the *UniCats agents*, together with three different types of UniCats agents, wrappers, user agents and traders. We do not preclude other types of agents, though.

This infrastructure is supposed to support the idea of an open market: Participants should be free to enter and leave the market on their own decision. For the infrastructure, this means there must be no fixed bindings between agents. Each agent will be able to communicate with any agent in the framework, but must be able to cope if this agent gets lost. Another implication of the openness is that software components should be able to communicate with UniCats agents even if they are outside the environment. Hence, the communication technology and data exchange format should follow widely used standards.

3. Technical Infrastructure

In this section, we motivate the principal technical decisions of the UniCats environment.

3.1 COMMUNICATION TECHNOLOGY

Since we deal with a distributed and heterogeneous environment, the first impulse is to employ a middleware architecture. Most prominent among the architectures are CORBA [10] and DCOM [9]. Both support the distribution of objects among a heterogeneous computer network. Communication is done by remote method call. However, these middleware platforms presuppose the installation of special interface software on each participating computer or are not really system independent. The intention of such techniques is to distribute systems on an object level, and they offer quite efficient tools for this. Our aims are more modest, though: We exchange documents. So a market participant may be forced to purchase and install a software product which ties him/her to the platform but is unnecessary for many of his/her needs.

Together with the programming language Java comes a technique named RMI (Remote Method Invocation) [6]. This technique may be used for the access to Java objects that may be distributed in a computer network. But RMI has again the disadvantage of working on objects. Also, it is restricted to Java and has performance problems.

Consequently, we chose to base our communication framework on TCP/IP [16] directly. TCP/IP is widespread used (it is the Internet protocol), and it is freely available for practically every computer platform and programming language.

TCP/IP is restricted to the transmission of bit streams between two communication partners. But this is exactly the functionality we need to exchange documents. However, we need a common data exchange model to ensure that the semantics of the transmitted data are preserved.

3.2 DATA EXCHANGE MODEL

Data exchange concerns both queries and results, and also internal messages. The data exchange model defines the conceptual model to express the semantics of the data and the data exchange format. This model has to be very flexible, because the transmitted data are very heterogeneous and their structure cannot be fixed in advance (semi-structured data model). This model should allow that messages and transmitted documents can be understood everywhere, even by agents external to the UniCats environment. This prevents UniCats from being an isolated systems and opens the way to other platforms.

The data exchange model applied in the UniCats environment is XML (eXtensible Markup Language) [18]. XML is available free and is widely used. It permits a high level of independence from operating systems and programming languages. Communication inside the UniCats environment is performed by the exchange of XML documents exclusively.

The semantic of an XML document is contained in the DTD (Data Type Definition). The DTD used in the UniCats environment follows the Open Trading Protocol (OPT) [1] which is the most common protocol set for electronic commerce based on XML.

3.3   CONNECTION ARCHITECTURE

In an electronic commerce environment, fixed connections between the market participants are counter-productive. Instead we need a communication model that allows to open and close connection between two agents at will. The simplest solution would be a central communication server inside the environment which establishes the connections dynamically during a user session. The server would have to know the names and addresses of all participating agents, and each agent would have to be connected to the server. Messages would have to be sent to the server which routes them to the recipient.

This central solution, like all central solutions, is weak on system scalability and robustness. Since each delivered document and each message between two agents has to be sent via the server, the server will become the bottleneck in the system. If the server fails or is unreachable even for a short period of time, the complete system will become inoperable.

Consequently, we chose a fully decentralised architecture for the UniCats environment. There are no components other than the agents. They communicate in one of two ways:

- *Direct communication* between two agents;
- *Group communication* between agents joint in a *communication group*.

The second communication way is established by multicast. A message broadcast from any agent in the group will be delivered to all agents that are currently members of this group. Communication groups may be installed and dissolved at runtime with the exception of one distinguished group ('UniCats'). Every agent in the environment belongs to this group which is necessary when a new agent enters the environment. By sending a group message to this group, the agents may become known to the environment, usually by announcing name, type and address. Of course, an agent may prefer to stay hidden, just listening to the other agents.

4.   Architecture of a UniCats Agent

In this section, we take a closer look at the UniCats agents. We employ a layered architecture which follows the usual rules where each layer uses only the services of the layer immediately below and provides services only for the layer immediately above. Hence, a layer may be exchanged without affecting the higher layers. Figure 1 shows the different layers of an agent.

4.1   COMMUNICATION PLATFORM

The communication layer contains the functionality necessary to establish direct communication and group communication. It is directly based on TCP/IP.

Direct communication uses bi-directional connections between two agent. The connections are based on *exchanges* that determine which data will be exchanged and which protocol will be used for this. Exchanges represent the protocols an agent may use in the different communication situations it may be involved in. They may be added or removed at runtime.

For an exchange, an agent can act as client or as server. On the server side, each exchange has a distinct port. A client may open a connection to a server by sending a message, and addresses the exchange by giving the port number assigned to this exchange. If the agent acts as a server, it has to create a listener first. As shown in Figure 2, whenever the listener guarding a special port receives a request, it calls the server's connection manager. For each connection the agent is involved in at this time, the connection manager creates a connection object, which will execute the communication process with the client until the connection is closed. Each server can handle several connections at the same time, although a limit can be set according to capacity. The connection object creates a (server-side) exchange for this connection.

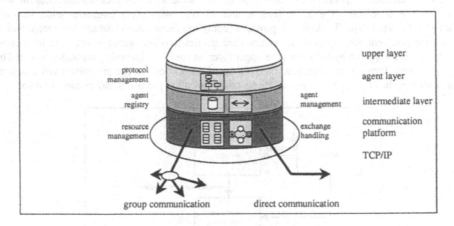

Figure 1. Structure of a UniCats agent

Exchanges are executed by *protocol engines*. For each state, a protocol engine may have one or more *exchange rules*. Any incoming message will be checked if it fits one of the exchange rules assigned to the current state of the protocol engine. Since the semantic of the exchange is expressed in a DTD, our communication platform requires that the message fits a DTD. Exchange rules also support synchronisation between different exchanges.

Group communication is used to broadcast messages to every agent or to a group of agents. Resource management filters the incoming messages and selects those messages that are relevant for the agent. To do this, it compares each incoming message with a list of templates generated by the agents. If the message matches one or more templates, the message will be given to the higher layers. Otherwise, it may be deleted or queued for a later check when the templates change.

4.2   INTERMEDIATE LAYER

The intermediate layer shields the higher agent layers - which may differ from one agent type to the other - from the technical details of the communication and operating system platform. It establishes a neutral level of agent communication functionality and thus can be seen as some sort of UniCats middleware. It starts exchanges, sends commands and receives status reports. Likewise, it sends and receives group messages and sets up the list of templates used in resource management.

These functions are encapsulated in two components. Agent management contains the basic interactions between agents. Among others, these are connection setup, address exchange, control requests, and receipts. In the agent repository, the agent holds the names, types and addresses of all agents known (at least those that the agent is interested in).

For the higher layers, the intermediate layer supports a set of methods that start or react to group messages and exchanges and set up the necessary DTDs. They establish a primitive kind of *transactional control*.

4.3   AGENT LAYER

The agent layer establishes a neutral functionality as well, this time on the level of standard behaviour of an agent. Agents of the same type act the same as far as their communication with other agents is concerned. The agent layer is able to cope with every communication situation declared for the agent type. To do this, it provides (complex) *transactions* that are interpreted within protocol management. Examples of transactions are queries to other agents or reactions to queries. Transactions are triggered by calls from the upper layer and react on incoming messages reported by the lower layers. Protocol management maps the agent transactions to the primitive transactions of the intermediate layer in order to start and direct communication protocols and to transmit data.

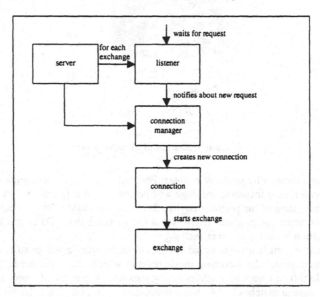

Figure 2. Server-side connection management

4.4   UPPER LAYER

The beauty of our layered architecture is that differences in agent type are confined to just one layer, the upper layer. This layer contains the algorithms that allow the agent to perform its task in an efficient way. It contains repositories for data that have to be stored as well as the user interface of the agent. The latter is of particular importance for an agent that has direct contact to human users other than administrators.

5.   Agent Types

As stated in section 2, we foresee at least three types of agents: wrappers, traders and user agents. In this section, we describe these agents. To motivate them, we first introduce a high-level architectural view of the UniCats systems as seen by users and providers.

5.1   ARCHITECTURE

Figure 3 shows the high-level architecture of the UniCats system. For each provider that takes part in the market, we install a wrapper that establishes the connection between the provider and the UniCats environment. In general, we expect that the provider furnishes the wrapper because it ought to represent the provider's interests. However, we allow others to place wrappers anywhere in the Internet. For example, it could be installed by a library or by a (possibly commercial) third party. An interesting consequence is that there may be more than one wrapper for a provider. Each wrapper should be registered to at least one trader.

The customer enters the market with the help of a user agent. We expect that libraries will provide, as a service, user agents to the campus users, but do not preclude that individuals install a user agent somewhere in the Internet. Given a customer's request, the user agent finds a set of relevant providers with the help of traders that are supposed to know the market and give recommendations. Then the user agent sends a query to the selected providers by using the wrappers and displays the results of these queries to the customer.

Of course, scenarios can be more complex, containing several successive queries to wrappers and traders, document delivery, billing, and payment.

The architecture must be able to reflect the dynamism of the market: old customers may go and new customer may come, old providers may leave and new providers may enter, but also old UniCats agents may vanish and new agents will be created.

5.2   WRAPPER

For a provider, it is possible to enter the market by implementing a UniCats agent. However, we think most providers will shy away from the efforts and costs. Also, it is not practicable to demand a direct access to the provider's database or the installation of a special interface. Moreover, to support an open market, adding a new source should be done fast and easy, so intending to change the provider's computer system is not a good idea.

The classical solution is to wrap the source. Since practically every information provider offers WWW access, we base our wrappers on a communication with the provider source via HTTP. This means, for a provider no additional efforts and costs will incur when it enters the market.

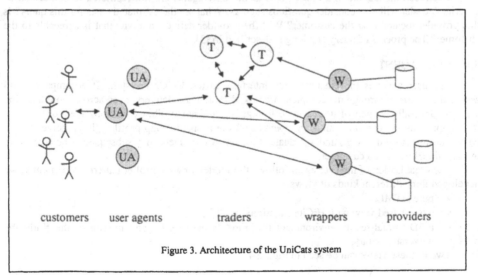

| customers | user agents | traders | wrappers | providers |

Figure 3. Architecture of the UniCats system

When a query is sent to the wrapper (typically by a user agent), the wrapper translates this query into a query plan that may involve several Web pages. The query plan simulates a user when he/she fills out the forms manually. However, since the wrapper knows the information source and its Web site, it can act more efficiently (and, of course, much faster). On return, the wrapper extracts the desired information from the result pages, translates the results into the data exchange format of the UniCats system, and sends them back to the user agents.

Wrappers can be extended beyond this basic functionality. For example, for commercial information sources, query translation and optimisation must consider the costs that will arise for each step of the query. To do this, the wrapper may include modules for cost pre-calculation and monitoring. [11] shows how a query will be performed.

Wrappers are always tailored to an information source. Consequently, they have to be adapted when the information source or its Web site undergoes changes. We built a wrapper generator [12] that provides an easy way to create a new wrapper and to modify an existing wrapper. With the help of this tool, wrapper generation is possible for people who are usually not trained to work with grammars and programming languages, e.g., librarians. In general, this will make it easier for a provider to enter the market.

5.3   TRADER

Traders are supposed to know the market and hold addresses and profiles of the providers that are currently available.

The main problem for the trader, then, is to gather the necessary information about a provider. Moreover, because the dynamism in the market the trader must detect each change in the market, such as new providers that have entered or changes in the pricing model or delivery conditions of an already connected provider. We foresee that the trader will get assistance from the wrappers registered with it, by supplying with current metadata about the providers. However, a trader should not entirely rely on the wrappers. Additionally, they may gain metadata by test queries and by the analysis of the feedback sent back from the user agents. This suggests that traders may themselves be specialised. Therefore, we also developed an approach of different traders working together in the form of co-operation or even federation.

The recommendations the trader gives to the user agents are not restricted to content-based criteria. A trader will also consider questions such as: What are the estimated costs for this query? Is this provider located near the customer? Will the provider deliver in a way that is agreeable to the customer? The process of query handling is described in [3].

5.4   USER AGENT

The user agent is the customer-side interface to the UniCats system. It accompanies and assists the customer through the complete process of search and delivery, even across more than one session. Generally, as part of its service offerings, the university library will provide a user with a stereotypical user agent. Such an agent operates on the basis of group profiles giving defaults for a typical customer groups, e.g., undergraduate students. A user agent may subsequently be adapted to the individual traits of a customer.

The organisation of the user agent follows the model-view-controller pattern. In particular, we developed three different kinds of views:
- pure HTML,
- a tree-based view with HiCite-functionality [17],
- a 3D virtual-reality environment that models the exterior and interior of the Karlsruhe university library.

Two of these views can be seen in Figure 4.

An important task of the user agent is the integration of the result sets received from different information sources into a single result set that is shown to the customer. During integration, operations such as duplicate detection and elimination, grouping and sorting are applied.

Integration is done incrementally: Results will be shown to the user as soon as they arrive. The customer has not to wait for the slowest provider but can work on the results immediately. Even if a provider is temporary offline or has left the market, the customer will get no greater problems and can work with the remaining results. Incremental result integration brings additional challenges to the integration algorithms. For instance, if a document has already been shown to the customer and the user agent receives new informations about it (e.g., an abstract), the user agent has to add this information in the displayed entry. Details of the integration process can be found in [14]

6. Related Work

Meta search engines offer a uniform interface for the access to catalogues. For example, the Karlsruher Virtueller Katalog [7] provides access to a great number of national and international catalogues. However, it provides neither post-processing operations such as duplicate elimination nor any support for commercial services or provider comparison. Result presentation is restricted to few bibliographic informations displayed on a HTML page. To get further information, the customer has to go to the provider's Web site.

In most cases, the integration of services in existing digital library systems is restricted to those provided by a single library. This library is supposed to reorganise its software installation and transfer its collections into the new digital library system. For example, IBM DB2 Digital Library [5] offers access to various collections of multimedia documents - texts, graphics, audio, and video - via the Internet. The central part of the system is the library server that holds catalogues of the entire collection and routes customers of this library to the requested document. DB2 Digital Library offers several tools for search and access, but also services like authentication, signatures and encryption. However, it provides no assistance for an open and dynamic market with many providers and heterogeneous data sources.

Current digital library projects usually do not assume a market situation. Instead their emphasis is on versatile access to a variety of underlying databases. In the Stanford Digital Library Project [15], for each collection a proxy has to be installed providing an interface for the internal protocol of the project. They offer a large toolkit of different utilities for document visualisation or

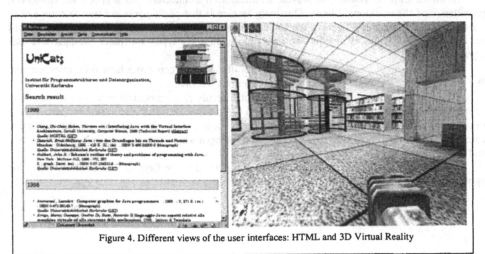

Figure 4. Different views of the user interfaces: HTML and 3D Virtual Reality

information retrieval, including a glossary service that can be used for service selection. Since they work on a more or less known set of providers, they have no use for a trader that compares services with different criteria.

Commercial services are considered in the MeDoc project [8], which is restricted to computer science literature. Similar to UniCats it is based on a three-tier architecture with user agents, provider agents and brokers. With the MeDoc computer science library, they have installed a new service providing full text documents of some computer science books. With the MeDoc brokers, a trading service is offered. However, MeDoc is not an open system so that wrapping has much less ambitious goals, and traders limit themselves to calculating costs.

In the field of electronic commerce platforms, commercial solutions are well established. To give an example, e-speak from Hewlett-Packard [4] is a platform that includes services like billing, security, and brokerage. Openness is limited, though, because both customers and providers are forced to install interfaces for the e-speak system and are rather tightly bound to the functionality of the e-speak system. Service specification must follow special rules.

GEM [13] is an electronic commerce platform containing a complex and distributed structure of trading facilities based on brokers and a central market server. GEM simulates a trading floor by bringing together requests and bids collected by the brokers. GEM also supports multiple markets but provides no solution for a market where the participants come and leave on their own will. Moreover, customers and providers either interact directly with the broker (so we have no common interface at all), or they have to implement a special interface component on their own computer system.

7. Conclusion and Future Work

The premise of this paper was the field of scientific literature supply has evolved into an information market. Any approach for the integration of services for search and delivery of scientific literature must consider this market situation. We claimed that no system architecture - platform and service components - exists as yet that supports a market that is open to new providers and transparent to users. We suggested that this situation offers dangers but also new opportunities to university libraries. The objective of this paper has been to find answers to these problems and to develop an architecture for the integration of information services in the field of scientific literature under the premise of an open, heterogeneous and dynamic market.

With the UniCats system, we provide an integration architecture that supports all, customers, providers, and the traditional library. One main feature is that participants are free to enter and to leave the market. Technical basis of the UniCats system is the UniCats environment, a framework for communicating UniCats agents. The most important agent types are trader, wrapper and user agent.

A first version of the platform and prototypes of the three agent types have been implemented. We plan to test the complete system in the daily campus practice.

The system needs extensions in two directions: secure data transmission and digital payment. We also plan studies regarding the legal situation (e.g., copyrights and intellectual property rights) in different countries, especially for cross-border transactions. In addition to the necessary extensions of the first three agent types, other types of agents are planned, e.g., certification centers and servers for digital payment.

We feel that although our studies have been restricted to the field of scientific literature, our approaches should give useful ideas to other kinds of markets.

References

1. Burdett, D. *Internet Open Trading Protocol Version 0.9.9*. The Open Trading Protocol Consortium, 1998.

2. Christoffel, M. Pulkowski, S., Schmitt, B., Lockemann, P. Electronic commerce: the roadmap for university libraries and their members to survive in the information jungle. *ACM Sigmod Record*, **27**(4), 1998, pp. 68-73.

3. Christoffel, M. A trader for services in a scientific literature market. In *Proceedings of the 2nd International Workshop on Engineering Federated Information Systems (EFIS'99)*, Kühlungsborn, 1999, pp. 123-130.

4. Hewlett Packard. *E-Speak - the platform for E-services*. http://www.e-speak.hp.com.

5. IBM. *DB2 Digital Library*. http://www-4.ibm.com/software/is/dig-lib/about.html.

6. JavaSoft. *Java Remote Method Invocation Specification*. Technical Report, Sun Microsystems, 1997. http://www.javasoft.com/products/jdk/1.1/docs/guide/rmi/.

7. *Karlsruher Virtueller Katalog*. http://www.ubka.uni-karlsruhe.de/kvk.html.

8. *MeDoc – The Online Computer Science Library*.
   http://medoc.informatik.tu-muenchen.de/english/medoc.html.

9. *Microsoft. DCOM Technical Overview*. Technical Report, Microsoft Corporation, Redmond, 1996.

10. Object Management Group. *CORBA 2.0/IIOP Specification*. Technical Report PTC/96-03-04, Framingham Corporate Center, Framingham (MA), USA, 1996.

11. Pulkowski, S. Making information sources available for a new market in an electronic commerce environment. In *Proceedings of the International Conference on Management of Information and Communication Technology (MICT'99)*, Copenhagen, 1999.

12. Pulkowski, S. Intelligent wrapping of information sources: getting ready for the electronic market. In *Proceedings of the 10th VALA Conference on Technologies for the Hybrid Library*, Melbourne, 2000.

13. Rachlevsky-Reich, B., Ben-Shaul, I. et. al. GEM: A Global Electronic Market System. In *Information Systems*, **24**(6), 1999, pp. 495-518.

14. Schmitt, B., Schmidt, A. METALICA: An Enhanced Meta Search Engine for Literature Catalogs. In *Proceedings of the 2nd Asian Digital Library Conference (ADL'99)*, Taipei, 1999.

15. *Stanford Digital Library Project*. http://www-diglib.stanford.edu/diglib/.

16. Stevens, W.R. *TCP/IP Illustrated, Volume 1, The Protocols*. Addison Wesley, Reading, 1995.

17. Wang Baldonado, W., Winogred, T. Hi-Cites: dynamically created citations with active highlighting. In *Proceedings of the International Conference on Human factors in computing systems (CHI '98)*, Los Angeles, 1998, pp. 408-415.

18. World Wide Web Consortium. *Extensible Markup Language Recommendation*. 1998.
    http://www.w3.org/TR/1998/REC-xml-19980210.

Heterogeneous Database Browsing in WWW Based on Meta Model of Data Sources

Guntis Arnicans, Girts Karnitis

University of Latvia
Faculty of Physics and Mathematics
Raina Blvd. 19, Riga LV-1586, Latvia
garnican@lanet.lv, girts@di.lv

Abstract

This paper describes a development principle and technique for a simple universal multiple database browser. The browser operates by getting information from metamodel of data sources and actual data from legacy data sources. Every element such as entity, field, and relation is mapped to some component of HTML page with appropriate structure and layout. Many templates of information layouts can be created allowing to dynamical changing of HTML page to acceptable user interface. The wrappers are used to provide browser with actual data and to act as mediators between data sources and browser. This approach allows to quickly describing new data sources, creating wrappers, making modifications later and managing data browsing in a simple unified style. The browser architecture is flexible enough to incorporate data sources with a variety of data models and query capabilities by various protocols. It is possible to select logically tied information from all available legacy data sources.

Keywords: Web-based information system, distributed information system, metamodels, database browsing.

1. Introduction

Organisations, both governmental and business, have to manage large amount of information stored in some form of databases or files. One of the main problems to deal with information managing is the weak interoperability between various databases and information systems. Especially this problem is serious when we want organise collaboration between the information systems of various organisations.

In nowadays a significant fraction of new information systems or services bases on the Web solutions. Usually developers use Web applications to organise communications between data source and data consumer (user) but data sources sometimes remain the old ones from the current or previous information systems. This leads to the operation with very heterogeneous data. To deal with problems the metadata of the data sources (data structure, content, attributes, etc.) are used to describe the heterogeneous information models. This approach supports the creating of very dynamical systems and it is easy to maintain system in the rapidly changing world.

In this paper we describe some results achieved during the development of two projects - the Integrated State Significance Information System (Megasystem) and the Baltic States Government Data Transmission Network (Network) [2, 5]. The goal of these projects is to provide fundamental improvements in the exchange of telecommunications and data among the administrative institutions of the Baltic States. The principles described in this paper were used to build up the first implementation of *Communication server*. A Communication server is a set of software and

J. Barzdins and A. Caplinskas (eds.), Databases and Information Systems, 167–178.

computer equipment that allows a wide range of users to receive information from variety of sources (governmental registers, databases, information systems) through a single contact point. Among the other significant functions the Communication server fulfils a requests that involves several information sources, merges together information, allows users to learn where information is stored and what kind of information it is, and to receive information from various registers without any need for in-depth knowledge about the technical aspects of its storage.

Data retrieval from different autonomous sources has become a hot topic during the last years in the other countries and large enterprises also. There are many different approaches to deal with this task. For instance, the systems described in [3, 4, 6, 7] allow data querying from different Data Sources (DS). All those systems are very complex, with their own query processor, but without universal user end. The development of these systems consumes many resources (time, money, people).

Our first aim was to make a simple Universal Browser (UB) that acts on model of data sources and is very useful in practice (relative to consumed development resources). Main ideas of the UB are described in [1], where the idea of database browsing based on the ER model is described. Our approach is a modified UB that can browse multiple DS, which can be made in different technologies and with limited access rights and possibilities. Access to the DS is made via wrappers. Information retrieval bases on logical data models, information between different data model are tied via special logical data entities. The simple means are offered to obtain information and display it on WWW page – the set of functions that allows to create executable formulas.

2. Repository of Conceptual Data Models of Data Sources

Repository is a database that contains information about data sources (DS) and the links between them – the specific ER model. Repository also contains a description of functions that can be executed by DS.

2.1 METAMODEL OF REPOSITORY

Figure 1 shows an ER model of Universal Browser's (UB) repository. There are different parts in this model that are used for different purposes:

- Entities *Data Source, Entity, Field, Relation, Relation Field* contain DS models and information about entities and relations.
- Entities *Function, Input, Input Function, Output, Output Function* contain information about functions that query information from DS and input and output fields of these functions.
- Entities *Representation* and *Field List* contain information about visual representations for each entity i.e. what fields in what order have to be shown. For instance, let us take the entity *Citizen* that contains information about a person. In *short* representation fields *PK, Name, Surname* are visible, but in *long* representation fields *PK, Name, Surname, Address* have to be shown.
- Entities *Frame Set, Frame* and *Content* contain information about visual representation.

2.2 CONCEPTUAL MODEL OF DATA SOURCE

DS is a real existing legacy data source that exposes its data to other systems. Any DS can be made with different technologies, and expose its data in different ways. Any DS has some functions that can be executed to get information from DS. It is not necessary for the user to know technical details of DS to get information from it. The user needs a simple and understandable logical information representation that is related to the objects from the real world.

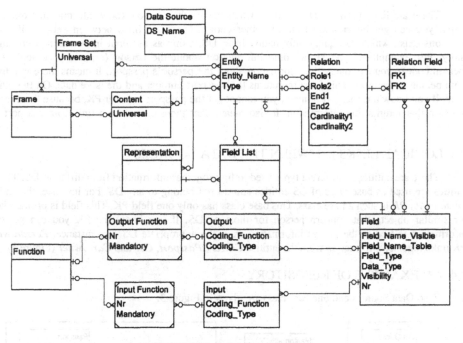

Figure 1. Metamodel of repository

For example, information about cars can be stored in many tables in the real system. We are interested in conceptual data model, without technical details. It means a car can be represented with one entity in the conceptual model.

There can be such technological fields in the real database, that are essential for the real system functioning, but they are not necessary for user and are not shown in the conceptual model.

There are two types of fields in the conceptual data model of DS:
- Fields that can be queried with some function,
- Fields from which we cannot query information. It means there are no functions where any of those fields are outputs. Usually these fields are not showed to the user, and they are used as input fields for some function. These fields are also used to link different entities.

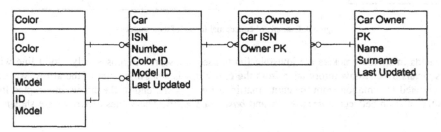

Figure 2. Example of physical data model

There are links between DS entities, which means that, if you know information from one entity, you can get information from the other entity. There are links between entities, if such functions exist, which can query information from DS, using as an input information from other entity. For example, if you know some information about the person (especially person's PK (person code)), you can query the information about the person's passport. It means there is a link from person to passport. This function returns the passport number and the issue date. On the other hand, if you know the passport number, you cannot get the passport's owner PK, because there is no function that returns this information. It also means that there cannot be a link from passport to citizen.

2.3 LOGICAL LINKS BETWEEN THE DATA SOURCES

There are entities of different types used to link together information from different DS. These entities are used as base class of DS entities and do not belong to any DS. For instance, the entity *Person with PK* is such a base class. This base class has only one field PK. This field is primary key for similar objects that concern person for most of DS. If you know the PK you can get the information related to the person information from the appropriate DS. For instance, *Person with PK* links together information from the entities *Citizen, Passport, Car* and *Car Owner* (Figure 3).

2.4 AN EXAMPLE OF REPOSITORY

Two Data Sources and one base class are given in Figure 3.

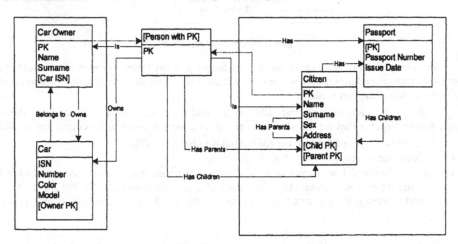

Figure 3. Example of conceptual model of data sources

Fields in square brackets are invisible fields used for search purposes only. Solid line with arrows means if you know information from the entity that is a starting point of the arrow, you can get the related information from the entity that is at the opposite end of the arrow. Interrupted line shows the relation between *normal entity* and *base class entity*. The values of arrows are shown in Table 1.

Table 1. Description of relations

End1	PK	End2	PK2	Relation name
	1			
Citizen	PK	Citizen	Child PK	Has Parents
Citizen	PK	Citizen	Parent PK	Has Children
Citizen	PK	Passport	PK	Has
Citizen	PK	Person With PK	PK	
Car Owner	PK	Car	Owner PK	Owns
Car Owner	PK	Person With PK	PK	
Car	IS	Car Owner	Car ISN	Belongs To
	N			
Person With PK	PK	Car Owner	PK	IS
Person With PK	PK	Car	PK	Owns
Person With PK	PK	Passport	PK	Has
Person With PK	PK	Citizen	PK	Is
Person With PK	PK	Citizen	Child PK	Has Parents
Person With PK	PK	Citizen	Parent PK	Has Children

3. Browsing Principles

General idea for dynamic browsing of various data sources is to generate Web pages with predefined information layout and functionality, get data from data sources and put them into page.

A Web page consists of a set of frames (Frame) – FrameSet. The FrameSet has a prefixed count of Frames, its layout and sizes. We can define as many as we need different FrameSets to organise and display information for the user. The FrameSet is a view to related data from one or many data sources. One of the Frames is the main Frame. The information in any other Frame is logically connected with data in the main Frame. The Frames can contain controls to manage the content in the other Frame.

The layout of the Frame is defined by rule, lets call it Content. Theoretically the Content is a formula or function: *Content(frameEntity, filterExpr)* where *frameEntity* is any entity from the metamodel of data sources and *filterExpr* is logical expression that filters data from appropriate data source. The Content defines:

1) what is the structure and principles of layout,
2) what data from metamodel and from actual legacy data sources are required to display information,
3) what actual instances of the defined entity are retrieved,
4) what controls are used to manage the content of the other Frame or to open the other FrameSet,
5) what related entities are involved from the same or any other data source. If we have various predefined Contents, then we can dynamically apply any Content to the Frame and get another data presentation for the same *frameEntity* and *filterExpr*.

4. Defining the Content of Frame

Let us assume that Content is the function *Content(frameEntity, filterExpr)*. Let us determine the means how we can define Content.

We introduce the following data types:
- **entity** - determines the entity from the metamodel,
- **field** - determines the field of the entity from the metamodel,

- **relation** - determines the relation for two entities from the metamodel,
- **record** - determines the actual data from the data source for one fixed instance of the entity,
- **value** - determines the actual data of the field for one fixed instance of the entity,
- **string** - determines the character string,
- **list** - determines the list of elements with any other allowed data type, we denote such types by the element type followed by postfix "List",
- **updateAction** - determines the action that updates Frame,
- **navigateAction** - determines the action that navigates browsing to another FrameSet,
- **sObject** - determines the HTML object that contains string to display,
- **aObject** - determines the HTML object with assigned some action to perform,
- **fObject** - determines the HTML object that is formatted for displaying,
- **frame** - determines the Frame,
- **frameSet** - determines the FrameSet,
- **view** - determines the list of fields that must be displayed.

Let us rewrite the Content as a function *Content(entity, expr(entity))*.

Let us introduce several additional functions to work with the metamodel and data sources, and to format HTML page.

- Functions to work with the metamodel:
  1. *SourceName(entity) →string* – returns the source name the entity belongs to.
  2. *EntityName(entity) →string* – returns the entity name.
  3. *RelationList(entity) →relationList* – returns all direct relations from the given entity to another entity (including itself) from the same data source.
  4. *MetaRelationList(entity) →relationList* – returns all indirect relations from the given entity to another entity from all available data sources.
  5. *FieldList(entity, view) →fieldList* – returns the list of all the fields of the entity.
  6. *RelationName(relation) →string* – returns the name (role) of the relation.
  7. *FieldName(field) →string* – returns the name of the field.
  8. *RelationEntity(relation)) →entity* – returns the entity at the opposite end of relation.

- Functions to work with data sources through wrappers:
  1. *RecordList(entity, expr(entity)) →recordList* – returns the list of instances (records) of the entity according to the given filtering expression.
  2. *ValueList(record, view) →valueList* – returns the list values of the given entity instance (record).
  3. *Value(value) →string* – returns the field value as character string.

- Functions to work with the list:
  1. *List(element_1, element_2, ..., element_i) →list_1* – returns the list of given elements and the list type *list_1* is appropriate to the element type.
  2. *IterateList(n%list_1, function(n%)) →list_2* – returns the list *list_2* that has as elements the results applying the given function. The function is executed with each parameter *n%* that is taken from the list *list_1* denoted by the identifier *n%* (n is any unique integer) and the list type *list_2* is appropriate to the function return type.
  3. *Concatenate(list_1, list_2) →list_3* – returns the concatenation of two lists with the same element type.

- Functions to format HTML page:
  1. *SO(string) →sObject* – creates sObject from the character string.
  2. *StringListObject(stringList, separatorString) →sObject* – creates sObject from the list of character strings separated by *separatorString*.
  3. *Update(frame, entity, expr(entity), content) →updateAction* – activates information update into the frame with the given entity, filter expression and layout.
  4. *Clear(frame) →updateAction* – clears the given frame .
  5. *Navigate(frameSet , entity, expr(entity), content) →navigateAction* – navigates to another FrameSet and update main Frame with the given entity, filter expression and layout.
  6. *Link(sObject, navigateAction, updateActionList) →aObject* – converts sObject into aObject and assign the navigation action and set of update actions to it. Any of action parameters may be empty.
  7. *AO(sObject) →aObject* – converts sObject into aObject with empty action.
  8. *FO(aObject) →fObject* – converts aObject into fObject without any special formatting.
  9. *HorizontalTable(aObjectListList) → fObject* – creates fObject from the list of lists, this frame object is displayed as table, and internal lists are placed in rows.
  10. *VerticalTable(aObjectListList) → fObject* – creates fObject from the list of lists, this frame object is displayed as table, and internal lists are placed in columns.
  11. *ListBox(aObjectList) → fObject* – creates fObject from the list, this frame object is displayed as listbox.
  12. *Horizontal(fObjectList) → fObject* – creates new fObject by arranging the given list horizontally.
  13. *Vertical(fObjectList) → fObject* – creates new fObject by arranging the given list vertically. Only frame objects with the type fObject may be displayed in the Web page.

5. Data Wrappers

Function ***RecordList*** must be implemented to get information from DS. The technology we use is simple, but effective. UB gets information from DS via Wrappers. This approach has the following advantages:
- It allows accessing DS via different protocols and methods – ODBC™, OLE DB™, SQL*Net™, DCOM™, COM+™, XML, HTTP.
- DS usually are made well suited for specific business tasks. DS are not primary made for data access from UB. The access to DS data usually is limited, it is allowed to execute some stored procedures to query data. Wrapper allows us to execute only authorised functions.
- Querying DS via functions allows us to have easy transfer real data from DS physical data model to logical data model that is more understandable for the user.

Information about functions is stored in the UB meta database: defined input and output fields for each function. Each input field may be mandatory or optional.

During development of the prototype, we discovered some rules for function implementation and developing conceptual model of DS.
- First rule - it is desirable to have input and output fields from one entity. It simplifies development of DS model and wrappers.
- Second rule - two approaches possible for making DS model and functions. One approach is that we already have functions, and we make conceptual data model of DS using the first rule. In case DS is a system we maintain and own, it is often possible to make functions according to conceptual data model of DS. In such a case we make conceptual data model of DS at first and

then we make data access functions according to conceptual data model and the first rule. It is helpful to make two types of functions:

1. The function gets information identifying the object from DS by some search criteria. For example, get person's PK by its name and surname (might be partial). The answer usually is a list of person's identifying information according to search criteria.
2. The function gets information about one object from one entity by its identifier. An example - get all information about the citizen by its PK.

For instance, we have two functions for the entity Citizen:

- Input data – Name, Surname (might be partial). Output data – PK, Name, Surname (full).
- Input data – PK. Output data – PK, Name, Surname, Address.

There are also 2 functions to get information about the citizen's parents and children:

- Input data – Parent PK. Output data – Children PK, Name, Surname.
- Input data – Child PK. Output data – Parents PK, Name, Surname.

There is a procedure that implements the function **RecordList**. This procedure gets the entity and filter expression as input and returns data from DS as output. In our implementation this procedure gets information from the meta database about functions that can be executed over entity from which we need information. In our implementation the filter expression is fields and corresponding values for these fields, e.g. PK="123456-111111". There is "brute force" algorithm that finds functions we can execute e.g. those are functions that have enough input data from the filter expression to be executed, executes these functions and returns result. There can be, of course, other implementations.

DS data access via wrappers allows connecting new DS to our system easily and quickly. We have to write a new wrapper and add information about new DS to the meta database. With some experience the writing of wrappers is easy and fast process, and there is no need to make any modification in DS.

6. Templates for Web Page Structure and Functionality

The design of FrameSet and Frames is based on template principle. With some experience the new FrameSets and Frames can be developed quickly. The design has two main steps – FrameSet structure planning and creating formulas for Frame Contents. We give some templates and ideas how the Web pages can be designed. The above given functions are used. Formulas are logically divided into several subparts only for easier understanding. Some formulas use subparts of other previously defined formulas. The example of visual presentation for each formula is given.

6.1 SIMPLE ENTITY INSTANCE PRESENTATION IN TABLE

The first column contains field names and the second – field values. The field values are retrieved according to the selected *view*.

```
A(entity, record) = VerticalTable(List(A1, A2))
A1 = IterateList(1%FieldList(entity, view), AO(SO(FieldName(1%))))
A2 = IterateList(2%ValueList(record, view), AO(SO(Value(2%))))
```

PK	12121211111
Name	Andris
Surname	Kalns
Sex	M
Address	Riga, Liepu 1-12, LV-1000

Figure 4. Example of entity instance presentation

6.2 ENTITY INSTANCE PRESENTATION AS TEXT

Instance field values are concatenated according to the order of the selected *view*.

B(record) = FO(AO(SO(StringListObject(B1, " "))))
B1 = IterateList(3%ValueList(record, view), Value(3%))

12121211111 Andris Kalns M Riga, Liepu 1-12, LV-1000

Figure 5. Example of entity instance presentation as text

6.3 ENTITY RELATIONS PRESENTATION IN VERTICAL LIST

Each relation is represented as relation name concatenated with entity name at the opposite relation end.

C(entity) = Vertical(IterateList(4%RelationList(entity), C1))
C1 = Horizontal(List(C2, FO(AO(SO(" "))), C3))
C2 = FO(AO(SO(RelationName(4%))))
C3 = FO(AO(SO(EntityName(RelationEntity(4%)))))

| Has Passport |
| Has Parents Citizen |
| Has Children Citizen |

Figure 6. Example of relations presentation

6.4 ALL RELATION PRESENTATION IN TABLE

The data about all relations (relation name, entity name and data source) are placed in table with headings.

D(entity, expr(entity))=HorizontalTable(Concatenate(D1,D2))
D1 = AO(StringListObject("Relation", "Entity name", "Data source"))
D2 = IterateList(5%MetaRelationList(entity),List(D3, D4, D5))
D3 = AO(SO(RelationName(5%)))
D4 = AO(SO(EntityName(RelationEntity(5%))))
D5 = AO(SO(SourceName(RelationEntity(5%))))

Relation	Entity name	Data source
Is	Citizen	Register of Residents
Has	Passport	Register of Residents
Has Parents	Citizen	Register of Residents
Has Children	Citizen	Register of Residents
Is	Car Owner	Register of Motor vehicles
Owns	Car	Register of Motor vehicles

Figure 7. Example of relation presentation

6.5 AN EXAMPLE OF FRAMESET

Let us look how a FrameSet can be built. Let us assume FrameSet *FRS_1* with four Frames – *FR_1, FR_2, FR_3, FR_4*. See Figure 8.

FR_1 (upper left) – to list instances of entity,
FR_2 (upper right) – to show details of fixed instance in FR_1,
FR_3 (lower left) – to list all relations to other entities in all data sources,
FR_4 (lower right) – to show details of another related entity instances of FR_2.

At first let us create three presentations or Contents (E, F, G) for viewing entities. We use formulas created before in this paper.

- Content formula E() for Frame FR_4 (from FR_4 we can update all Frames in FRS_1)

```
E(entity, expr(entity)) = Vertical(E1, E5)
E1 = Horizontal(List(FO(E2), FO(AO(SO(" "))), FO(AO(SO(SourceName(entity))))))
E2 = Link(SO(EntityName(entity)), E3, E4)
E3 = Navigate("FRS_1", entity, expr(entity), "" )
E4 = List(Clear("FR_2"), Update("FR_3", entity, expr(entity), """"), Clear(FR_4))
E5 = Vertical(IteateList(6%RecordList(entity, expr(entity)), A(entity, 6%)))
```

- Content formula F() and G() for Frame FR_2 (from FR_2 we can update this frame or update FR_4)

```
F(entity, expr(entity)) = Vertical(H, FO(AO(SO(" "))), E5)
G(entity, expr(entity)) = Vertical(H, FO(AO(SO(" "))), Vertical(E5, G1))
G1 = C(entity), where C3 is substitute with G2 in all places (we have added the action)
G2 = FO(Link(SO(EntityName(RelationEntity(4%))), NULL, G3))
G3 = List(Update("FR_4", RelationEntity(4%), expr(RelationEntity(4%)), "E"))
H = ListBox(List(Link("Presentation F", NULL, H1), Link("Presentation G", NULL, H2)))
H1 = Update("FR_2", entity, expr(entity), "F")
H2 = Update("FR_2", entity, expr(entity), "G")
```

- Content formula I() for Frame FR_1 (from FR_1 we can update FR_2, FR3, FR_4)

```
I(entity, expr(entity))  = Vertical(I1, I2)
I1 = Horizontal(List(FO(EntityName(entity)), FO(AO(SO(" "))), FO(AO(SO(SourceName(entity))))))
I2 = HorizontalTable(IterateList(7%RecordList,Link(B(7%), NULL, I3))
I3 = List(Update("FR_2", entity, expr(entity) and expr(7%), "F"),
Update("FR_3", entity, expr(entity) and expr(7%), ""), Clear("FR_4"))
```

- Content formula J() for Frame FR_3 (from FR_3 we can update FR_4)

J(entity, expr(entity)) = D(entity, expr(entity)), *where D4 is substitute with J1 in all places (we have add the action)*

J1 = Link(SO(EntityName(RelationEntity(5%))), NULL, J2)

J2 = List(Update("FR_4", RelationEntity(5%), expr(RelationEntity(5%)), "E"))

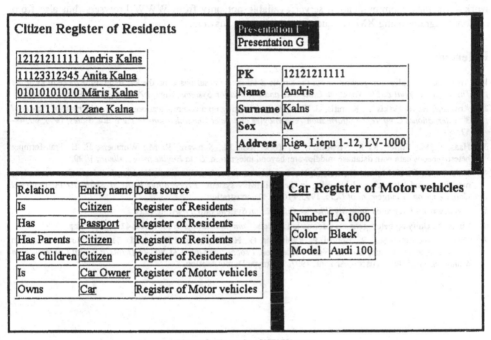

Figure 8. Example of WWW page

7. Conclusions and Future Directions

The prototype of the UB is made during developing Megasystem and Communication Server. Four state significance registers test databases are connected to the UB for testing purposes. Two of them use Oracle™ as DBMS, other two use Microsoft SQL Server™.

The UB prototype shows the effectiveness of our approach and is being initiated as first version of the real system at present time.

Our approach differs from other systems by several aspects:

- We have developed simple universal user-end that still allows us to show to users information in many different ways. We achieved this goal by implementing user-end using formal formulas.
- UB operates using logical models of DS. Related objects from these models are bound together with base classes that do not belong to any particular DS.
- We transfer physical model of DS to our internal logical representation which is much more comfortable for end-user. We do it by using of data wrappers.
- Our approach allows us to maintenance system and to connect new DS or modify existing one without interrupting operation of Communication server.

There are many aspects that are very important in real life application, but not covered in this article – security, user authorisation, logging, query cost calculation. All these features also are incorporated in the UB. The UB is useful in many large enterprises having many autonomous data sources as a browser for these systems with integrated view.

Future direction of our work is to develop a query processor that can take as input SQL-like query and return as output the result queried from multiple data sources. Other directions of future work – to make Communication server available not only from WWW browsers, but also from custom programs using XML to query data and return answers.

References

1. Arnicans, G. Application generation for the simple database browser based on the ER diagram. *Proceedings of the Third International Baltic Workshop Databases and Information Systems*, Riga, 1998, pp. 198-209.

2. Arnicans, G., Bicevskis, J., Karnitis, G. The concept of setting up a communications server. *Abstracts of Papers of 3rd International Conference Information Technologies and Telecommunications in the Baltic States*, 1999, pp. 48-57.

3. Haas, L. M., Miller, R. J., Niswonger, B., Tork Roth, M., Schwarz, P. M., Wimmers, E. L. Transforming heterogeneous data with database middleware: beyond integration. *Data Engineering Bulletin*, 1999.

4. Hammer, J., Garcia-Molina, H., Ireland, K., Papakonstantinou, Y., Ullman, J., Widom, J. Information translation, mediation, and Mosaic-based browsing in the TSIMMIS system. *Proceedings of ACM SIGMOD International Conference on Management of Data*, 1995, Project Demonstration.

5. *Megasystem - Integrated State Significance Information System.* http://www.mega.lv.

6. Singh, N. Unifying heterogeneous information models. *Communications of the ACM*, 41(5), 1998, pp. 37-44.

7. Tomasic, A., Amouroux, R., Bonnet, P., Kapitskaia, O., Naacke, H., and Raschid, L. The distributed information search component (disco) and the World Wide Web. *Proceedings of ACM SIGMOD International Conference on Management of Data*, Tuscon, Arizona, 1997, Prototype Demonstration.

Building Digital Video Editing System Based on Dynamic Synchronous Transfer Mode Network

Algirdas Pakstas

University of Sunderland, School of Computing, Engineering and Technology
Sunderland SR1 3SD, England
Institute of Mathematics and Informatics
Akademijos 4, LT-2600 Vilnius, Lithuania
E-mail: a.pakstas@ieee.org

Abstract

For the compilation of the edited video stream, normally at least two others are manipulated (A/B roll). With conventional "linear editing", video/audio sequences are stored on the magnetic media with compilation via replication in real time. This causes some limitations in flexibility, since final compilation must be in the correct chronological sequence and is constrained by the serial linear tape access time. "Non-linear editing" systems require all clip/sequence data to be stored on the random access medium, which affords play-out and manipulation/compilation abilities. Digital formats afford the opportunity for non-linear editing but certain constraints must be considered. Volume of data associated with audio and video streams is very large and requires high capacity storage. While adequate storage is often available, the communications between the workstations and access to the storage becomes a bottleneck. Paper is devoted to investigation of the existing experience of building Distributed Digital Video Editing Systems and use in them widely available computing platforms such as PCs in order to apply this for the project DIVIDEND (DIgital VIDeo Editing based on the Network testbeD). Project DIVIDEND addresses the demand of the media industry and video producers in particular, for non-linear editing facilities which are currently unavailable. It intends to build an experimental testbed based on high speed network technology called Dynamic synchronous Transfer Mode (DTM). System architecture and specifications characteristics are described.

Keywords: digital video editing, distributed systems, Dynamic synchronous Transfer Mode (DTM) network.

1. Introduction: From Linear to Non-Linear Digital Video Editing

For the compilation of the edited video stream, normally at least two others are manipulated (so called *A/B roll*) [13]. With conventional "linear editing", video/audio sequences are stored on the magnetic media. Access to the video/audio sequences (clips) involves physically moving of the media across the magnetic head for reading/writing. Thus, compilation of the edited video stream is achieved via replication from the sources in real time.

The University of Sunderland currently uses two linear editing systems, namely "Video-Machine" of FAST Multimedia AG, Germany [33], configured as A/B roll "hybrid" systems. This causes some limitations in flexibility, since final compilation must be done in the correct chronological sequence and is constrained by the serial linear tape access time.

The other approach is called "non-linear" editing. The University of Sunderland currently uses two non-linear editing systems ES-7 of SONY [32]. This technology requires all clip/sequence data to be stored on some medium which allows random access, preferably in real-time, play-out ability,

179

as well as manipulation and compilation the programme sequences from the stored clips according to the editor's needs [25]. The arrival of digital video equipment in the broadcast industry brought high expectations of increased efficiency and convenience in addition to improved picture quality [31]. Many believed that video and audio material would be treated similarly to computer files for managing, processing, and transferring via computer networks and servers.

Recent moves towards digitising of the video production as well as start of the digital TV broadcasting (in UK since 1999) shows that the future is going to be digital. However, while digital formats afford the opportunity for non-linear editing, certain constraints must be considered.

This paper aims to investigate existing experience of building Distributed Digital Video Editing Systems and use in them widely available computing platforms such as PCs. The rest of the paper is organised as following. Section 2 is discussing typical features of the video stream and related problems of its storing and retrieving in digital format. Review of the related works aiming use of the inexpensive PC platforms as an editing stations or storages as well as approaches to build video distribution architectures and video delivery protocols are presented in the Section 3. Section 4 introduces DTM (Dynamic synchronous Transfer Mode) network technology and benefits of its use for carrying video traffic. Project DIVIDEND and more details about DTM network technology are presented in Section 5. Section 6 presents conclusions.

2. Video Stream and Problems Related to Digital Video Editing

The analogy to computer data systems, as used for example in office automation, is too simplistic and cannot be applied directly to the demanding video and audio system architecture of a broadcast facility. Stringent requirements must be placed on broadcast A/V systems to deliver high volumes of data, in continuous streams, to a multitude of users. Real-time throughput and predictable delays are all essential for editing and on-air applications [31].

Television program compilation, storage and transmission in the digital domain demands high speed data handling. One of the factors that makes implementation of such facilities especially difficult is the volume of data associated with audio and video streams. For example, the data rate required for 16-bit colour video with 720x570 resolution at 25 frames per second is 27 MBytes per second (as in CCIR601 4:2:2 standard - now ITU-R601 [4]) per stream.

Further, with the volume of data comes the need of high capacity storage [34]. For example, storing of 5 seconds (i.e. size of the typical video clip) of the above mentioned video stream will need 131.8 MB and storing of 5 minutes (= 300 seconds) will need approximately 6GB of memory. For uncompressed studio quality video or High Definition TV (HDTV) this would require correspondingly even greater storage.

For editing workstations where audio/video streams are compiled, access and rendering time is often crucial in real-time operations (such as re-play of situations during the broadcasting of live sports). Both real-time and post-production (non-real-time) environments may have additional need for shared used of materials. Demands for video storage can include re-usable components such as production house logos, credits and graphics. It is beneficial to store these on the shared access storage rather than retain many copies directly on the workstations.

3. Related Works

3.1 USE OF THE PC PLATFORMS FOR DIGITAL VIDEO EDITING

Interest to the development of the digital video editing system using relatively powerful and inexpensive hardware and software available on personal computers and workstations was expressed relatively early [22]. At that time the video editing application category has been dominated by visual, easy-to-use, direct manipulation interfaces. These systems were able to bring high-bandwidth human-computer interaction to a task formerly characterised by slow, inflexible, indirectly-operated machines. However, the direct manipulation computer interfaces are limited by their manual nature, and cannot easily accommodate algorithmically-defined operations. The paper proposed a melding of the common direct manipulation interfaces with a **programming language** enhanced to manipulate digital audio and video. The result was a system which can automate routine tasks as well as perform tasks based on sophisticated media recognition algorithms.

Video server system for **continuous media (CM)** data is described in [24]. Server consists of a low-priced personal computer (PC) and a **disk array**. The bit rate of the data stream varies depending on which applications are being used, which include video on demand (VOD) and digital video editing systems. Moreover, due to large data volumes, arranging and controlling data with different bit rates on the disk array presents a number of problems. A new file system which utilises two-layer hierarchical media management rate has been proposed. It is using the concept of packages based on the management of contents and disk space, and CM-records based on the management of bit-rate and disk access. The size of the packages and the sizes of CM-records are flexible so that a range of bit-rate streams are supported. The site of disk access is decided by taking into account access efficiency, which in turn depends on the continuous media data bit rate. Using these methods it is possible to reduce dramatically the memory space for administration, even for large volumes of data. The file system and the experimental video server have been implemented on a standard PC platform. This prototype system achieved 230.8 Mbps of I/O capability for continuous media.

The necessary high-speed transfer rates and fast access dictates the use of **storage devices** controlled by the SCSI or even faster interface. **Fibre Channel (FC)** is usually thought of as a system-to-system or system-to-subsystem interconnection standard. FC uses optical cable in a point-to-point or switch configuration [1, 6, 29]. One of the goals in the development of the FC interface was to improve or eliminate SCSI shortcomings, particularly in the areas of connectivity, performance, and physical robustness. FC is a standard which is especially actively promoted for video storage applications. In theory, FC operates at up to 2 Gbps, however, most installations don't actually achieve this speed [19].

Thus, adequate storage is often available but communications between the different types of the workstations and access time becomes a bottleneck [16, 26, 27]. Specialised RAID systems [11] such as EIDE-based high-speed, low-cost disk arrays VideoRaid pci of Medea Corporation [23] are capable of sustainable 27-40MB/sec datarates.

One of the approaches to speed-up communications with the storage is to design the parallel video server architecture [18]. In order to do so three central architectural issues should be addressed: server striping policies, video distribution architectures, and video delivery protocols.

3.2 VIDEO DISTRIBUTION ARCHITECTURES AND VIDEO DELIVERY PROTOCOLS

Video distribution in a local area network (LAN) can impede or even paralyse normal data transmission activities. The problem can be solved, at least for a while, by compression and by increasing the bandwidth, but that solution can become excessively costly or otherwise impractical. Moreover, experience indicates that usage quickly expands to test the limits of bandwidth.

It is a current practice to view **Asynchronous Transfer Mode (ATM)** networks as the only choice for high-speed networking [28, 16]. ATM is a link layer protocol which is related to ISDN and broadband ISDN. ATM uses T1 services or SDH/SONET as a physical layer. SDH/SONET, however, lacks switching commands and a signalling protocol. ATM is connection-oriented packet switching technology.

Project [17] is an example of the approach of using **ATM broadband networks** (LAN and WAN) in building DDVES. This project was a part of the European ACTS project and aimed to build a central to the distributed video production. Various distributed pilot applications for professional digital video production has been developed and described in the paper.

Article [10] reports about experiments on defining **relationship between MPEG video quality and ATM network performance**. Recommendations are made on acceptable ranges for cell errors, cell loss, and cell delay variation parameters. Advanced MPEG techniques such as scalability and error concealment are discussed, including their application on ATM networks.

Thus, here has been demonstrated that even with the use of the broadband ATM there is no any talk about **loss-less error-free transmission** or **100% Quality of Service**. Even fast ATM network is not enough for achieving of acceptable quality and some additional efforts are required anyway. Some other approaches are focusing on the alternative solutions rather than simply applying of the broadband networks.

A telecommunication system for the transmission of video and audio signals over optical fibre is investigated in [30]. A new multiplexing scheme for **digitised uncompressed video and audio signals** is proposed and is analysed at system level. The special frame developed to support the system allows expandability for the multichannel transmission of audio-video signals multiplexed with other types of data.

In the paper [9] is introduced and analysed the architecture of a **hybrid analog/digital video network (ADViNet)** which separates video distribution from standard data-handling functions. The network preserves the features of a standard digital network and, in addition, provides efficient real-time full-screen video transmission through a separate analog communication medium. System employs a specially developed control and management protocol. For all practical purposes, ADViNet may be used when graphical images have to be distributed among many nodes of a LAN. It relieves the burden of video distribution and allows users to combine efficient video data transmission with normal, regular network activities.

While many approaches for implementing of the digital broadcast environments are available, the paper [31] discusses the concept and implementation of a novel **peer-to-peer networking system** that addresses the specific requirements of the news broadcast environment. The paper emphasises the merit of a simple solution to manage A/V material between MPEG-2 4:2:2 MP@ML Betacam SX workstations.

Thus, we may conclude that for the **isochronous nature of the video stream**, some kind of circuit switching rather than connected-oriented packet switching of ATM would be preferred for video transfer across a distributed system.

4. DTM: Alternative Technology for the DDVES Network Backbone

DTM (Dynamic synchronous Transfer Mode) network technology is based on the use of fiber optics [2, 3, 7, 8, 12, 14, 15, 21, 20]. DTM can achieve datarates of 100 Gbits/sec but this is not the most important its feature for DDVES.

4.1 WHY DTM IS GOOD FOR DDVES

The DTM network architecture is based on circuit switching augmented with dynamic and priority reallocation of available bandwidth. The protocol is designed to be used in integrated services networks and has support for point-to-point, multicast and broadcast communication. A DTM network could be used for both distribution and unicast communication. Non-the-less, DTM maintains many of the advantages of circuit-switched networks, namely guaranteed capacity, flow isolation and simple and deterministic Quality of Service (QoS) differentiation.

The **isochronous service** provided by DTM also ensures a good support of both existing PDH/SDH structures as well as increasing data traffic. Benefits from using a DTM backbone as a DDVES network backbone are:

- DTM enables 270 Mbps ITU-R 601 channels to be switched on demand.
- A high capacity DTM network enables to edit/create films remotely and hence reduce production costs.

Thus, a DTM network also gives a new perspective on feature film production, leading to new services and markets.

4.2 DTM APPLICATIONS AND IP-OVER-DTM

A DTM network can be used directly for real-time application-to-application communication or can be used as a carrier network for higher layer protocols, such as ATM or IP. The IP switch using DTM's switching capabilities handles data, voice and video smoothly and solves many of the problems associated with IP traffic in today's networks, e.g., provides bandwidth on demand, allows for preferential resource reservation, and supports multicasting.

4.3 DTM VS. SDH/SONET: SIMILARITY AND INTEROPERABILITY

DTM has the same type of framing structure as existing transport networks, i.e. SDH/SONET, using 125 µs frames that are divided into time slots. Due to the similarity to SDH/SONET data frames, it can interoperate with existing SDH/SONET infrastructures, conversely DTM networks can carry SDH/SONET streams. It belongs to the same class of **circuit switching technologies** as SDH/SONET but is dynamic not static. DTM, however, operates at OSI layers one to three and thus, in contrast to i.e. SDH/SONET, includes switching commands and a **signalling protocol**.

5. DIVIDEND: Digital VIDeo Editing over Network testbeD

From the above it could be concluded that currently there are no satisfactory (or for many organisations affordable) solutions for non-linear editing based on the existing distributed networking technologies. There however could be formulated certain principles for building system architecture with defined real-time operating parameters. Project DIVIDEND (Digital VIDeo Editing over Network testbeD) is intended to address some problems of non-linear editing by building an experimental testbed based on the DTM network technology.

It is assumed that the compilation of the video data stream is done on non-linear editing **workstations** with access to the **Video Storage** via the **Network Backbone**. System Architecture is shown in Fig.1. Compilation of the video data stream is done at the **workstations** (WS1,... WSn) comprising the non-linear editing facilities with shared access to the **Video Storage** via **Network Backbone**.

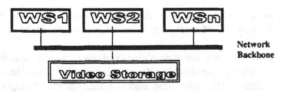

Figure 1. DIVIDEND System Architecture

Workstation specifications include:

- Limited local disk storage (sufficient for at least 5 minutes of video stream) with high-speed transfer/access rates.

- Local operating memory (to allow manipulation of data equal to at least 5 seconds of the video stream).
- High speed CPU.
- The video editing software package.

From this specification and data rate for CCIR601 4:2:2 video stream [4], it seems reasonable that currently available PCs with 256 MB RAM and 20 GB of hard disk storage would be sufficient for manipulating and editing (including manipulating in RAM and storing on the disk) the video data required. However, even some "normal" EIDE disk servers with 9.5msec access time and 10GB capacity could be acceptable in low-end configurations, where real-time access is not critical, as a building component for larger storage.

Typical distributed video editing activity is shown in Fig.2 with Editing Unit, Film Bank and Recording Studio being connected to the switches of the DTM network. This configuration uses the 270 Mbps Video Module (referred as 601) which is an Interface Card for the DTM-switch the Nimbra One. Based on the BT.601 video standard (derivative of CCIR601), the 270 Mbps Video Module is targeted at the video/TV production and distribution market. A configuration consisting of the Nimbra One and the Video Module supports full **uncompressed streaming of studio quality video**. Due to its modularity, the switch can be set to function as a pure video switch or as an integrated switch for video, voice, and data. It is capable of switching and transporting multiple streams of video (BT.601/(656), 270 Mbps), data (Ethernet 10/100 Mbps) and voice (E1/T1) simultaneously on the same physical fibre and with **100% guaranteed Quality-of-Service** (QoS).

The modules have two Serial Digital Interfaces for incoming traffic, and two for outgoing traffic. Fully configured for video, the Nimbra One switch supports 12 interfaces for incoming video, and 12 for outgoing video.

As a true multi-service platform, the Nimbra One DTM Switch transports IP traffic for purposes such as controlling video equipment, carrying MPEG streams for compressed video, and telephony traffic for inter PBX communication with guaranteed QoS alongside the 270 Mbps video streams.

The minimum channel size is 512 Kbps, which can be scaled in increments of 512 Kbps up to the total capacity of the fibre cable. The channel can be connected between one sender and one receiver, or between one sender and many receivers.

To set up a channel with a certain capacity, DTM allocates the required number of time slots to the channel. For example:

- 4 time slots are necessary to set up a 1,5-Mbps channel for a PSTN switch or other leased line.
- 6 time slots is enough to send 3-Mbps MPEG video with guaranteed service quality.
- 530 time slots are required for transferring studio-quality video at 270 Mbps.
- 1900 time slots are needed to set up a channel for the capacity of the Gigabit Ethernet traffic.

Different traffic types run simultaneously in the network, each in its own channel and at the desired bandwidth. In this way, DTM complies with all the demands of a well functioning multiservice network.

Since the Nimbra One switches are cascadable and switching is distributed, co-located switches can increase the number of possible interfaces significantly. This allows to have several possible video units connected at the same time and choose, via the management system, the interfaces to which the streams should be directed, either locally or remotely.

Using the Nimbra One and its modules in a WAN or MAN environment (see example in Figure 3) allows save money, thanks to centralisation and more cost-effective use of expensive editing and storage equipment.

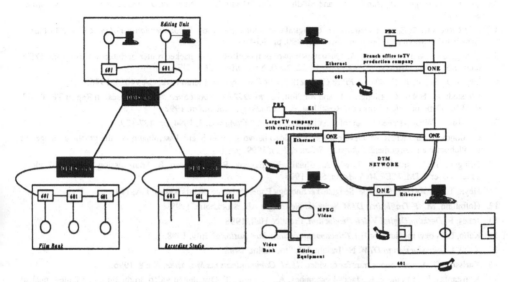

Figure 2. Typical video editing system using DTM.
(This picture is a courtesy of NetInsight)

Figure 3. Distributed video production in MAN
environment. Here ONE is DTM switch Nimbra One.
(This picture is a courtesy of NetInsight)

6. Conclusions

The high speed communications capability of the DTM system, makes the concept of high resolution multi-channel uncompressed video transfer between nodes in real-time not only possible, but feasible. Non-linear editing and graphics for instance would be afforded a much greater degree of flexibility when data is stored and manipulated between available server capacity anywhere on a network in real-time.

Project DIVIDEND addresses the demand of the media industry and video producers in particular, for non-linear editing facilities which are currently unavailable. Additionally, the School of Computing, Engineering and Technology at the University of Sunderland plans to use this testbed for the following goals:

- As an educational facility;
- For production of the educational video projects.

Future research activity presumes research of the video traffic behaviour under various circumstances. In particular, study [5] could be useful in the planning of the simulation approach and fulfilling experiments with CACI COMNET III simulation tool.

References

1. Anderson, D. *Fibre Channel-Arbitrated Loop: The Preferred Path to Higher I/O Performance, Flexibility in Design.* Seagate Technology Paper #MN-24, Seagate, Scotts Valley, CA, 1995.
2. Bohm, C., Hidell, M., Lindgren, P., Ramfelt, L., and Sjödin, P. Fast circuit switching for the next generation of high performance networks. *IEEE Journal on Selected Areas in Communications,* 14(2), 1996, pp. 298-305.

3. Bohm, P., Lindgren, P., Ramfelt, L., and Sjödin, P. The DTM Gigabit Network. *Journal of High Speed Networks*, 3(2), 1994.

4. CCIR Rec. 601-2. Encoding parameters of digital television for studios. *Recommendations of the CCIR*, XI - Part 1, Broadcasting Service (Television), Geneva, 1990, pp. 95-104.

5. Chang, C. J. and Nilsson, A. A. Queueing networks modeling for a packet router architecture using the DTM technology. *Proc. IEEE ICC'2000*, June 18-22, 2000, New Orleans, LA, USA.

6. Dedek, J., Stephens, G. *What is Fibre Channel?* Ancot Corporation, Menlo Park, CA 94025, 1996.

7. Elmstedt, L., Bohm, C., Lindgren, P. and Ramfelt, L. *The DTM Protocol Specification*. Research Report TRITA-IT R 93:02. Dept. of Teleinformatics, Royal Inst. of Technology, Stockholm, 1992.

8. Gauffin, L. What we need for an information society. *IFIP Congress*, 3, 1994, pp. 127-129.

9. Gordonov, A. and Kress, M. Development of a video network for efficient dissemination of the graphical images in a collaborative environment. *Informing Science*, 2(1), 1999, pp. 1-8.

10. Gringeri, S., Khasnabish, B., Lewis, A., Shuaib, K., Egorov, R., and Basch, B. Transmission of MPEG-2 video streams over ATM. *IEEE MultiMedia*, 5(1), 1998.

11. Heyn, T. *The RAID Advantage*. Seagate Technology Paper, Seagate, Scotts Valley, CA, 1995.

12. Holmlund, M. *IP Traffic in a DTM Network*. NetInsight AB, Stockholm, 1998.

13. Jones, F. *Desktop Digital Video Production*. Prentice Hall, 1998.

14. Kahn, L. A new medium for IP? *Telecommunications International*, July, 1998.

15. Kahn, L. *Introduction to DTM*. NetInsight AB, Stockholm, 1998.

16. Karlsson, G. Asynchronous transfer of video. *IEEE Communications Magazine*, No. 8, 1996.

17. Konstantas, D., Milanese, R., Jacot-Descombes, A., and Pun, T. Distributed video production, distributed musical rehearsal and distributed video editing and retrieval. *ComTec.*, 78(2), 2000, p. 30-37.

18. Lee, J. Y. B. Parallel video servers - a tutorial. *IEEE MultiMedia*, 5(2), 1998.

19. Liebman, S. Long live the router! *Videography*, February, 1999.

20. Lindgren, P. *A Multi-Channel Network Architecture Based on Fast Circuit Switching*. Doctoral Dissertation, Royal Institute of Technology, Stockholm, May, 1996.

21. Lindgren, P. and Bohm, C. Fast connection establishment in DTM. *Proc. of High Performance Networking Conference*, Grenoble, France, June 1994.

22. Matthews, J., Gloor, P., and Makedon, F. VideoScheme: a programmable video editing system for automation and media recognition. *Proceedings ACM Multimedia 93*, ACM, New York, NY, USA, 1993, pp. 419-426.

23. *Medea VideoRaid pci*. http://www.videoguys.com/medea.htm

24. Nishikawa, J., Okabayashi, I., Mori, Y., Sasaki S., Migita M., Obayashi Y., Furuya, S., and Kaneko, K. Design and implementation of video server for mixed-rate streams. *Proceeding of the IEEE 7th International Workshop on Network and Operating Systems Support for Digital Audio and Video*, IEEE, New York, NY, USA, 1997, p. 3-11.

25. Ohanian, T. A. *Digital Nonlinear Editing: New Approaches to Editing Film and Video*. Butterworth-Heinemann, 1998.

26. Perkins, C., Crowcroft, J. Real-time audio and video transmission of IEEE Globecom'96 over the Internet. *IEEE Communications Magazine*, No. 4, 1997.

27. Plank, B. Video disk and server operation. *International Broadcast Engineer*, September, 1995.

28. de Prycker, M. *Asynchronous Transfer Mode: Solution for Broadband ISDN*. Ellis Horwood, New York, 1993.

29. Sachs, M. W., Varma, A. Fibre channel and related standards. *IEEE Communications Magazine*, No. 8, 1996.

30. Sotiropoulos, S., Hawkins, I., Darwazeh, I. A novel digital architecture for high quality uncompressed digital video and audio transmission. *NOC '98: Long-Haul, ATM and Multi-Media Networks*, IOS Press, Amsterdam, Netherlands, 1998, pp. 49-54.

31. Takeuchi, H., Tansek, D., Golson, C., and Sato, N. SXnet: a practical approach to digital video networking: a migration path to digital video distribution as applied to the broadcast news operation. *SMPTE Journal*, 108(3), 1999, pp. 168-172.

32. *Video Editing System ES-7*. Sony, 1995.

33. *Video-Machine: Reference Guide*. FAST Multimedia AG, 1995, Munich, Germany.

34. Whitaker, J. Data storage systems. J. C. Whitaker, (ed.), *The Electronics Handbook*, CRC Press, Boca Raton, FL, 1996.

Part 5: Information Systems and Software Engineering

The Use of Aggregate Approach for Formal Specification and Simulation of Real-Time Systems[*]

Henrikas Pranevicius and Dalius Makackas

Business Informatics Department,
Kaunas University of Technology
Studentu 50, LT-3031 Kaunas, Lithuania
E-mail: {hepran, d.makackas}@if.ktu.lt

Abstract

Paper presents model of Control Area Network (CAN) protocol. The model was created using piece-linear aggregate formalism. CAN protocol is a component part of Anti-lock Braking System (ABS). The goal of performed investigations was to analyse protocol application possibilities in ABS. Created simulation model of CAN protocol permitted to evaluate waiting times of transmitted information packets. Requirements for this parameter are defined by ABS dynamical characteristics.

Keywords: CAN protocol, aggregate approach, real-time systems, simulation, formal specification.

1. Introduction

The stage of formal specification creation is one of the most important during the design of the software for real-time systems. Such formal specification usually is used for analysis and implementation purposes. During analysis stage it is necessary to resolve two tasks: analysis of logical correctness and evaluation of the systems functioning timing parameters.

Different mathematical schemes are used for creation of systems formal description, such as forms of automata models, Petri-nets, data flow and state transition diagrams, temporal logic of actions technique, abstract communicating methods, Quirk methodology [3], mixed and others.

While choosing a formalisation method it is preferable to resolve both fore mentioned analysis tasks on the base of a single formal specification. Analysis task can be resolved on the base of a single formal description. Piece-linear aggregate approach or simply aggregate approach [7] has such property—it can be successfully used both for correctness analysis [5] and for evaluation of system functioning timing parameters. Specification language ESTELLE/Ag and specification analysis tool PRANAS-2 [6] were created on the base of Aggregate method. There are some differences between ESTELLE/Ag and the ESTELLE ISO standard: a model of piece-linear aggregate is used in ESTELLE/Ag (abbreviation "Ag" denotes Aggregate approach). The use of such a model instead of a finite-state automaton, which is the formal background of the standard ESTELLE, enables to create a single model both for validation and simulation. This is possible due to the special structure of the piece-linear aggregate. Apart from the discrete components describing the state of the modules of specified system, there are also continuous components to control event sequences in the module. These continuous components are called operations. Sequences of actions are described by means of operators. Intermediate results of operators are invisible to the outside. If

---

[*] Investigations have been supported by COPERNICUS programme according LIMITS project.

189

J. Barzdins and A. Caplinskas (eds.), Databases and Information Systems, 189–198.
© 2001 *Kluwer Academic Publishers.*

such an operation sequence is being performed at a given instance of time the corresponding operation is called "active". Thus, an individual module evolves two types of events: arrival of input signal and completion of an active operation. Specification analysis system PRANAS-2 consists of the following software tools: specification editor, validation subsystem and simulation subsystem. Specification editor provides a capability to create initial specifications in ESTELLE/Ag language. The validation subsystem permits to construct a validation model for the program by generating reachability graph. After construction of the reachability graph the following specification characteristics may be verified: completeness, deadlock freeness, boundedness, absence of static and dynamic deadlocks and termination.

An initial specification generated by specification editor has to be supplemented with additional code. This is necessary in order to define the duration of operations and to introduce additional variables for gathering statistics about evaluated system parameters.

There are two classes of real-time systems: *Hard* and *Soft*. *Hard* real-time systems must do a certain activity before a priory defined time T, i.e. $t_{act} < T$, where t_{act} – time instant when activity occurs. *Soft* real-time systems should perform activity before time T for example in 92% of the cases, i.e. $P(t_{act} < T) = 0.92$.

Usually *Hard* systems are analysed by carrying out analytical calculation of time intervals during which systems events occurs. *Soft* systems are investigated by means of simulation.

The possibility of using the aggregate approach for analysis of real time systems is illustrated by creation of simulation model of Control Area Network (CAN) protocol when this protocol is used in Anti-lock Braking System (ABS). The conceptual and functional descriptions and timing parameters of that system are taken from [9].

The goal of this investigation was to analyse CAN protocol application possibilities in ABS. CAN interface has to provide fast transmission of information packets. ABS forms requirements for high-speed transmission of information packets through CAN interface. Created CAN protocol simulation model was used for check of this requirement.

The paper is structured in the following way. Section 2 gives short introduction about aggregate approach. Section 3 gives formal specification of CAN protocol using piece-linear aggregate formalism. Simulation results showing waiting times for packets with different priorities are presented in section 4. The last section presents requirements for transmission time of information packets through CAN interface, there it is also discussed how these requirements are fulfilled.

2. Aggregate Approach

In the application of the aggregate approach for system specification, the system is represented as a set of interacting piece – linear aggregates (PLA) [6]. The PLA is taken as an object defined by a set of states Z, input signals X, and output signals Y. The aggregate functioning is considered in a set of time moments $t \in T$. The state $z \in Z$, the input signals $x \in X$, and the output signals $y \in Y$ are considered to be time functions. Apart from these sets, transition H and output G operators must be known as well. The state $z \in Z$ of the piece-linear aggregate is the same as the state of a piece-linear Markov process, i.e.:

$$z(t) = (v(t), z_v(t)),$$

where $v(t)$ is a discrete state component taking values on a countable set of values; and $z_v(t)$ is a continuous component comprising of $z_{v1}(t), z_{v2}(t), ..., z_{vk}(t)$ co-ordinates.

When there are no inputs, the state of the aggregate changes in the following manner:

$$v(t) = \text{const}, \quad \frac{dz_v(t)}{dt} = -\alpha_v,$$

where $\alpha_\upsilon = (\alpha_{\upsilon 1}, \alpha_{\upsilon 2}, ..., \alpha_{\upsilon k})$ is a constant vector.

The state of the aggregate can change in two cases only: when an input signal arrives at the aggregate or when a continuous component acquires a definite value. The theoretical basis of piece-linear aggregates is their representation as piece-linear Markov processes.

Let us consider an aggregate as a system with N input and M output interaction points (IP). Input signals $x_1, x_2, ... x_N \in X$ arrive at the input IP. Here, the signals $x_i \in X_i$, $i = \overline{1, N}$ are treated as elementary ones, X_i is a set of elementary signals. In the general case, an elementary signal is of a vector structure $x_i = \{x_i^1, x_i^2, ..., x_i^n\}$, i.e., can be described by several quantities, each of which has a value from some set X_i^j, so that $x_i^j \in X_i^j$, $j = \overline{1, r_i}$.

Thus, a set of elementary signals coming to the i-th IP of the aggregate is:

$$X_i = X_i^1 * X_i^2 * ... * X_i^n, \ i = \overline{1, N}.$$

A set of the aggregate input signals is presented as a union of sets X_i:

$$X = \bigcup_{i=1}^{N} X_i,$$
$$Y = \{y_1, y_2, ..., y_M\}, \ y_1 = \{y_1^1, y_1^2, ..., y_1^{s_i}\} \in Y_1,$$
$$y_1^k \in Y_1^k, \ l = \overline{1, M}, \ k = \overline{1, s_i}.$$

A set of elementary output signals taken from the l-th IP:

$$Y_l = Y_l^1 * Y_l^2 * ... * Y_l^{s_i}, \ l = \overline{1, M}.$$

and a set of output signals is of the form:

$$Y = \bigcup_{l=1}^{M} Y_l.$$

Aggregate functioning is examined on a set of time moments $T = \{t_0, t_1, ..., t_m, ...\}$ at which one or several events take place, resulting in the aggregate state alternation. The set of events E which may take place in the aggregate is divided into two non-intersecting subsets $E' = E' \cup E''$. The subset $E' = \{e_1', e_2', ..., e_N'\}$ comprises classes of events (or simply events) e_i', $i = \overline{1, N}$ resulting from the arrival of input signals from the set $X = \{x_1, x_2, ..., x_N\}$. The class of events $e_i' = \{e_{ij}', j = 1, 2, 3, ...\}$, where e_{ij}' is an event from the class of events e_i' taking place the j-th time since the moment t_0. The events from the subset E' are called external events. A set of aggregate input signals is unambiguously reflected in the subset E' i.e., $X \rightarrow E'$. The events from the subset $E'' = \{e_1'', e_2'', ..., e_f''\}$ are called internal events where $e_i'' = \{e_{ij}'', j = 1, 2, 3, ...\}$, $i = \overline{1, f}$ are the classes of the aggregate internal events. Here, f determines the number of operations taking place in the aggregate. The events in the set E'' indicate the end of the operations taking place in the aggregate.

The events of the subsets E' and E'' are called the evolutionary events of the aggregate. The main evolution events are sufficient for unambiguous determination of the aggregate evolution. Apart from the basic evolutionary events, auxiliary evolutionary events may be considered, which are simultaneous to the basic ones and determine the start of the operations.

Additional events, associated with the gathering of statistics, the determination of the steady state, the end of system simulation, etc. are introduced in the aggregate. Let a set of additional events be denoted E'''. The events from the subset E''' are internal also. Let the additional events, having no impact on the evolutionary ones be called auxiliary events.

In accordance with the input subsets of events, a set of time moments T is divided into two subsets: T' – a subset of input signals arrival and T''– a subset of internal events occurrence. Moreover, $T = T' \cup T''$.

For every class of events e_i'' from the subset E'', control sequences are specified $\{\xi_j^{(i)}\}$, where $\xi_j^{(i)}$ – the duration of the operation which is followed by the event e_{ij}'' as well as event counters $\{r(e_i'', t_m)\}$, where $r(e_1'', t_m)$, $i = \overline{1, f}$ is the number of events from the class e_i'' taken place in the time interval $[t_0, t_m]$.

In order to determine start and end moments of operation, taking place in the aggregate the so called control sums $\{s(e_i'', t_m)\}$, $\{w(e_i'', t_m)\}$, $i = \overline{1, f}$ are introduced, where $s(e_i'', t_m)$ – the time moment of the start of operation followed by an event from the class e_i''. This time moment is indeterminate if the operation was not started; $w(e_i'', t_m)$ is the time moment of the end of the operation followed by the event from the class e_i''. In case of no priority operations, the control sum $w(e_i'', t_m)$ is determined in the following way:

$$w(e_i'', t_m) = \begin{cases} s'(e_i'', t_m) + \xi_{r(e_i'', t_m)+1}, & \text{if at the moment } t_m \text{ an operation is taking place,} \\ & \text{which is followed by the event } e_i; \\ \infty, & \text{in the opposite case.} \end{cases}$$

The infinity symbol (∞) is used to denote the undefined values of the variables.

3. Aggregate Specification of CAN Protocol

The conceptual model of the CAN protocol is prepared using ISO standard [1], PHILIPS[4] and SIEMENS [8] documents. Figure 1 presents aggregate system interconnection scheme using these standards. The names of aggregates are following A_1 - the sending of the 1st bit of a message; A_2 - an arbitration procedure; A_3 - the transmission of informational part of a message; A_4 - the transmission of control information of message; A_5 - a bus, A_6 - an intermission between the transmission of messages.

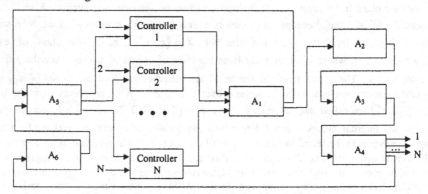

Figure 1. Aggregate system interconnection scheme of CAN protocol

Aggregate A_1. (The aggregate describes the sending of the 1st bit of a message).
1. The set of input signals:
    $\{x_1, \ldots, x_N\}$, where x_i – signal from i-th controller.

2. The set output signals:
    $\{y_1, y_2\}$, where y_1 – signal denoting start of transmission, y_2 – signal denoting start of arbitration procedure.

3. The set of external events:

   $\{e_1',...,e_N'\}$, where e_i' – means that i-th controller starts to send packet of l-th priority.

4. The set of internal events:

   $\{e_1'',e_2''\}$, where e_1'' – means that transmission of start of frame bit has ended; e_2'' – means that initialisation of packet transmission has ended.

5. Controlling sequence:

   $e_1'' \rightarrow \{\eta_i\}_{i=1}^{\infty}$, where $\eta_i = 1$, $e_2'' \rightarrow \{\xi\}_{i=1}^{\infty}$ where $\xi = 0.2$.

6. The set of discrete components:

   $z(t_m) = \{\chi_1(t_m), \chi_2(t_m)\}$,

   where $\quad \chi_1(t_m) = \begin{cases} 0, & \text{bus is empty;} \\ l, & \text{bus is occupied by } l \text{ - th priority packet;} \end{cases}$

   $\chi_2(t_m) = \begin{cases} 0, & \text{bus is empty;} \\ 1, & \text{bus occupation phase;} \\ 2, & \text{bus is occupied.} \end{cases}$

7. The set of continuous co-ordinates:

   $z_v(t_m) = \{w(e_1'', t_m), w(e_2'', t_m)\}$.

8. Initial state:

   $w(e_1'', t_0) = \infty$, $w(e_2'', t_0) = \infty$, $\chi_1(t_0) < 0$, $\chi_2(t_0) < 0$.

9. Transition operators:

   $H(e_i')$ $i = \overline{1,N}$:

   $\chi_1(t_{m+1}) = \begin{cases} x_i, & \chi_1(t_{m+1}) < x_i \wedge w(e_1'', t_{m+1}) \neq \infty \wedge w(e_2'', t_{m+1}) \neq \infty; \\ \chi_1(t_m), & \text{otherwise;} \end{cases}$

   $\chi_2(t_{m+1}) = \begin{cases} t_m, & \chi_1(t_{m+1}) \leq 0; \\ \chi_2(t_m), & \text{otherwise;} \end{cases}$

   $w(e_1'', t_{m+1}) = \begin{cases} t_m + \eta_m, & \chi_1(t_{m+1}) \leq 0; \\ w(e_1'', t_m), & \text{otherwise;} \end{cases}$

   $w(e_2'', t_{m+1}) = \begin{cases} t_m + \xi_m, & \chi_1(t_{m+1}) \leq 0; \\ w(e_2'', t_m), & \text{otherwise.} \end{cases}$

   $H(e_1'')$:

   $\chi_1(t_{m+1}) = 0;$
   $\chi_2(t_{m+1}) = 0.$

   $G(e_1'')$:

   $Y = \{y_2\} y_2 = \chi_1(t_m)$

   $H(e_2'')$:

   $\chi_2(t_{m+1}) = 2.$

$G(e_2^*)$:
$$Y = \{y_1\}.$$

Aggregate A$_2$ (The aggregate describes an arbitration procedure in CAN)

1. The set of input signals:

   $\{x_1\}$, where x_1 – a signal initiating an arbitration procedure, its value corresponds to a transferring message.

2. The set of output signals:

   $\{y_1\}$, where y_1 – a signal indicating the end of an arbitration procedure, its value is a transferring message.

3. The set of external events:

   $\{e_1'\}$, where e_1' – the start of an arbitration procedure.

4. The set of internal events:

   $\{e_1''\}$, where e_1'' – the end of an arbitration procedure.

5. Controlling sequence:

   $e_1'' \rightarrow \{\eta_i\}_{i=1}^{\infty}$, where $\eta_i = const$.

6. The set of discrete components:

   $z(t_m) = \{\chi(t_m)\}$, where $\chi(t_m)$ - transmitted message.

7. The set of continuous co-ordinates:

   $z_v(t_m) = \{w(e_1'', t_m)\}$.

8. Initial state:

   $w(e_1'', t_0) = \infty$.

9. Transition operators:

   $H(e_1')$:
   $$\chi(t_{m+1}) = x_1;$$
   $$w(e_1^*, t_{m+1}) = t_m + \eta_m.$$
   $G(e_1^*)$:
   $$Y = \{y_1\}, y_1 = \chi(t_m).$$

Aggregates A$_3$, A$_4$, A$_6$ (The aggregate A$_3$ describes the transmission of informational part of a message and A$_6$ — an intermission between the transmission of messages; A$_4$ aggregate describes the transmission of control information of message)

The description of these aggregates is identical to the previous one with exception that the set of discrete co-ordinates of aggregate A$_6$ is empty.

The description of A$_4$ aggregate is the same as of A$_2$ excepting the set of output signal that is equal to $\{y_1, ..., y_N\}$ and transition operator $G(e_1')$: $Y = \{y_1, ..., y_N\}, y_i = \chi(t_m), i = \overline{1, N}$.

Aggregate A$_5$ (The aggregate describes occupation of bus)

1. The set of input signals:

   $\{x_1, x_2\}$, where x_1 – the start of a message transmission; x_2 – the end of an intermission between message transmission.

2. The set of output signals:

   $\{y_1,...,y_N\}$, where y_i – a bus state.

3. The set of external events:

   $\{e_1',e_2'\}$, where e_1' – the start of a bus occupation, e_2' – the end of a bus occupation.

4. The set of internal events is empty.

5. Controlling sequence: none.

6. The set of discrete components:

   $z(t_m) = \{\chi(t_m)\}$, where $\chi(t_m) = \begin{cases} 0, & \text{if a bus is idle;} \\ 1, & \text{otherwise.} \end{cases}$

7. The set of continuous co-ordinates:

   $z_v(t_m) = \varnothing$.

8. Initial state:

   $\chi(t_0) = 0$.

9. Transition operators:

   $H(e_1')$:
   $$\chi(t_{m+1}) = 1.$$

   $G(e_1')$:
   $$Y = \{y_1,...,y_N\}, y_i = \chi(t_m), i = \overline{1,N}.$$

   $H(e_2')$:
   $$\chi(t_{m+1}) = 0.$$

   $G(e_2')$:
   $$Y = \{y_1,...,y_N\}, y_i = \chi(t_m), i = \overline{1,N}.$$

Aggregate Controller (This aggregate describes the flow of messages, which have to be transmitted using CAN)

1. The set of input signals:

   $\{x_1,x_2\}$, where x_1 – a bus state; x_2 – a message is received.

2. The set of output signals:

   $\{y_1\}$, where y_1 – a transmitted message, which value is its priority.

3. The set of external events:

   $\{e_1',e_2'\}$, where e_1' – the change of a bus state, e_2' – next message was transmitted through a bus.

4. The set of internal events:

   $\{e_1''\}$, where e_1'' – the end of a generation of a new message.

5. Controlling sequence:

   $e_1'' \rightarrow \{\eta_i\}_{i=1}^{\infty}$, where η_i – a duration between successful transmission of messages and the generation of a new message.

6. The set of discrete components:

$z(t_m) = \{\chi_1(t_m), \chi_2(t_m)\}$, where

$$\chi_1(t_m) = \begin{cases} 0, & \text{if a bus is idle;} \\ 1, & \text{otherwise;} \end{cases} \quad \chi_2(t_m) = \begin{cases} 0, & \text{if there are nothing to transmit;} \\ 1, & \text{otherwise.} \end{cases}$$

7. The set of continuous co-ordinates:

$z_v(t_m) = \{w(e_1'', t_m)\}$.

8. Initial state:

$w(e_1'', t_0) = t_0$, a – the priority of transmitted messages from controller.

9. Transition operators:

$H(e_1')$:

$$\chi_1(t_{m+1}) = x_1.$$

$G(e_1')$:

$$Y = \begin{cases} \{y_1\}, & \text{if } \chi_1(t_{m+1}) = 0 \wedge \chi_2(t_m) > 0; \\ \varnothing, & \text{otherwise;} \end{cases}$$

where $y_1 = a$.

$H(e_2')$:

$$\chi_2(t_{m+1}) = \begin{cases} \chi_2(t_m) - 1, & \text{if } x_2 = a, \\ \chi_2(t_m), & \text{otherwise;} \end{cases}$$

$$w(e_1'', t_{m+1}) = \begin{cases} t_m + \eta_m, & \text{if } \chi_1(t_m) = 0 \wedge x_2 = a, \\ w(e_1'', t_{m+1}), & \text{otherwise.} \end{cases}$$

$H(e_1'')$:

$$\chi_2(t_{m+1}) = \chi_2(t_m) + 1.$$

$G(e_1'')$:

$$Y = \begin{cases} \{y_1\}, & \text{if } \chi_1(t_{m+1}) = 0 \wedge \chi_2(t_m) = 1; \\ \varnothing, & \text{otherwise;} \end{cases}$$

where $y_1 = a$.

Presented above aggregate specification of CAN protocol was used to develop ESTELLE/Ag specification. The protocol was investigated using PRANAS-2 simulation system. The relationship between an intensity of incoming flow of packets and their waiting time where investigated. Waiting time was calculated separately for the packets with different priorities.

4. Simulation Results of CAN Interface

Simulation results are presented in Figure 2, where *Waiting time* – the mean waiting time till packet transmission is started, τ – mean time interval between two successfully of arrived packets to CAN interface. Each dependency in Figure 2 is for flow of packets with different priorities. The *2nd* curve in Figure 2 is for the first priority flow (highest priority). The *1st* curve is for the fourth priority flow (lowest priority).

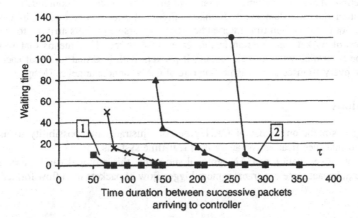

Figure 2. Waiting time dependencies (the scale of axis is measured in microsecond)

Simulation experiments were carried out at the following parameters of CAN interface:
- Four flows of packets with different priorities and equal intensities were transmitted;
- Lengths of packets are the same and equal to 80 bits;
- Transmission rate of CAN monochannel is 1Mbps.

5. Requirements for Packet Transmission Time through CAN Interface

In order to prevent wheels locking, both response time of braking system mechanical part and transmission time of packets through CAN interface have to be less than time interval of wheel locking.

It is considered that braking system response time is approximately 0.06 sec. Figure 3 presents dependencies of car wheel angular velocity change during braking either on asphalt or an ice when car velocity is 72 km/h. According to Figure 3 a wheel is locked after 0.07 sec on an ice while on asphalt locking lasts two-times longer.

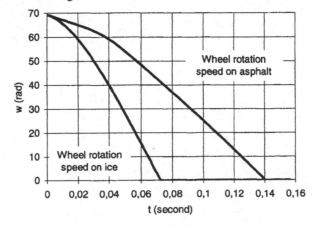

Figure 3. Dependencies of angular velocities of a car wheels

Considering wheel locking time at worst conditions (on an ice) we conclude that packets have to be transmitted not less than every 10 msec. Figure 2 shows that queues in CAN interface practically are not formed when time interval between successive packets arriving to controller is 10 msec. Duration of packet transmission in this case is 80 μ sec. This means that wheels braking process can be controlled without their locking if packets with information about each wheel state are transferred every 10 msec and transmission rate of CAN monochannel is 1Mbps.

6. Conclusions

Developed simulation model of CAN protocol illustrates the possibility to use aggregate approach for formal specification and analysis of real-time systems.

Carried out investigation of CAN protocol show that this protocol can be used in Anti-lock Braking System, because one can transfer more bigger flow of packets then flow formed by ABS.

References

1. *ISO 11898:1993, Road Vehicles - Interchange of Digital Information - Controller Area Network (CAN) for High-Speed Communication.*

2. Mikuckas, A., Makackas, D. Modelling car braking temporal characteristics. *Informacines Technologijos'97*, Technologija, Kaunas, 1997, pp. 218-224 (in Lithuanian).

3. Motus, L., Rodd, M. G. *Timing Analysis of Real-Time Software.* Pergamon, 1994.

4. *Philips Semiconductors. CAN Specification.* Version 2.0, 1991.

5. Pranevicius, H., Chmieliauskas, A. *Correctness Analysis and Performance Prediction of Protocol by means of Aggregate Approach and Control Sequences Method.* Academy of Science. USSR, Moscow, 1983, 32 p.

6. Pranevicius, H., Pilkauskas, V., Chmieliauskas, A. Aggregate Approach for Specification and Analysis of Computer Network Protocols. Technologija, Kaunas, 1994.

7. Pranevicius, H. Aggregate approach for specification, validation, simulation and implementation of computer network protocols. *Lectures Notes in Computer Sciences*, **502**, Springer-Verlag, Berlin, 1991, pp. 433-477.

8. *SAE 81C90/81C91, Stand Alone Full CAN Controller.* Siemens Semiconductor Group, 1994.

9. Valatka, A. *Anti-Lock Braking and Traction Control Systems of Car.* Smaltija, Kaunas, 1996 (in Lithuanian).

Using Software Reuse to Drive Requirements

Ronald J. Leach

Department of Systems and Computer Science
Howard University
Washington, DC 20059
E-mail: rjl@scs.howard.edu

Abstract

Software reuse can reduce development and maintenance costs. Reuse of software artefacts early in the life cycle increases potential savings, with the greatest savings possible when reuse is used to drive the requirements for a system.

COTS software has great potential for improving reuse. However, the indiscriminate use of COTS or other reusable components can actually increase total life cycle costs because of inexact matches to requirements or unexpected high costs of system integration, testing, and maintenance.

In this paper we report on a new paradigm for a software development process based on using reuse to modify software requirements. A simple cost model for this approach is presented.

We describe two different development approaches to the same large software system, one using only existing components with requirements largely determined by the existing software, and the other using conventional software development techniques. Both the software development processes used to create the two systems and the systems themselves are compared.

Keywords: software reuse, requirements, COTS, cost estimation.

1. Introduction

Software reuse is very appealing because it has the potential to reduce development and maintenance costs. Reusing software artefact early in the life cycle produces the greatest cost savings, because many later life cycle activities can be reduced or even eliminated.

It is clear that reusing a set of requirements for a subsystem provides the greatest potential for cost savings for that subsystem. Thus, at least theoretically, the least expensive type of software system is one built entirely from an existing collection of reusable subsystems, which act as high level building blocks chosen at the time of requirements analysis of the system.

Reusing the requirements for a building block is the highest level of reuse. This is true, regardless of the life cycle model used [2, 8, 11]. Reuse can be incorporated into nearly all software life cycle development models, including the classic waterfall model [13, 14], the rapid prototyping model [13, 14], and the spiral model [3]. Reuse is also the basis of the two software development models described in the references [1, 18].

A 1993 report on the status of research and practice in the field of requirements engineering indicated that many of the same problems observed in the 1970s are still present today [9]. Functional requirements given in textual form are hard to translate to formal specifications. Usability requirements present additional difficulties because of subsystem interaction. Improvements in the requirements process are welcome, especially if they are consistent with increased software reuse, because of potential cost savings. Requirements techniques that promote effective use of appropriate commercial off-the-shelf (COTS) products are especially appealing.

J. Barzdins and A. Caplinskas (eds.), Databases and Information Systems, 199–208.

Unfortunately, realistic applications rarely reuse entire sets of requirements exactly. Technical specifications for a system are rarely the same as the requirements for an existing system that we wish to reuse. (Frequently, these technical specifications are simply not available from the software vendors; this is due primarily to confidentiality issues.) Even if all detailed specifications were available at the subsystem level, the technical specifications for subsystems will generally not be identical with those of the existing building blocks that we wish to reuse.

The usual approach in this situation is to make a decision to modify an existing building block based on the perceived percentage of reuse in the requirements. The exact breakpoints differ from organisation to organisation, but an estimated reuse factor that is typically in the range of 75 to 90 percent or higher usually means that the existing subsystem will be modified in order to meet the requirements. Lower estimated reuse factors generally means that the desired subsystem will be built from scratch, with no attempt to reuse the subsystem. Different levels of reuse are often reflected in different cost estimates, with the cost models depending on the amount of code that can be reused as is; the amount that needs a "small" amount of change, usually in the 75 to 90 percent range; and the amount of new code that must be designed, written, tested, integrated, maintained, and documented. This process is repeated for each subsystem.

Of course, the subsystem can itself be decomposed and the process of looking for a match with one or more reusable software components can continue. In many cases, however, the search for reusable components focuses on source code modules instead of higher-level components. Thus the software development process cannot achieve maximum savings because reuse will only occur relatively late in the software life cycle.

We note that object-oriented frameworks have promise for reducing software development costs. However, at present, such frameworks do not appear to be adequate for describing systems in the application domain used as the primary example in this paper. It is unclear if this limitation is due to a difficulty with the framework model or with the rate of technology change in the application domain.

In this paper we will suggest a different approach – changing the new system's requirements to meet the known requirements, functionality, and quality of the existing system or subsystems. This reuse-driven requirements approach can use both locally-developed and COTS software.

We note that several authors are reporting on the problems associated with heavy use of COTS software [6, 10, 17].

2. The Reuse-Driven Requirements Paradigm

The objective of this paradigm is to change iteratively the requirements for a new system to a set that is inexpensive (because of reuse) and also satisfactory to any customers. The extreme case of this paradigm is the use of COTS software to affect system requirements, without any new software development, in order to meet the requirements of a new software system. The requirements team must know the functionality, quality, run-time efficiency, and interface standards of locally-developed software and COTS products in the application domain and must include an expert on classification using domain analysis.

The high level description of the reuse-driven requirements process is given below. For simplicity, we will only describe the interaction of the development team with a known customer. The modification for new systems that have a target set of likely end users, but no fixed customer, is similar and will not be discussed in this paper.

1. Develop an initial set of requirements. This should be done in concert with the customer, using standard elicitation methods. If no customer is known, then the requirements should be chosen according to the perceived needs of the system's end users. Step one is consistent with most organisation's requirement processes.

2. Determine if there is an existing reusable system that meets the set of requirements. If there is such a system, stop the requirements process and return the existing reusable system. This step depends upon detailed knowledge ("domain analysis") of nearly all existing reusable systems in the relevant application domain [15].

3. Determine if there is an existing reusable system that meets "nearly all" the requirements. If such a system exists, provide the customer with a description of the existing system's requirements, how they differ from the original requirements, and the expected costs of using the existing system to "nearly meet" the customer's requirements. If the customer accepts the modified requirements and the reused existing system at the estimated cost, stop the requirements process and return the existing reusable system. Step three depends upon good, often empirical estimates of the degree of "nearness" for both the existing software system and the set of requirements.

4. If no existing system meets or "nearly meets" the customer's requirements, then the set of requirements should be separated into sets of requirements for subsystems. The most effective way to do this is to partition the set of requirements using a decomposition that is consistent with an existing classification scheme for categorising existing reusable software systems and COTS products. Smaller-grained components can also be used at this time, although the greatest cost saving arise from larger components or systems.

5. Steps 2 through 4 should be carried out for each subsystem. Each reused subsystems must meet appropriate interface and performance standards. This should be done during a check of the certification of the reused subsystem.

6. New software development is limited to those subsystems in which no agreement can be made between the customer's fixed requirements and the existing reusable subsystem's functionality.

7. After agreement between customer and the software team on the final set of requirements for the subsystems, the remainder of the software development process begins. Any filters or glueware necessary to interface existing components is developed at this stage. Existing subsystem building blocks are integrated together with any new code into the new system, which is then configured, tested, documented, and delivered to the customer.

This process is different from requirements techniques in which the goal is to develop requirements that meet the needs (actual or perceived) of the customer. Our goal is to develop the cheapest system that meets the customer's minimal needs, while letting the customer determine which features are not readily available and what their true system cost will be.

The role of prototypes in the reuse-driven requirements development paradigm can vary, depending on the preferences of the organisation doing the software development and the financial commitment of the customer. Prototypes could be developed at any of steps 3, 4, or 5. Certainly good prototypes can make negotiation of enhancements with the customer easier.

Prototype development is expensive and it is not realistic to proceed with costly prototype development at the early, request for proposal stage, unless there is reasonable assurance that the software development organisation will be awarded a contract.

3. A Simple Cost Model for the Reuse-Driven Requirements Technique

In certain circumstances, the potential benefits of this reuse-driven requirements approach to requirements can be enormous. The cost savings depend upon the number of iterations until the customer accepts the set of modified requirements, the costs of searching reuse libraries and evaluating COTS products, the costs of developing multiple cost estimation models, and the amount of testing and integration effort.

Note that the reuse-driven requirements approach involves a considerable amount of effort before the final system requirements are set. On the other hand, obtaining the requirements is one of the most costly steps in this approach.

Note also that both the successful, but relatively recent "win-win" approach of Boehm and the much more widely publicised iterative spiral and rapid prototyping approaches to software development are closer to this reuse-driven requirements paradigm than the classical waterfall model. This is because at each iteration of the reuse-driven requirements process, the previous set of requirements is discarded. Other reused-based cost models are given in the references [4, 7, 11].

We will use the common estimate that the amortised cost of a systematic reuse program with extensive use of software metrics is between ten and fifteen percent of the cost of software development references [2, 8, 11]. For simplicity, we will use the average of 12.5%. The overhead can be recovered by early notification of problems and elimination of later life cycle costs.

The difficulty in accurately estimating some of the individual costs needed for the simple linear models presented here makes more complex models impractical. We will be satisfied with cost models that provide a first approximation to true life cycle costs for the reuse-driven requirements method. The cost model for the reuse-driven requirements method is given below:

cost = cost of initial requirements for non-reuse system +
        sum (for all iterations) of
                {cost to examine reuse library and COTS +
                cost to develop requirements +
                cost to evaluate non-reuse system}
        + 1.125 * (cost to develop new code)
        + cost to purchase COTS products
        + integration costs (non-reuse-based system)
        + cost to test system
        + cost to maintain system

It follows that the most pessimistic and optimistic cost estimates for software development using the reuse-driven requirements method are, respectively:

cost = cost of requirements for non-reuse system +
        .125 * (cost to evaluate non-reuse system) +
        1.0 * (cost to develop non-reuse system) +
        cost to maintain system

and

cost = cost of requirements for non-reuse system +
        .125 * (cost to evaluate non-reuse system) +
        cost to maintain system

The pessimistic estimate assumes that there is no relation between the future development path of the system and the initial requirements. This is not very likely for appropriate application domains for this technique.

Integration costs are generally substantial, even in systems that use only COTS products. Consider the cost of a UNIX-based system of COTS products, in which each COTS application reads its input from the standard input file, stdin, and writes its output to the standard output file, stdout. Assume also that each COTS application acts as a filter on some data as in the hypothetical UNIX shell command

    cat data > COTS_app1 | COTS_app2 | COTS_app3

The input to the first COTS application COTS_app1 is read from the output of the file stdout, which is, of course, is where the UNIX cat utility ordinarily writes its data. In turn, the COTS application COTS_app1 writes its output to the input of the COTS application COTS_app2, and so on. In this situation, there is little or no integration problem because the different components have restricted interfaces that are standard in the UNIX environment.

However, most COTS applications do not fit this situation, even in the UNIX world. Many applications are transaction-oriented, rather than following the stream-oriented, transformation flow model described above. For example, applications might access an operating system's services using system calls, interface to a query language for a data base, or use some existing user interface management system. As such, there is a possibility of running out of essential system resources, such as the maximum number of open files or runnable processes at any one time.

Clearly the estimation of integration costs for COTS products is a difficult matter and requires considerable knowledge of the application domain. In particular application domain, developing the glueware or filters for system integration is relatively inexpensive; one interface was created in a single week by one person. We note that Ellis [6] and Kontio [10] have developed some techniques for estimation of the cost of COTS in several application domains.

The system integration problem is much worse in a modern, distributed environment, such as one based on the client-server paradigm. There may be some problem with the number of remote procedures that can be operating at any one time, because of a limit on the number of socket descriptors available for connection by remotely-executing processes. There may be other problems due to concurrency and associated synchronisation problems. Thus any systems integrator must know the level of resources required for the application.

Note that an investment in COTS application does not guarantee that it will be easy to maintain the system over time, due to company failures. Many purchasers of COTS systems will only buy systems for which source code is available. This makes maintenance possible if the COTS vendor leaves the business or stops supporting the product. However, this strategy greatly increases initial costs to purchase the COTS application.

In many organisations, some of the development team is assigned to maintenance for a short time after the system is delivered. These software engineers have an easier time understanding the source code because they are already familiar with at least some portion of the software. Thus these people would have an easier time fixing software faults than people who are unfamiliar with the software. This potential disadvantage of COTS in maintenance will be eliminated over time as more of the original development team moves away from maintenance of a non-COTS product.

4. A Case Study

One of the responsibilities of NASA's Goddard Space Flight Centre is the development of software systems for ground control of spacecraft. One of the most successful projects is the Transportable Operations Control Centre (TPOCC), which provides a reusable software core for use by multiple spacecraft missions, each of which has its own additional mission-specific software. The mission-specific software and enhancements to TPOCC are in response to requests of the scientific managers of the spacecraft missions. The SAMPEX (Solar Anomalous and Magnetospheric Particle Explorer) spacecraft uses TPOCC as the reusable central core of its ground control system. The total SAMPEX system consists of approximately five hundred thousand combined lines of code including the TPOCC subsystem, but not included software.

The TPOCC project was developed by a skilled team and has resulted in considerable cost savings over its lifetime [12]. It uses standard interfaces to TCP/IP, HP-UX, Motif, and the Oracle database system. It has an extremely low defect ratio as measured in faults per KLOC, primarily due to the high levels of reuse. Most of the code for TPOCC is written in C. The TPOCC system consists of approximately two hundred thousand lines of code by itself. A high-level view of the relation of TPOCC to SAMPEX and other missions is shown in Figure 1.

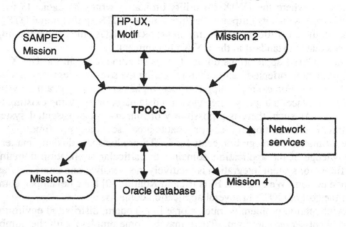

Figure 1. Software interfaces of the SAMPEX ground control software system as developed traditionally using the TPOCC software system

However, continuing economic pressures force consideration of other techniques besides the reuse of locally written components. The evolution of some commercial software for ground control of spacecraft written outside the existing NASA environment has made it possible to create a control system in 90 days, using only COTS software. The new ground control software system was developed using availability of COTS to drive the requirements process, rather than use the standard approach [3]. The project was known as the IMACCS (Integrated Monitoring Analysis and COTS Control System) project. The IMACCS team was lead by M. Bracken [5].

The IMACCS project was intended to demonstrate that a COTS-driven technique was feasible, at least in a specialised application domain with knowledgeable personnel who were experts in the application domain. The IMACCS software was to be compared with a ground control software system developed using conventional techniques for the same SAMPEX spacecraft. The existing method used TPOCC and had a high degree of reuse.

The SAMPEX mission is one of the simplest missions carried out by NASA in the 1990s. It has little of the complexity of the Hubble Space Telescope, for example. The SAMPEX mission has relatively few absolute requirements and therefore was more likely to have these few requirements met by COTS packages. The software architecture of the SAMPEX ground centre control system as developed by the IMACCS project is shown in Figure 2.

IMACCS was developed as a prototype that needed to meet all existing requirements for handling spacecraft data transmitted by the SAMPEX spacecraft, using NASA-standard timing and accuracy constraints. This was considered to be an essential, non-negotiable requirement for a spacecraft ground control software system. Many other non-essential requirements were modified or eliminated. Validation that the IMACCS system met the essential requirements was given by a demonstration using the actual SAMPEX spacecraft. Work essentially stopped on the IMACCS project after the demonstration was complete.

The SAMPEX spacecraft was operated with only one ground control software system at any one time. Thus it is impossible to compare the IMACCS and standard approaches in detail, since IMACCS never went through the extensive testing, maintenance, and usage that the standard system did. Therefore we will not make exact cost comparisons but will present instead a high-level overview. The best estimate is that the IMACCS project would have required one year for production of a complete system that was tested according to typical NASA standards, as opposed to the two years for the traditional software development process.

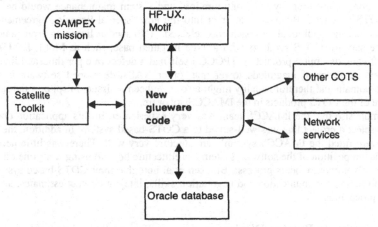

Figure 2. Software interfaces for the SAMPEX ground control software system as developed using a COTS and reuse-based software approach in the IMACCS project

The IMACCS system satisfied 127 of the 143 functional requirements that were originally given for the SAMPEX control system. This represents 88.8% of the system requirements. The unmet requirements were not spread uniformly over three major identifiable subsystem architectural areas, but instead were concentrated primarily in the control centre subsystem, with 15 of 85 requirements not met by the IMACCS system.

Unfortunately, it is difficult to quantify directly the benefits of this procedure, given the often-stated rule of thumb that 80% of the software development effort is allocated to meet 20% of the requirements. We do note however, that the IMACCS project did produce software capable of operating the SAMPEX spacecraft at the system demonstration. Table 1 provides an overview of the best available information for the three types of software development processes used in this application domain: traditional, based on the TPOCC reusable core, and COTS-based.

Table 1. Comparison of methods used in this case study

	Traditional Approach	TPOCC-based Approach	IMACCS (COTS-based) Approach
Total cost	10M	2-3M	unknown
Cost excluding maintenance	9M	1.7-2.5M	1-2M (estimated)
Time to develop prototype from requirements	N/A	9 months	95 days
Time to develop system from requirements	varies	27 months	1 year (estimated)
Size in KLOC	500-1000	500	unknown
Defects/KLOC	.3	.03	unknown
Percent of requirements met	100	100	88.8

Bracken et al. note that the development process used to create their COTS-based system placed special emphasis on communication and negotiation skills, integration cost estimates, and product assessment procedures [6]. This result is consistent with the recommendations made earlier in this paper.

It is reasonable to consider the rationale for the selection of the TPOCC-based system. One major unresolved question is the level of co-operation needed between the vendor of a special-purpose COTS product and the licensing organisation. It is clear that a special arrangement to provide additional consulting, system configuration, and system maintenance would be necessary for these COTS products. Reluctance to enter into the new "special licensing agreements" was a major reason that the traditional approach was selected. (No special licensing arrangements were deemed necessary for COTS products with a large installed base, such as Motif, HP-UX, Oracle database software, or similar products.) TPOCC itself had a defect rate per thousand lines of code approximately an order of magnitude lower than other NASA-developed software in the same applications domain and therefore quality might also have been an issue, in spite of the satisfactory performance of the COTS products in the IMACCS software.

We emphasise that the IMACCS team was very experienced in this application domain and was able to select a project that was well-suited to a COTS-based system. In addition, the available COTS software fitted the IMACCS system's architecture very well. There was little need for any additional decomposition of the software system's architecture beyond using steps one through four of the reuse-driven requirements process. Bracken et al note that their COTS-based system placed special emphasis on communication and negotiation skills, integration cost estimates, and product assessment procedures [3].

5. Comparisons to Related Work

Ahrens and Prywes [1] describe a reuse-based life cycle using both top-down and bottom-up domain engineering techniques in the context of a larger software development process, with customer feedback used to develop software systems. Their analysis suggests that hybrids of the top-down and bottom-up domain engineering techniques are most effective when incorporating legacy systems into new systems to meet customer's needs. Reuse appears primarily in the design step in their life cycle model.

Wilkening, Loyall, Pitarys, and Littlejohn [18] consider reuse primarily in the context of software reengineering. Their primary concern is the migration of FORTRAN code into Ada. They discuss automatic program translation and program transformation that is a combination of automatic and manual processes. They develop a life cycle process to aid in this translation.

Their paper also discusses of options when direct translation yields an unsatisfactory result in the sense that the Ada code produced has little modular structure. The consider approaches that develop Ada interfaces to some FORTRAN components, leaving these FORTRAN components as is, and translating others. Here reuse affects requirements, but only in the sense that the existing system to be translated is taken as fulfilling most of the target system's requirements.

Many organisations have been pursuing the use of COTS products or other high-level reusable systems to improve their software development productivity. The published work by Waund [17] on the nature of a COTS-based methodology and the related work by Ellis [6] on cost modelling provide an excellent insight into the process being used at Loral Federal Systems. Ellis has developed a weighted scale to be used for cost estimation. His scale includes several different aspects of quantitative analysis of COTS software, including assessment of vendor stability [6].

One major problem with most weighted scales used for cost modelling is that the weights of the individual inputs to the models frequently are not validated. A calibration step is needed in order to determine the best estimators using a linear regression or similar technique. The Ellis cost estimation models have been calibrated against data for a variety of projects. Thus his cost models have some validity, at least within the appropriate application domains for which the models are valid.

The work by Kontio at the University of Maryland provides a different approach to selection of appropriate COTS products [10]. He uses the Analytic Hierarchy Process originally developed by Saaty [16] for decision making. Kontio's evaluation process defines a hierarchy of factors, with a preference determined for each alternative branch in the hierarchy. That is, each of several alternatives is compared with each other. Other than a weighting scale of the individual factors on each level of the hierarchy, no use of a weighting scale is made.

Both Ellis' and Kontio's work focus on the process of selection of COTS products, rather than on the requirements modification technique. The work of Ahrens and Prywes, and Wilkening et al each suggest some potential improvements to current life cycle processes. None of these papers consider the approach of changing requirements to be consistent with existing reusable software in the application domain.

6. Conclusions

It is possible to reduce the cost of complex software systems by incorporating software reuse at the beginning of the software life cycle when initial software requirements are being set. The process includes attempting to match capabilities of existing systems, subsystems, or components to the desired requirements. The process also requires the team setting the system requirements to be flexible, in the sense that a workable, relatively inexpensive software system may meet the real needs of its users, even if not all the original requirements were met by the new system with somewhat reduced capabilities. The process requires considerable domain knowledge on the part of the requirements team.

The IMACCS project illustrates clearly the effectiveness of this approach in a realistic software project of moderate size. A system was produced with substantially lower cost than even systems developed with heavy use of large reuse libraries.

7. Future Work

Validated methods of estimating both the size and functionality of COTS products are critical, as are more accurate cost models. Detailed and accurate fault-analysis models of component interactions are essential, especially if the resulting systems are safety-critical or very expensive. Finally, a set of simple criteria to determine in advance whether a particular project can be developed using this method is also needed.

8. Acknowledgements

This research was partially supported by NSF grant CCR-9706058, NASA grant NAG 5-2904 and the Air Force Office of Scientific Research, grant 49620-95-1-0526.

References

1. Ahrens, J. D., Prywes, N. S. Transition to a legacy- and reuse-based software life cycle. *IEEE Computer*, 28(10), 1995, pp. 27-36.

2. Biggerstaff, T., Perlis, A. (eds.). *Software Reusability*. ACM Press, New York, 1989.

3. Boehm, B. A spiral model of software development and enhancement. *IEEE Computer*, 21(2), 1988, pp. 61-72.

4. Bollinger, T., Pfleeger, S. L. Economics of reuse: issues and alternatives. *Information and Software Technology*, September, 1990.

5. Bracken, M. R., Hoge, S. L., Sary, C., Rashkin, R., Pendley, R. D., Werking, R. D. IMACCS: an operational COTS-based ground system proof-of-concept project. *Proceedings of the European Space Conference*, 1995, pp. 37.1-37.8.

6. Ellis, T. COTS integration in software solutions: a cost model. In *Systems Engineering in the Global Marketplace, NCOSE International Symposium*, St. Louis, MO, July 24-26, 1995.

7. Gaffney, J., Cruickshank, R. D. *A General Economics Model for Software Reuse.* Software Productivity Consortium, 1991.

8. Hooper, J. W., Chester, R. *Software Reuse: Guidelines and Methods.* Plenum Press, New York, 1991.

9. Hsia, P., Davis, A., Kung, D. Status report: requirements engineering. *IEEE Software*, 10(6), 1993, pp. 75-79.

10. Kontio, J. *OTSO: A Systematic Process for Reusable Software Component Selection.* University of Maryland, College Park Technical Report CS-TR-3478, UMIACS-TR-95-63, December, 1995.

11. Leach, R. J. *Software Reuse: Methods, Models, Costs.* McGraw-Hill, New York, 1997.

12. Mahmot, R., Koslosky, J., Beach, E., Schwarz, B. Transportable Payload Operations Control Center reusable software: building blocks for quality ground data systems. *Proceedings of the Third International Symposium on Space Mission Operations and Ground Data Systems*, NASA Goddard Space Flight Center, Greenbelt, Maryland, November 15-18, 1994, 2, NASA Publication 3281, pp. 1161-1169.

13. Pfleeger, S. L. *Software Engineering: The Production of Quality Software.* Macmillan, New York, 1989.

14. Pressman, R. *Software Engineering: A Practitioner's Approach.* 4th. *Edition*, McGraw-Hill, New York, 1997.

15. Prieto-Diaz, R., Arango, G. (eds.). *Domain Analysis and Software Sytems Modeling.* IEEE Press, Los Alamitos, California, 1991.

16. Saaty, T. L. *The Analytic Hierarchy Process.* McGraw-Hill, New York, 1990.

17. Waund, C. COTS integration and support model. In *Systems Engineering in the Global Marketplace: National Conference on Systems Engineering, NCOSE International Symposium*, St. Louis, Missouri, July 24-26, 1995.

18. Wilkening, D. E., Loyall, J. P., Pitarys, M. J., Littlejohn, K. A reuse approach to software reengineering. *J. Systems Software*, 30(1-2), 1995, pp. 117-125.

An Approach to Modelling Expertise in the Environment Pollution Evaluation System

Dale Dzemydiene

Institute of Mathematics and Informatics, Law Academy of Lithuania,
Akademijos 4, LT-2600 Vilnius, Lithuania
E-mail: daledz@ktl.mii.lt

Abstract

The article presents a summary of research activities performed in the field of knowledge representation of rapidly changing and complex environmental protection domain. The consideration is attached to the representation of expertise that could relate the use and analysis of information base and evaluation of circumstances of enterprise functioning that influence the environment pollution characteristics. The knowledge structures simultaneously express mutual object communication and decision-making processes in time. A unified framework is developed through the analysis of various types, aspects, and the role of knowledge relevant to the decision support system using Evaluation nets (the extension of Petri nets). The attention is paid to the representation of dynamic and static aspects of a target system and to the specification of decision-making processes describing general reasoning courses at different levels of detailing.

Keywords: decision support system (DSS), knowledge representation, goal structure, E-nets, environment protection.

1. Introduction

Environmental protection problems are very important now, and a significance of their solution will rise in near future. An ecological situation of a region may be considered as rapidly changing environment. In this subject area we face the problem of representing process development dynamism and rapid information change. In addition, the process poses rather a complex inherent inner structure and mechanisms of interaction between subsystems that are frequently express by temporal, geographic, and space dependence conditions.

The decision support system first of all may secure a possibility of modelling and assessing the situation as well as to enable one to reason defining the presentation of alternative decisions and decision making by choosing one of them. The problem addressed in this research is that of developing an approach that integrates problem solving and model-based knowledge acquisition within an extensive model of different knowledge types, describing a changing information environment and decision-making processes in a decision support system (DSS). Some exceptional features of the changing environment, especially dynamic components, require additional means for knowledge representation, data verification and assurance of efficiently making decision processes.

In the KADS project [2] an approach to modelling of problem solving expertise has been developed, based on the four layers of expert knowledge:

- The domain layer contains definitional knowledge of the domain;
- The inference layer describes the structure of reasoning and inference mechanisms that operate upon domain layer;

J. Barzdins and A. Caplinskas (eds.), Databases and Information Systems, 209–220.
© 2001 *Kluwer Academic Publishers.*

- The task layer explicates knowledge about when a certain inference is to be made;
- The strategic layer sets up the plan for achieving a goal, thereby controlling the reasoning in the task layer.

According to [1] the expertise is knowledge in broadest interpretation of the term and includes factual knowledge of domain, problem solving strategies and methods, and learning strategies. Some components of the expertise model are distinguished in our decision support system. As well: the fundamental knowledge that describes the application domain in static (semantic model of information structure) and dynamic (the imitation model of tasks and processes) perspective. The model of the problem solution strategy is introduced in control level (e.g., plans, diagnostic, strategies of correcting task), and the reasoning model that embraces stepwise decision support structure.

Rapidly changing environment may include additional techniques for planning, operation control and decision support. A new viewpoint and approaches are needed allowing us to concentrate the attention on the organisational aspects that ensure information for decision support. The technology for building such systems must provide methods for acquisition, structural representation of many types of knowledge taking into consideration the large, shared and distributed databases [3, 10].

Some issues for knowledge representation including the acquisition and structural analysis stages are considered in this paper. The knowledge elicitation process tries to extract knowledge form specialist and experts of application domain. This initially unstructured knowledge is analysed and structured into an intermediate knowledge model. We propose the Evaluation nets (E-nets) formal means, following [9], which allowed to express the behavioural aspects of events, processes and actions and relate the use and analysis of information structures with the strategy of decision making in time. This model may be viewed as a specification of behavioural aspects of the target system. When modelling problem solution definitely, we combine expertise knowledge and associate it with its purposes and goals in the problem solution process.

2. Decision Making in the Dynamic Environment

One part of a DSS is the model of decision-making processes. Referring to a decision support performance analysis the problem is in a representation of goals, plans and in a specification of interaction between the individual steps in decision making and general information environment. The network can ensure the proper application of the information and the reasoning with respect to the knowledge base. A description of a meta-model can include the model of goals, plans and must represent the practice and strategy of reasoning of specialist-experts in making the decision. At the stage of analysis and evaluation of the enterprise performance, the use of this meta-model could allow:

- to recognise what changes in the environment may induce changes in decision goals;
- to decide is the situation relevant for the really application of existing rules or not;
- to specify the process of identification of possible courses of actions and alternatives and to control the choice of concrete variant of these actions by evaluating attractiveness of the consequences of each action.

Decision-maker must constantly pay attention to the process because the state of it changes dynamically. Process environments are further characterised by being dynamic, by having multiple and possibly conflicting goals and by having incomplete information. Some characteristics are needed for a great deal of data to properly model and verify these problems [2, 6]. We must construct a precise structure of information due to their time and geographical links.

The problems of expression of behavioural aspects of dynamic environmental domain (temporal relationships of process interaction and their determination in time, synchronisation of decision making and information processing, communication between the objects, etc.) causes a necessity of designing a conceptual model witch enabled to specify requirements for such type decision support systems [4, 5].

Temporal knowledge representation aspects are of primary interest in the decision- making context when the problems of retrospective analysis and prognosis are concerned. In the prognosis of further evolution of the target area and the system behaviour it is important to design the adequate imitation model of the target system functioning. Our consideration of information system aimed at helping in organisational management processes by means of imitation modelling [8, 10].

The system for evaluation of enterprises as stationary contamination objects was developed using the theoretical results obtained in [6, 7]. In order to evaluate the contamination level of sewage from the enterprise our decision support system analyses the indices of pollution provided in the project compares monitoring data, inspection data and reports, etc. Decision determines whether to permit a future exploitation or building enterprises and new facilities that pollute or can potentially contaminate surroundings. Decision making is also related with the problem of estimation of the general ecological situation of the given region, the indices of pollution provided in the project, the risk factors related to the preservation of links that are of biological significance and time-dependent, etc.

3. Possibilities of E-Nets to Specify Functional Requirements

The Evaluation nets (i.e., E-nets are the extension of Petri nets) were introduced in [9] and proposed in [4]. The structure and behavioural logic of E-nets give new features in conceptual modelling and imitation of domain processes and decision-making processes. Apart from time evaluation property, E-nets have a much more complex mechanism for description of transition work, some types of the basic transition structures, a detailing of various operations with token parameters. In addition to Petri nets, two different types of locations are introduced (peripheral and resolution locations). The exceptional feature is the fact that the E-net transition can represent a sequence of smaller operations with transition parameters connected with the processes. However, a direct application of E-nets to decision-making processes requires additional analysis and the modification of their interpretation.

Following [9] it is possible to consider the E-net as a relation on (E, M_0, Ξ, Q, Ψ), where E is a connected set of locations over a set of permissible transition schemes, E is denoted by a four-tupple $E=(L, P, R, A)$, where L is a set of locations, P is the set of peripheral locations, R is a set of resolution locations, A is a finite, non-empty set of transition declarations; M_o is an initial marking of a net by tokens; $\Xi = \{\xi_j\}$ is a set of token parameters; Q is a set of transition procedures; Ψ is a set of procedures of resolution locations.

The E-net transition is denoted in [9] as $a_i = (s_i, t(a_i), q_i)$, where s_i is a transition scheme, $t(a_i)$ is a transition time and q_i is a transition procedure. In order to represent the dynamic aspects of complex processes and their control in changing environment it is impossible to restrict ourselves on the using only one temporal parameter $t(a_i)$ which describes the delaying of the activity, i.e. the duration of transition. Therefore, a transition description is extended as follows:

$$a_i = (s_i, t_i^P, \Delta \tau_i, \Pi t_i, q_i),$$

where i is an index of transition; s_i is a transition schema and may consist of $(L'_i, L''_i, \psi(r'_i, r''_i))$, where L'_i is the set of input locations of the transition; L''_i is a set of output locations of the transition; r'_i is the location of complex input conditions of a transition (i.e., input resolution location); r''_i is the resolution location for the transition output; $\psi(r'_i, r''_i)$ is a procedure of resolution locations (see Figure 1). We introduce T as a time scale and $t_i \in T$ as time moments denoted on this scale. According to the property of continuity of time, we can define the time interval by starting and terminating moments: $\tau_k=[t_i,t_j]$, where $i<j$. The duration of the time interval $\Delta(\tau_k)$ is defined by a numerical expression of difference $\Delta(\tau_k)=t_j-t_i$. The period and the base define the periodical time Πt_i. The period is defined as duration of an interval, and the base may be either a time moment t_i or a time interval τ_k.

The t_i^p is defined as a planned moment of transition firing, $t_i^p \in T^*$, where $T^*=T \cup \{t_v^*\}$ and $\{t_v^*\}$ is the set of time moments determined approximately, relatively and etc.

$\Delta\tau_i$ is the duration of the transition working time; Πt_i is the periodic transition time. $q_i \in Q$ is a transition procedure, which according to the rules of transition maps $M \times L' \times \Xi'$ into $M \times L'' \times \Xi''$ and determines the flow of tokens $m_s \in M$ with parameters $\{\xi'_j\}$ from input locations $\{b'_j\}_i$ into output locations taking account the results of procedure $\psi(r'_i, r''_i)$ at the actual time moment t_i^f, where $\Xi', \Xi'' \subset \Xi$.

A concrete parameter of token obtain a concrete value according to its identification, when the token is introduced into the location $b_j(\xi_k)$. Such a combination of locations with the tokens in them, the parameters of which obtain concrete values, describes a situation for process execution.

Such an understanding of the transition procedure enables us to introduce the time aspects into procedure of control of processes and determine operations with token parameters in time dimension. The exceptional feature is the fact that the E-net transition can represent a sequence of smaller operations with transition parameters connected with the event/process. Operations are described in the transition procedure with these parameters.

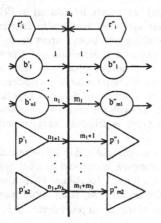

Figure 1. The E-net transition schema

The E-nets support a top down design in graphical representation manner. The hierarchical construction of dynamic model is simplified by representing macro-transition and macro-location constructions. The input locations L_i' of the transition correspond to the pre-conditions of the activity (represented by the transition in Figure 1). The output locations L_i'' correspond to post-conditions of the activity. The complex rules of transition firing are specified in the procedures of resolution locations Ψ and express the rules of process determination.

4. Description of Decision-Making Circumstances

Decision processes may be structured by a certain number of typical processes that reflect different phases of problem analysis, diagnostics, estimation, choice of the object priority, resource planning, decision realisation, etc. We consider a decision making process by analysing a space of possible problem solutions. Every decision is a result of a dynamic process influenced by many factors. In each of these stages we identify and define a problem, analyse alternative decision versions. Having estimated all the conditions and risk factors, an optimal decision is selected that is realised.

The basic sequences of functional reasoning are joined with information processes for expressing the structure of a decision making process. As a result the 'states of knowledge' are obtained. Such states are involved into the process of decision-making. This analysis is significant for identifying the strategies of information processing which are efficient at different phases of the sequences of decision-making steps.

In order to identify necessary data, control structures, and information processing possibilities, we have to imitate cognitive tasks. In each case, it is of importance to find criteria such that would make it possible to choose more useful and reliable decisions out of possible alternatives.

We have distinguished three levels of knowledge representation in the system: the semantic data model of static aspects of the target system, the model of behavioural analysis of activities in target system, and a model of decision making processes (Figure 2.). The main attention is paid to the representation of dynamic aspects of the application domain and to the specification of decision-making processes. The decision support is represented as inference engine of different levels of reasoning courses that combine the analysis of a model of dynamic changes in the domain.

The model of behavioural analysis of the target system shows the dynamics of observable processes. The adequate imitation model of the behavioural analysis allows to predict further evolution of the target system and to increase the quality of decision-making.

The multiple objective decision making deals with the analysis of information obtained from the static sub-model taking into account all possible measurement points revealed in dynamic sub-model of such a system (Figure 2.).

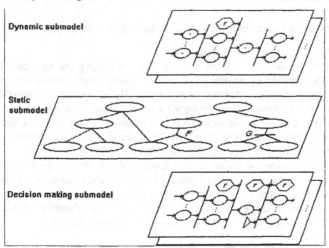

Figure 2. Three levels of knowledge representation in the decision support system

The task structure relationship with information elements, the course of decision-making processes and presentation of alternative variants of decisions are represented in this sub-model. The modelled system is regarded as direct mapping of the real enterprise system, and decisions can be based on decisive facts and followed rather deterministic rules.

4.1 INTERPRETATION OF DECISION MAKING PROCESSES BY E-NETS

The rules in a given system are interpreted by the set of transitions $A=\{a_1,a_2,...,a_n\}$ of the E-net. The locations $L=\{b_1,b_2,....,b_m\}$ are corresponded to conditions (facts), so that the condition of applicability of each rule consists of simultaneous accomplishment of a certain totality of conditions $\{b_{i1},...,b_{is}\}$. Using means of E-nets the representation of decision-making processes are very similar to the form of a production rule system, where production rules are of the form: *IF* <*conditions/premise/situation*>*THEN* <*conclusions/situation*>.

Each condition from the given totality may be a compound vector, i.e., may consist of the set of elementary conditions:

$$\vec{b_{ik}}=\{b_{ik}(\xi_{j1}),b_{ik}(\xi_{j2}),....,b_{ik}(\xi_{jn})\}.$$ The "truth" or "falsity" of various combinations of elementary conditions determines rule applicability. The condition

$$\vec{M(b_{ik})}=1$$ means that the token is in the location b_{ik} and is confirmation of this condition.

The transition having a resolution location allows the situation to be described by using various combinations of conjunctions and disjunction among such conditions:

$$\vec{M(b_{ik})}.$$

The result of a rule may be either the combination of conditions making another rule, or a final inference. The purpose of the analysis of the rule system is finding the sequence of the rules implying the fact we are interested in. The net allows representation of various procedures forming sequences of rules that may include consecutive, recurrent, parallel or mixed inferences. The whole inference process may be described as the evolution of the dynamic system. The terminal or objective set of states is interpreted by set of output (terminal) locations $\{p''_j\}$. The purpose of inference will be achieved if condition:

$$\vec{M(p''_j)}=1,$$ i.e. the state is achieved: $M(p''_j(\xi_{j1}))^\wedge M(p''_j(\xi_{j2})^\wedge...^\wedge M(^\wedge p''_j(\xi_{jn}))=1$

where $\{\xi_{jk}\}$ are the token parameters in the location p''_j.

The complexity of the decision making task consists in finding the best decision under multiple criteria. As the number of alternative increases, multi-criteria evaluation involves a mechanism for rejecting a number of those alternatives. By analysing the possible choice mechanisms (under lack of information about the importance of criteria, or assuming the criteria are equivalent), the acceptable decision variant seems to be not so easily chosen. It is expedient to make a choice according to a weighed criterion. Then the basis for choosing the decision variant is qualitative information on the relative importance of each separate criterion.

It is possible to determine the set of final inferences $\{p''_j\}=P''\subset P$ as a discrete set of decisions or alternatives (variants) available for choice. In the real choice tasks, the variants are not in arbitrary order: some variants may exclude others, while others are always accompanied. The set of criteria functions is denoted as $G=\{g_1,g_2,...,g_n\}$. The function f allows depiction of the variant g_k (p''_j) according to the criterion g_k is designated by $p''_j(\xi_k)$. We call the collection

$$\vec{p''_j}=(p''_j(\xi_1),p''_j(\xi_2),...,p''_j(\xi_d))$$ the vector estimation of the variant p''_j.

Choice according to the weighted criterion g_k, $k=1,..,d$, is based on the weight $w_j \geq 0$ which estimates characterising relative importance of the criterion.

The choice function:

$$C_w(P'')=\{p''_i\in P''\,|(\,\forall p''_j\in P'')(\,(\hat{w},p''_i)\geq(\hat{w},p''_j))\}$$ is determined by weighted sum:

$\sum_{1 \le k \le d} \hat{w}_k p''_i(\xi_k) = (\hat{w}, p''_i)$, where $\hat{w} = (w_1, ..., w_d)$.

The goals are means for orienting the organisation activities towards desired results. In the general process of creating an information control system, the stage of goal formulation is one of the main stages that affect both the general organisation structure and decisions. In addition, the process poses rather a complex inherent inner structure and mechanisms of interaction between subsystems that are frequently expressed by temporal, geographic, and space dependence conditions.

4.2 THE MODEL OF GOAL STRUCTURE OF DSS

The existence of goals is one of the main characteristics of an organisation. The goals (aims, objectives) form motivation factors in order that the tasks (problems) of the organisation can be accomplished. The model of goal structure of the organisation (e.g. enterprise) can be expressed by an asymmetric graph that has no cycles:

$S = (G, R)$, where $G = \{G_k | G_k$ is the kth goal (aim, wish, objective)$\}$, $k = 1, ..., K$.

R is the set of all the relations between goals; its elements are: $R = \{r_{kl} | r_{kl} = (G_k, G_l)\}$.

Each relation $r_{kl} = (G_k, G_l)$, $k = 1, ..., K$ ir $l = 1, ..., K$ reflects a direct contribution of the goal G_k to G_l.

On the strategic control level plans and meta-rules are formulated, functioning interference of the system identified, and the failure probability is established. These control objects determine object structures and tasks on the level of task formulation. On the level of reasoning derivation of these structures apply knowledge sources, meta-classes, and formulate derivation structures. Descriptions of subject area concepts, relations and their structures as well as the axiom system are used on the level of derivation.

In order to make a decision on estimating several criteria whose values can be formally calculate for any plan (object), one has to estimate it quantitatively. If there is a single goal G_l, then the actual value of 'action – result' is equal to the contribution into the desirable value:

If there is more than one final goal, then there is more than one actual value of the pair 'action-result'.

$$v_{ij} = \tilde{G}^{ij}_l, \text{ where } i = 1, ..., m, \ j = 1, ..., n \quad (5.1).$$

Let the goals (i.e., aims, wishes) of a decision maker correspond to a set GD:

$$GD = \{G_{d1}, G_{d2}, ..., G_{dD}\} \quad (5.2).$$

The decision-maker according the contribution to the concrete goal of the set GD measures the significance of the pair 'action-result'. If there is any way to estimate the contribution of 'action-result' to the goal, then one can estimate the unique 'action-result' value as the sum of their contributions weighted according to priority factors $\{q_{dk}(t)\}$:

$$v_{ij}(t) = q_{d1}(t)\tilde{G}^{ij}_{d1} + q_{d2}(t)\tilde{G}^{ij}_{d2} + ... + q_{dD}(t)\tilde{G}^{ij}_{dD}, \text{ where } i = 1, ..., m, j = 1, ..., n \quad (5.3)$$

Here $q_{dk}(t)$ is the goal priority factor established by the decision maker that describes a relative importance of the goal G^{ij}_{di} at a certain time moment t. The relative importance of the goal is compared with other objects in the set GD.

The goal of the manufacture enterprises is to rationally develop an ecologically clean production. It means that enterprises (e.g. factories, plants, etc.) must guarantee the manufacture of products with minimal pollution of the environment and damage to nature, not exceeding the permissible standards.

Thus we have a problem of two objectives/goals:

G_1 – increase in capacity of production and profits of the enterprise under consideration;

G_2 – decrease in the environmental pollution within the permissible limits.

The first criterion $\tilde{N}$ – the profit of production has to be maximised while the second criterion $\tilde{O}$ – the environmental pollution has to be minimised. The importance of the first criterion is determined by various economic industrial parameters. The maximisation of its importance is of direct interest to and care of the producers. The main task of our decision support system is to maintain the importance of the second criterion $\tilde{O}$ within the permissible limits and thus act on the first criterion. The $\tilde{O}$ criterion is stipulated by three factors: water pollution, air pollution and contamination of harmful solid wastes: $\tilde{O}=\{W,A,H\}$.

More in details we consider the example of the analysis of water resources and the pollution of sewage of the enterprise. The pollutants from the production are entering into the water in some types of cases. Such cases we find out by the construction of E-net distribution processes of sewage in the enterprise (Figure 3).

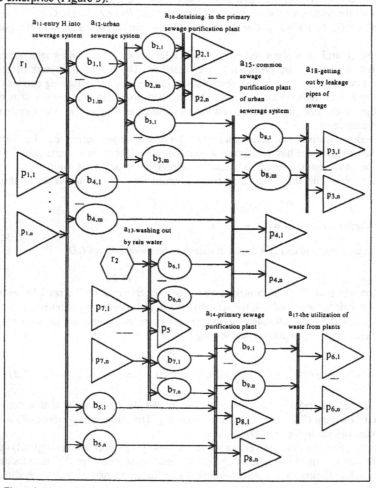

Figure 3. The E-net of distribution processes of harmful materials in the water of enterprise

The tasks and sub-processes are shown as transitions, while inputs/outputs from the processes are shown as positions of E-net.

The initial task of expertise is always data gathering, resulting in a set of observed findings.

The materials are classified by the rate of their harmfulness. Such materials (which are ecologically dangerous) are the *main decision variables* of the sewage analysis task:

H_1 – are pollutants of first rate of harmfulness into water bodies, which are especially dangerous;

H_2 – are pollutants of second rate of harmfulness;

H_3 – are pollutants of third rate of harmfulness;

H_4 – are pollutants of unidentified effect.

The highest permissible contents or interim permissible concentrations of these substances in water are established dependent on the type of the water reservoir the polluted sewage eventually gets into.

The harmful materials that are represented by peripheral locations of the E-net (in Fig. 3) are very important for evaluation of water pollution of an enterprise:

$p_{1,1},...,p_{1n}$ are materials included in water efflux;

$p_{2,1},...,p_{2,n}$ are waste materials from the primary sewage purification plant;

$p_{3,1},...,p_{3,n}$ are waste materials from the common sewage purification plant;

$p_{4,1},...,p_{4,n}$ are materials entering into open reservoirs, that are not detained in the sewerage system of the enterprise;

$p_{5,1},...,p_{5,n}$ are materials entering into open reservoirs, if there is no rainwater collection system;

$p_{6,1},...,p_{6,n}$ are utilised wastes from primary purification plants;

$p_{7,1},...,p_{7,n}$ are materials entering into rain water if they are stored openly in the territory of enterprise;

$p_{8,1},...,p_{8,n}$ are materials entering into the external reservoir from the primary sewage purification plant.

The E-net structure, which describes the decision-making process, gives visually the parameters needed for control and the control structure relation with tasks and decisions.

The highest permissible contents or interim permissible concentrations of these substances in water are established dependent on the type of water reservoir the polluted sewage gets into. The example presented in Figure 4 represents the conceptual structure of data for norms of greatest permissible concentrations of materials.

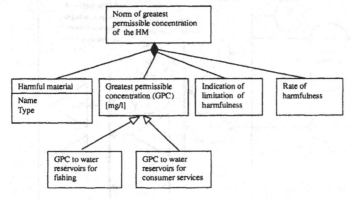

Figure 4. The static structure diagram of the norms of greatest permissible concentration of harmful materials for water reservoirs

Harmful materials, and their usage and distribution during the production process, are the information units that may be established in information system and analysed dynamically with regard to the extent of enterprise contamination.

5. The Representation of Expertise Structure

The main steps of diagnosis are suggesting a fault and undesirable performance of functioning enterprise on the basis of the problem description. Such task is highly complex, since solving a problem often involves iterative loops, backtracking, shortcuts, etc.

A large amount of measurement points at different time and conditions causing overlapping and conflict between different observations, and the inaccuracy of measurements and reports.

Another essential aspect of such application domain is their spatial dimension. While in many other application domains the problems study are within very precise and, usually, narrow framework, for instance a plant, factory or firm contamination problem deals with spatially and temporally varying phenomena with very unbounded limits.

The multiple objective decision support level deals with the analysis of information obtained from the all measurement points revealed in the dynamic sub-model of DSS. The modelled system is regarded as direct mapping of real enterprise system and decisions can be based on decisive facts and follows rather deterministic rules.

Decision support is also related with the problems of estimation of general ecological situation of the given region, the indices of pollution provided in the project, the risk factors related to preservation of links that are of biological significance and time dependent, etc.

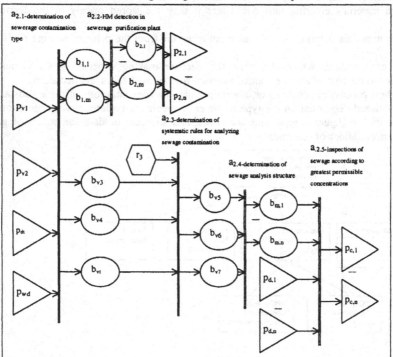

Figure 5. The E-net of evaluation making for water diagnosis task

The expertise may include the following aspects of analysis: usage of materials and natural resources in the production process; emission of harmful materials into the air and into territorial waters and soil; utilisation of waste materials from the production process; usage of the purification equipment. The structure of determination of systematic rules for analysing sewage contamination is represented by the E-net in Figure 5.

The information needed for such evaluation are represented in positions:

p_{v1} is outlet amount of sewage released into urban net;

p_{v2} is outlet amount of sewage released into open reservoir;

p_{dt} is amount of working days;

p_{dt} is time period with respect of accounting is done;

$b_{1,1} - b_{1,n}$ are materials detected in purification plant of enterprise;

$b_{v2,1} - b_{v2,n}$ are amounts of harmful materials accumulated in purification equipment;

b_{v3} is amount of sewage released into urban net per day;

b_{v4} is the amount of sewage released into open reservoir per day;

b_{vt} is the type of sewage

b_{v5} is the established character of analysis;

b_{v6} is a frequency of analysis;

b_{v7}– is the co-ordinates of inspection of sewage according to the water receiver;

$b_{m,1} - b_{m,n}$ are materials which may estimate;

$b_{c,1} - b_{c,n}$ are results of determination of sewage contamination according to greatest permissible concentration norms for separate type of receivers;

$p_{d,1} - b_{d,n}$ are norms of contamination (greatest permissible concentration-GPC) of the harmful materials (HM).

The rule r_3 is applied in E-net for $a_{2,3}$ transition description is specified as in Table 1. Rain and mixed water is treated as sewage from industrial processes.

Table 1. Sample of rule for determining the frequency and character of sewage analysis

IF			THEN	
Sewage			Character of sewage analysis	Frequency of sewage analysis
Character	Outlet amount of sewage			
	Released into urban net [m³/day]	Released into open reservoir [m³/day]		
From industrial processes	$b_{v3} > 500$		Common analysis and determination of specific obligatory materials	Once a month
	$100 \leq b_{v3} \leq 500$		Common analysis and determination of specific obligatory materials	Once a quarter
	$b_{v3} < 100$		Analysis not carried out	
		$b_{v4} \geq 100$	Extended analysis	Once a month
		$b_{v4} \leq 100$	Extended analysis	Once a quarter
From consumer services	$b_{v3} > 500$		Dynamic characteristic of separate specific materials	Once a month
	$100 \leq b_{v3} \leq 500$		Dynamic characteristic of separate specific materials	Once a quarter
	$b_{v3} < 100$		Average contamination characteristic	Once a quarter
		$b_{v4} \geq 100$	Dynamic characteristic of separate specific materials	Once a month
		$b_{v4} \leq 100$	Extended analysis	Once a quarter

In conformity with the values of analysis variables and exceeding permissible standards the decision support system has to make one of these following decisions:

(1) to permit the functioning of enterprise and give the permission in which the drinking water amount to be used during certain time period is determined as well as the amounts and characteristic of sewage into appropriate water collection system or water reservoir;

(2) to impose a fine on a enterprise for environmental pollution within certain range;

(3) to restrict the functioning of an enterprise production processes.

6. Conclusions

Dynamic environment have a significant dynamic component, which means that the conditions of the real system at the time the decision is made, are the results of all the past history of the system and influence its subsequent behaviours. Some issues for a qualitative knowledge representation including the acquisition and representation stages are considered.

The approach of applying E-net formal means to conceptual modelling of dynamic aspects of the domain and to specifying decision making allowed expressing the behavioural aspects of processes in a hierarchical construction and levelling manner without making complicated schemes. The functional requirement specification interrelated with the use and analysis of information structures and the strategy of decision-making processes. The decision making sub-model represents all reasoning courses at different levels of detailing. The decision support generates the alternative variants of decisions at actual conditions. The inference engine (represented by using E-nets) applies the knowledge to the solution of an actual problem and it acts as a control system.

References

1. Aamodt, A. *A Knowledge-Intensive, Integrated Approach to Problem Solving and Sustained Learning.* Knowledge Engineering and Image Processing Group, University of Trondheim, 1991.

2. Breuker, J. and Wielinga, B. Models of expertise in knowledge acquisition. In G. Giuda (ed.), *Topics in Expert System Design*, Elsevier, North-Holland, 1989, pp. 265-295.

3. Chaturvedi, A.R. Acquiring implicit knowledge in a complex domain. *Expert Systems with Applications.* 6(1), 1994, pp. 23-36.

4. Dzemydiene, D. An extension of E-nets for the specification and effective planning and management of system automatic control. *Computer Programming,* 12, Institute of Mathematics and Informatics, Vilnius, 1988, pp.94-104 (in Russian).

5. Dzemydiene, D. Data reliability problems for impartial multi-criteria decision support. *Informatica,* 3(3), 1992, pp. 393-417.

6. Dzemydiene, D. Representation of decision making processes for the ecological evaluation system. *Annals of Operation Research,* 51, 1994, pp. 349-366.

7. Dzemydiene, D. and Pranevichius, H. Description of a dynamically changing environment in a decision support system. *Proceedings of the Baltic Workshop on National Infrastructure Databases: Problems, Methods, Experiences,* 2, Vilnius, 1994, pp. 102-111.

8. Dzemydiene, D. Conceptual architecture for dynamic domain representation. *Mathematical Modelling and Analysis,* 5, Vilnius, Technika, 2000, pp. 55-66.

9. Noe, J.D. and Nutt, G.J. Macro E-nets for representation of parallel systems. *IEEE Transactions on Computers,* C-22(5), 1973, pp. 718-727.

10. Pranevichius, H. Specification and analysis of real-time systems by means of aggregate approach. In *Proc. of the 3rd Baltic Summer School on Information Technology and System Engineering,* Kaunas, Technologija, 1995, pp. 60-87.

11. Schreft, M. Behaviour modelling by stepwise refining behaviour diagrams. In H. Kangassalo (ed.), *Entity-Relationship Approach: the Core of Conceptual Modelling,* North-Holland, 1991, pp. 119-134.

An OOAD Approach to Resolve Conflicting Management of Shared Objects among Components

Izuru Kume

Nara Institute of Science and Technology,
Takayama-cho 8916-5, Ikoma, Nara 630-0101, Japan
E-mail: kume@is.aist-nara.ac.jp

Abstract

Component-based development is an important and a practical topic of software engineering. Object-oriented analysis and design (OOAD) approach, and component-based development go particularly well together because the former provides software architecture that increases the merit of component-based development. However, Components that work well independently do not always work correctly. Often, it is because unwilling dependencies among the components are introduced. In this paper we study a kind of dependency caused by inconsistent management of objects that are shared by several components. We propose an OOAD approach to specify disciplined management of shared objects.

Keywords: object-oriented analysis and design, UML, object sharing.

1. Introduction

Recently component-based system development[1] [25, 26] and Object-Oriented Analysis and Design (OOAD) approach [16, 28, 22, 4] are important topics of software engineering. As shown by successful practical examples component-based system development does decrease implementors' effort. Moreover, component-based system development and object approaches go particularly well together. OOAD approaches show the architecture that describes the collaboration among components and their responsibility [14, 3, 28]. An architecture is also useful for system development, reconstruction and evolution because it helps developers to decide which component should be developed, reused and replaced in the analysis level or design level [9, 15].

On the other hand, it is difficult to guarantee that a system which is built by assembling components works correctly without any conflict among the components. In [10] conflicts among code components are explained as mismatches of architectural assumptions of components and connectors. Several cases of mismatches are listed and explained in detail with examples from a real project. In this paper we pay attention to an example shown in [10] where a conflict occurs by the inconsistent management of shared object. The example shows a management conflict of visualisation objects with hierarchical structure. In this example, the visualisation objects are intended to be shared by several code components. One code component, which plays the role of user interface management

---

[1]Throughout this paper, we use a term "components" to indicate reusable artifacts including program codes, design diagrams and so on. In order to indicate a reusable program code, we use a term "code component". The term "component-based system development" means a development style by reusing, integrating and replacing existing components.

J. Barzdins and A. Caplinskas (eds.), Databases and Information Systems, 221–235.

system, assumes that each visualisation object is manipulated through its parent object in the hierarchy of the visualisation objects. On the other hand, others try to manipulate the object directly without any notice to the code component that assumes the top-down management. The code components are mutually dependent because their acts on the shared objects affect each other.

Even if we adopt an OOAD approach or other object technology, this kind of dependency doesn't usually come to the surface. Suppose that two code components share an object which is passed from one code component to another through several other code components after a series of independent tasks. The dependency of the two code components will not come to the surface at the design phase because they have no explicit association and they don't participate in the same collaboration.

The contribution of this paper is to propose a way to solve this problem. In the following, we list the conditions for a desirable solution.

- We need a specification in the analysis and design model so that system designers can decrease the chance to create dependency among code components.

- The specification should be simple and has same style for any kind of data and application logic.

- The specification should, if possible, tell the dependency among code components which otherwise doesn't come to the surface.

Then we explain why we select these conditions. The first condition tells that our solution should be integrated into an OOAD approach. The specification should make it clear which code components do a collaborative task through shared data objects and which are not. The code components are introduced to realize some tasks expressed in an analysis model. Whether they collaborate or not is obviously decided in analysis models. Our approach proposes to start by analysing the dependency among the tasks caused by shared data objects. Our basic idea is to prevent update operations on the same object for the tasks that are not intended to cooperate each other[2]. The second condition guarantees uniform specification means, which means we don't use expressions, for example, logical formulae that include model-specific data types.

The last condition is important. Whether the dependency arise or not depends on the implementation of the code components. It is possible to reflect the implementation detail in the design model. Then, however, we face the famous dilemma [8] that if we do so, we lose the encapsulation of the code component which is needed to make the code component reusable. We need a novel idea that indicate the correct implementation but doesn't touch the implementation detail.

2. Background and Related Work

The types of conflicts in components integration range so widely. In [10] they are classified based on assumption mismatch. There are four kinds of conflicting assumptions: *nature of components* (behaviour inside of component), *nature of connectors* (collaboration among components) , *global architecture* and *construction process*. The problem of **conflicting management of shared object** that we study in this paper belongs to the first three categories. First, shared objects are managed inside of components. Second, sharing arises because there are object exchanges among the

---

[2]We focus on the update context of shared objects rather than sharing itself.

components. (This is not pointed out in [10].) Third, however, there might not be any explicit collaboration among the components after the exchanges. We need to think the situation as a problem of global architectural structure. (This is not pointed out in [10] also.) In this paper, we only deal with the problem of shared object that we solve by our architectural approach.

Recently pre-condition and post-condition are thought to be a part of interfaces of components, called *Contracts* [11]. The concepts of contracts and invariant are integrated into OOAD approaches that support component-based development [7, 13]. Several OOAD approaches offer the ways to describe global architecture assumption. In [2] existential dependency among classes is thought as a basic modelling concept and represented by a special notation. In [27] constraints are introduced into frameworks in order to integrate components on a large scale where all participating components correctly cooperate with each other. Dependency among components arises in a process of system evolution. The solution in [20] is to express the changes on components explicitly, thus make it possible to do several kinds of automatic conflict checking.

The above approaches are quite useful to cope with a range of problems that appear in analysis or design level. However, they can't so well cope with the conflicts that are brought by wrong implementation. We adopt a solution to check implementation by warning unwilling dependencies of analysis and design components. Apart from OOAD, to control object sharing is a big problem. The concept of *composite object* is introduced as a solution [18, 5]. Its basic idea is to control the management of the objects called *component objects* which are parts of a unique object, *composite object*. This approach is only applicable to the cases that we can easily find the relationship between component objects and their composite object.

For more general cases, there are several approaches that use type systems to restrict the management of shared object [12, 1, 21, 6, 19]. These approaches can cope with a wider range of case than composite object approach and we integrate it into OOAD approaches. In [19] we proposed a way to specify the restriction of shared data management by assigning annotation called *access modes*. Though the notation is very similar to other type-based approaches, our notation generates a code for the test phase that does extra runtime checking of shared data management in a component. The main contribution of this paper is to make a bridge between our previous work and OOAD approaches.

3. Motivating Example

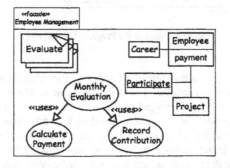

Figure 1. Package for Employee Management

Throughout this paper we use Unified Modelling Language (UML) [23] to describe our example. We borrow a term *component systems* from [17] to indicate the packaged components that are reused as a unit to do a task. In general, a component system contains three kinds of types[3], entity types, control types and interface types. It also contains use cases, design classes and code components (a collection of implementation classes). In this paper we don't deal with interface types. The contents of our component system and the way to develop it are explained in section 4. In the following we see two component systems, which seem to be independent each other but bring an unexpected conflict when they are integrated as the parts of a system.

The first component system Employee Management in Figure 3. provides a function of the accounting management of employees. The figure shows that the component system includes a use case diagram, code components and a class diagram. A code component Evaluate implements the task of Monthly Evaluation use case in the figure. The class diagram illustrates that an employee participates in a project and has his career record. We represent the participation as an association class Participate so that we can record the information about participation of employees such as position, working attitude and etc. Career is the class for the working record of Employee. In the task Monthly Evaluation, the value of Salary is calculated based on the information of Career. There is an implicit assumption that for each Employee his participation in a project is preserved until Monthly Evaluation is executed by Evaluate. In the architecture of the class diagram, it means that the association class Participate is preserved.

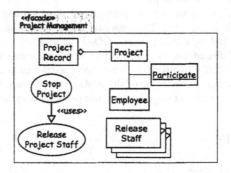

Figure 2. Package for Project Management

Employee may appear in other component systems. Figure 3. shows the appearance of Employee in another component system Project Management. The main task of this component system is to manage the members of a project (an instance of Project). An Employee instance appears as a member of a project. When a project finishes, its termination is recorded and all members are released, which is achieved by a code component Release Project Staff. Each Employee instance itself is not modified at all, but is only removed from the finished project. At the first glance, it looks that the two component systems Employee Management and Project Management can be combined in a new component system Enterprise Management without

---

[3]Throughout this paper the term "types" is used to mean "classes in the analysis phase" [17].

any trouble.

Suppose that the task in Employee Management to set Career references some attributes of Participate in the execution of Monthly Evaluation. Then a conflict arises. When a project finishes, all members are released. From the viewpoint of Employee, it means that the association class Participate is deleted and the information of its project participation is lost. This situation is illustrated in Figure 3.. The figure shows a runtime situation that Release Staff affects the execution of Evaluate because both code components deal with the same instance of Participate. Therefore, there arises the mismatch of architectural assumption between Employee Management and Project Management because of the shared instance of Participate. The former component system assumes that no one else deals with the instance of Participate while the latter never recognises the assumption of Evaluate.

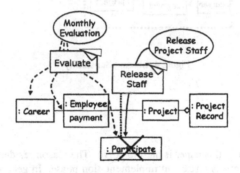

Figure 3. Management Conflict

It looks that such a situation can easily be avoided by careful checking of analysis and design models without any special solution. It might be correct if we design the system from scratch. However, systems are not always built from scratch but often are developed by restructuring existing systems. For example, in the old system the information in Career contains only the age and the years for which an Employee worked. After the restructuring, the information about project participation is considered to be a part of Career. For another example, there were several kinds of employees and those who participated in a project were paid their salary according to an accounting system different from Employee Management. The system was restructured so that the employment style was unified and one accounting system is now applied to all employees. We think that it looks quite hard to examine and make component dependencies explicit for every kind of system restructuring.

From the consideration above, we try not to make all dependencies explicit but to prevent unexpected conflicts with respect to shared object management. A component protected in this meaning is called *sharing sensible* or we say that *the component has sharing sensibility*. Once a component has sharing sensibility, it recognises the objects to be referred or modified by itself and its collaborators (if any) only. The component system holds instances of the types. As we show in Figure 3., any trial to modify the instances by any components other than itself or its collaborators is forbidden by default. Notice that sharing sensibility is represented in the models in analysis phase and design phase but works in their implementation. In our example, Participate instances should be surrounded by `Employee Management` as long as the instance of `Employee` that holds the `Participate` instances are subject of employee management.

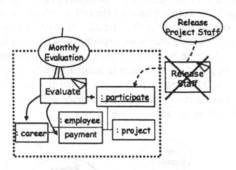

Figure 4. Sharing Sensibility

4. Process Scenario

The problem shown in this paper is hard to solve. The reason resides in the gap between the representation levels of analysis phase and implementation phase. In general, the representation of model elements in the analysis phase is simple and their nature is clear. It is easy to find the possibility of the conflicting management of shared object. In the implementation phase, the simplicity is lost. An analysis model is repeatedly refined; the original model elements gain more complex representation and many new model elements are possibly added in the design phase. We must keep the sharing sensibility in the early analysis model in the result of the refinement. Figure 4. shows an example of refinement. The class diagram in the refined model has more classes and associations than the corresponding diagram in the original model. [4] In general, given these two diagrams in the models before and after refinement, it is difficult to show the correspondence among their components unless we investigate the refinement process. The intention of system analysts tends to be lost and implementors may write a code that causes conflicts in shared data management.

In order to solve this problem, we propose an OOAD method that helps system analysts indicate their intention also in later development phases. Our method has two core parts: (1) a refinement style from abstract model elements to more concrete ones, and (2) automatic test code generation for the dynamic check of conflicts with respect to shared data management. The generated test code works in a test run to show runtime errors caused by the management of shared object. These two parts work as a pipeline. Roughly speaking, the first part enables the development of sharing sensible components. In general, one of the results of the design phase is the design interfaces of implementation classes. Our refinement method assigns additional information about object sharing [5] to the interfaces. This is the result of the first core part of our method. The interfaces with the additional information are

---

[4]Of course, the less abstract model may have simpler structure. For such cases, our proposal is valid, although in this paper we focus on simple cases only in order to simplify our discussion.

[5]A kind of type system called *access mode*

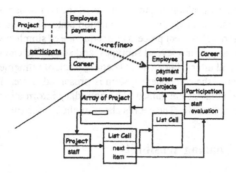

Figure 5. Refinement Example

called *an exclusive schema*. We need an exclusive schema for the automatic test code generation. We explain exclusive schema in detail in section 6.

Implementors might write a code that introduces conflicting management of shared object. It is desirable to detect the code in the test phase. We realize the run-time check by generating a sharing sensible test code. It is achieved by automatically inserting pieces of test code into the implementation classes according to the information generated by the first process. The second part has been already discussed in our previous work [19] and we put more emphasis on the first part in this paper.

Jacobson's Reuse-driven Software Engineering Business (RSEB) [17] deals with component-based system development in UML. The UML representation of a component is a package called *a facade package* that contains a code components and other design artifacts. In our method, a component is represented as a package also. Our method proposes guidelines for the design of sharing sensible component packages. In the rest of this section, we explain the rough sketch of our design process. The important details are explained using concrete example in section 5.

The process of our method begins when system analysts find several tasks cooperating through the management of a group of shared data objects. They might find such tasks and shared data objects when they decompose a task, such as `Employee Management` in section 3., into several subtasks or when they extend an existing system by adding new functions. Such cooperation can be found at a stage in analysis and design phase[6]. Each of the cooperating tasks is represented as a use case, or it is included in a task that is represented by a use case. Such use cases are embodied later by class diagrams, interaction diagrams, and etc. We say that *the use cases and these artifacts belong to the cooperating tasks*.

In our method a package is introduced in order to include all artifacts that belong to particular cooperating tasks. This package is called *a component system*. It is obvious that the component system includes the class diagrams of the object sharing for the cooperation. The purpose of the component system is to restrict the treatment of the shared data object by specifying an architectural boundary that tells which object belongs inside and which are not. When the data objects are shared and updated outside of the boundary, it possibly causes a conflict. Such a boundary is easy to form in a simple model in the earlier phases of a system development cycle. The boundary in the earlier phases should be preserved in later phases as analysts' intention.

---

[6]The difference between analysis phase and design is not very clear. UML doesn't provide any notational difference in these phases [24] later than the analysis phase.

In the progress of system development, the contents of the component system are refined several times in order to give implementation details. In our method static class diagrams are important in the refinement process. We regard refinement process as a sequence of simple actions such as introduction of a new type, separation of a type into several subtypes, and so on. We can get the correspondence of the model elements before and after refinement by keeping track of refinement actions. The boundary specified at the introduction of the component system is preserved. After the refinement process the interfaces of implementation classes are gained. The boundary information is translated in the form of exclusive schema mentioned above. The details about exclusive schema is explained in section 6.

5.   Refinement with Sharing Sensibility

5.1   SHARING PACKAGE

In this section, we explain what artifacts in a component system constitute a specification of sharing sensibility. First, we specify a collection of use cases. It is called a *session* of the component system. Use cases in the same session may be dependent with respect to the management of shared objects. In other words, they may share data objects to accomplish a task. We assume that the component developer take care of the dependency caused by the shared objects. On the other hand, use cases inside of the session should not be affected by those outside of the session through shared objects. A session forms a boundary of use cases that accomplish a task using shared data objects.

Second, we need to select the types, associations and attributes in the component system that are not to be changed by the tasks outside of the session. We call those selected model elements *shared elements of the session*. The component system may be designed without considering the changes on the shared elements that happen outside of the session.

Next we explain the process of our specification more precisely than section 4. The modelling process of a component system with respect to sharing sensibility begins by the specification of a *sharing package*. A sharing package includes a session and its shared elements. For our specification we introduce several stereotypes. A sharing package is assigned a stereotype ≪ *sharing* ≫. We show an example of sharing package in Figure 5.1. The session specified here consists of only one use case **Monthly Evaluation**. Types, associations and attributes assigned a stereotype ≪ *managed* ≫ are the subjects of the exclusive management by the session of the package. In this case, attribute **payment**, the association between **Employee** and **Career**, and association type **Participate** are the shared elements. Any update operations on these elements outside of the **Monthly Evaluation** session should be refused.

An association class of UML is a class to represent an association. When we select an association class as a sharing elements, it means that the association represented by the class is also selected as a shared element. When, instead of the whole association class, only some of its attribute are selected, the represented association are not the subject of exclusive management. In our example, the association between **Employee** and **Project** should not be broken by any operations outside of session of **Monthly Evaluation**.

5.2   RECEPTIONISTS

Given an analysis model and a sharing package, we introduce several new analysis types called *receptionists* as the first refinement step. A receptionist represents a session. There must be at least one receptionist for a session, and no single receptionist can represent more than one session. Figure 5.2

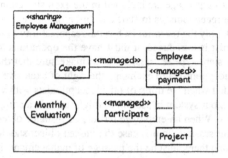

Figure 6. Sharing Package for Employee Management

shows that a receptionist named **Evaluate** is introduced. A receptionist must be connected by at least one class with a newly introduced association. The association is called an *exclusive association*. Exclusive associations are designated by an assigned stereotype ≪ *exclusive* ≫.

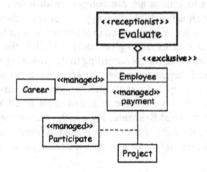

Figure 7. Introduction of Receptionist

A receptionist has three roles with respect to sharing sensibility. First role is similar to that of composite object. It decides the shared elements that should be under the exclusive management of the session it represents. All types, attributes and associations that can be reached from a receptionist by passing its exclusive association are said to be in *the exclusive connection* of the receptionist. In the implementation phase, the exclusive connection is represented as a collection of instance variables that can be reached from the instance variable that is the implementation of the exclusive association. We call the collection *an instance of the exclusive connection.*

The receptionist thus restrict the collection of all objects to be taken care of in order to guarantee the sharing sensibility. In terms of the instance of the exclusive connection, sharing sensibility means that for any instance variable corresponding to a shared element, its value can be changed only in the session specified in the sharing package. We can introduce the exclusive association between the receptionist and any types. However, the introduction must satisfy a constraint that all shared elements specified in the sharing package are included in the exclusive connection.

The second role of the receptionist is to start execution of the session specified in the sharing package. In terms of OOAD, only the receptionist has the responsibility to manage its exclusive connection. When the receptionist is introduced, it must have the operations to start the corresponding session [7]. We may assign a stereotype ≪ *session* ≫ to make sure that the action embodies a session. The third role of the receptionist is to exchange the right of exclusive management with object exchanges. This role is needed when we think of other receptionists with which the receptionist exchange objects. For example, our system in section 3. might include a component system to manage the data of retired employees. When an employee retires, its instance object is passed to the receptionist to execute a retirement session. In this case the passed object should not be managed by the **Evaluate** session any more and there must be the passage of management right of the passed object.

5.3 REFINEMENT

As we explained in section 4., a refinement process is a sequence of simple refinement steps. In [7], refinement gives details to class diagrams, splits an action in interaction diagrams into a sequence of more simpler actions among several objects or inside of an object, and introduces intermediate states in state charts. We must pay attention to the steps to refine actions and static structure diagrams. Refinement steps with respect to actions are not complex with respect to sharing sensibility. We only have to take care so that an action with stereotype ≪ *session* ≫ always starts the successive collaboration to implement a session. We may need to introduce actions to exchange the management right of an object in the instance of its sharing connection. When the action is represented as an operation, assign a stereotype ≪ *exclusive* ≫ according to the following rule. When it gains the right to manage the object passed as an argument, assign ≪ *exclusive* ≫ to the position of the argument. If the object returned from the receptionist with management right, assign ≪ *exclusive* ≫ at the position of return value. In Figure 5.3 we can see an intermediate result of a refinement process. The receptionist has a session trigger named **Evaluate**. It gains the management right of the object passed as an argument of **hire**. It loses the right of the object passed to other receptionists as an argument of **retire**. Notice that the management right is passed with a stereotype ≪ *exclusive* ≫.

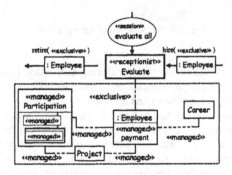

Figure 8. Result of Refinement

As a result of the above design process, we can specify for each session the timing to catch and release the right of exclusive management of shared objects by assigning ≪ *exclusive* ≫ in operation declarations. We can also specify at some abstraction level the connection between a receptionist and the objects under its exclusive management. At implementation level, this connection will be described by in terms of instance variables of implementation classes. It is achieved by the refinement of class diagrams. As we explained in section 4. the sharing sensibility specification should be translated properly. In this paper, we pose a constraint on refinement steps that the number of model elements never decrease and different model elements remains different after any refinement step. A model element can be refined only in the way that it gains more complex structure, or new model entities are introduced. At the same time, the sets of model elements corresponding to different model elements must be disjoint. Though there are many kinds of refinement steps, the thing we must keep in our mind is simple, "A shared element only change its shape into one or several shared elements". Here we explain it using examples.

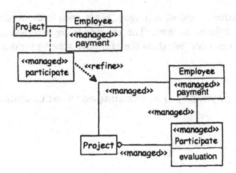

Figure 9. Refinement of Association Class

Figure 5.3 shows a refinement of association class **Participate**. As a result of this step, three associations are introduced to connect each pair of **Employee**, **Project** and **Participate**. In this case, we think that the association between **Employee** and **Project** are split into the new three associations. Because the original association was a shared element, the new associations are assigned a stereotype ≪ *managed* ≫. Figure 5.3 shows a refinement step of **Participate** itself. It has a new name and a type of its sub-object inside. In this case, we assign ≪ *managed* ≫ to the renamed type, the new type inside, and the association among them. We continue such refinement steps until we have one-to-one corresponding between types and implementation classes, between actions and methods, and between associations and instance variables.

6. Operation Refinement by Access Mode

After all refinement steps, we implement classes and an exclusive schema as explained in section 4. should be generated. The result of a refinement process doesn't affect the implementation of classes except for the fact that each receptionist class should be Singleton in order to keep the uniqueness of session [9].

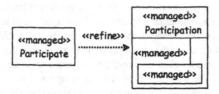

Figure 10. Refinement of Class

Stereotypes ≪ *exclusive* ≫ and ≪ *managed* ≫ assigned to the model elements also appear as keywords in the resulting exclusive schema. The key words are assigned to the types of parameters, return values and instance variables. We show the exclusive schema for our example in Figure 11.

```
class Employee{
  Money [managed] payment; // <<managed>> attribute

  ...

}

class EvaluateReceptionist{
  public ListOfEmployee [exclusive] employees;
  // <<exclusive>> association

  public evaluateAll();  // <<session>> action
  public hire(Employee [exclusive]); // <<exclusive>> parameter

  ...

}
```

Figure 11. Exclusive schema for employee management

Notice that only two stereotypes ≪ *managed* ≫ and ≪ *exclusive* ≫ are rest. Only receptionist classes have ≪ *exclusive* ≫ instance variables. Therefore, ≪ *receptionist* ≫ is needed only for explanation of the nature of types in the analysis and design phases. Stereotype ≪ *session* ≫ is not needed neither, for a similar reason.

The semantics of assigned keywords and how to translate implementation code for test phase, are explained in our previous work [19]. To show in detail and formally how these assigned keywords works and why they guarantee exclusive management needs future work. In this paper, we only address key points.

Now we briefly explain how the transformed code components work at the test phase. The assignment of an object to an instance variable with `exclusive` succeeds if and only if the right of its exclusive management is released by the other receptionists. The successful assignment means the passed object now participates in the task of the receiver (a receptionist). Each object that is the subject of exclusive management holds the information who has the right to manage it. The `exclusive` keywords assigned at the position of argument or return value change this information. At the moment that the object is passed to someone with `exclusive` keyword, the management right is released. In this situation anyone but only one object can assign the object to an `exclusive` instance variable. At the moment of assignment, the management right goes to the object who has the instance variable. After that no one can gain the management right unless the new owner release it.

As for the object, say object A, which is held directly in an `exclusive` instance variable, who owns A's management right is obvious. Then, how about those objects linked from A? Should and can the owner of A claim the management right of those objects.Those objects might be shared by other objects who are their potential owners. Our answer is that the owner of A should and can claim their management right also. We solved this problem in [19], although in an informal way. We pose a restriction that in order to do an update operation on an object, the updated object must be accessed along a link that starts from an `exclusive` instance variable of the right owner. In this paper we release the restriction so that only those instance variables with a keyword `managed` are the subject of restricted management. However this slight modification affect the explanation just shown above.

7. Conclusions

In this paper we did two contributions. First, we pointed out a problem in the combination of code components where they affect each other unconsciously by the same object that is accidently shared. We pointed out the difficulty to assume and prevent such a conflict even if OOAD approaches are combined. Second, we propose our OOAD approach to solve this problem. Our approach make it enable to decrease dependency of a component system under development with respect to shared data management.

One of the essence of our solution is a specification means for the disciplined management of shared objects in analysis and design models. Another essence is our refinement process. As a result of a refinement process, we can gain an exclusive schema that is useful for the test of code combination with respect to shared data management.

There are many topics to be done as our future research. We must consider the case that we must resolve a mismatch of type representation. In this paper we implicitly assume an ideal situation that there is no difference in the representation of shared data management. We didn't consider the limitation of the usefulness of our exclusive schema neither. Because it is not possible that the gained exclusive schema tells all possibility of unexpected object sharing. Therefore we must propose the guidelines so that the exclusive schema can tell useful results as much as possible.

References

1. Almeida, P. S. Balloon types: Controlling sharing of state in data types. In *ECOOP*, Lecture Notes in Computer Science, **1241**, 1997.

2. van Baelen, S., Steegmans, J. L. E., and Swennen, B. Constraints in object-oriented analysis. In *JSSST Int. Symp. Object Technologies for Advanced Software,* Lecture Notes in Computer Science, **742**, KANAZAWA, Springer-Verlag, November 1993, pp. 393-407.

3. Beck, K. and Cunningham, W. A laboratory for teaching object-oriented thinking. In *ACM OOPSLA,* 1989, pp. 1-6.

4. Booch, G. *Object Oriented Analysis and Design with Applications.* The Benjamin Cummings Publishing Co. Inc., second edition, 1994.

5. Civello, F. Roles for composite objects in object-oriented analysis and design. In *ACM OOPSLA,* 1993, pp. 376-393.

6. Clarke, D. G., Potter, J. M., and Noble, J. Ownership types for flexible alias protection. In *ACM OOPSLA,* 1998, pp. 48-64.

7. D'Souza, D. F. and Wills, A. C. *Objects, Components, and Frameworks with UML: The Catalysis Approach.* Addison Wesley, 1998.

8. Edwards, S. H., Weide, B. W., and Hollingsworth, J. A framework for detecting interface violations in component-based software. In *IEEE Int. Conference on Software Reuse,* 1998, pp. 46-55.

9. Gamma, E., Helm, R., Johnson, R., and Vissides, J. *Design Patterns.* ADDISON-WESLEY, 1994.

10. Garlan, D. and Ockerbloom, R. A. J. Architectural mismatch: why reuse is so hard. *IEEE Software,* **12,** November 1995, pp. 17-26.

11. Helm, R., Holland, I. M., and Gangopadhyay, D. Contracts: specifying behavioral compositon in object-oriented systems. In *ECOOP/OOPSLA,* 1990, pp. 169-180.

12. Hogg, J. Islands: aliasing protection in object-oriented languages. In *ACM OOPSLA,* 1991, pp. 271-285.

13. Hollingsworth, J., Sreerama, S., Weide, B. W., and Zhupanov, S. RESOLVE components in ada and c++. In *ACM SIGSOFT Software Engineering Notes,* October 1994, pp. 52-63.

14. Jacobson, I. A large commercial success story based on objects. *Object Magazine,* May 1996.

15. Jacobson, I. Succeeding with objects: reuse in reality. *Object Magazine,* July 1996.

16. Jacobson, I., Christerson, M., Jonsson, P., and Övergaard, G. *Object-Oriented Software Engineering: A Use Case Driven Approach.* The ACM Press, 1992.

17. Jacobson, I., Griss, M., and Jonsson, P. *Software Reuse.* ADDISON WESLEY Longman Limited, 1997.

18. Kim, W., Bertino, E., and Garza, J. F. Composite objects revised. In *ACM SIGMOD Record,* **18,** 1989, pp. 337-347.

19. Kume, I. Semantically consistent system integration on object-oriented databases. In *International Conference on Management of Data,* 1998.

20. Mens, T., Lucas, C., and Steyaert, P. Supporting disciplined reuse and evolution of UML models. In *The Unified Modeling Language,* Lecture Notes in Computer Science, **1618,** Springer-Verlag, 1998, pp. 378-392.

21. Noble, J., Vitek, J., and Potter, J. Flexible alias protection. In *ECOOP,* 1998.

22. Rumbaugh, J., Blaha, M., Premerlani, W., Eddy, F., and Lorensen, W. *Object-Oriented Modeling and Design.* Prentice Hall, 1991.

23. Rumbaugh, J., Jacobson, I., and Booch, G. *The Unified Modeling Language Reference Manual.* Addison-Wesley, 1999.

24. Rational Software, Microsoft, Hewlett-Packard, Oracle, Sterling Software, MCI Systemhouse, Unisys, ICON Computing, IntelliCorp, i Logix, IBM, ObjecTime, Platinum Technology, Ptech, Taskon, Reich Technologies, and Softeam. *UML Summary, version 1.1,* September 1997.

25. Szyperski, C. *Component Software*. Addison-Wesley, 1997.

26. Udell, J. Componentware. *BYTE*, May 1994, pp. 46-56.

27. Wills, A. Frameworks and component-based development. In *International Conference on Object Oriented Information Systems*, 1996, pp. 413-430.

28. Wirfs-Brock, R., Wilkerson, B., and Wiener, L. *Designing Object-Oriented Software*. Prentice Hall, 1990.

Object-Oriented Design Frameworks: Formal Specification and Some Implementation Issues

Ivica Crnkovic

Department of Computer Engineerig, Mälardalen University
721 23 Västerås, Sweden
E-mail: Ivica.Crnkovic@mdh.se

Juliana Küster Filipe*

Abt. Informationssysteme, Informatik, Technische Universität Braunschweig
Postfach 3329, D-38023 Braunschweig, Germany
E-mail: J.Kuester-Filipe@tu-bs.de

Magnus Larsson

ABB Automation Products AB, LAB
721 59 Västerås, Sweden
E-mail: Magnus.Larsson@mdh.se

Kung-Kiu Lau

Department of Computer Science, University of Manchester
Manchester M13 9PL, United Kingdom
E-mail: kung-kiu@cs.man.ac.uk

Abstract

In component-based software development, object-oriented design (OOD) frameworks are increasingly recognised as better units of reuse than objects. This is because OOD frameworks are groups of interacting objects, and as such they can better reflect practical systems in which objects tend to have more than one role in more than one context. In this paper, we show how to formally specify OOD frameworks, and briefly discuss their implementation and configuration management.

Keywords: object-oriented design frameworks, component-based software development.

1. Introduction

Object-Oriented Design (OOD) frameworks are groups of (interacting) objects. For example, in the CBD (Component-based Software Development) methodology *Catalysis* [10], a driver may be represented as the OOD framework shown in Figure 1.[1] A driver is a person who drives a car, or in

---

*The second author was supported by the DFG under Eh 75/11-2 and partially by the EU under ESPRIT-IV WG 22704 ASPIRE.

[1] *Catalysis* uses the UML notation, see e.g. [21].

J. Barzdins and A. Caplinskas (eds.), Databases and Information Systems, 237–251.

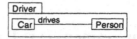

Figure 1. The Driver OOD framework

OOD terminology, a driver is a framework composed of a car object and a person object, linked by a 'drives' association (or attribute).

OOD frameworks are increasingly recognised as better units of reuse in software development than objects (see e.g. [12, 20]). The reason for this is that in practical systems, objects tend to have more than one role in more than one context, and OOD frameworks can capture this, whereas existing OOD methods (e.g. Fusion [6] and Syntropy [8]) cannot. The latter use classes or objects as the basic unit of design or reuse, and are based on the traditional view of an object, as shown in Figure 2, which regards an object as a closed entity with one fixed role. On the other hand, OOD frameworks

Figure 2. Traditional view of an object

allow objects that play different roles in different frameworks to be composed by composing OOD frameworks. In *Catalysis*, for instance, this is depicted in Figure 3.

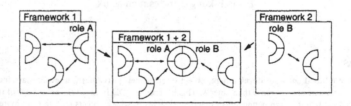

Figure 3. Objects by composing OOD frameworks

For example, a person can play the roles of a driver and of a guest at a motel simultaneously. These roles are shown separately in the PersonAsDriver and PersonAsGuest OOD frameworks in Figure 4. If we compose these two frameworks, then we get the PersonAsDriverGuest OOD framework as shown in Figure 5. In this OOD framework, a person object plays two roles, and is a composite object of the kind depicted in Figure 3.

OOD frameworks should play a crucial role in the design and implementation of next-generation component-based software systems. In this paper, we show how to formally specify them, and briefly discuss their implementation (in COM) and configuration management.

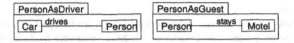

Figure 4. PersonAsDriver and PersonAsGuest OOD frameworks

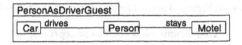

Figure 5. PersonAsDriverGuest OOD framework

2. Formal Specification of OOD Frameworks

In this section, we describe formal specification of OOD frameworks. First we consider the *static* aspects, i.e. *without* time or state transitions, then we consider the *dynamic* aspects, i.e. *with* time and state transitions.

2.1 STATIC ASPECTS

We have considered the static aspects of OOD frameworks in [17, 18]. In this section, we briefly outline this semantics.

As we have seen in Section 1., OOD frameworks are composite objects/classes. In our approach, we define OOD frameworks and objects/classes in terms of a basic entity that we call a *specification framework*, or just a *framework*, for short.[2]

A *framework* $\mathcal{F} = \langle \Sigma, X \rangle$ is defined in the context of first-order logic with identity. It is composed of a signature Σ (containing sort symbols, function declarations and relation declarations), and a finite or recursive set X of Σ-axioms. The purpose of a framework is to axiomatise a problem domain and to reason about it. In our approach, a problem domain contains the ADT's and classes needed to define the objects of the application at hand.

A framework is thus a (first-order) theory, and we choose its intended model to be a *reachable isoinitial model*, defined as follows:[3]

Let X be a set of Σ-axioms. A Σ-structure i is an *isoinitial model* of X iff, for every other model m of X, there is one isomorphic embedding $i : \mathsf{i} \to \mathsf{m}$.

A model i is *reachable* if its elements can be represented by ground terms.

We distinguish between *closed* and *open* frameworks. The relationship between open and closed frameworks plays a crucial role in our interpretation of objects. Roughly speaking, in object-oriented programming terminology, open frameworks represent *classes*, and closed frameworks represent their instances, i.e. *objects*.

A framework $\mathcal{F} = \langle \Sigma, X \rangle$ is *closed* iff there is a reachable isoinitial model i of X.

An *open* framework $\mathcal{F}(\Omega) = \langle \Sigma, X \rangle$ does not have an isoinitial model, since its axioms leave open the meaning of some symbols Ω of the signature, that we call *open* symbols. Non-open symbols

---

[2]To avoid confusion with OOD frameworks, in this section we will use 'framework' to refer to a specification framework only, and not to an OOD framework.

[3]See [18] for a justification of this choice and [3, 16] for a discussion of isoinitial theories.

are called *defined* symbols.

Open frameworks can be *closed*, i.e made into closed frameworks, by instantiating its open symbols. We will use only open frameworks which have reachable isoinitial models for all their instances. Such frameworks are called *adequate*, and they can be constructed incrementally from small (adequate) closed frameworks (see [17, 18]).

Example 2..1 The Car class in Figures 4 and 5 can be defined as the following *open* framework:

> **OBJ-Framework** $\mathcal{CAR}(.km, .option)$;
>
> IMPORT: $\mathcal{INT}, year96$;
>
> DECLS: $.km$: $[\,] \to Int$
>
> $.option$: $[year96.opts]$
>
> CONSTRS: $.km \geq 0$

where $\mathcal{INT}$ is a predefined ADT of integers,

and $year96$ is an object that contains the sort $year96.opts$ of the possible options for a car in the year 96. The constraint $.km \geq 0$ is an axiom for the open symbol $.km$.

We call a framework like this an *OBJ-framework*, since it is a class of objects. To obtain objects we instantiate an OBJ-framework, i.e. by closing the OBJ-framework.

The axioms used to close $\mathcal{F}(\Omega)$ into an object represent the *state* of the object, and are called *state axioms*. State axioms can be updated, i.e. an object is a dynamic entity.

An object of class $\mathcal{CAR}$ is created, for example, by:

> NEW $spider : \mathcal{CAR}$;
>
> CLOSE: $spider.km$ BY $spider.km = 25000$;
>
> $spider.option$ BY $spider.option(x) \leftrightarrow x = Airbag \lor x = AirCond$.

where $spider.km = 25000$ and $spider.option(x) \leftrightarrow x = Airbag \lor x = AirCond$ are (explicit) definitions that close the constant $spider.km$ and the predicate $spider.option(x)$ respectively.

The state of a spider object can be updated, by redefining its state axioms:

> UPDATE $spider : \mathcal{CAR}$;
>
> $spider.km = 27000$
>
> $spider.option(x) \leftrightarrow x = Airbag \lor x = AirCond$

As we can see, the constant $spider.km$ has been changed.

An OOD framework is a composite OBJ-framework. It can be viewed as a *system* of objects, in which objects can be created (and deleted) and updated dynamically.

Example 2..2 The PersonAsDriver OOD framework in Figure 5 can be formalised as the following framework:

> **OOD-Framework** $\mathcal{DRIVER}[\mathcal{PERSON}, \mathcal{CAR}]$;
>
> DECLS: $.drives : [obj]$;
>
> CONSTRS: $`X.drives(c) \to PERSON(`X) \land `X.age \geq 18 \land CAR(c)$;
>
> $(\exists c : obj)(.drives(c))$;

where *obj* is a reserved sort symbol that contains the set of names of all existing objects in the system; 'X is a meta-symbol that stands for any object name; and the OBJ-framework $\mathcal{PERSON}$ may be something like:

OBJ-Framework $\mathcal{PERSON}$;

IMPORT . . .;

DECLS: .*name* : → *string*;

            .*age* : → *int*; . . .

CONSTRS: .*age* ≥ 0

Here the composite object is built via links between its components, which constrain object creation (and deletion) methods. We cannot create an object $n.\mathcal{DRIVER}$, if n is not a person. Furthermore, we need at least one car c.

2.2 DYNAMIC ASPECTS

In this section, we consider how to introduce time and state changes. We will combine the static formalisation outlined in the previous section with the logic MDTL presented in [13]. MDTL is an extension of the TROLL logic [11] for describing dynamic aspects of large object systems.

2.2.1 State Transitions

In MDTL, an OBJ or OOD framework has a local logic consisting of a *home* and a *communication* logic. The *home* logic allows us to express internal state changes, whereas the *communication* logic describes framework interactions. The *home* logic of a framework is mainly a first-order temporal logic with (true) concurrency. We do not deal with concurrency explicitly in this paper, and so we will use axioms that are just first-order temporal formulae. Also, in this paper, we will not use the communication logic, since we do not deal with framework interactions.

In MDTL, in addition to attributes, an object also has *actions*,[4] which will affect its current state. Actions may be either *enabled* or *occurring* in a particular state. The *state* of an object is given by the current values of the attributes, and the current status of its actions. Thus in MDTL, a state formula is a conjunction of facts (the current values of the attributes) and actions (enabled or occurring).

If an action is *enabled*, then it may occur in the next state. When an action occurs, the state of the object changes. In the logic, $\odot a$ is used to denote the occurrence of action a, and $\triangleright a$ that the action a is enabled. If an action occurs, then it must have been enabled in the previous state: $\odot a \Rightarrow Y \triangleright a$. In this formula, Y is the temporal operator *Yesterday* referring to the previous state. Enabling ($\triangleright$) is useful for expressing *preconditions*, and occurrence ($\odot$) for expressing *postconditions*.

In the sequel, we shall also use the temporal operators X (next state), F (sometime in the future including the present), and P (sometime in the past including the present).

The state of an OOD framework is given by the states of the current objects belonging to the framework.

We illustrate how to specify state transitions of an OOD framework in MDTL with a simple example.

Example 2..3 Consider the OOD framework for employees as depicted in Figure 6, in which a per-

---

[4]More commonly known as *methods* in object-oriented programming.

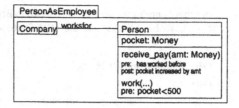

Figure 6. PersonAsEmployee OOD framework

son plays the role of an employee of a company. A person as an employee has an attribute *pocket* representing the amount of money he possesses, and two actions *receive_pay* and *work*. In this example, a person as an employee only works if he has less than £500 (precondition for *work*). A person only receives a payment if he has worked before (precondition for *receive_pay*). If a person receives a payment, the money in his pocket increases by the amount received. Here, we express the pre- and postconditions only informally, and we omit the parameters and the postcondition of *work*, as well as the definition of the OBJ-framework for Company.

The class Person might be formalised by the following OBJ-framework:

OBJ-Framework $\mathcal{PERSON}$;

IMPORT: $\mathcal{MONEY}$

DECLS: *.pocket*   : $[\,] \rightarrow Money$;
        .receive_pay : $[Money]$;
           .work   : $[\ldots]$;

AXIOMS: ...

ST-AXIOMS: $\forall_a \triangleright .receive\_pay(a) \Rightarrow P \odot .work(\ldots)$;
              $\forall_{a,n} \odot .receive\_pay(a) \Rightarrow Y(.pocket = n) \Rightarrow .pocket = n + a$;
              $\triangleright .work(\ldots) \Rightarrow .pocket < £500$.

where the ST-AXIOMS are the *state transition axioms*.

Pre- and postconditions allow us to define the state transitions of a framework. The state transition axioms do not affect the (static) isoinitial model of the OBJ-framework, and are relevant only for the behaviour model. The first axiom states that if the action *receive_pay* is enabled, then sometime in the past (temporal operator P) the action *work*(...) must have occurred. The second axiom says that the occurrence of action *receive_pay*(a) implies that if in the previous state the value of *pocket* was n, then its current value is $n + a$. Finally, the third axiom states that if the action *work*(...) is enabled (it might occur in the next state) then the value of *pocket* must be less than £500.

We can create an object *joe* of Person class as follows:

NEW *joe* : $\mathcal{PERSON}$;
CLOSE: *joe.pocket* BY $joe.pocket = £100$;
        joe.work   BY $\triangleright joe.work(\ldots)$;
         joe.pay   BY $\neg \triangleright joe.receive\_pay(a)$.

When an object is created, its initial state is defined. In the initial state of *joe*, (attribute) *pocket* is £100, (action) *receive_pay*(a) is disabled for any a, and (action) *work*(...) enabled.

In MDTL we can also express general properties of objects. For example,[5]

$$joe.pocket < \pounds 500 \Rightarrow F \exists_a \odot joe.receive\_pay(a)$$

means 'if *joe* has less than £500 then he will receive a payment sometime'.

2.2.2 Event Structures

MDTL is interpreted over *labelled prime event structures* ([24]). A labelled prime event structure is thus a model for an OOD framework if it satisfies all the axioms of the framework (both the static and the state transition axioms).

A labelled prime event structure consists of a prime event structure and a labelling function. Prime event structures can be used to describe distributed computations as event occurrences together with a *causal* and a *conflict* relations between them. The causal relation implies a (partial) order among event occurrences, and the conflict relation denotes a choice. Events in conflict cannot belong to the same *run* or *life cycle*. The labelling function associates each event with a state.

Example 2..4 Consider the event structure in Figure 7. It shows a small part of a (sequential) be-

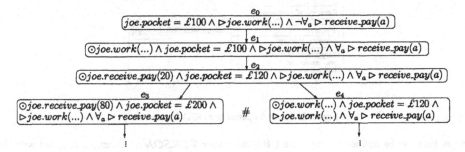

Figure 7. Event structure for *joe* as an employee

haviour model for *joe*.

In general, in event structures, *boxes* denote events $\{e_0, e_1, \ldots\}$, *arrows* between boxes represent event *causality*, and $\#$ denotes event *conflict*. The state of the object at a given event is written inside the box as a state formula.

For the object *joe*, the events in the event structure are labelled by the formulae of the state logic of the Person class. Event e_0 corresponds to the initial state. The occurrence of e_1 depends on the previous occurrence of e_0. With the occurrence of action $joe.receive\_pay(20)$ at event e_2, the current value of attribute *pocket* changes to £120. Events e_3 and e_4 are in conflict, which means that either one or the other occurs but not both. A conflict thus denotes a choice.

There are therefore two life cycles for *joe* in Figure 7. One consists of events $\{e_0, e_1, e_2, e_3, \ldots\}$ and the other $\{e_0, e_1, e_2, e_4, \ldots\}$. In the former, *joe* receives two payments after working. In the latter, *joe* works, then receives a payment and then works again.

Finally, it is easy to see that this event structure satisfies the state transition axioms of the OBJ-framework $\mathcal{PERSON}$.

---

[5]We are not saying that this property necessarily follows from the ST-axioms of the object *joe*.

In general, labelled event structures provide models for concurrent computations. Other such models include transition systems, Petri nets, traces, and synchronisation trees. Petri nets and transition systems allow an explicit representation of the (possibly repeating) states in a system, whereas trees, traces and event structures abstract away from such information, and focus instead on the behaviour in terms of patterns of occurrences of actions over time. Furthermore, event structures are a "true" concurrency model, as opposed to transition systems that model systems as non-deterministically interleaved sequential computations. A detailed survey and comparison of some of these models can be found in [24].

2.2.3   Composing Event Structures

In order to create objects by composing OOD frameworks with state transitions in the manner depicted in Figure 3, we need to be able to compose event structures.

Example 2..5 In the previous example, a person plays the role of an employee. This partial definition of person could be combined with another view of a person, e.g., a person as a consumer. The PersonAsConsumer OOD framework in Figure 8 defines this role for a person object. The class

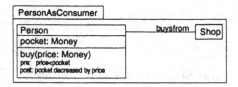

Figure 8. PersonAsConsumer OOD framework

Person here can be defined by the same OBJ-framework $\mathcal{PERSON}$ in Example 2..3, but with the action $buy(p)$ instead of the actions $receive\_pay(a)$ and $work(\ldots)$. We omit the definition of the OBJ-framework for Shop.

A consumer has an action $buy(p)$, where p represents the price of the item bought. Pre- and postconditions for this action are the expected ones. A consumer may only buy something if he has enough money, and after buying an item the money in his pocket decreases by the amount of money spent. The state transition axioms for $buy(p)$ are thus:

$$\forall_p \rhd .buy(p) \Rightarrow .pocket > p$$
$$\forall_{p,n} \odot .buy(p) \Rightarrow Y(.pocket = n) \Rightarrow .pocket = n - p$$

Let joe be a person playing now the role of a consumer. In the event structure for joe as a consumer, a life cycle is a linear sequence of buy events starting from the initial state in which $joe.pocket$ is initialised. In Figure 9, we show two possible life cycles with distinct initial states.

We may compose the OOD frameworks for PersonAsEmployee and PersonAsConsumer, to obtain a person with both roles together. A person now has all the actions of both roles, namely $receive\_pay$, $work$ and buy, and the attribute $pocket$ in both roles. The composition is illustrated by Figure 10.

The composite PersonAsEmployeeConsumer framework contains the union of the state transition axioms of its component OOD frameworks. An event structure, i.e. a model, for a person as an

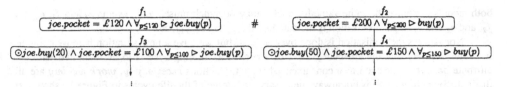

Figure 9. Event structure for *joe* as a consumer

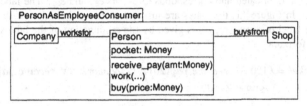

Figure 10. PersonAsEmployeeConsumer OOD framework

employee and consumer is obtained by composing a model for person as an employee with one for person as a consumer in a special manner. Several constructions for sequential and parallel composition of event structures have been defined in the literature, e.g. [23, 19]. What we need for composing roles is in fact a combination of *interleaving* of the models and *synchronisation*. Interleaving (sequential composition), because we are combining models for the same object in different roles (and objects are considered to behave sequentially), and therefore the composed model must be sequential. Synchronisation, because some attributes and/or actions for distinct roles may be identified as the same (e.g. *pocket*).

Figure 11 shows the composed model for *joe* as an employee and consumer based on the models of Figures 7 and 9 for *joe* as an employee and *joe* as a consumer respectively. In this case, event

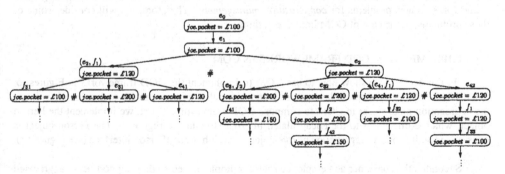

Figure 11. Event structure for *joe* as an employee and a consumer

synchronisation is done over the value of the common attribute *pocket*. That is, only those events of both models that have the same value for pocket may be synchronised, e.g., events e_2 and f_1, e_3 and f_2, and e_4 and f_1. Synchronisation is indicated by the pairs (e_2, f_1), etc.

Normally, synchronisation is done over actions, but we have a new situation here by combining roles, namely that the attribute *pocket* of a person as an employee is to be identified with the attribute *pocket* of a person as a consumer, whereas the actions *receive_pay*, *work* and *buy* are all distinct. Synchronisation is not always necessary, and some of the life cycles in Figure 11 show just interleaving.

The construction of composite event structures sometimes leads to the duplication of events, e.g., event e_3 has been duplicated and corresponds to events e_{31} and e_{32}. The labels of these events are the same as e_3. In Figure 11, the states are just indicated by the value of the attribute *pocket* for simplicity. The label of event (e_2, f_1) is given by the conjunction of the labels e_2 and f_1, i.e., it corresponds to the formula

$$joe.pocket = £120 \wedge \odot receive\_pay(20) \wedge \triangleright joe.work \wedge \forall_a receive\_pay(a) \wedge$$
$$\forall_{p \leq 120} \triangleright buy(p)$$

Parallel composition of event structures with synchronisation is useful for modelling interacting frameworks (e.g., [15]), whereas without synchronisation it models non-interacting frameworks.

3.   Some Implementation Issues

Having shown how to formally specify OOD frameworks, we now turn to practical concerns. In particular, we will discuss how we might construct such frameworks in practice using currently available technology, and the issues involved in such constructions.

Of the current technologies for developing component-based software systems, COM [5] seems to lend itself most readily to the implementation of OOD frameworks. Therefore, we will briefly show how to implement OOD frameworks in COM.

The fact that OOD frameworks are composite objects/classes means that constructing these frameworks creates problems for *configuration management*. Therefore, we will consider some of these problems, in the case of COM implementations.

3.1   IMPLEMENTING OOD FRAMEWORKS IN COM

In this section, we show how to use COM to implement the OOD frameworks in Figures 6, 8 and 10. COM suits multiple roles because it can use multiple interfaces for each role. We will use the aggregation mechanism in COM to compose OOD frameworks. First, we implement the Person object, which corresponds to the encapsulated internal structure in Figure 2. The Person object is constructed so it supports aggregation of role objects and it has one IPerson interface (see Figure 12).

Secondly, the consumer and employee roles are implemented so they support being aggregated into a person object. Figure 12 shows the consumer role with one IConsumer interface. The consumer object also needs a reference to the person object to be able to work on the pocket variable. The person reference is set up when the consumer is aggregated into the person object (see Figure 13). In a similar way the employee role is implemented. Using aggregation we can reuse the different

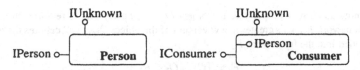

Figure 12. A COM object for the person object and the consumer role

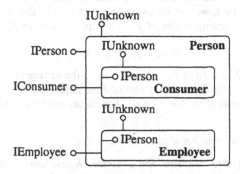

Figure 13. The Consumer and Employee roles are aggregated into the Person object

components that we have created. Figure 13 shows how Person aggregates the two already defined COM objects. Frameworks are created at run-time by adding roles to an object.

The COM implementation of the framework concept has some limitations. The COM model defines frameworks as aggregates of the completed objects created at run-time, while a general framework model allows us to use incomplete objects (at run-time) or classes (at build-time).

3.2 CONFIGURATION MANAGEMENT

Using OOD frameworks instead of traditional objects yields several advantages, but it also introduces an additional level of complexity when building these frameworks. Frameworks are composite types of entities – they have an internal structure which is built from objects, or from parts of them. A framework entity also has relations to other frameworks, and can be composed from other (sub)frameworks. The definition and creation of such a composite entity introduces configuration problems. Some of them will be illustrated here for a COM implementation.

Let us consider the following cases:

- Sharing objects in several frameworks;

- Composing frameworks from objects and frameworks.

3.2.1 Sharing Objects in Several Frameworks

Suppose framework F_1 includes objects O_1 and O_2 with a relation R_{12} between them, and framework F_2 contains objects O_1 and O_3 with a relation R_{13}. The object O_1 is shared by two frameworks:

$$F_1 = \{O_1\ O_2\ ;\ R_{12}\}, \quad F_2 = \{O_1\ O_3\ ;\ R_{13}\} \tag{1}$$

Suppose we now add a new property to the object O_1, a property that is required in (an improved version of) framework F_2. This creates a new version of the object $O_{1;v2}$, ($v2$ denotes the new version) which is included into the framework F_2:

$$F_2 = \{O_{1;v2}\ O_3\ ;\ R_{13}\}$$

However, if we do not take versioning into consideration, then the framework specifications will remain the same. In this case, we can be aware of the change of the object O_1 in the context of framework F_2, but not necessarily in that of F_1. Our specification of F_1 is defined by (1), but in reality we have

$$F_1 = \{O_{1;v2}\ O_2\ ;\ R_{12}\}$$

If the role of the object $O_{1;v2}$ used in F_1 is changed, then the behaviour of F_1 will be changed unpredictably, and a system using F_1 can fail. To avoid these unpredictable situations we can introduce basic configuration management methods – a version management of objects and configuration of frameworks [7]:

- An object is identified by its name and version.

- A framework is identified by a name and a version. A new framework version is derived from object versions included in the framework.

These rules imply that new versions of frameworks will be configured when a new object version is created, as shown in our example:

$$F_{1;vi} = \{O_{1;vm}\ O_{2;vn}\ ;\ R_{12}\},\quad F_{2;vk} = \{O_{1;vm}\ O_{3;vk}\ ;\ R_{13}\}$$

$$F_{1;vi+1} = \{O_{1;vm+1}\ O_{2;vn}\ ;\ R_{12}\},\quad F_{2;vk+1} = \{O_{1;vm+1}\ O_{3;vk}\ ;\ R_{13}\}$$

As several frameworks can share one object, and a framework can contain several objects, the number of generated frameworks can grow explosively. It is, however, possible to limit the number of interesting configurations. Typically, in a development process, we would implement the changes on all the objects we want, collect the versions of objects we want in a baseline and derive the frameworks from the baselined object versions. In such a case, experience for similar cases [2] shows that the number of derived entities does not necessarily grow rapidly.

A shared object is not necessarily completely shared, but different parts of the object, defined by the object's roles, are used in the frameworks. In the COM implementation a complete object will be included, but a part of it will be used. In a general framework model, a class (or an object at run-time) includes only those parts which are specified in the object's role. When we define a new role for an object in a framework or re-define the existing one, we need to change a specific part of the object class. We call this specific part an object aspect. The change of an object aspect will affect only those frameworks where the aspect is included. Other frameworks, though containing the object (or part of it), are not affected by the change. In this case, it is better to keep version control on the aspect level, and relate a framework configuration to the object aspects.

If we declare an aspect as a subset of an object $A_i(O_k) \subseteq O_k$, then an object version is defined as a set of aspect versions:

$$O_{i;vk} = \{A_{j;vl}\}$$

and a framework version is defined as a set of aspect versions with relations between the aspects:

$$F_{vk} = \{\{A_{j;vl}(O_{i;vk})\}\ ;\ R_{jl}\}$$

Having control over changes on the aspect level, we can gain control over the changes on the framework level. Now we can more precisely identify the frameworks being affected by changes in object roles.

3.2.2 Composing Frameworks from Objects and Frameworks

In the framework model it is possible to compose new frameworks from existing frameworks. A new framework is a superset of the classes and relations from the frameworks involved. If a new framework is created at run-time, as in a COM implementation, then the objects from the selected frameworks comprise the new framework. The following example illustrates the merging process of two frameworks F_1 and F_2 into $F3$:

$$F_1 = \{O_1 \, O_2 \; ; \; R_{12}\}, \quad F_2 = \{O_1 \, O_3 \; ; \; R_{13}\}, \quad F_3 = \{O_1 \, O_2 \, O_3 \; ; \; R_{12}, R_{13}, R_{23}\}$$

The composition works fine as long as we do not need to consider the changes of objects within one framework.

Suppose we create a new object version (or a new object aspect version) in F_2 and keep the old version of the same object in F_1:

$$F_{1;vi} = \{O_{1;v1} \, O_{2;vk} \; ; \; R_{12}\}, \quad F_{2;vj} = \{O_{1;v1+1} \, O_{3;vl} \; ; \; R_{13}\}$$

In the merging process we have to recognise if different versions of the same objects are included in the frameworks being merged. If that is the case, we have two possible solutions:

- Selecting one specific version of the object (for example the latest):

$$F_{3;v1} = \{O_{1;v1+1} \, O_{2;vk} \, O_{3;v1} \; ; \; R_{12}, R_{13}, R_{23}\}$$

- Selecting both versions and enable their consistence in the new framework:

$$F_{3;v1} = \{O_{1;v1} \, O_{1;v1+1} \, O_2; vk \, O_{3;v1} \; ; \; R_{12}, R_{13}, R_{23}\}$$

For the second case there must be support for identifying object versions. This support can be provided by introducing an identification interface [14] as the standard interface of an object. There must also be support for managing different versions of the same object in the running system.

4. Conclusion

In this paper we have shown how to formally specify OOD frameworks using MDTL and event structures. In particular, we have shown a semantics for composing OOD frameworks with state transitions in the manner depicted in Figure 3.

Our work here is closely related to TROLL [11], which is used for specifying large distributed/concurrent object systems, and to [4], which formalises an algebraic semantics for object model diagrams in OMT [22]. The main difference is that they take the traditional view of objects (Figure 2), whereas we adopt the multiple-role, more reusable approach (Figure 3). Their semantics is based on initial theories, as opposed to isoinitial theories that we use.

Overall, our approach to specification is model-theoretic, whereas other approaches are mostly proof- or type-theoretic. For example, our model-theoretic characterisation of states and objects stands in contrast to the type-theoretic approach, e.g., [1]. Our model-theoretic approach also enables us to define a notion of correctness that is preserved through inheritance hierarchies, which is particularly suitable for component-based software development.

We have also presented a possible implementation of OOD frameworks using the COM technology. This implementation has some limitations, and we need to do further work to investigate how to improve this implementation.

Finally we have discussed configuration management for frameworks. We emphasise a need for using configuration management methods for managing frameworks as composite objects. The configuration management issues are complicated and need further investigation: Questions of managing relations, concurrent versions of frameworks, inclusion of change management [9], etc., must be addressed. Since aspects and objects are not entities recognised by standard configuration management tools (which recognise entities such as files, directories, etc.), new, semantic-based rules must be incorporated into such tools. For different object-oriented and component technologies, different tools have to be made. How different do they need to be, and are there possibilities to define common rules and implementation? These are questions for future investigation.

ACKNOWLEDGEMENTS

We would like to thank the referee who pointed out some minor mistakes.

References

1. Abadi, M. and Cardelli, L. *A Theory of Objects*. Springer-Verlag, 1996.
2. Asklund, U., Bendix, L., Cristensen, H. B., and Magnusson, B. The unified extensional versioning model. In J. Estublier, (ed.), *Proc. System Configuration Management SCM-9*, Springer, 1999, pp. 17-33.
3. Bertoni, A., Mauri, G., and Miglioli, P. On the power of model theory in specifying abstract data types and in capturing their recursiveness. *Fundamenta Informaticae*, VI(2), 1983, pp. 127-170.
4. Bourdeau, R. H. and Cheng, B. H. C. A formal semantics for object model diagrams. *IEEE Trans. Soft. Eng.*, 21(10), 1995, pp. 799-821.
5. Box, D. *Essential COM*. Addison-Wesely, 1998.
6. Coleman, D., Arnold, P., Bodoff, S., Dollin, C., Gilchrist, H., Hayes, F., and Jeremaes, P. *Object-Oriented Development: The Fusion Method*. Prentice-Hall, 1994.
7. Conradi, R. and Westfechtel, B. Version models for software configuration management. ACM Computing Surveys, 30(2), 1998, pp. 232-282.
8. Cook, S. and Daniels, J. *Designing Object Systems*. Prentice-Hall, 1994.
9. Crnkovic, I. Experience with change oriented SCM Tools. In R. Conradi, (ed.), *Proc. Software Configuration Management SCM-7*, Springer, 1997, pp. 222-234.
10. D'Souza, D. F. and Wills, A. C. *Objects, Components, and Frameworks with UML: The Catalysis Approach*. Addison- Wesley, 1999.
11. Grau, A., Küster Filipe, J., Kowsari, M., Eckstein, S., Pinger, R. and Ehrich, H.-D. The TROLL approach to conceptual modelling: syntax, semantics and tools. In T.W. Ling , S. Ram and M.L. Leebook, (eds.), *Proc. 17th Int. Conference on Conceptual Modeling, LNCS*, **1507**, Springer, 1998, pp. 277-290.
12. Helm, R., Holland, I. M., and Gangopadhay, D. Contracts - Specifying behavioural compositions in OO systems. *Sigplan Notices*, **25**(10) *(Proc. ECOOP/OOPSLA 90)*, 1990.
13. Küster Filipe, J. Fundamentals of a module logic for distributed object systems. *J. Functional and Logic Programming*, **2000**(3), 2000.
14. Larsson, M. and Crnkovic, I. New challenges for configuration management. In J. Estublier, (ed.), *Proc. System Configuration Management SCM-9*, Springer, 1999, pp. 232-243.

15. Lau, K.-K., Liu, S., Ornaghi, M., and Wills, A. Interacting frameworks in *Catalysis*. In J. Staples, M. Hinchey and S. Liu, (eds.), *Proc. Second IEEE Int. Conf. on Formal Engineering Methods*, IEEE Computer Society Press, 1998, pp.110-119.

16. Lau, K-K. and Ornaghi, M. Isoinitial models for logic programs: A preliminary study. In J.L. Freire-Nistal, M. Falaschi, and M. Vilares-Ferro, (eds.), *Proceedings of the 1998 Joint Conference on Declarative Programming*, A Coruña, Spain, 1998, pp. 443-455.

17. Lau, K.-K. and Ornaghi, M. On specification and correctness of OOD frameworks in computational logic. In A. Brogi and P. Hill, (eds.), *Proc. lst Int. Workshop on Component-based Software Development in Computational Logic*, September 1998, Pisa, Italy, pp. 59-75.

18. Lau, K.-K. and Ornaghi, M. OOD frameworks in component-based software development in computational logic. In P. Flener, (ed.), *Proc. LOPSTR'98, LNCS, 1559*, Springer-Verlag, 1998, pp. 101-123.

19. Loogen, R. and Goltz, U. Modelling nondeterministic concurrent processes with event structures. *Fundamenta Informaticae*, **XIV**(l), 1991, pp. 39-73.

20. Mauth, R. A better foundation: development frameworks let you build an application with reusable objects. *BYTE*, **21**(9):40IS, 1996.pp. 10-13.

21. Pooley, R. and Stevens, P. *Using UML: Software Engineering with Objects and Components*. Addison-Wesley, 1999.

22. Rumbaugh, J., Blaha, M., Premerlani, W., Eddy, F., and Sorenson, W. *Object-Oriented Modeling and Design*. Prentice-Hall, 1991.

23. Vaandrager, F. W. A simple definition for parallel composition of prime event structures. Technical Report CS-R8903, Centre for Mathematics and Computer Science, P.O. Box 4079, 1009 AB Amsterdam, The Netherlands, 1989.

24. Winskel, G. and Nielsen, M. Models for concurrency. In S. Abramsky , D. M. Gabbay, and T.S.E. Maibaum, (eds.), *Handbook of Logic in Computer Science, 4, Semantic Modelling*, Oxford Science Publications, 1995, pp. 1-148.

Problem Resolution Process for Software Porting Project – A Case Study

Janis Plume and Juris Strods

Riga Information Technology Institute
Kuldigas 45, LV-1083 Riga, Latvia
Phone: +371- 7067735
Fax: +371- 7619573
E-mail: J.Plume@alise.lv   juris.strods@dati.lv

Abstract

This article contains summary of experience and lessons learned during a software porting project. The main goal of the project is to move a product from 16 bit Windows 95 platform to the 32 bit Windows NT. Problem resolution process is taken as the central for this project and it gives the context for all activities performed in the project. Some product and process measures are gathered from the project and analysed to show the main characteristics of the project in general and problem resolution process in particular.

Keywords: software porting, software engineering processes, software measurements.

1. Introduction

Together with the enormous extent of the software products developed up to now, more and more urgent becomes a need to provide product's functioning with the new technologies. Effort necessary for product maintenance increases. A relatively new discipline is developing – reengineering, that is closely related to the maintenance problems. Reengineering usually is a unique activity that aims to resolve some particular maintenance problem. Especially if the problem can not be resolved locally and the product need some extensive changes. Typical example of such changes is software porting, or in other words, adaptation of software for some other platform (e.g. hardware, operating system).

Reengineering in its classical meaning appears as two-direction process with so-called reverse engineering and forward engineering [4]. In case when target environment of the product does not differ significantly from the source environment (e.g. implementation language remains the same), so-called "quick-fix" [1] method for software porting project can be applied. In this approach reengineering can be performed without specific reverse engineering phase. There is no need for requirements and/or design reengineering for software porting project. The existing source code can be updated to ensure correct operation in the new environment.

Development of Windows operating system has also experienced few significant leaps. This has created problems for continuity of existing products' development or even for operation. Problem of this type is also to ensure operation of the 16 bit Windows application for 32 bit functioning under Windows NT. Experience of such project is reported in this article, special attention attaching to the project results and lessons learned from the point of view of development process.

253

J. Barzdins and A. Caplinskas (eds.), Databases and Information Systems, 253–258.

2. Context of the Project

2.1 PRODUCT CHARACTERISTICS AND PROJECT GOALS

The product to be ported is a CASE tool that implements both basic concepts of structured and object-oriented analysis. The CASE tool is implemented in the C++ programming language using the Borland C++ compiler and C++ views class library. CASE tool's repository is implemented in a data base management system.

The main goal of the project is to ensure that product will work under the Windows NT operating system. Simultaneously, it was decided to switch to the Microsoft C++ compiler to build the NT version of the product.

The product initially was developed in another software company located in other country. As a consequence of that was the fact that initially no project team member had any knowledge about the product architecture and implementation. The project team had a very essential background in the area of CASE tools and that helped to get necessary knowledge and skills to carry out the porting project.

2.2 PROJECT PHASES

Product was received in the situation when some porting activities were already completed. As a result of these activities, it was possible to compile the source code of the product with the Microsoft compiler. Approximately 75 person-months were spent in those porting activities at the moment when the project was overtaken.

At this stage project development was divided in two phases:
- Getting familiar with the product and establishment of basic functionality in the new environment.
- Through the problem resolution process [2, 3] fix and remove problems.

The initial phase in the software re-engineering project traditionally is the know-how building. In this project know-how building proceeded quickly because of project team's familiarity with the development environment and subject area of the product.

Although it was possible to start the problem resolution process at once, it was decided not to do so. Such decision reduced the size of project's actual information. The level of stability was too low initially. Problem report registration too early could create a very high stack of the problem reports.

2.3 PROJECT ORGANISATION

Project was performed on time-material base. The customer was paying for 5 positions and the project had to be completed in 15 months. Great emphasis was put on the testing effort and project team was structured in two divisions – testing team and programming team.

The main tasks for testing team were:
- Extend the product coverage by automated test cases
- Regularly operate the automated test cases
- Retest the problems resolved by the programming team

Results of both former activities were problem reports. The results of the last activity were quality assurance (validation) of the work done by programmers.

Programming team performed problem resolution by identifying problem source and making updates in the source code.

2.4 STATES OF PROBLEM REPORT

The problem status (state) concept was introduced that helps to track the advance of resolution of a particular problem. Problems change their status after completion of some particular activity. Following problem states were introduced in this project:

1. **Actual**. All problems receive this state immediately after problem is identified.
2. **Processing**. If it is decided to start resolution of the problem, there is a responsible person assigned for that problem. After that, problem report changes its state to the "processing".
3. **Temporary suspended**. This state usually is assigned to the problems because of low priority. In case when additional resources will be available, problem may become "Actual" once more.
4. **Rejected**. Problem report is decided as not applicable for this project.
5. **Retest it**! Problem is corrected, but some member of the testing team must check it (retest).
6. **Lost**. If a problem with unclear reasons can not be reproduced after some time, it is supposed as lost. However, there is possibility that the problem reappears.
7. **OK**. Problem is corrected and retested.

The Figure 1 shows state transition [5] diagram, which illustrates possible state transitions of problem report in this project. State transition diagram of such kind is project convention and shows only one possible way of problem status change.

Normally, no problem report could reach a final state without accept of at least 2 project members. Regular problem report reviews were performed together with the customer representative.

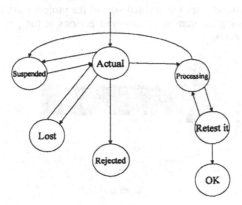

Figure 1. Problem report state transitions

3. Measurements and Results

3.1 PRODUCT SIZE

Basic functionality of the product is divided across 40 DLL (dynamic link library) files. The sizes of the DLL files differ very much. These DLL files are compiled from a number of C++ files, and we will refer to the set of C++ files that form one DLL file as cluster. Further measurements will use the concept of cluster as the least unit for making some assumptions.

The total size of the product is 750 KLOC. The Figure 2 shows distribution of the source code among the clusters. The clusters are ordered according to the size of cluster. Differences between the sizes are significant, the biggest one being by approximately factor 90.

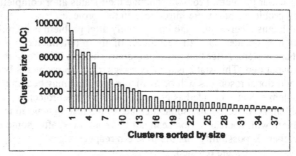

Figure 2. Cluster size

3.2 PROJECT SCHEDULE AND EFFORT

Project was performed on the time-material basis. At the moment of overtaking, there were already 75 person-months invested in the porting of the product.

At the very beginning of the project the activities were started by two persons, which acquired initial knowledge for product overtaking. The number of involved persons was gradually increased and about 5 months after project start, the planned size of the project team was reached. There is a graph in the Figure 3 showing the number of involved persons in the project and division of the persons in test and coding teams.

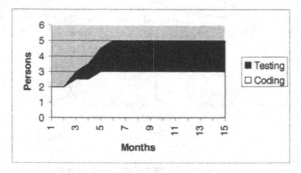

Figure 3. Persons involved in the project

During the 15 months of the project, about 70 person-months were invested. Summing up this number with the effort invested by the previous developer, it makes about 145 person-months for the porting of the whole product.

Thus, the total productivity of the porting of the product (including the work done by the first developer) is 5000 lines of code per person-month (5 KLOC/PM).

Not all of the effort was spent effectively, the reasons of the wasting being:
- Costs of the project overtaking.
- Problems with the first developer's level of quality of development.

Considering those two conditions an assumption can be made, that project could be performed with the 110 or 120 person-months. Thus the porting productivity could reach 7 KLOC/PM.

3.3 PROBLEM REPORTS AND UPDATES DONE

This section contains statistics gathered at the moment when 15 months had passed since the beginning of the project. At that moment the first version of the 32bit product was released.

The next table contains statistics of problem reports:

Problem report category	Number
Total	198
Including:	
Resolved (OK)	161
Lost	2
Rejected	3
Suspended	32
Including:	
16 bit problem reports with low priority	12
16 bit change requests	10
low priority	6
problems from related tools	4

Thus, the defect (problem) density during the 12 months of the project is 2.23 defects on the 1000 lines of code (DEF/KLOC).

At the moment of the release, program source texts were updated 1627 times. All these updates were done to fix the problems.

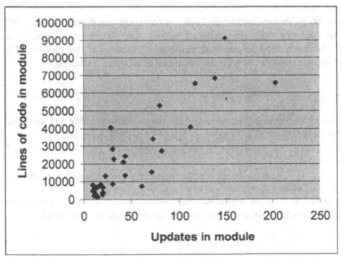

Figure 4. Updates in clusters

Pareto principle [6] asserts that most of all problems (up to 80 percent) detected in software can be tracked to the 20 percent of all possible reasons of errors. This hypothesis very often is interpreted as assumption that 20 percent of source code (modules) contains 80 percent problems that have to be resolved in maintenance projects.

Information about updates done in the clusters was analysed to validate this hypothesis. There was no direct information about problem relation to the clusters gathered. The information of updates were used instead, because, all updates were done to fix the problems detected.

7 clusters (20 percent of total number) that contained the highest number of updates showed 54 percent of total updates. Considering the very big difference of the cluster size, the statistic proved to be another. It proved that the 7 modules contained 57 percent of total code. Thus the interpretation of Pareto principle mentioned above did not hold.

Final conclusion is that number of updates in this project mostly depends on the size of the cluster (module). The dependence is shown in the graph in the Figure 4. The correlation between size of cluster and the updates done is significant and is approximately 0.885.

Thus, there is basis to say that measurements gathered in this project did not prove the hypothesis about concentration of the problems in some small chunk of code. The reason of this is that portability aspect obviously was not considered during development of the product.

4. Conclusions and Lessons Learned

Summarising the information about measurements gathered in the project, following main conclusions can be done:

1. Problem resolution process is applicable in the software porting project, but it requires some particular level of product stability.
2. Regression test automation is the only solution for cases when comparatively large product experiences regular changes. Daily performance of all test coverage allows immediately identify those changes that has involved some negative side effects.
3. Maintenance of automated test cases and test coverage extension is a very time-consuming job. In the porting project it took about 40 percent of total effort. The big graphical interface is the main reason of it.
4. There were no evidence found that 20% source code (modules) contains 80% problems. The defects were very evenly disseminated across the source code. Measurements show high correlation between module size and number of updates in the module. Thus, in the porting project developer must count with the necessity of extensive changes.

References

1. Basili, V. Viewing maintenance as reuse-oriented software development. *IEEE Software*, 7(1), 1990, pp. 19-25.
2. ISO/IEC 12207:1995. *Information Technology – Software Life Cycle Processes*.
3. ISO/IEC TR 15504-2:1998. *Information Technology – Software Process Assessment* – Part 2: A Reference Model for Processes and Process Capability.
4. Klosch, R., Gall, H. Objektorientiertes reverse engineering. *Von klassischer zu objektorientierter Software,*. Springer, 1995 (in German).
5. Martin, J., McClure, C. *Diagramming Techniques for Analysts and Programmers*. Prentice-Hall, 1985.
6. Pressman, R. *Software Engineering – a Practitioner's Approach*. McGraw-Hill, 1997.

Part 6: Knowledge Bases, Artificial Intelligence, and Information Systems

Model Transformations for Knowledge Base Integration within the Framework of Structural Modelling

Janis Grundspenkis and Janis Jekabsons

Systems' Theory professor's group, Riga Technical University, Riga, Latvia
E-mail: jgrun@itl.rtu.lv, jajek@parks.lv

Abstract

A plethora of different methods and models has been worked out for model-based diagnosis of complex technical systems. Models are described using a distinctive language that is serious obstacle towards effective reuse of already developed models taken from different approaches. It remains valid even for rather similar modelling methods such as structural modelling and multilevel flow modelling. Both were invented several decades ago and have accumulated a wide spectrum of structural models used in different application areas. It is impossible to integrate these models in a knowledge base due to their syntactically different description languages. This paper reflects results obtained in a pilot project where transformation methods and algorithms have been worked out for structural models of complex technical systems developed in the structural modelling and in the multilevel flow modelling approaches. It is supposed that a set of knowledge bases constitutes a repository of syntactically different models developed for diagnosis problem solving. Problem of reuse and integration of models captured in a knowledge base is reduced to the problem of model transformations from one specific modelling method to another. Principles of transformation method are shown. Similarities of model elements are proposed. Two transformation algorithms are presented.

Keywords: structural modelling, multilevel flow modelling, model transformation, knowledge base integration.

1. Introduction

Nowadays technical systems often are hybrid and consist of different types of components: software, hardware, electronic, mechanical, hydraulic, pneumatic and even chemical [8]. Many different modelling methods have been developed and used for a model-based diagnosis of complex technical systems. Some researchers (for example [1]) argue that for complex hybrid systems better diagnosis results may be achieved by integration of different modelling approaches. There are many obstacles along the way towards integral models for diagnosis. First, no universal models are known and it is doubtful that such models may be developed for large-scale classes of technical systems. Second, frequently models are so specific that it is hard to imagine how they may be integrated. Thus, integration of different methods and models is a problem itself that must be solved to achieve more efficient diagnosis.

This paper deals only with one of possible model transformations, namely, structural model transformation. The reason why this model transformation is chosen is that most of the modelling methods (structural, functional, causal, behavioural and others) are based on or have to deal with a structure of a system. A structural model of the technical system is a description of system's physical structure in terms of specified components and connections between them. The components represent physical objects of the real system and the connections represent physical flows. It is well known that systems structure determines possible functions, behaviour and causal

J. Barzdins and A. Caplinskas (eds.), Databases and Information Systems, 261–274.
© 2001 *Kluwer Academic Publishers.*

relationships in the system. That is why modelling of structure, in particular, in form of various modifications of tree structure or networks are widely used in technical systems' diagnosis. Considerations of the role and the importance of a structural model is the cornerstone of the proposed approach for integration of different modelling methods which are based on concepts of structural models.

Current results obtained in the pilot project of structural model transformations allow to carry out model transformations only if they belong to quite similar modelling methods based on different kinds of structures. In particular, the paper deals with structural model transformations that are developed for two modelling methods: the Multilevel Flow Modelling [9] and the Structural Modelling [6].

These two modelling methods have been chosen taking into account several aspects. First, we look at the problem of method and model integration from the point of view of knowledge base integration. Let suppose that there is a collection of different methods and models for model-based diagnosis problem solving. All knowledge is stored in corresponding knowledge bases, i.e., a collection of knowledge bases are available (we call this collection "a repository of models", see Figure 1).

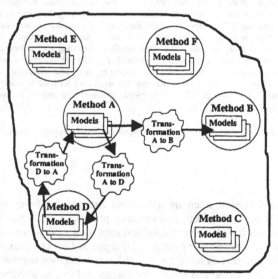

Figure 1. The repository of models

There may be several cases where knowledge base integration is a pressing problem. The most important case is that where powerful knowledge processing is necessary but from different modelling methods only one supports all kinds of reasoning. In other words, all already existing models (built using different modelling methods and languages) must be transformed and integrated in one particular model. The integration of knowledge bases can not be a straightforward task due to the different schemes used for knowledge base construction and difference of languages used for model description. Consequently, the reuse of some early built models depends on success of model integration or, in other words, it depends on possibilities of knowledge base integration. From this aspect it must be pointed out that structural modelling supports various kinds of reasoning [3] while multilevel flow modelling (MFM) has much weaker possibilities. At the same time the MFM is rather widely used method for diagnosis problem solving [2, 7]. Its applications to real life problems allowed to create a number of models of complex technical systems which can be successfully reused in other applications.

The contents of the paper are organised in five sections. First section is devoted to the general principles of model transformations. In the second section a short discussion of structural modelling concepts and knowledge bases used to support various kinds of reasoning are presented. In the third section we give a short overview of the MFM. Similarities of model elements are discussed in the fourth section. The algorithms of structural model transformation are presented in the fifth section. We conclude with the short discussion of obtained results and with the outline of further work.

2. Principles of Structural Model Transformations

Consider the situation of model development of a complex system. Practically there are two alternatives: to build a model from scratch or to reuse some already developed, tested and approbated models. A wide variety of modern technical systems that often are hybrid ones and consist of components of different types have caused the development of different methods and models for diagnosis problem solving. Within each framework many models have been developed that, in fact, are unique in sense that they are used only in one particular application. Even if it is known that suitable model for some part of the complex system already exists one can not use it because diagnosis requires a model of the system as a whole (fragmentary models without their integration are helpless). Therefore, the question is how to reuse already developed models if they are appropriate in the specific diagnosis problem solving. Suppose we have a repository of technical systems' elements and subsystems together with their models that are taken from sets of different models of different modelling methods. In this case models and methods in a repository may be considered as a set of knowledge bases where the user can find the most appropriate models for his/her specific task. A repository may be utilised for reuse and model reconstruction but additional obstacles appear, namely, different schemes used for knowledge representation. A simple transformation of knowledge bases by rewriting their contents using one common knowledge representation schema, for example, rules, frames or semantic nets followed by integration of knowledge bases will not allow to achieve the goal - to develop a model of the complete system as a whole. The solution must be found at the model level. The idea is that first of all the model integration must be provided. Due to the wide variety and complexity of the technical systems, especially, the hybrid ones, it is hard to expect the appearance of a universal modelling method at least in near future. That is why the model reengineering approach seems to be more perspective. In this paper, the notion "model reengineering" is used to denote the procedures of multiple model integration.

In general, there are three options for integration:
1) model integration using one common and universal interface (see Figure 2);
2) model integration using many pair-wise different interfaces (see Figure 3);
3) model integration using different types of transformations (see Figure 4).

In all figures, the term "modelling process" represents model-based reasoning that is a dynamic process utilising knowledge represented by models. In this context, models are passive components and modelling is an active component.

In the first case, it is needed to design universal enough interface that provides information exchange among models. The complexity of an interface is proportional to the number of models. The implementation of the second case also is limited by the increasing number of needed interfaces. The third option suggests to develop as many transformation methods as there are modelling methods. This approach is effective in cases when considered modelling methods are rather similar.

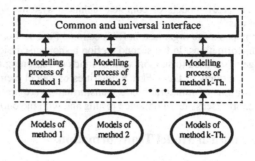

Figure 2. Model integration using common and universal interface

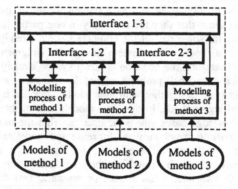

Figure 3. Model integration using many pair-wise different interfaces

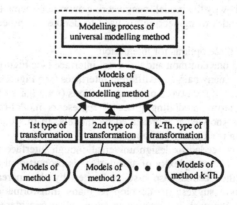

Figure 4. Model integration using universal modelling method

Common features of all three model integration options are that, in fact, model transformations change a model of one modelling method into a model of another modelling method. Transformation always causes some losses of information (knowledge) captured in models. The determination of permissible level of knowledge losses is a hard issue. It is an area for future research and is not discussed in this paper. In ideal case all knowledge that is captured in an original model (an input of transformation) and is necessary for use in diagnosis of technical systems is transformed into a destination model (an output of transformation). The transformation must transform not only the elements of the models but also should remain the semantical aspects for to be able to use this destination model in the reasoning of the destination modelling method. Figure 5 illustrates basic principles of transformation.

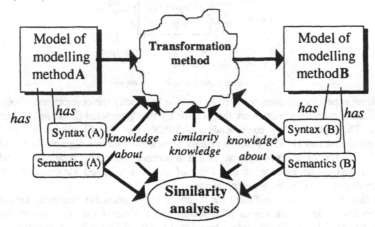

Figure 5. Basic principles of transformation

Each of modelling methods has its own syntax and semantics of models. Note the significant difference: syntax of a model can be represented in a formal way but usually it is much harder to give a formal description of semantics of modelling elements and models as a whole.

In the development of transformation method, it is necessary to take into account syntax, semantics and similarity of elements of both modelling methods, too. Similarity analysis of elements is based on the principle of finding for each element of transformation input an appropriate element of transformation output. It is worth to stress that, in general, all kinds of relations may exist between transformation input and output (one-to-one, one-to-many, many to one and many-to-many). In the model transformation, a similarity means knowledge that describes replacement of elements of one model by elements of another model. Process of similarity analysis also needs knowledge about syntax and semantics of models. The examples of similarities will be shown further in this paper.

3. Structural Modelling Concepts and Construction of Knowledge Bases to Support Reasoning

Structural modelling is a systematic model-based knowledge acquisition framework [4]. An abstract causal domain model built within the framework of structural modelling consists from three models, namely, a model of morphological structure (MSM, in brief) and two kinds of models of functional structures (FSM). Building of these models is essentially a method for encapsulating domain knowledge into small, independent, composable and decomposable units of knowledge (see

[3, 4]). The basic units of abstract domain model are called *objects*. These primitives have *input* and *output contacts* as it is shown in Figure 6. When interpreted in an application domain, abstract objects correspond to physical components of a given system, and contacts represent their inputs and outputs, respectively. Thus, each object captures knowledge about names of its causal inputs and outputs which is the mechanism for linking objects together. The connection of one object's output to another object's input is the only path by which the components may interact. The interactions between objects are called *flows*.

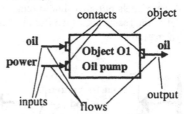

Figure 6. An example of an object

In general, an expert (user) does not need to be able to specify the connections of objects because within structural modelling framework this is done by the Automated Structural MOdelling System (ASMOS). The execution of corresponding ASMOS tool [4, 6] allows to get a *model of morphological structure* (MSM) which is visualised as a diagram or a digraph. The MSM represents a physical structure of a given system, i.e., it represents structural relationships which can be reasoned in logic. The essence of this kind of reasoning, called structural reasoning, is the exploration of paths and cycles between objects.

In fact, the MSM is insufficient for diagnostic and predictive reasoning because it doesn't contain the knowledge about causal relationships in a direct form. To support these kinds of reasoning the MSM is transformed into a functional model. Two models of functional structure are defined, namely, a *functional model in a space of functions* (FSM FS) and a *functional model in a space of parameters* (FSM PS). To support reasoning about processes proceeding in physical elements, the FSM FS encodes knowledge about functions of a system that operates in normal conditions, i.e., when a given system has no faults. If visualised, the FSM FS is displayed by a corresponding diagram. Expert's understanding of how a given system works is organised as a representation that describes purpose why particular function is accomplished. Arcs of the FSM FS represent cause-consequence relations between functions. In this sense, the FSM FS is a representation language for a causal dimension. To represent functions we use two notions - *behaviour* of a component and a *behaviour state* of a contact of a given component. Behaviour specifies an action that component performs upon its "substance", i.e., it specifies how a reaction to a given stimulus is achieved. In other words, behaviour is a characteristic of an input/output relation that may be considered as a causal explanation how structure insures the fulfilment of functional specifications. Behaviour states, in turn, specify how flows "act" in corresponding inlets and outlets of components. So, each object described in MSM has its own behaviour and contacts of object are mapped on corresponding behaviour states. For example, the behaviour of a fuel pump, if it operates normally, is "pumping" (in this case fuel may be considered as default "substance"). The behaviour state of input contact of a fuel pump is "fuel flows through the input of fuel pump" and the behaviour state of output contact of a fuel pump is "fuel flows through the output of fuel pump". Having notions of behaviour and behaviour state the question is "what is the semantic of a function?" We suppose that function closely relates with a purpose (a goal) why the designer has included certain component in a system. More precisely, *function* captures the intended purpose of the object (component), that is, function specifies what the response is to a given stimulus. In other words, function specifies what is the result of proper behaviour (functioning) of a given component. Therefore, our notion of function is similar with that used in multilevel flow modelling [10]. Thus, "to provide fuel flow under pressure" is the purpose why a fuel pump is included in the system. To achieve this goal, the pump must behave properly, i.e., its behaviour must be "pumping". It is worth to stress that in the structural modelling framework a topology of the FSM FS is derived from the MSM automatically [3, 4].

When some changes occur in the system's components or some links between components change, the result usually is that the functional effectiveness decreases or we may notice that the behaviour of the system deviates from that of normal operation. In terms of structural modelling that means changes of behaviour states and, as consequences, changes of behaviour of the system as a whole. In diagnosis we need to detect changes in normal operation, and if they are detected, we need to make a decision "why system's behaviour have changed". We also can consider the inverse task, namely, to find the answer to the question "what will happen if definite change will occur?" In both cases we need a model to support these two kinds of behaviour reasoning, called diagnostic and predictive reasoning, respectively. In the framework of structural modelling behaviour states as well as functions are qualitative characteristics (because they are not characterised by numerical parameters) of processes taking place in physical components. In engineering practice the notion "variables" (or parameter values) is used to get quantitative characteristics. It is rather obvious that each pair of serial behaviour states, i.e., each function must be characterised by a certain variable to allow to detect changes in system's behaviour. Thereby, we can construct the second model of functional structure called a *model of functional structure in a space of parameters* (FSM PS) using a transformation from the FSM FS to the FSM PS. In ideal case (not always held in real world) only one parameter corresponds to each function. Thus, the transformation is straightforward, i.e., the topology of the FSM PS will be isomorphic with the topology of the FSM FS. This makes the systematic problem domain knowledge acquisition supported by structural modelling much easier because all topologies of models are generated automatically using ASMOS and the user (problem domain expert) adds semantics in accordance with interpretation of structural modelling primitives in a particular problem domain.

The acquired knowledge about morphological and functional structures represented by a network of frames is captured in *a topological knowledge base*, or the TKB in brief [5]. In order to use well known reasoning mechanisms of AI, namely, forward and backward chaining the TKB is used to obtain a deep knowledge rule base (DKRB). To achieve the transformation from the TKB to the DKRB the model of functional structure in a parameter space is decomposed into substructures. This transformation is described in [4]. These substructures are called *event trees*. Each event tree reflects cause-consequence relations between a subset of possible faults and changes of parameter values, i.e., failures. There is the straightforward transformation of event tree into a subset of IF - THEN rules or, so called, cause-consequence rules (C-C rules). The set of cause-consequence rules that compiles the DKRB is a deep causal model of the system under diagnosis. The main distinction between the DKRB and the commonly used rule base in diagnosis expert systems is that the DKRB can support reasoning with the goal to establish what really is going on in the system under faults, i.e., we can get a "full picture" of failure propagation. In commonly used rule bases the set of rules, in fact, represents only so called shallow knowledge acquired from experience. Each rule may be considered as a mapping of a subset of faults to a subset of observed symptoms without any information about the real chain of failure propagation from causes (faults) to consequences (symptoms). Paper [5] has shown an easy way how the set of rules stored in the DKRB may be transformed into the set of production rules.

It is important that structural modelling proposes an automated way of deep knowledge rule base building [4] because it is based on the formal algorithms of decomposition of the FSM PS and the change of knowledge representation schema from the event tree form to the C-C rule form.

So, the architecture of the knowledge base used in structural modelling includes two parts:
1) a topological knowledge base (TKB) that captures all acquired knowledge and consists from three models: the MSM, the FSM FS and the FSM PS described above;
2) a deep knowledge rule base (DKRB) that supports various kinds of reasoning about the investigated system.

For already explored systems all models that have been built should be stored in a repository. A repository makes it possible to reuse models when necessary. The effectiveness of a process of new model building depends not only on the ability to identify a suitable model when specifications of current situation are available but also from the number and variety of already modelled systems. That is a reason why an addition of models is so important. In this paper we discuss one of the options, i.e., how within the structural modelling framework use models that have been built for different applications and have been implemented using different modelling techniques. These models are added to the topological knowledge base. This process is interpreted as knowledge base integration based on model transformations. Due to the limited scope of this paper we describe knowledge base integration only for the case if we have models which are developed using multilevel flow modelling techniques.

4. A Short Overview of the MFM

Multilevel Flow Modelling (MFM, in brief) is developed by Professor Morten Lind at the Technical University of Denmark (see [7, 9, 10]). Its purpose is to model a system as a man-made system with certain intentions. An important feature of the MFM is the representation of system at multiple levels of abstraction where system description is made in terms of goals, functions and physical components (devices). This aspect is equal to the description of system along two dimensions, namely, means-ends and whole-part dimensions. Means-ends dimension describes how the certain goals of a system are achieved by functions and what components carry out these functions. The complexity of a system or its parts is reduced by using abstraction principles along a whole-part dimension. The abstraction and decomposition principles are used to represent system's parts at the proper level of granularity. The MFM uses a set of previously defined primitive function concepts related to the processing of material, energy and information flows. Using these concepts, the knowledge of process plant is represented.

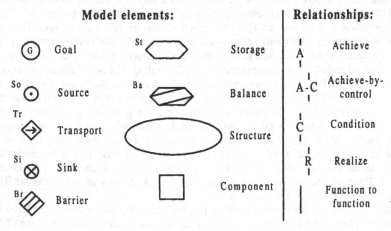

Figure 7. Graphical representations of model elements and their relationships

The MFM deals with five elements of modelled system that are displayed in Figure 7:

1) goals - represent the intentions of designed system;
2) functions - show how goals can be achieved. There are six functions: Source, Sink, Transport, Barrier, Balance and Storage;
3) functional structures - connected functions of one certain level of abstraction, e.g., water circulation structure, thermal energy supply structure; etc.
4) components - show how the functions of the system can be implemented;
5) relationships - connect goals to functional structures, goals to goals, components to functions and functions to functions.

5. Similarities of Model Elements

In accordance with the proposed transformation method for each model element of one modelling method it is necessary to find analogous or similar element of another modelling method. If such element does not exist then there is a need to find a possible construction of number of elements to replace this one. If this effort also fails then the transformation of the particular element is impossible (knowledge losses take place). The alternative way is to change syntax or/and semantics of the destination modelling method with the goal to adapt it for element transformation. In practice, it may be consuming work or even impossible task. Let's look at some examples of element transformations from the Multilevel Flow Modelling to the Structural Modelling. The transformation of a balance function of the MFM to the object of the MSM is depicted in Figure 8.

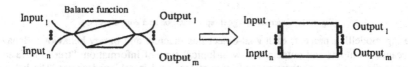

Figure 8. The transformation of a balance function

It is easy to see one-to-one correspondence between these two primitives. Transformation of a storage function is analogous. It is very simple also to transform a source function to the object with only one contact - the output contact. Similarly, a sink function is transformed to the object with one input contact and a transport function - to the object with one input and one output contact.

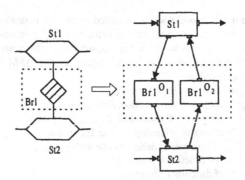

Figure 9. The transformation of a barrier function

The transformation of a barrier function (Br1) concerns determination of one element similarity with the construction of two elements - objects O_1 and O_2. This case is showed in Figure 9. Dotted area bounds the elements of transformation. Barrier function represents a hindrance for flow that is inadmissible (undesirable) between elements St1 and St2 of a storage function. In the case of system's damage this undesirable flow may exist in one or another direction (from St1 to St2 or from St2 to St1).

The concept of the goal in the Structural Modelling does not exist. From the viewpoint of syntax of model, we can easily depict a goal in the MSM as a specific object with at least one input contact. We name it a goal-object. In general, the goal-object can have from 1 to many inputs and from 0 to many outputs (see example in Figure 10).

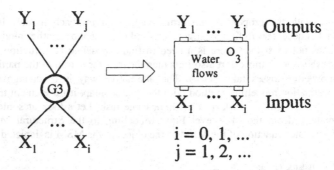

Figure 10. Example of a goal representation as a goal-object O_3

During modelling process, each goal-object has discrete and binary behaviour. Behaviour is binary because all inputs and outputs deal with logical type of information: "true" or "false" only. Behaviour is discrete because there are only two states: goal is achieved or not. The behaviour is defined by the following expression:

$$Y_1 = Y_2 = \ldots = Y_j = \ldots = Y = \bigcap_i X_i$$

In each output (Y_1, Y_2, ...) is the same one value that is equal to the logical conjunction of all inputs X_i. Function objects that are connected to goal-object need special additional inputs and outputs for connections to the goals.

Cases that are more difficult occur when so called nested transformation is needed. It means that one construction is transformed into another construction and afterwards there is necessity to apply element to element transformation inside the construction. The nested transformation of the functional structure of MFM to the set of connected objects of the MSM is depicted in Figure 11. Symbols have the following meaning:

m - the number of output goals of functional structure;
k - the number of output goal groups of the functional structure;
r - the number of goals in the 1st group of goals (r=1,2,3,...);
T1 -the label ("A" or "A-C") of goal relationship for the 1st group;
Tk - the label ("A" or "A-C") of goal relationship for the k-th group;
f - the number of functions in the functional structure;
n - the number of input goals of functional structure;
i - the number of objects;
j - the number of functional structures in the model;

G1,...,Gm - the output goals of the functional structure;
Ga, Gb - the input goals of the functional structure.

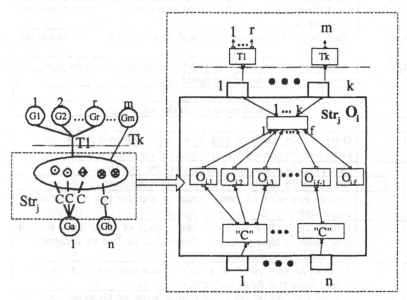

Figure 11. General example of functional structure transformation

6. Transformation Algorithms

The first step of the development of the transformation method is the linguistic description of the transformation algorithm. It represents the strategy and steps of transformation of model constructions and elements at certain level of details. Linguistic descriptions of two different transformation algorithms are given in Table 1 and Table 2. More detailed description is used for practical needs. The input of the transformation process is a model of Multilevel Flow Modelling. In accordance with defined similarity of model elements, functional structures and functions are changed into similar elements of Structural Modelling. The output of transformation process is the MSM of Structural Modelling.

Table 1. The linguistic description of 1st transformation algorithm

Step	Action
1.	*MFM model changing:*
1.1.	Create joining knot points with label "A" or "A-C" for replacement of grouped (by similar type) output goals of functional structure.
1.2.	Create joining knot points with label "A" or "A-C" for replacement of grouped (by similar type) input goals of functional structure.
1.3.	Create knot points with label "A" or "A-C" for each independent (not grouped) goal.

Table 1. The linguistic description of 1st transformation algorithm (continued)

Step	Action
1.4.	Place the knot points of functional structure output goals outside of the structures.
1.5.	Place the knot points of functional structure input goals inside the structures.
1.6.	Assign dependency-direction for all flow connections in the model.
1.7.	Determine the number of functional structures – j.
1.8.	*For each functional structure S_j do the following:*
1.8.1.	Determine the number of output goal groups of structure – k.
1.8.2.	Determine the number of output goals of the structure – m.
1.8.3.	Determine the number of input goals of the structure – n.
1.8.4.	Determine the number of functions within the structure – f.
1.8.5.	Replace ellipse of functional structure with the functional structure object with k output and n input contacts.
1.8.6.	Reconnect the flow nodes of knot points of input goals to their corresponding input goals (not directly but via free input contacts of functional structure object).
1.8.7.	Connect all knot points of functional structure output goals to the output contacts of functional structure object
1.8.8.	Create one special object of output goals of functional structure inside the structure. It will have f input and k output contacts.
1.8.9.	Connect each output contact of output goal object to the output contact of functional structure object.
1.8.10.	*Within the functional structure object S_j for each function F_f do the following:*
1.8.10.1.	Determine the number of input goals that are connected with conditional relationship to this function – c.
1.8.10.2.	Replace function with a similar object keeping (or restoring) connections with other functions or objects of functional structure object. (Reminder: a barrier function should be replaced by two objects!)
1.8.10.3.	If replaced (in previous step) function had a "R" type relationship with component then assign the name of the component as the name of the object. If the connected component has left only this one "R" type relationship function-component then eliminate the component. Eliminate the "R" type relationship of the replaced function.
1.8.10.4.	Supplement the object of function with c control inputs. Each control input connect to the corresponding knot point of functional structure input goal.
1.8.10.5.	Supplement a function with one output contact of functional state of the object.
1.8.10.6.	Connect the functional state output contact to any still free input contact of the output goal object of the functional structure object.

Table 1. The linguistic description of 1st transformation algorithm (continued)

Step	Action
1.9.	Replace each knot point of goal with additional goal object assigning the name of the knot point ("C", "A" or "A-C") as the name of the goal object.
1.10.	Replace each goal of the model with a goal object assigning the label of the goal as the name of the goal object.
2.	***Simplification of MSM model (it is not obligatory):***
2.1.	If it is necessary exclude all abstract transport objects replacing them by connecting flows.
2.2.	If it is necessary exclude all additional goal objects outside the functional structure objects that has only one input and only one output.
2.3.	Number the objects.

Table 2. The linguistic description of 2nd transformation algorithm

Step	Actions
1.	***Multilevel Flow Modelling model changing:***
1.1.	Delete all relationships of goals
1.2.	Delete all goals
1.3.	Attach labels of the functional structure to each flow inside the functional structure
1.4.	Delete functional structures
1.5.	Assign directions to flows
1.6.	Transform each function in accordance with similarity
1.7.	If replaced (in previous step) function had a "R" type relationship with component then the name of component assign as the name of the object. If the connected component has left only this one "R" type relationship function-component then eliminate the component. Eliminate the "R" type relationship of the replaced function.
2.	***Morphological Structure model simplification:***
2.1.	Combine repeated objects
2.2.	If it is necessary, exclude all abstract transport objects replacing them by connecting flows.
2.3.	Number the objects

The first algorithm includes goal transformation and multilevel transformation features while the second - transforms multilevel structure of the MFM model to the one level structure of the MSM. The first algorithm requires the extension of the MSM that is achieved by adding the concept "goal". When using the second algorithm, no changes of structural modelling are needed but the loss of knowledge about goals and multilevel constructions take place.

Due to the scope of this paper, the examples of model transformations are not included.

7. Conclusions

Model transformations supporting knowledge base integration within the structural modelling framework have been proposed. In general, the purpose of transformations is to support model integration from different approaches because model-based diagnosis requires a model of the system as a whole. In fact, transformations are closely related to the interface development problem. There are three options, namely, to use a universal interface, pair-wise interface or to use a universal modelling method. It is shown that in the case of rather similar modelling methods the transformation to universal modelling method is the most appropriate approach for model integration. One can find similarities of model elements to carry out the corresponding transformation. The paper deals only with transformations of models of multilevel flow modelling (MFM) to models of structural modelling (SM). Model transformations from the SM techniques to the MFM are under the development.

It is worth to point out that if one have an integrated knowledge base containing models of morphological structure then using ASMOS tools it is possible to generate functional models semi-automatically and to develop a deep knowledge rule base. Deep knowledge rule base supports several kinds of reasoning, namely, structural, behavioural and causal (diagnostic and predictive) reasoning [3].

Future work is connected with investigations of models from different classes and with looking for their similarities that will allow to expand the approach to other classes of models and to work out corresponding model transformation methods. The similarity aspects of semantics of models, i.e., the investigation of permissible level of knowledge losses during the model transformations, will be a topic of future research, too.

References

1. Abu-Hanna, A. *Multiple Domain Models in Diagnostic Reasoning.* Ph.D. Thesis, University of Amsterdam, Amsterdam, 1994.
2. Fang, M. *MFM Model Based Diagnosis and Implementation.* Report 94-D-712, Institute of Automatic Control Systems, Technical University of Denmark, Lyngby, 1994.
3. Grundspenkis, J. Reasoning supported by structural modelling. *Lecture Notes of the Nordic-Baltic Summer School'98: Intelligent Design, Intelligent Manufacturing and Intelligent Management,* Kaunas University of Technology Press "Technologija", Kaunas, 1999, pp. 57-100.
4. Grundspenkis, J. Structural modelling of complex technical systems in conditions of incomplete information: a review. *Modern Aspects of Management Science,* No. 1, Riga Technical University, Riga, 1997, pp. 111-135.
5. Grundspenkis, J. The extension of structural modelling approach for procedural knowledge representation. *Data Bases and Information Systems: Proceedings of the Third International Baltic Workshop,* 1, Latvian Academy Library, Riga, 1998, pp. 152-166.
6. Grundspenkis, J. The synthesis and analysis of structure in computer aided design. *Computer Applications in Production and Engineering: Proceedings of the First International Conference,* Amsterdam, 1983, pp. 301-316.
7. Jaako, J. *The Extension of Multilevel Flow Modelling.* PhD Thesis, Department of Process Engineering, University of Oulu, Oulu, 1996.
8. Kurki, M. *Model-Based Fault Diagnosis for Mechatronic Systems.* PhD. Thesis, Technical Research Centre of Finland, VTT Publications 223, Espoo, 1995.
9. Lind, M. *Representing Goals and Functions of Complex Systems - an Introduction to Multilevel Flow Modelling.* Institute of Automatic Control Systems, Technical University of Denmark, Lyngby, 1990.
10. Lind, M. Status and challenges of intelligent plant control. *Proceedings of 4th IFAC Symposium on Dynamics and Control of Chemical Reactors,* Helsingor, 1995.

Methods of Partial Logic for Knowledge Representation and Deductive Reasoning in Incompletely Specified Domains

Anatoly Prihozhy and Liudmila Prihozhaya

Information Technologies and Robotics Department,
State Politechnical Academy, Minsk, Belarus
aprihozhy@bspa.unibel.by

Abstract

This paper presents a new partial logic that generalises the traditional proposition and first order predicate logics for incompletely specified domains. Three values are considered in the partial logic (false, true, and don't care) instead of two values considered in the traditional logic. The operations, formulas, laws, and inference rules constitute a basis for knowledge representation and deductive reasoning when the world is not completely specified. The Robinson's resolution principle is generalised for situation when a clause can take the don't care value. Methods for the transition from partial deductive reasoning to inference in the first order predicate logic are proposed. The presented theoretical results are illustrated with examples. The proposed models and methods speed up the deductive reasoning process and decrease the number of clauses needed for knowledge representation.

Keywords: don't care value, partial logic, incompletely specified domain, knowledge representation, deductive reasoning, generalisation of Robinson's resolution principle.

1. Introduction

The use of knowledge-based systems technology simplifies modelling a large class of complex situations involving symbolic reasoning and eases the task of stating complicated things about irregular domains. Several knowledge-based systems environments have been developed, both in research institutions and commercially. These environments use technologies such as pattern-action rules, frames, variants of procedural attachment and others [2]. Such environments provide not only the internal representational structures of their chosen paradigm, but also interface facilities that understand and can manipulate these structures.

Logic systems mostly constitute a theoretical basis for knowledge-based technologies. Logic approaches can be classified on [1, 2, 3, 4, 5, 6, 7, 8, 9, 10, 11]:

- the set of truth values,
- methods of construction assertions and definition of semantics,
- methods of reasoning.

Taking account of the set of truth-values, the following logic systems are used:

- two-valued Boolean logic with the set of truth-values {false, true},
- multiple-valued logics with a finite or infinite set T of elements,
- probability-based logic with the truth-values belonging to interval $[0,\ldots 1]$,
- fuzzy logic with the set of truth-values consisting of fuzzy subsets of set T, and other logics.

Taking account of methods of constructing assertions and defining semantics, the logic systems are listed as follows:

J. Barzdins and A. Caplinskas (eds.), Databases and Information Systems, 275–295.

- two-valued proposition, first-, and higher-order predicate logics,
- multiple-valued proposition, first-, and higher-order predicate logics,
- probability-based and fuzzy proposition and first-order predicate logics, and others.

The existing logics use the following reasoning methods:
- inference rules (modus ponens and others),
- resolution principle,
- Bayes rule,
- solution of non-linear program in fuzzy logic and other methods.

Very often we deal with incompletely specified domains where assertions can be made for a part of situations. In this paper we propose a new partial logic that is based on three truth-values: *false, true*, and *don't care*. The logic is a generalisation for the traditional proposition and first order predicate logics. The key results of Robinson's work [8] hold in the partial logic as well. Although the value *don't care* has been used for many years, a novel aspect is that the partial logic allows for manipulation of the clause domains and simplification of the clauses during logic inference.

The paper is organised as follows. In section 2 we give a background of knowledge representation and reasoning. Basic concepts of partial proposition logic are considered in section 3. The syntax, semantics, and transformation procedures of partial first order predicate logic are presented in section 4. In section 5 the Robinson's resolution principle is generalised in the partial logic. Methods of transition from the partial to traditional first order predicate logic are proposed in section 6. Section 7 includes some experimental results. We conclude the work in section 8.

2. Methods of Knowledge Representation and Reasoning: Background

In a knowledge-based system [2, 8, 10, 11] the fundamental assumption is *"knowledge is power"*. The key idea is to separate knowledge of the task area as much as possible from the procedures that manipulate it.

A representation is a set of conventions for describing the world. The results of artificial intelligence research have been used to establish convenient ways of describing parts of the world. The current representation methods are not the final word. However, they are well enough developed that they can be used for problem solving in interesting domains. By separating a knowledge base from the inference procedures that work with the knowledge, a lot of systems were built that are understandable and extendable. The basic requirements on a knowledge representation scheme are extendibility, simplicity, and explicitness. To achieve these goals, three types of representation framework have been used: rule-based, frame-based, and logic-based systems [2, 3, 4, 5, 6, 7, 8].

Instead of viewing computation as a pre-specified sequence of operations, production systems view computation as the process of applying transformation rules in a sequence determined by the data. A classical production system has three major components: a global data base, rule base, and rule interpreter.

One approach to representing knowledge that allows rich linkages between facts is a generalisation of semantic nets known as frames. A frame is an encoding of knowledge about an object, including not only properties (slots) and values, but points to other frames and attached procedures for computing values.

A logic-based representation scheme is one in which knowledge about the world is represented as assertions in logic, usually first order predicate logic or a variant of it. This mode of representation is normally coupled with an inference procedure based on theorem proving. The rigor of logic is an advantage in specifying precisely what is known and knowing how the knowledge will be used. Besides the proposition and first order predicate logics, the multiple-valued [9], temporal

[3], and other logics constitute very important tools for solving various problems of computer science and artificial intelligence. A disadvantage is difficulty in dealing with the imprecision and uncertainty of plausible reasoning.

For many years, artificial intelligence research has focused on heuristic reasoning [10, 11]. Heuristics are an essential key to intelligent problem solving because computationally feasible, mathematically precise methods are known for only a relatively few classes of problems.

Incompletely specified functions that take values of the set *{false, true, don't care}* are a very useful mechanism for modelling incompletely specified domains, in particular, the process of logic synthesis of digital systems [1]. The application potential of the functions is restricted by the fact that their arguments can take only the truth-values *true* and *false*.

3. Partial Proposition Logic

The proposition variables and truth values are the primitive elements that are used for definition of more complex concepts in the partial proposition logic.

3.1 PARTIAL VALUES, VARIABLES AND FUNCTIONS

The traditional total logic considers two values: *true (1)* and *false* (0). The partial logic [5, 6, 7, 8] considers three values: *true (1), false (0)*, and *don't care (dc or -)*. The *don't care* value can be replaced with *true* or *false* arbitrarily. A total function $f(x_1,...,x_n)$ is a mapping $f: B^n \rightarrow B$ where $B=\{0,1\}$. A partial function $g(y_1,...,y_m)$ is a mapping $g: M^m \rightarrow M$ where $M=\{0,1,-\}$. An incompletely specified function $h(x_1,...,x_n)$ is a mapping $h: B^n \rightarrow M$. A variable that takes values from the set B will be called a *total variable*, and a variable that takes values from the set M will be called a *partial variable*.

A partial function $g(y_1,...,y_m)$ is valid if for all vectors $a', a'' \in M^m$ such that $g(a')=1$ and $g(a'')=0$ the vectors a' and a'' are orthogonal. The vectors $a'=(a'_1,...,a'_m)$ and $a''=(a''_1,...,a''_m)$ are orthogonal if an integer j exists such that $a'_j=0$ and $a''_j=1$, or $a'_j=1$ and $a''_j=0$.

A *Value-Domain Representation (VDR)* is the following encoding of a partial variable y_i with a pair $(v_i|d_i)$ of total variables [4, 5, 6, 7]:

$$y_i = \begin{cases} 0 & \text{if } v_i=0 \text{ and } d_i=1 \\ 1 & \text{if } v_i=1 \text{ and } d_i=1 \\ dc & \text{if } v_i \in \{0,1\} \text{ and } d_i=0. \end{cases} \qquad (3.1)$$

The variable v_i is called a value variable and the variable d_i is called a domain variable. Due to VDR, a partial function $z=g(y_1,...,y_m)$ of m three-valued arguments is represented as an incompletely specified function $z'=g'((v_1|d_1),...,(v_m|d_m))$ of $2*m$ two-valued arguments. The partial function z' can be considered as a pair $(v|d)$ of total functions depending on the primary variables $v_1, d_1, ... , v_m, d_m$. In this case the Boolean space is broken down into three parts as shown in Fig. 1:

- on-set g^{on} is a part (a set of vector values) where the function takes value 1, the part is described by the expression $g^{on}=(v\&d)^{on}$ where $\&$ is the total *conjunction* operation,
- off-set g^{off} is a part where the function takes value 0, the part is described by the expression $g^{off}=(\sim v\&d)^{on}$ where $\sim$ is the total *negation* operation,
- don't care set g^{dc} is a part where the function takes value *don't care*, the part is described by the expression $g^{dc}=(\sim d)^{on}$.

Logic assertions that can be formulated concerning the third part take value don't care that can be replaced with value *true* or value *false* arbitrarily.

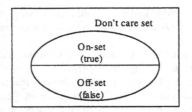

Figure 1. Structure of Boolean space

3.2 PARTIAL LOGIC OPERATIONS

Monadic and dyadic partial operations are basic ones in the partial logic. They allow for representation of all the partial functions through using a composition operation. There exist 27 monadic partial operations. Five of them are defined in Table 1: *constant 0, constant 1, constant dc, identity*, and *negation*. The third to fifth columns of the table describe the operation values for various values of the three-valued argument y. The sixth column indicates an operator that is used for corresponding operation, and the seventh column presents a Value-Domain Representation of the operation, where v_1 and d_1 are Boolean variables that encode the partial variable y_1.

Exactly 19683 dyadic partial operations are possible. Ten of them that generalise the traditional dyadic logical operations are defined in Table 2. For the partial operations, we use underlined operators that are similar to the operators used for the traditional Boolean operations. The dyadic operations are as follows: *conjunction, disjunction, Sheffer stroke, Pierce arrow, implication, implication negation, consequence, consequence negation, exclusive OR, and equivalence*. The third to eleventh columns of the table present the operation values for various values of partial variables y_1 and y_2. The thirteenth column presents a Value-Domain Representation of each dyadic partial operation, where v_1, d_1 v_2, and d_2 are Boolean variables that encode the partial variables y_1 and y_2.

In the pair *(v|d)* function d is fixed. The function v can be replaced with another total function v_i such that *$(v_i|d)=(v|d)$* or $v_i\&d=v\&d$. In other words, the VDRs *$(v_i|d)$* and *(v|d)* represent the same incompletely specified function. If V is the set of functions v_i then for each $v_i \in V$ the inequality as follows

$$(v\&d)^{on} \subseteq v_i^{on} \subseteq (v+\sim d)^{on} \tag{3.2}$$

holds where + is the total *disjunction* operation. A minimisation operation *min(v|d)* is a mapping *min*: $F \times F \rightarrow F$ where F is the set of total functions $f: B^n \rightarrow B$. The operation selects one function from the set V. Different definitions for *min(v|d)* are possible [7]. These depend on which representation forms for v and d are used.

Table 1. Monadic partial logical operations

N	Operation name	Partial variable y			Operator	Representation in VDR
		0	1	−		
1	Constant 0	0	0	0	$\underline{c0}(y_1)$	$\underline{c0}(v_1|d_1)$
2	Constant 1	1	1	1	$\underline{c1}(y_1)$	$\underline{c1}(v_1|d_1)$
3	Constant −	−	−	−	$\underline{c-}(y_1)$	$\underline{c-}(v_1|d_1)$
4	Identity	0	1	−	$\underline{\equiv}(y_1)$	$\underline{\equiv}(v_1|d_1)$
5	Negation	1	0	−	$\underline{\sim}(y_1)$	$\underline{\sim}(v_1|d_1)$

Table 2. Dyadic partial logical operations

N	Operation name	0	1	–	0	1	–	0	1	–	Operator	Representation in VDR
		0	0	0	1	1	1	–	–	–		
1	Conjunction	0	0	0	0	1	–	0	–	–	$y_1 \& y_2$	$(v_1|d_1) \& (v_2|d_2)$
2	Disjunction	0	1	–	1	1	1	–	1	–	$y_1 \pm y_2$	$(v_1|d_1) \pm (v_2|d_2)$
3	Sheffer stroke	1	1	1	1	0	–	1	–	–	y_1 / y_2	$(v_1|d_1) / (v_2|d_2)$
4	Pierce arrow	1	0	–	0	0	0	–	0	–	$y_1 \downarrow y_2$	$(v_1|d_1) \downarrow (v_2|d_2)$
5	Implication	1	0	–	1	1	1	1	–	–	$y_1 \rightarrow y_2$	$(v_1|d_1) \rightarrow (v_2|d_2)$
6	Consequence	1	1	1	0	1	–	–	1	–	$y_1 \leftarrow y_2$	$(v_1|d_1) \leftarrow (v_2|d_2)$
7	Negation of implication	0	1	–	0	0	0	0	–	–	$y_1 \sim> y_2$	$(v_1|d_1) \sim> (v_2|d_2)$
8	Negation of consequence	0	0	0	1	0	–	–	0	–	$y_1 <\sim y_2$	$(v_1|d_1) <\sim (v_2|d_2)$
9	Exclusive OR	0	1	–	1	0	–	–	–	–	$y_1 \oplus y_2$	$(v_1|d_1) \oplus (v_2|d_2)$
10	Equivalence	1	0	–	0	1	–	–	–	–	$y_1 \equiv y_2$	$(v_1|d_1) \equiv (v_2|d_2)$

3.3 EXPRESSIONS

A formula that is interpreted using a two-valued truth function will be called a total formula. A formula that is interpreted using a truth function taking a value from the set M will be called a partial formula. As we allow for using only Boolean primary variables, a partial formula has to contain at least one pair $(F|G)$ of total formulas F and G. The partial logical operators are used for construction of partial formulas. If the total logical operators such as *negation* (~), *conjunction* (&), *disjunction* (+), *Sheffer stroke* (/), *Pierce arrow* ($\downarrow$), *implication* ($\rightarrow$), *negation of implication* (~>), *consequence* ($\leftarrow$), *negation of consequence* (<~), *exclusive OR* ($\oplus$), and *equivalence* ($\equiv$) are used as well, then the formula will be called a mixed total-partial formula. The formula as follows

$$(x1|x2) \underline{\&} ((x2|x3) \underline{\pm} (x3|x2) \underline{\rightarrow} (x4|x1)) \tag{3.3}$$

is a partial formula, and the following formula:

$$(x1 \& x2|x2 \rightarrow x3) \oplus (x2|x1 + x3 + x4) \underline{\pm} (\sim x3 + \sim x4|x1) \tag{3.4}$$

is a mixed total-partial formula where $x1$, $x2$, $x3$, $x4$ are total Boolean variables. The expressions of the considered type represent incompletely specified functions through using partial operations.

Example 3.1. The incompletely specified function defined in Table 3 is represented by the following total-partial expression: $f=(\sim x_1 + \sim x_2 + \sim x_3|x_1 \& x_2 + \sim x_3 \& (x_1 + x_2))$.

Table 3. Example incompletely specified function

x_1	x_2	x_3	f
0	0	0	–
0	0	1	–
0	1	0	1
0	1	1	–
1	0	0	1
1	0	1	–
1	1	0	1
1	1	1	0

Example 3.2. Let we have three total assertions as follows:
"*The student studies at a state university*" – X
"*The student will work at a state institution*" – Y
"*He / she is a belarusian student*" – Z.

Based on the total assertions and the proposition variables X, Y, and Z the following partial assertion can be constructed:

Y if X on Z $\Rightarrow$ $(Y \leftarrow X \mid Z)$.

The partial assertion consists of two parts: the value part Y if X (or $Y \leftarrow X$) and the domain part Z. The assertion is interpreted with the partial truth function presented in Table 4. It is easy to see, the assertion $Y \leftarrow X$ is essential if the student is a belarusian one and is not essential in opposite case.

Table 4. Partial truth function

Proposition variables			Partial assertion
X	Y	Z	
false	false	false	don't care
false	false	true	true
false	true	false	don't care
false	true	true	true
true	false	false	don't care
true	false	true	false
true	true	false	don't care
true	true	true	true

3.4 PARTIAL LOGIC LAWS

We formulate a partial logic law as

$$Lp = Rp, \tag{3.5}$$

where Lp and Rp are the left and right parts respectively in the law. The parts Lp and Rp are partial formulas. The values of the formulas have to belong the set M and have to be the same at any values of total proposition variables v, d, v_1, d_1, v_2, and d_2 occurring in the formulas. In this section we consider three types of laws:

- the laws that maintain transformation of an arbitrary partial proposition logic formula to a pair of total formulas,
- the laws that are generalisations for appropriate laws in the traditional logic,
- the novel laws of partial logic that maintain an equivalent transformation of a partial formula.

3.4.1 Transforming partial operations to pairs of total formulas

The monadic partial logical operations are transformed to pairs of total formulas through using the laws as follows:

$$\underline{c0}(v \mid d) = (0 \mid 1) \tag{3.6}$$
$$\underline{c1}(v \mid d) = (1 \mid 1) \tag{3.7}$$
$$\underline{c\sim}(v \mid d) = (v \mid 0) \tag{3.8}$$
$$\underline{=}(v \mid d) = (v \mid d) \tag{3.9}$$
$$\underline{\sim}(v \mid d) = (\sim v \mid 0). \tag{3.10}$$

The following laws constitute a basis for transformation of the dyadic partial operations to pairs of total formulas:

$$(v_1 \mid d_1)\underline{\&}(v_2 \mid d_2) = (v_1 \& v_2 \mid d_1 \& d_1 + \sim v_1 \& d_1 + \sim v_2 \& d_2), \tag{3.11}$$
$$(v_1 \mid d_1)\underline{+}(v_2 \mid d_2) = (v_1 + v_2 \mid d_1 \& d_1 + v_1 \& d_1 + v_2 \& d_2), \tag{3.12}$$
$$(v_1 \mid d_1)\underline{/}(v_2 \mid d_2) = (v_1 / v_2 \mid d_1 \& d_1 + \sim v_1 \& d_1 + \sim v_2 \& d_2), \tag{3.13}$$
$$(v_1 \mid d_1)\underline{\downarrow}(v_2 \mid d_2) = (v_1 \downarrow v_2 \mid d_1 \& d_1 + v_1 \& d_1 + v_2 \& d_2), \tag{3.14}$$
$$(v_1 \mid d_1)\underline{\rightarrow}\&(v_2 \mid d_2) = (v_1 \rightarrow v_2 \mid d_1 \& d_1 + \sim v_1 \& d_1 + v_2 \& d_2), \tag{3.15}$$

$$(v_1|d_1)\underleftarrow{}\&(v_2|d_2)= (v_1\leftarrow v_2|d_1\&d_1+v_1\&d_1+{\sim}v_2\&d_2), \quad (3.16)$$

$$(v_1|d_1)\underrightarrow{\geq}(v_2|d_2) = (v_1{\sim}{>}v_2|d_1\&d_1+{\sim}v_1\&d_1+v_2\&d_2), \quad (3.17)$$

$$(v_1|d_1)\underline{\leq}{\sim}(v_2|d_2) = (v_1{<}{\sim}v_2|d_1\&d_1+v_1\&d_1+{\sim}v_2\&d_2), \quad (3.18)$$

$$(v_1|d_1)\underline{\oplus}(v_2|d_2) = (v_1\oplus v_2|d_1\&d_1), \quad (3.19)$$

$$(v_1|d_1)\underline{\equiv}(v_2|d_2) = (v_1{\equiv}v_2|d_1\&d_1), \quad (3.20)$$

A proof of equivalence (3.11) is presented in Table 5 where two last columns are identical. The values of pairs $(v_1|d_1)$, $(v_2|d_2)$, and $(v_1\&v_2|d_1\&d_1+{\sim}v_1\&d_1+{\sim}v_2\&d_2)$ are computed through (3.1), and the values of expression $(v_1|d_1)\underline{\&}(v_2|d_2)$ are computed through using row 1 of Table 2. It is easy to see, the proof of other equivalencies is performed in the similar way.

Table 5. Proof of equivalence (3.11)

v_1	d_1	v_2	d_2	$(v_1|d_1)$	$(v_2|d_2)$	$v_1\&v_2$	$d_1\&d_1+{\sim}v_1\&d_1+{\sim}v_2\&d_2$	$(v_1|d_1)\underline{\&}(v_2|d_2)$	$(v_1\&v_2|d_1\&d_1+{\sim}v_1\&d_1+{\sim}v_2\&d_2)$
0	0	0	0	–	–	0	0	–	–
0	0	0	1	–	0	0	1	0	0
0	0	1	0	–	–	0	0	–	–
0	0	1	1	–	1	0	0	–	–
0	1	0	0	0	–	0	1	0	0
0	1	0	1	0	0	0	1	0	0
0	1	1	0	0	–	0	1	0	0
0	1	1	1	0	1	0	1	0	0
1	0	0	0	–	–	0	0	–	–
1	0	0	1	–	0	0	1	0	0
1	0	1	0	–	–	1	0	–	–
1	0	1	1	–	1	1	0	–	–
1	1	0	0	1	–	0	0	–	–
1	1	0	1	1	0	0	1	0	0
1	1	1	0	1	–	1	0	–	–
1	1	1	1	1	1	1	1	1	1

The domain parts of pairs appearing in the right parts of (3.11) to (3.20) are represented as a sum of products. In the following versions of the laws the domain part is represented as a product of sums:

$$(v_1|d_1)\underline{\&}(v_2|d_2) = (v_1\&v_2|(d_1+d_1)\&({\sim}v_2+d_1)\&({\sim}v_1+d_2)) \quad (3.21)$$

$$(v_1|d_1)\underline{+}(v_2|d_2) = (v_1+v_2|(d_1+d_1)\&(v_2+d_1)\&(v_1+d_2)) \quad (3.22)$$

$$(v_1|d_1)\underline{/}(v_2|d_2) = (v_1/v_2|(d_1+d_1)\&({\sim}v_2+d_1)\&({\sim}v_1+d_2)) \quad (3.23)$$

$$(v_1|d_1)\underline{\downarrow}(v_2|d_2) = (v_1{\downarrow}v_2|(d_1+d_1)\&(v_2+d_1)\&(v_1+d_2)) \quad (3.24)$$

$$(v_1|d_1)\underrightarrow{}\&(v_2|d_2)= (v_1{\rightarrow}v_2|(d_1+d_1)\&(v_2+d_1)\&({\sim}v_1+d_2)) \quad (3.25)$$

$$(v_1|d_1)\underleftarrow{}\&(v_2|d_2)= (v_1{\leftarrow}v_2|(d_1+d_1)\&({\sim}v_2+d_1)\&(v_1+d_2)) \quad (3.26)$$

$$(v_1|d_1)\underrightarrow{\geq}(v_2|d_2) = (v_1{\sim}{>}v_2|(d_1+d_1)\&(v_2+d_1)\&({\sim}v_1+d_2)) \quad (3.27)$$

$$(v_1|d_1)\underline{\leq}{\sim}(v_2|d_2) = (v_1{<}{\sim}v_2|(d_1+d_1)\&({\sim}v_2+d_1)\&(v_1+d_2)). \quad (3.28)$$

If $d_1=d_2=1$ then the partial operations become completely specified. In particular, the partial conjunction $(v_1|1)\underline{\&}(v_2|1)$ is transformed to the total traditional conjunction $v_1\&v_2$ in the following way: $(v_1|1)\underline{\&}(v_2|1) = (v_1\&v_2|1+{\sim}v_1\&1+{\sim}v_2\&1) = (v_1\&v_2|1) = v_1\&v_2$.

3.4.2 Generalisation of traditional logic laws

The key laws of the traditional two-valued logic are generalised in the partial logic as:

$${\sim}{\sim}(v|d) = (v|d) \quad (3.29)$$

$$(v_1|d_1)\underline{\&}(v_2|d_2) = (v_2|d_2)\underline{\&}(v_1|d_1) \tag{3.30}$$

$$(v_1|d_1)\underline{\&}((v_2|d_2)\underline{\&}(v_3|d_3)) = ((v_1|d_1)\underline{\&}(v_2|d_2))\underline{\&}(v_3|d_3) \tag{3.31}$$

$$(v_1|d_1)\underline{+}(v_2|d_2) = (v_2|d_2)\underline{+}(v_1|d_1) \tag{3.32}$$

$$(v_1|d_1)\underline{+}((v_2|d_2)\underline{+}(v_3|d_3)) = ((v_1|d_1)\underline{+}(v_2|d_2))\underline{+}(v_3|d_3) \tag{3.33}$$

$$(v_1|d_1)\underline{\&}((v_2|d_2)\underline{+}(v_3|d_3)) = ((v_1|d_1)\underline{\&}(v_2|d_2))\underline{+}((v_1|d_1)\underline{\&}(v_3|d_3)) \tag{3.34}$$

$$(v_1|d_1)\underline{+}((v_2|d_2)\underline{\&}(v_3|d_3)) = ((v_1|d_1)\underline{+}(v_2|d_2))\underline{\&}((v_1|d_1)\underline{+}(v_3|d_3)) \tag{3.35}$$

$$\underline{\sim}((v_1|d_1)\underline{\&}(v_2|d_2)) = \underline{\sim}(v_1|d_1)\underline{+}\underline{\sim}(v_2|d_2) \tag{3.36}$$

$$\underline{\sim}((v_1|d_1)\underline{+}(v_2|d_2)) = \underline{\sim}(v_1|d_1)\underline{\&}\underline{\sim}(v_2|d_2) \tag{3.37}$$

$$(v_1|d_1)\underline{\&}((v_1|d_1)\underline{+}(v_2|d_2)) = (v_1|d_1) \tag{3.38}$$

$$(v_1|d_1)\underline{+}((v_1|d_1)\underline{\&}(v_2|d_2)) = (v_1|d_1) \tag{3.39}$$

$$(v|d)\underline{\&}(v|d) = (v|d) \tag{3.40}$$

$$(v|d)\underline{+}(v|d) = (v|d) \tag{3.41}$$

$$(v|d)\underline{\&}\underline{\sim}(v|d) = (0|d) \tag{3.42}$$

$$(v|d)\underline{+}\underline{\sim}(v|d) = (1|d) \tag{3.43}$$

$$(v|d)\underline{\&}(1|1) = (v|d) \tag{3.44}$$

$$(v|d)\underline{+}(0|1) = (v|d) \tag{3.45}$$

$$(v|d)\underline{\&}(0|1) = (0|1) \tag{3.46}$$

$$(v|d)\underline{+}(1|1) = (1|1) \tag{3.47}$$

$$(0|1)\underline{\rightarrow}(v|d) = (0|1) \tag{3.48}$$

$$(v|d)\underline{\rightarrow}(v|d) = (1|d) \tag{3.49}$$

$$(v|d)\underline{\rightarrow}(1|1) = (1|1) \tag{3.50}$$

$$(v_1|d_1)\underline{\rightarrow}(v_2|d_2) = \underline{\sim}(v_1|d_1)\underline{+}(v_2|d_2) \tag{3.51}$$

$$(v_1|d_1)\underline{\rightarrow}(v_2|d_2) = \underline{\sim}(v_2|d_2)\underline{\rightarrow}\underline{\sim}(v_1|d_1). \tag{3.52}$$

Equivalence (3.29) is the *double negation* law. Equivalencies (3.30) and (3.32) are the *commutative* laws for partial conjunction and partial disjunction respectively. Equivalencies (3.31) and (3.33) are the *associative,* and equivalencies (3.34) and (3.35) are the *distributive* laws for partial conjunction and disjunction. Equivalencies (3.36) and (3.37) are the *de Morgan's* laws. The *absorption* laws are represented by equalities (3.38) to (3.50). Laws (3.51) and (3.52) allow for transformation of partial implication.

3.4.3 Novel laws in partial logic

The partial logic has own novel laws that constitute a mechanism for manipulation of value and domain parts of pairs representing incompletely specified functions:

$$(v_1|d)\underline{\&}(v_2|d) = (v_1\&v_2|d) \tag{3.53}$$

$$(v_1|d)\underline{+}(v_2|d) = (v_1+v_2|d) \tag{3.54}$$

$$(v|d_1)\underline{\&}(v|d_2) = (v|d_1\&d_2+\sim v\&(d_1+d_2)) \tag{3.55}$$

$$(v|d_1)\underline{+}(v|d_2) = (v|d_1\&d_2+v\&(d_1+d_2)) \tag{3.56}$$

$$(v|v) = (1|v) \tag{3.57}$$

$$(\sim v|v) = (0|v) \tag{3.58}$$

$$(v\&d|d) = (v|d) \tag{3.59}$$

$$(v+d|d) = (1|d) \tag{3.60}$$

$$(v\&\sim d|d) = (0|d) \tag{3.61}$$

$$(v+\sim d|d) = (v|d) \tag{3.62}$$

$$(v|v\&d) = (1|v\&d) \tag{3.63}$$

$$(v|\sim v\&d) = (0|\sim v\&d) \tag{3.64}$$

$$(v|v\&d) = (v|d)\underline{+}(v|0) \tag{3.65}$$

$$(v|\sim v\&d) = (v|d)\underline{\&}(v|0) \tag{3.66}$$

$$(v|v+d) = (v|1)\underline{+}(0|d) \tag{3.67}$$
$$(v|{\sim}v+d) = (v|1)\underline{\&}(1|d) \tag{3.68}$$
$$({\sim}v|v+d) = ({\sim}v|1)\underline{\&}(1|d) \tag{3.69}$$
$$({\sim}v|{\sim}v+d) = ({\sim}v|1)\underline{+}(0|d) \tag{3.70}$$
$$(f|x_i) = (f(x_i=1)|x_i) \tag{3.71}$$
$$(f|{\sim}x_i) = (f(x_i=0)|x_i) \tag{3.72}$$
$$(f(v)|v\oplus d) = (f({\sim}d)|v\oplus d) \tag{3.73}$$
$$(f(v)|v\equiv d) = (f(d)|v\equiv d). \tag{3.74}$$

Equivalencies (3.53) and (3.54) prove that partial logical operations do not modify the domain part if the part is the same in the both operands. Equivalencies (3.55) and (3.56) show how the domain part is determined when the partial conjunction is applied to two source pairs with the same value part. Laws (3.57) to (3.64) allows for simplification of the value part in special cases. Equivalencies (3.65) to (3.70) are expansions of an incompletely specified function on partial conjunction and partial disjunction. Laws (3.71) to (3.74) constitute a mechanism for transformation of the total function appearing in the value part.

4. Partial First Order Predicate Logic

The syntax and semantics of the partial first order predicate logic are described in this section. We also present a method for transforming a formula to a form that can be efficiently used for logic inference in the partial logic.

4.1 SYNTAX

The *alphabet* of our language consists of:
1) delimiters ',', '(', ')', '|',
2) variables of a set V,
3) total logical operators $\sim$, $\&$, $+$, $\rightarrow$, $\oplus$, and others,
4) partial logical operators $\underline{\sim}$, $\underline{\&}$, $\underline{+}$, $\underline{\rightarrow}$, $\underline{\oplus}$, and others,
5) functional symbols $f_1^{n_1},...,f_i^{n_i},...$ of degree $n_i \geq 0$; a functional symbol f^0 of degree $n=0$ is an individual constant,
6) predicate symbols $P_1^{n_1},...,P_i^{n_i},...$ of degree $n_i \geq 0$; a predicate symbol P^0 of degree $n=0$ is a proposition variable,
7) total universal quantifier $\forall$, total existential quantifier $\exists$, partial universal quantifier $\underline{\forall}$, and partial existential quantifier $\underline{\exists}$.

The alphabet symbols are used for building expressions.

Terms:
1) an individual constant f^0 is a term,
2) a variable $v \in V$ is a term,
3) a functional symbol $f_i^n(t_1,...,t_n)$ followed by n terms is a term.

Atomic formulas:
1) a proposition variable P^0 is an atomic formula,
2) a predicate symbol $P_i^n(t_1,...t_n)$ followed by n terms is an atomic formula.

Literals:
i) an atomic formula is a literal,
2) if A is an atomic formula then $\sim A$ is a literal.

A literal containing no variables is called a ground literal. Two literals A and $\sim A$ constitute a complementary pair.

Total formulas:
1) an atomic formula is a total formula,
2) if F is a total formula then $(\sim F)$ is a total formula,
3) if F and G are total formulas then $(F\&G)$, $(F+G)$, $(F{\rightarrow}G)$, $(F{\oplus}G)$, ... are total formulas,
4) if F is a total formula and x is a variable, then $(\forall x)F$ and $(\exists x)F$ are total formulas.
Sometimes we will omit the parentheses, taking into account the priority of operations.
Partial formulas:
1) a pair $(F|G)$ of total formulas is a partial formula,
2) if R is a partial formula then $(\underset{\sim}{\sim}R)$ is a partial formula,
3) if R and Q are partial formulas then $(R\underline{\&}Q)$, $(R\underline{+}Q)$, $(R{\underline{\rightarrow}}Q)$, $(R\underline{\oplus}Q)$, ... are partial formulas,
4) if R is a partial formula and x is a variable, then $(\underline{\forall}x)R$ and $(\underline{\exists}x)R$ are partial formulas.

4.2 SEMANTICS

The semantics of our language is defined as follows.

With each total logical operator we associate a truth function $B^n{\rightarrow}B$ where n is the arity of operator. The truth functions for operators $\sim$, $\&$, $+$, $\rightarrow$, and $\oplus$ are well known.

The incompletely specified function $B{\times}B{\rightarrow}M$ defined in Table 6 is put into accordance with the pair $(F|G)$. With each partial logical operator we associate a partial function $M^n{\rightarrow}M$ from Table 1 and Table 2. The semantics of the universal and existential quantifiers $(\underline{\forall}x)R$ and $(\underline{\exists}x)R$ is represented by the functions described in Table 7. The functions are mappings $M^+{\rightarrow}M$, where M^+ is the set of all subsets of set M excluding the empty set. The ordinary universal and existential quantifiers $(\forall x)R$ and $(\exists x)R$ are defined in the traditional way.

Table 6. Truth function for pair $(F|G)$

F	G	(F|G)
0	0	-
0	1	0
1	0	-
1	1	1

Table 7. Functions for $(\underline{\forall}x)R$ and $(\underline{\exists}x)R$

The set of values of R	$(\underline{\forall}x)R$	$(\underline{\exists}x)R$
{0}	0	0
{1}	1	1
{-}	-	-
{0,1}	0	1
{0,-}	0	-
{1,-}	-	1
{0,1,-}	0	1

Let a set D be the domain. We assign a function $D^n{\rightarrow}D$ to each n-place functional symbol f_i^n, and assign a function $D^n{\rightarrow}B$ to each n-place predicate symbol P_i^n. Each variable of V is mapped to an element of D. An evaluation function $v_I(R)$ computes the value of a partial formula R for interpretation I. An interpretation I satisfies a partial formula R if $v_I(R){\in}\{1,-\}$. The formula R is called unsatisfiable if there is no interpretation that satisfies R.

4.3 TRANSFORMING A PARTIAL FORMULA

Now we describe a method of transforming any partial formula to the following special form:

$(F|G)$.   (4.1)

The parts F and G are total formulas without any quantifiers. Each total formula is a conjunction of sentences and each sentence is a disjunction of literals. The transformation procedure includes the steps as follows:

- eliminating the total logical operators except negation, conjunction, and disjunction,
- introducing a unique variable for each quantifier,
- reducing the scope of negation operations,
- eliminating the existential quantifiers,
- moving the universal quantifiers to the formula prefix,
- removing the formula prefix,
- eliminating all the partial logical operators,
- transforming the partial formula matrix to a pair of sets of total clauses.

Example 4.1. Each step of the transformation procedure will be illustrated through using the following example partial formula:

$$(\underline{\forall}x)((\underline{\forall}y)(\sim Q(c,x){\rightarrow}R(a,y) \mid Q(y,b)) \underline{\&} (\underline{\exists}z)\underline{\sim}(\underline{\exists}y)(R(y,z){+}P(x) \mid P(b))),$$ (4.2)

where x, y, and z are variables, a, d, and c are individual constants, and P, Q, and R are predicate symbols.

Step 1. Eliminating the total logical operators except $\sim$, $\&$, and $+$. The known equivalencies are used for this purpose. Performing the step for formula (4.1) we eliminate implication in the value part of first pair and obtain the formula as follows:

$$(\underline{\forall}x)((\underline{\forall}y)(Q(c,x){+}R(a,y) \mid Q(y,b)) \underline{\&} (\underline{\exists}z)\underline{\sim}(\underline{\exists}y)(R(y,z){+}P(x) \mid P(b))).$$ (4.3)

Step 2. Introducing a unique variable for each quantifier. Formula (4.3) uses three variables: x, y, and z. Each of them is under a quantifier. The variable y is used twice. Therefore, we rename the variable at the second existential quantifier and have the following formula:

$$(\underline{\forall}x)((\underline{\forall}y)(Q(c,x){+}R(a,y) \mid Q(y,b)) \underline{\&} (\underline{\exists}z)\underline{\sim}(\underline{\exists}v)(R(v,z){+}P(x) \mid P(b))).$$ (4.4)

Step 3. Reducing the scope of the total $\sim$ and partial $\underline{\sim}$ negation operators. The double negation and de Morgan's laws for conjunction and disjunction are used. Besides, one has to use the equivalencies as follows:

$$\underline{\sim}(F|G) = (\sim F|G)$$ (4.5)
$$\underline{\sim}(\underline{\forall}x)(F|G) = (\underline{\exists}x)\underline{\sim}(F|G)$$ (4.6)
$$\underline{\sim}(\underline{\exists}x)(F|G) = (\underline{\forall}x)\underline{\sim}(F|G).$$ (4.7)

It is easy to proof equivalence (4.5). Equivalencies (4.6) and (4.7) are proved by Table 8. Columns 5 and 7 are identical (this proves (4.6)) and columns 4 and 8 are identical as well (this proves (4.7)).

Formula (4.4) contains one total negation operator. Applying equivalencies (4.7), (4.5), and one of the de Morgan's laws to the formula, we generate the formula as follows:

Table 8. Proof of equivalencies (4.6) and (4.7)

$(F|G)$	$\underline{\sim}(F|G)$	$(\underline{\exists}x)(F|G)$	$\underline{\sim}(\underline{\exists}x)(F|G)$	$(\underline{\exists}x)\underline{\sim}(F|G)$	$(\underline{\forall}x)(F|G)$	$\underline{\sim}(\underline{\forall}x)(F|G)$	$(\underline{\forall}x)\underline{\sim}(F|G)$
{0}	{1}	0	1	1	0	1	1
{1}	{0}	1	0	0	1	0	0
{-}	{-}	-	-	-	-	-	-
{0,1}	{0,1}	1	0	1	0	1	0
{0,-}	{1,-}	-	-	1	0	1	-
{1,-}	{0,-}	1	0	-	-	-	0
{0,1,-}	{0,1,-}	1	0	1	0	1	0

$(\underline{\forall}x)((\underline{\forall}y)(Q(c,x)+R(a,y) \mid Q(y,b)) \underline{\&} (\exists z)(\underline{\forall}v)(\sim R(v,z)\&\sim P(x) \mid P(b)))$.   (4.8)

Step 4. Eliminating the total and partial existential quantifiers by means of introducing a function symbol instead of the variable under the quantifier. If the existential quantifier is located after n universal quantifiers then the symbol is of degree n. If there are no universal quantifiers before the existential quantifier then $n=0$. Analysing formula (4.8), we conclude that the existential quantifier $(\exists z)$ is located after the universal quantifier $(\underline{\forall}x)$. Therefore, the variable z is replaced with a function symbol $f(x)$:

$(\underline{\forall}x)((\underline{\forall}y)(Q(c,x)+R(a,y) \mid Q(y,b)) \underline{\&} (\underline{\forall}v)(\sim R(v,f(x))\&\sim P(x) \mid P(b)))$.   (4.9)

Step 5. Moving the total and partial universal quantifiers to the formula prefix. To perform the moving, equivalencies as follows are used:

$((\forall x)F \mid G) = (\underline{\forall}x)(F \mid G)$ (4.10)

$((\underline{\forall}x)R)\underline{\&}Q = (\underline{\forall}x)(R\underline{\&}Q)$ (4.11)

$((\underline{\forall}x)R)\underline{+}Q = (\underline{\forall}x)(R\underline{+}Q)$.   (4.12)

Equivalence (4.10) allows for moving the ordinary total quantifier from the value part of a pair and replacing the total quantifier with a partial quantifier. The equivalence is proved by the contents of Table 9: columns 4 and 6 of the table are identical. Equivalencies (4.11) and (4.12) allow for moving the quantifier from the operands of conjunction and disjunction operators. They are proved by the contents of Table 10: columns 4 and 6 as well as columns 7 and 9 are identical. While moving to the prefix, the ordinary quantifiers may be replaced with partial quantifiers.

In order to move the universal quantifier from a partial formula to the prefix we additionally need the equivalence as:

$(F \mid (\forall x)G) = (\underline{\forall}x)(F \mid G)$.   (4.13)

Analysing Table 11, we conclude that the equality holds in all the cases except case 3, where the formula $(F \mid (\forall x)G)$ takes value '-' and the formula $(\forall x)(F \mid G)$ takes value 0. The transition from value '-' to value 0 is eligible; therefore equivalence (4.13) can be used during the formula transformation. Applying equivalence (4.11) to formula (4.9), we generate formula (4.14):

$(\underline{\forall}x)(\underline{\forall}y)(\underline{\forall}v)((Q(c,x)+R(a,y) \mid Q(y,b)) \underline{\&} (\sim R(v,f(x))\&\sim P(x) \mid P(b)))$ (4.14)

Step 6. Removing the formula prefix. After the removing, the formula consists of a matrix. Formula (4.14) is directly transformed to

$(Q(c,x)+R(a,y) \mid Q(y,b)) \underline{\&} (\sim R(v,f(x))\&\sim P(x) \mid P(b)))$.   (4.15)

Table 9. Proof of equivalence (4.10)

F	G	$(\forall x)F$	$((\forall x)F \mid G)$	$(F \mid G)$	$(\underline{\forall}x)(F \mid G)$
{0}	0	0	-	{-}	-
{1}	0	1	-	{-}	-
{0,1}	0	0	-	{-}	-
{0}	1	0	0	{0}	0
{1}	1	1	1	{1}	1
{0,1}	1	0	0	{0,1}	0

Table 10. Proof of equivalencies (4.11) and (4.12)

R	Q	$(\forall x)R$	$((\forall x)R)\&Q$	$R\&Q$	$(\underline{\forall}x)(R\&Q)$	$((\underline{\forall}x)R)\underline{+}Q$	$R+Q$	$(\underline{\forall}x)(R+Q)$
{0}	0	0	0	{0}	0	0	{0}	0
{1}	0	1	0	{0}	0	1	{1}	1
{-}	0	-	0	{0}	0	-	{-}	-
{0,1}	0	0	0	{0}	0	0	{0,1}	0
{0,-}	0	0	0	{0}	0	0	{0,-}	0
{1,-}	0	-	0	{0}	0	-	{1,-}	-

Table 10. Proof of equivalencies (4.11) and (4.12) (continued)

R	Q	$(\forall x)R$	$((\forall x)R)\&Q$	$R\&Q$	$(\forall x)(R\&Q)$	$((\forall x)R)+Q$	$R+Q$	$(\forall x)(R+Q)$
{0,1,-}	0	0	0	{0}	0	0	{0,1,-}	0
{0}	1	0	0	{0}	0	1	{1}	1
{1}	1	1	1	{1}	1	1	{1}	1
{-}	1	-	-	{-}	-	1	{1}	1
{0,1}	1	0	0	{0,1}	0	1	{1}	1
{0,-}	1	0	0	{0,-}	0	1	{1}	1
{1,-}	1	-	-	{1,-}	-	1	{1}	1
{0,1,-}	1	0	0	{0,1,-}	0	1	{1}	1
{0}	-	0	0	{0}	0	-	{-}	-
{1}	-	1	-	{-}	-	1	{1}	1
{-}	-	-	-	{-}	-	-	{-}	-
{0,1}	-	0	0	{0,-}	0	-	{1,-}	-
{0,-}	-	0	0	{0,-}	0	-	{-}	-
{1,-}	-	-	-	{-}	-	-	{1,-}	-
{0,1,-}	-	0	0	{0,-}	0	-	{1,-}	-

Table 11. Proof of equality (4.13)

N	G	F	$(\forall x)G$	$(F\backslash(\forall x)G)$	$(F\backslash G)$	$(\forall x)(F\backslash G)$
1	{0}	0	0	-	{-}	-
2	{1}	0	1	0	{0}	0
3	{0,1}	0	0	-	{0,-}	0
4	{0}	1	0	-	{-}	-
5	{1}	1	1	1	{1}	1
6	{0,1}	1	0	-	{1,-}	-

Step 7. Eliminating all the partial logical operators. The elimination is based on laws (3.6) to (3.28). As a result we obtain a pair of total formulas. Applying equivalence (3.21) to formula (4.15), the following formula without partial operators is generated:

$$((Q(c,x)+R(a,y)) \& \sim R(v,f(x))\&\sim P(x) \mid (Q(y,b)+P(b))\&$$
$$(Q(y,b)+\sim(\sim R(v,f(x))\&\sim P(x)))\&(P(b)+\sim(Q(c,x)+R(a,y)))) \qquad (4.16)$$

Step 8. Transforming the total formulas in the value and domain parts of the pair to a conjunction of disjunctions of literals. Two sets of total clauses are obtained. Performing step 8 for formula (4.16), the resulting sets contain 3 and 4 total clauses respectively:

$$((Q(c,x)+R(a,y)) \& \sim R(v,f(x))\&\sim P(x) \mid \qquad (4.17)$$
$$(Q(y,b)+P(b))\&(Q(y,b)+R(v,f(x))+P(x))\&(P(b)+\sim Q(c,x))\&(P(b)+\sim R(a,y)))).$$

In this paper, we also use other representation forms for a partial formula.

4.4 KNOWLEDGE REPRESENTATION IN INCOMPLETELY SPECIFIED DOMAIN

Additionally to form (4.1), for knowledge representation we will also use a partial conjunction of sentences that are partial clauses:

$$Knowledge=C_1 \& \dots \& C_m, \qquad (4.18)$$

$$C_i = (\forall x_1)\dots(\forall x_n)\,(P_{i,1} \pm \dots \pm P_{i,m}), \qquad (4.19)$$

where $P_{i,j}$ is a pair $(F\backslash G)$ of total formulas. In particular, formulas F and G can be literals. The universal quantifiers will be omitted. After that the partial clause

$$(L_1\backslash D_1)\pm\dots\pm(L_k\backslash D_k)\pm(\sim L_{k+1}\backslash D_{k+1})\pm \quad \pm(\sim L_m\backslash D_m) \qquad (4.20)$$

contains k positive and $m-k$ negative literals in the value part of pairs. The empty clause includes one pair $(0|D_i)$.

Similarly to the *Horn* clause in the traditional first order predicate logic we introduce a *Horn partial clause* with one positive literal:

$$(L|D)\pm(\sim L_1|D_1)\pm \quad \pm(\sim L_m|D_m) \tag{4.21}$$

It is easy to see that partial clause (4.20) is transformed to a pair the value part of which is a total clause and the domain part is a total formula:

$$(L_1+...+L_k+\sim L_{k+1}+...+\sim L_m \, | $$
$$D_1\&...\&D_m+L_1 \, \&D_1+...+L_k\&D_k+\sim L_{k+1}\&D_{k+1}+ \, +\sim L_m\&D_m). \tag{4.22}$$

Horn partial clause (4.21) is transformed to a partial consequence:

$$(L|D)\pm(\sim L_1|D_1)\pm \quad \pm(\sim L_m|D_m) = $$
$$(L|D)\pm \, \sim((L_1|D_1)\& \quad \&(L_m|D_m)) = $$
$$(L|D)\Leftarrow((L_1|D_1)\& \quad \&(L_m|D_m)). \tag{4.23}$$

Consequence (4.23) will be called a partial rule. One pair $(L|D)$ *will be* called a partial fact.

5. Deductive Reasoning in Partial Logic

Presented in work [8] is a formulation of first order logic that is specifically designed for use as the basic theoretical instrument of a computer theorem-proving program. Traditionally, a single step in a deduction has been required, for pragmatic and psychological reasons, to be simple enough. In the system described in [8], one inference principle is used. It is called the resolution principle. It is machine-oriented and forms a complete system of first order predicate logic. In this paper the resolution principle is generalised for incompletely specified domains.

We use the deductive reasoning formalism that is based upon the notions of Herbrand interpretation, unsatisfiability and refutation. A set of clauses is satisfiable if there is a model containing no complementary pair of the two literals L and $\sim L$.

5.1 GOALS AND THEOREMS

Given a set $S=\{C_1,...,C_m\}$ of partial clauses (pieces of knowledge) and a target partial formula (goal) R, we formulate the following theorem:

$$C_1 \& ... \& C_m \Rightarrow R. \tag{5.1}$$

The formula R represent a new piece of knowledge that has to be inferred from $C_1,...,C_m$. In order to proof the theorem we find a model being a set of variable values satisfying formula (5.1). The formula is satisfied if it takes value 1 or value *don't care* that can be replaced with value 1.

5.2 PROVING BY REFUTATION

To prove formula (5.1) be satisfiable we use a refutation procedure and prove the formula as follows be unsatisfiabile:

$$C_1 \& ... \& C_m \& \sim R. \tag{5.2}$$

Based on the resolution principle and starting with the clauses $C_1, ... C_m$ and $\sim R$.a sequence of additional clauses (resolvents) is generated until a clause consisting of one pair $(0|L)$ appears.

5.3 GENERALISATION OF RESOLUTION PRINCIPLE

First, we consider a generalisation of the resolution principle for the ground [8] partial clauses. Given two partial clauses

$C_1 = (L_1|D_1)\pm(L_2|D_2)$ (5.3)

and

$C_2 = (\sim L_1|D_3)\pm(L_3|D_4)$ (5.4)

where L_1 and $\sim L_1$ is a complementary pair of ground literals, the following additional partial clause (resolvent) is added to the source clauses:

$C = (0|D_1\&D_3+\sim L_1\&D_1+L_1\&D_3)\pm(L_2|D_2)\pm(L_3|D_4)$.   (5.5)

The pairs $(L_2|D_2)$ and $(L_3|D_4)$ from the source clauses are included in the resolvent. An additional pair containing the logical value 0 in the value part appears.

To prove C be the resolvent we have to prove that $C_1\&C_2$ is satisfied if $C_1\&C_2\&C$ is satisfied. The partial conjunction $C_1\&C_2$ of two clauses is transformed as follows:

$C_1\&C_2 = ((L_1|D_1)\pm(L_2|D_2)) \& ((\sim L_1|D_3)\pm(L_3|D_4)) =$
$(L_1+L_2|D_1\&D_2+L_1\&D_1+L_2\&D_2) \& (\sim L_1+L_3|D_3\&D_4+\sim L_1\&D_3+L_3\&D_4) =$
$((L_1+L_2)\&(\sim L_1+L_3) | (D_1\&D_2+L_1\&D_1+L_2\&D_2)\&(D_3\&D_4+\sim L_1\&D_3+L_3\&D_4) +$
$D_1\&D_2\&\sim L_1\&\sim L_2 + D_3\&D_4\&L_1\&\sim L_3) =$
$((L_1+L_2)\&(\sim L_1+L_3) | D_1\&D_2\&D_3\&D_4 + D_1\&D_2\&D_3\sim\&L_1 +$ (5.6)
$\qquad\qquad D_1\&D_2\&D_4\&L_3 + D_1\&D_2\&\sim L_1\&\sim L_2 +$
$\qquad\qquad D_1\&D_3\&D_4\&L_1 + D_1\&D_4\&L_1\&L_3 +$
$\qquad\qquad D_2\&D_3\&D_4\&L_2 + D_2\&D_3\sim\&L_1\&L_2 +$
$\qquad\qquad D_2\&D_4\&L_2\&L_3 + D_3\&D_4\&L_1\&\sim L_3)$.

The resolvent C can be represented as:

$C = (0|D_1\&D_3+\sim L_1\&D_1+L_1\&D_3)\pm(L_2|D_2)\pm(L_3|D_4) =$
$\qquad (L_2 + L_3 | (D_1\&D_3+\sim L_1\&D_1+L_1\&D_3)\&D_2\&D_4 + (L_2\&D_2) + (L_3\&D_4)) =$
$\qquad (L_2 + L_3 | D_1\&D_2\&D_3\&D_4 + D_1\&D_2\&D_4\&\sim L_1 +$
$\qquad\qquad D_2\&D_3\&D_4\&L_1 + L_2\&D_2 + L_3\&D_4)$.   (5.7)

Performing the partial conjunction operation on the operand $C_1\&C_2$ presented by (5.6) and on the operand C presented by (5.7) we obtain the following partial formula:

$C_1\&C_2\&C = ((L_1+L_2)\&(\sim L_1+L_3)\&(L_2+L_3) |$ (5.8)
$\qquad D_1\&D_2\&D_3\&D_4 + D_1\&D_2\&D_3\sim\&L_1 + D_1\&D_2\&D_4\&L_3 +$
$\qquad D_1\&D_2\&\sim L_1\&\sim L_2 + D_1\&D_3\&D_4\&L_1 + D_1\&D_4\&L_1\&L_3 +$
$\qquad D_2\&D_3\&D_4\&L_2 + D_2\&D_3\sim\&L_1\&L_2 + D_2\&D_4\&L_2\&L_3 + D_3\&D_4\&L_1\&\sim L_3)$.

Comparing the formulas (5.6) and (5.8), it is easy to see that the domain parts of the pairs are the same, and the value part of formula (5.8) contains an additional total resolvent compared to the value part of formula (5.6). Therefore, formula (5.6) is satisfied if the formula (5.8) is satisfied.

Example 5.1. Given the partial formula

$(A+B|\sim C) \& (\sim A|B) \& (C+D|A) \& (\sim D|C)$,   (5.9)

we are going to prove that the formula is not satisfiable. The formula is broken down into the set of partial clauses as follows:

  1. $(A+B|\sim C)$ - source clause
  2. $(\sim A|B)$ - source clause   (5.10)
  3. $(C+D|A)$ - source clause
  4. $(\sim D|C)$ - source clause

Applying the resolution method to pairs of partial clauses, we generate partial resolvents until the empty partial clause appears:

  5. $(B|B\&\sim C)$ - resolvent for clauses 1 and 2

6. $(1|B\&\sim C) = (\sim C|B\&\sim C)$ - from clause 5
7. $(D|A\&B\&\sim C+A\&D)=(D|A\&(B+D)\&(\sim C+D))$ - resolvent for clauses 3 and 6
8. $(0|A\&D\&C)$ - resolvent for clauses 4 and 7

Clause 8 is the empty partial clause therefore formula (5.9) is not satisfiable.

5.4 GENERATION OF A RESOLVENT

If the source partial clauses look like

$$C_1 = (L_1 + L_2 \mid D_1) \tag{5.11}$$

and

$$C_2 = (\sim L_1 + L_3 \mid D_2) \tag{5.12}$$

then the resolvent derived from the clauses is as follows:

$$C = (L_2+L_3 \mid D_1\&D_2+L_2\&D_1+L_3\&D_2). \tag{5.13}$$

To prove (5.13) we transform clauses (5.11) and (5.12) in the following way: $C_1'=(L_1|D_1)\pm (L_2|D_1)$ and $C_2''=(\sim L_1|D_2) \pm (L_3|D_2)$. Based on expression (5.5), the following resolvent is constructed from the clauses:

$$C = (0|D_1\&D_2+\sim L_1\&D_1+L_1\&D_2) \pm (L_2|D_1) \pm (L_3|D_2) =$$
$$(L_2 + L_3 \mid D_1\&D_2+L_2\&D_1+L_3\&D_2). \tag{5.14}$$

If the clauses are not ground then the unification algorithm from [8] has to be used.

5.5 RESOLUTION PRINCIPLE FOR CLAUSES IN CONSEQUENCE FORM

Starting with a set of rules (clauses in the consequence form) and a target formula (goal), we transform the current goal to another one, step by step through using the resolution principle until an empty clause appears. The current goal is represented in the consequence form as follows:

$$(0\leftarrow L_1\&L_2|D_1). \tag{5.15}$$

The clause that is used for transforming the current goal to the next-step goal is also represented in the consequence form as:

$$(L_1\leftarrow L_3|D_2). \tag{5.16}$$

We translate the goal and rule to the form of disjuncts $(\sim L_1+\sim L_2|D_1)$ and $(L_1+\sim L_3|D_2)$. Applying the resolution principle, we obtain the following resolvent:

$$(\sim L_2+\sim L_3| D_1\&Q+\sim L_2\& D_1+\sim L_3\& D_2) \tag{5.17}$$

that is translated to the next-step goal:

$$(0\leftarrow L_2\& L_3| D_1\& D_2+\sim L_2\& D_1+\sim L_3\& D_2). \tag{5.18}$$

The value part of the goal can be simplified through using laws (3.57-3.63). If a fact as

$$(L_1| D_2) \tag{5.19}$$

is used instead of rule (5.16) to generate a resolvent, then the next-step goal is as follows:

$$(0\leftarrow L_2 \mid D_1\&(D_2+\sim L_2)). \tag{5.20}$$

6. Transition from Partial to Traditional Total Logic

In order to use the proposed mechanism in practice for knowledge representation and deductive reasoning, an appropriate software or hardware should be developed. We propose a method of transition from the partial to the traditional first order predicate logic consisting of four steps.

1. Transforming the partial formula to the pair *(F⌐G)* of total formulas.

2. Replacing the value part *F* of the pair with a total formula *Value_Part* from the range

$$F\&G \subseteq Value\_Part \subseteq F+\sim G. \tag{6.1}$$

The new pair is as follows:

$$(Value\_Part \mid G). \tag{6.2}$$

3. Transition from the pair with the domain part *G* to the pair with the domain part 1 and replacing all the partial universal quantifiers (that are omitted) with the traditional total quantifiers:

$$(Value\_Part \mid 1). \tag{6.3}$$

4. Transforming the *Value_Part* to a set of clauses in the traditional first order predicate logic:

$$C_1 \& \dots \& C_m. \tag{6.4}$$

Three methods are possible when selecting the *Value_Part* at step 3:
- to use both *0* and *1* for replacing '-' (method 1),
- to replace the value '-' with the value *1* (method 2),
- to replace the value '-' with the value *0* (method 3).

6.1 TRANSITION TO TOTAL LOGIC (METHOD 1)

When we use the both values *0* and *1* for replacing the value '-', the *Value_Part* is selected from the range $F\&G \subset Value\_Part \subset F+\sim G$. In particular, the *Value_Part=F* can be used.

Example 6.1. This example continues example 5.1. We transform partial formula (5.9) to a total conjunction of total disjuncts in the following way:

$$(A+B \mid 1)\underline{\&}(\sim A \mid 1)\underline{\&}(C+D \mid 1)\underline{\&}(\sim D \mid 1) = ((A+B)\&(\sim A)\&(C+D)\&(\sim D) \mid 1) =$$
$$(A+B)\&(\sim A)\&(C+D)\&(\sim D). \tag{6.5}$$

The following set of four total clauses is derived from (6.5):

1. A+B
2. ~A   (6.6)
3. C+D
4. ~D.

It is easy to see that it is impossible to infer the empty clause from clauses (6.6).

6.2 TRANSITION TO TOTAL LOGIC (METHOD 2)

If we use only the value *1* for replacing the value '-', then *Value_Part = F+~G*.

Example 6.2. Let us transform partial formula (5.9) to a total conjunction of disjuncts by means of replacing the value part of pairs with disjunction of their value and domain parts:

$$(A+B+C \mid \sim C)\underline{\&}(\sim A+\sim B \mid B)\underline{\&}(C+D+\sim A \mid A)\underline{\&}(\sim D+\sim C \mid C) =$$
$$(A+B+C \mid 1)\underline{\&}(\sim A+\sim B \mid 1)\underline{\&}(C+D+\sim A \mid 1)\underline{\&}(\sim D+\sim C \mid 1) =$$
$$((A+B+C)\&(\sim A+\sim B)\&(C+D+\sim A)\&(\sim D+\sim C) \mid 1) =$$
$$(A+B+C)\&(\sim A+\sim B)\&(C+D+\sim A)\&(\sim D+\sim C). \tag{6.7}$$

The following set of four clauses is derived from (6.7):

1. A+B+C
2. ~A+~B   (6.8)
3. C+D+~A
4. ~D+~C.

It is easy to see that it is impossible to infer the empty clause from clauses (6.8).

6.3 TRANSITION TO TOTAL LOGIC (METHOD 3)

If we use only the value 0 for replacing the value '-', then the *Value_Part* = *F&G*.

Example 6.3. Now we replace the value part of pairs in partial formula (5.9) with total conjunction of the pair's value and domain parts

$$((A+B)\&(\sim C)|\sim C)\&((\sim A)\&(B)|B)\&((C+D)\&(A)|A)\&((\sim D)\&(C)|C) =$$
$$((A+B)\&(\sim C)|\ 1)\&((\sim A)\&(B)|\ 1)\&((C+D)\&(A)|\ 1)\&((\sim D)\&(C)|\ 1) =$$
$$((A+B)\&(\sim C)\&(\sim A)\&(B)\&(C+D)\&(A)\&(\sim D)\&(C)\ |\ 1) =$$
$$(A+B)\&(\sim C)\&(\sim A)\&(B)\&(C+D)\&(A)\&(\sim D)\&(C). \tag{6.9}$$

The following set of eight clauses is derived from (6.9):

1. $A+B$
2. $\sim C$
3. $\sim A$
4. B (6.10)
5. $C+D$
6. A
7. $\sim D$
8. C.

It is easy to see that it is sufficient to generate only one resolvent in order to infer the empty clause from clauses (6.10). In particular, the literals C and $\sim C$ constitute a complementary pair.

Method 3 seems to be the most preferable, because it speeds up the generation of the empty clause and the technique for transition from the partial formula to a set of clauses in the traditional logic is the most efficient. Comparing methods 1, 2, and 3, we conclude that only method 3 can be used in practice.

6.4 TRANSLATION OF PARTIAL CONSEQUENCE

Now we consider the following rule in the form of partial consequence:

$$(A|1) \Leftarrow (C|Q). \tag{6.11}$$

In pair $(A|1)$ the domain function equals 1. Therefore, the pair value is equal to the value of literal A. The pair $(C|Q)$ takes one of three values: *false, true* and *don't care*. The *don't care* value can be replaced with *false* or *true* arbitrarily. As a result, one of the completely specified truth functions belonging to the range $C\&Q$ to $C+\sim Q$ can be obtained. In order to generate all the possible solutions for a given goal, we select the function $C+\sim Q$. Formula (6.11) is transformed to the following expression:

$$A \leftarrow (C + \sim Q). \tag{6.12}$$

It easy to see that expression (6.12) is equivalent to the following conjunction of two total consequences:

$$(A \leftarrow \sim Q) \& (A \leftarrow C). \tag{6.13}$$

Therefore, one consequence (6.11) in the partial logic is translated to two total consequences in the first order predicate logic.

7. Results

Now we consider an example of knowledge representation and deductive reasoning in an incompletely specified domain. The proposed methods of knowledge description and logic inference allow for reduction in the number of clauses and in the number of inference steps.

7.1 INCOMPLETELY SPECIFIED FINITE STATE MACHINE (FSM)

The finite state machine (FSM) model is widely used for modelling and synthesis of digital sequential circuits and systems. The FSM is a five-tuple

$$FSM = (X, Y, S, \varphi, \delta), \tag{7.1}$$

where X is a set of input symbols; Y is a set of output symbols; S is a set of internal states; φ: $SxX{\rightarrow}S$ is a next-state function; δ: $SxX{\rightarrow}Y$ is an output function. The FSM is incompletely specified if the next-state and output functions are incompletely specified, that is the functions take additionally the value *don't care* or '–' value. An example FSM is presented in Table 12 where the pair s/y defines the next state s and the output symbol y.

Table 12. FSM next-state and output functions

State	Input symbol			
	x1	x2	x3	x4
s0	– / y1	s0 / y3	s4 / y2	s1 / y2
s1	s2 / y3	s0 / –	s3 / –	– / y1
s2	– / y2	– / y2	s1 / –	s2 / y4
s3	s1 / –	s4 / –	– / y4	– / y3
s4	– / y4	s3 / y1	s2 / –	s3 / –

7.2 REPRESENTATION OF KNOWLEDGE ABOUT FSM

The *don't care* value used in the FSM definition is rather a value of the domain variables *next state* and *output symbol*, but is not a logical value. We could formulate a set of clauses for FSM without the theoretical results obtained in this paper. We show that a FSM representation in the partial logic requires a less number of clauses.

The input symbols $x1$, $x2$, $x3$, $x4$, the output symbols $y1$, $y2$, $y3$, $y4$, and the internal states $s0$, $s1$, $s2$, $s3$, $s4$ are represented by function symbols of degree 0, i.e. by individual constants. The sequences of input symbols, output symbols, and internal states are represented as lists.

In order to define clauses on the FSM, a set of predicates is introduced. Among them there are the predicates as follows: *next_state(s,x,sn)*, *state_specified(s,x,sn)*, *state_dontcare(s,x,sn)*, *output(s, x,y)*, *output_specified(s,x,y)*, and *output_dontcare(s,x,y)*, where s is the current state, sn is the next state, x is the input symbol, and y is the output symbol. Using these predicates, we could construct the three-valued clause as follows:

(next_state(s,x,sn) | 1) if (state_specified(s,x,sn) | not state_dontcare(s,x,sn)).

According to (6.12) and (6.13) the clause is split to following two-valued clauses:

next_state(s,x,sn) if state_dontcare(s,x,sn).
next_state(s,x,sn) if state_specified(s,x,sn).

Following this way, we obtain the Prolog program shown in Fig. 2.

7.3 LOGIC INFERENCE TASKS CONCERNING FSM

The knowledge presented in Fig. 2 allows for solving various logic inference tasks, including as follows:

- what is the output symbol sequence for the given input symbol sequence,
- what is the input symbol sequence if any exists, given the output symbol sequence,
- what is the FSM state sequence, given the input or output symbol sequence,
- are there any unreachable states,

and others.

The goal

    mapping(s0,Xl,[y3,y1,y2,y3,y2,y4]) and *write*("Xl=",Xl),

described in Fig. 2 denotes the task consisting in searching for an input symbol sequence *Xl*, given the output symbol sequence *[y3,y1,y2,y3,y2,y4]*.

    Comparing the models of knowledge representation and deductive reasoning constructed through using the proposed methods of partial logic with the existing logic inference techniques, we can conclude that our models speed up the logic inference process and increase the efficiency of knowledge representation in incompletely specified domains. Thus, the FSM representation presented in Fig. 2 contains 55 clauses. If the proposed methods are not used then 90 clauses are needed in order to describe the FSM.

Domains
   state=s0;s1;s2;s3;s4
   input_symbol=x1;x2;x3;x4
   output_symbol=y1;y2;y3;y4
   sequence_of_states=state*
   sequence_of_inputs=input_symbol*
   sequence_of_outputs=output_symbol*
predicates
   mapping(state,sequence_of_inputs,
               sequence_of_outputs)
   next_state(state,input_symbol,state)
   state_specified(state,input_symbol,state)
   state_dontcare(state,input_symbol,state)
   sx_y_dc(state,input_symbol)
   each_of_y(output_symbol)
   output(state,input_symbol,output_symbol)
   output_specified(state,input_symbol,
               output_symbol)
   output_dontcare(state,input_symbol,
               output_symbol)
   sx_s_dc(state,input_symbol)
   each_of_s(state)
goal
   mapping(s0,Xl,[y3,y1,y2,y3,y2,y4]) **and**
      write("Xl=",Xl).
clauses
   mapping(_,[],[]).
   mapping(S,[X|Xl],[Y|Yl]) **if** *output*(S,X,Y) **and**
               next_state(S,X,Sn) **and**
               mapping(Sn,Xl,Yl).
   Output(S,X,Y) **if** *output_specified*(S,X,Y) **or**
               output_dontcare(S,X,Y).
   output_specified(s0,x1,y1).
   Output_specified(s0,x2,y3).
   Output_specified(s0,x3,y2).
   Output_specified(s0,x4,y2).
   Output_specified(s1,x1,y3).
   Output_specified(s1,x4,y1).
   Output_specified(s2,x1,y2).
   Output_specified(s2,x2,y2).
   Output_specified(s2,x4,y4).
   Output_specified(s3,x3,y4).
   Output_specified(s3,x4,y3).

   output_specified(s4,x1,y4).
   output_specified(s4,x2,y1).
   output_dontcare(S,X,Y) **if** *sx_y_dc*(S,X) **and**
               each_of_y(Y).
   sx_y_dc(s1,x2).
   sx_y_dc(s1,x3).
   sx_y_dc(s2,x3).
   sx_y_dc(s3,x1).
   sx_y_dc(s3,x2).
   sx_y_dc(s4,x3).
   sx_y_dc(s4,x4).
   each_of_y(y1).
   each_of_y(y2).
   each_of_y(y3).
   each_of_y(y4).
   next_state(S,X,Sn) **if** *state_specified*(S,X,Sn) **or**
               state_dontcare(S,X,Sn).
   state_specified(s0,x2,s0).
   state_specified(s0,x3,s4).
   state_specified(s0,x4,s1).
   state_specified(s1,x1,s2).
   state_specified(s1,x2,s0).
   state_specified(s1,x3,s3).
   state_specified(s2,x3,s1).
   state_specified(s2,x4,s2).
   state_specified(s3,x1,s1).
   state_specified(s3,x2,s4).
   state_specified(s4,x2,s3).
   state_specified(s4,x3,s2).
   state_specified(s4,x4,s3).
   state_dontcare(S,X,Sn) **if** *sx_s_dc*(S,X) **and**
               each_of_s(Sn).
   sx_s_dc(s0,x1).
   sx_s_dc(s1,x4).
   sx_s_dc(s2,x1).
   sx_s_dc(s2,x2).
   sx_s_dc(s3,x3).
   sx_s_dc(s3,x4).
   sx_s_dc(s4,x1).
   each_of_s(s0).
   each_of_s(s1).
   each_of_s(s2).
   each_of_s(s3).
   each_of_s(s4).

Figure 2. Prolog-description of incompletely specified finite state machine

8. Conclusions

In this paper we have proposed the formalism for modelling the world in which an assertion is essential in one situation and is not essential in other situation. The formalism is the partial proposition and first order predicate logics developed through using three truth-values: *false, true,* and *don't care*. The difference between the partial logics and the traditional three-valued logics consists in that the *don't care* value is replaceable with other values.

Due to encoding the three-valued partial variables with a pair of two-valued Boolean variables, a knowledge is represented as a set of partial clauses constructed on a set of two-valued predicates through using partial operations and quantifiers. In order to perform deductive reasoning in an incompletely specified domain we generalised the Robinson's resolution principle to infer a partial resolvent from partial clauses. The inference rule supports manipulation of clause domains and simplification of clauses during reasoning.

Two approaches are possible for the implementation of the partial logics. The first one consists in development of special software handling partial clauses and performing partial reasoning. The second one is based on transition from the partial logics to the traditional two-valued logics. Three methods of transition are proposed in the paper. One of these is the most preferable and speeds up logic inference. Knowledge representation in an incompletely specified domain is illustrated with the incompletely specified finite state machine. The example proves reduction in the number of clauses when the proposed methods have been used.

9. Acknowledgements

The authors are grateful to Prof. E. Zavadskas and Prof. A. Kaklauskas who encouraged submitting the paper to the BalticDB&IS'2000 Conference. Our thanks are also due to Prof. R. Pliuskevicius and A. Pliuskeviciene for their interest to the topic and useful comments.

References

1. Damiani, M. and de Micheli, G. Don't care set specifications in combinational and synchronous logic circuits. *IEEE Trans. On CAD*, **12**, 1993, pp. 365-388.

2. Filman, R. Reasoning with worlds and truth maintenance in a knowledge-based programming environment. *Communications of the ACM*, **31**(4), 1988, pp. 382-401.

3. Pliuskevicius, R. The saturated tableaux for linear miniscoped horn-like temporal logic. *Journal of Automated Reasoning*, **13**, 1994, pp. 391-407.

4. Prihozhy, A. A. Methods of partial logic. *Proc. Int. Conf. on Neuro Computers and Artificial Intelligence*, Brest, 1999.

5. Prihozhy, A. A. Logic inference in partial logic. *Intelligent Systems*, Minsk, Belarus, 1998, pp. 123-140.

6. Prihozhy, A. A. Algebra of partial logic. *New Technologies for Computers and Mechanics*, Brest, Belarus, 1998, pp. 168-174.

7. Prihozhy, A. A. If-diagrams: theory and application. *PATMOS'97: Proc. European Workshop*, Belgium, 1997, pp. 369-378.

8. Robinson, J. A. A machine-oriented logic based on the resolution principle. *Journal of the Association for Computing Machinary*, **12**(1), 1965, pp. 23-41.

9. Sakalauskaite, J. *Ordered Resolution for Finitely-Valued First-Order Logics*. Preprintas Nr. 95-3, Vilnius, Lietuva, 1995, 10 p.

10. Zadeh, L. A. *The Role of Fuzzy Logic in the Management of Uncertainty in Expert Systems. Approximate Reasoning in Expert Systems*. Elsevier Science Publishers, North Holland, 1985, pp. 3-41.

11. Zavadskas, E., Peldschus, F., Kaklauskas, A. *Multiple Criteria Evaluation of Projects in Construction*. Vilnius, Technika, 1994.

Part 7: Activity Modelling and Workflow Management

Skill Management: A Building Block for Project Management with Flexible Teams

Reinhard Lucas and Thorsten Weber

Fraunhofer Institute Software and Systems Engineering
Joseph-von-Fraunhofer Straße 20, D-44227 Dortmund, Germany
E-mail: lucas@do.isst.fhg.de

Abstract

Skill management is becoming increasingly important as a form of personalised knowledge management achieved through changes in work organisation. Existing solutions only partly fulfil the necessary criteria. One reason is a lack of requirement analysis embedded in a holistic approach. This paper is a contribution to this type of requirements analysis.

Keywords: skill management, knowledge management, flexible teams.

1. Introduction

Continuing changes in industry and commerce mean that companies' organisation must be highly dynamic to support product and service development and to deal with projects.

Concentration, global co-operation, and new organisational concepts like virtual enterprises lead to larger company units or alliances in which the critical task of human resource management becomes very complex. Companies regularly report that they failed to apply for a given project because they did not know the skills required were available among their employees. This situation requires the possibility to compose a 'flexible team'. In the following, the term 'flexible team' is used for a group of employees who work together on a temporary task and do not stay together after the task is completed. If flexible teams are to be used for project management, employees' individual knowledge profiles must be known, raising the demand for an information system that supports this by managing and analysing qualifications and links to persons with specific experience. In this respect, this kind of information system becomes a knowledge management system but, unlike organisational memory information systems, the aim is not to document the knowledge explicitly. Instead, knowledge itself stays personalised and meta-information about knowledge owners is stored.

Accessing expert knowledge or identifying potential team members today often works in the classical way by using implicit personal information about who knows what in which area, by using 'expertise concierges' or by escalating the search as described in [6]. Meta-information about the knowledge owners is either stored in a personal notebook or is not documented at all. But if time restrictions increase and companies grow, become more global or virtual, this is no longer efficient enough and the need for technical support becomes evident. So some companies started building their own skill management systems, failed, and returned to the classical way of finding experts.

In this paper, neither a tool nor a complete solution to the problem can be presented. Instead, requirements for skill management systems are presented, as derived from several interviews with

J. Barzdins and A. Caplinskas (eds.), Databases and Information Systems, 299–305.

companies in different business sectors. They were structured and put into the context of a complete skill management approach. This approach consists of a language to describe qualifications and meta-information about experience, an information system to administrate and analyse this meta-information, and organisational concepts for introducing the system and motivating those involved. In this paper we focus on analysing the requirements for skill management systems and their relations to other information systems that play a central role in this area.

2. Definition of Skill Management System Functionality

The requirements for skill management systems are based on different project phases in which a skill management system can be used.

Building a team involves identifying persons with special qualifications or experiences and bringing them together with people who possess different knowledge. This team is then used to perform a defined and temporary task. To do this, information is required concerning employees' qualifications, both explicitly in the form of certifications as well as relating to prior experience that led to an implicit and "procedural" knowledge [5] of how to solve problems. To assess someone's aptitude for a task, the qualification profile can be used. This profile contains information about general aptitude and project experience.

Team building does not take place exclusively at the beginning of a project. In this phase, people with general knowledge are often needed to offer free capacity for analysing the project tasks and designing the project phases. The aim is to construct a balanced team possessing all the necessary knowledge as the sum of the different team members' individual knowledge. The criteria needed to decide if a team is balanced or not result from the overall task the project deals with. Later on single project phases may lack for experts in explicit areas.

As an example for different types of knowledge used in project work, a software development project can be used: first of all there is a need for people with application knowledge as well as for people with knowledge about the technology that will be used. Both knowledge types can be important in a general manner to get an impression of the project dimensions, tasks and costs, as well as in a detailed view in which special use cases or bug fixes have to be managed. Even if all tasks and subtasks are known at the start of the project, a balanced team may become unbalanced in later project phases as requirements and tasks change in the course of a project. For example, a project that deals with consulting in the context of document management systems changes if the project members detect that the customer problems could be better solved by a workflow management system. To get a solution in this case, it is necessary to train, change or enlarge the project team. Once again there is a need for skill management.

As described above during a project, there is often a need for persons who can supply the team with knowledge on the basis of special experience or qualifications. Such experience constitutes important information, but it cannot be generalised, as experience is always context-specific. Details of why a given project failed are important, but they often depend on conditions that existed at a former point of time. An explicit description of the reasons for the failure is only complete if the constraints posed by circumstances, individuals, former technology, etc. are also mentioned. This knowledge can be communicated, but it is a complex and time-consuming procedure. In this case, administration of meta-knowledge, i.e. links to people who could offer this information, is the more useful approach. Another reason why knowledge transfer based on personalisation (documenting meta-knowledge) is more useful than the codification of knowledge (documenting knowledge in a kind of organisational memory system) is that new knowledge often cannot be categorised. As an example, an employee who has obtained knowledge about a new technology by studying the literature can be used. At the point in time when he reads the article, it is impossible to tell which future context this knowledge may be used in, but by spreading the information he becomes an interesting contact for other employees.

Besides the search for persons who carry certain knowledge, a skill management system can also be used to identify people who lack certain qualifications or experience. To enable this kind of skill gap analysis, it is necessary not only to rate the employees' qualifications but also to appraise the qualifications needed for given tasks.

3. Requirements for Skill Management Systems

To achieve all of these aims, skill management approaches have to comply with numerous requirements, which are described in more detail in the following, starting with the technical aspects.

3.1 TECHNICAL REQUIREMENTS

The technical requirements mainly deal with how to structure information of employees qualification and experiences and how to administrate this data in an information system :

- The criteria used to structure employees knowledge vary depending on the system in question. If the system is used to build a team, i.e. finding people with knowledge of certain products, tools and processes or who have considerable work experience, it is helpful to categorise and structure their qualifications accordingly. It is relatively easy to express the role played and tools used by a given person in the past and to structure these keywords in a hierarchical order. Because tasks require knowledge of different categories, different hierarchies have to be defined. The dimension of the hierarchies depends on the category type and the area of business. Because of this, a skill management system has to offer a flexible knowledge category structure whose width and depth can be freely defined.
- Even more flexibility is needed if the system is used to initiate a knowledge transfer. This role of a skill management system is used to administrate meta-information about people with experience relating to certain tasks or projects. This experience is strongly linked to a specific context. It is quite individual and cannot be generalised. On the other hand, employees carry knowledge that can be generalised but is too new to fit the criteria structure because the appropriate keywords are missing or one cannot determine yet in which context this knowledge might be useful. Meta-information about both kinds of information cannot be structured or sorted into a hierarchic way very well. A skill management system therefore has to offer another way to administrate links to the knowledge owners. One way may be the use of keyword lists or semantic nets. But the use of both these options involves the problem of handling synonymous and homonymous terms, so that a kind of automated thesaurus is needed.
- While 'experience'-knowledge is hard to structure, 'qualification'-knowledge can be put in a kind of schema. The problem arises if employees have to rate their qualifications. This rating should be done by the employees themselves or in co-operation with the affected persons in order to guarantee the acceptance of the rating and also the system itself. A comparison of different profiles is only possible if a standardised assessment is used. A simple 'grade'-system like that used in school should be avoided because the interpretation differs. 'Good knowledge of foreign languages', for example, means reading specialist literature with the help of a dictionary for one person, while for another it means taking part at an international discussion. Because of this, it is necessary to create 'objective' criteria in a skill management system that help the users to rate themselves by explaining the qualification needed to reach a specific level.

- The distinction between strongly structured qualifications and weakly structured experience has an effect not only on the administration of criteria in a system but also on the frequency of data input and update. Relatively static qualification profiles do not need updating very often but can become large and complex so the task of documenting an employee's qualification initially becomes an activity that cannot be managed in one step and not in one day. Because of this, a skill management system has to offer methods that make it possible to save half-filled profiles, manage different versions, and automatically check for completeness. The use of different roles may reduce the amount of criteria that have to be dealt with. On the other hand, the weakly structured experience reports are characterised by a high degree of variance. So a skill management system has to offer methods that ensure that a permanent knowledge input is possible without a reaction of all system users as needed to request input to new category items. On the other hand, experience has a strong time-context, so a skill management system should offer methods to document the relevance of the information to the present situation and to delete old data.

- Beside the requirements concerning input, structure and update of data, skill management systems have to fulfil requirements concerning search and evaluation of data. 'Static' qualification profiles can be organised in hierarchical structures. But searching along the structures doesn't always return an answer to the users requests. First of all, the user of a skill management system doesn't want to have the structure in mind while searching for people. He wants to enter a keyword and find the adequate person immediately without knowing the structure context. Over and above that, there is the requirement to find a person with similar knowledge if no one with the exact qualification or experience can be found. For example, a user might search for someone who is familiar with databases in general if he cannot find someone who is especially familiar with object-oriented databases. Skill management systems have to support this kind of requests and sort the results by their appropriateness. Searching along non-structured experience profiles is even more difficult. To support this, an effective keyword or full-text search has to be implemented including solutions to solve the problems of synonymous and homonymous terms. Saving 'successful' search strings is a useful feature that makes it possible to repeat a query automatically as a kind of 'search agent' until the right person is available. Beside the search functionality, there is also a need for an analysing component capable of comparing the knowledge profiles of different persons, enabling users to select the most suitable one. Over and above that there should be a possibility to compare more general knowledge (e.g. modelling-know-how in relation to programming-know-how) without referring to a detailed view of modelling or programming languages.

- In addition to the above-mentioned requirements, the usual requirements for all software systems, described in the field of software ergonomics, have to be fulfilled with special respect to the fact that a large variety of users with different levels of experience in using software will be affected and a large amount of different systems platforms and software releases may be used.

- The collection of the personal data required for skill management demands high levels of organisational commitment to guarantee data protection for reasons of legality and acceptance by those involved. But ensuring data protection is not limited to organisational items, there are some technical methods that can be used for data protection, too. Because it is the aim of a skill management system to identify people, all methods based on making data anonymous are less useful but can be used in special cases to restrict access to personal data to a selected group of people. Reduction of data my be useful in those cases where statistical evaluations take place. A messaging service that automatically informs the affected people about access to their data is a useful method to ensure the transparency of the system.

3.2 ORGANISATIONAL REQUIREMENTS

Besides the technical aspects, the success of a system depends on the system acceptance that is based on some organisational aspects:

- To fulfil the organisational part of the approach, the first step is to find a concept for system introduction. Qualification categories have to be developed or configured to the needs of the specific organisation. This requires analysis of the organisational units and some units have to be designated to participate in a test phase. Timetables have to be developed and controlled, personal resources must be available to define the category structure. The results of a first test phase have to be analysed and possibly result in a structure update. The final structure used to reflect the employee's qualification must be easy understandable and the used terms unambiguous. This is a lot of work, but similar departments of different companies use similar profile structures, so predefined templates for different areas of business offered by a skill management approach may be a way to reduce work in the definition phase. The next step is to define the rating scheme and the explanations needed for each level. The amount of levels depends on the hierarchy of the qualification structure. The more general a category item is, the more levels are needed to rate one's qualification.

- Once a system is installed, the aim of organisational measures is to motivate the employees to fill the system with their data and to keep it up to date. This runs up against several fears, for example the fear of being bombarded with requests, the fear of throwing away knowledge, or the fear of abuse of data to monitor work. One advantage of skill management systems in this content is that the problem of 'knowledge hoarding' is less dramatic because meta-information not knowledge itself is encoded in a skill management system and the control of who gets which information is in the hands of the knowledge owner. To reduce fears of getting too much work by updating the system data, the system itself has to be effective and fast enough on the one hand, and on the other hand there have to be organisational commitments that define the right time for qualification updates, while experience can be updated continuously. Useful hints for these commitments may be the end of projects, reaching a milestone, exchange of team members, etc. If data can be kept up to date, searching for someone using a skill management system may be faster than using the classical methods. This is an important motivation for the acceptance of a system. If a skill management system is not only used to manage qualifications but also links to experts, the benefit for the individual user increases. But this statement is only true if all employees have a similar need for information. If there is only a small amount of people who have knowledge and a large amount of people who are searching for knowledge, additional organisational measures are necessary. This could involve financial incentives, but within the discussion of knowledge management, the accepted opinion is increasingly that changing the organisational culture in general has more effect than money.

4. The Use of Integrating Skill Management Systems

If a skill management system fulfils all described technical requirements and the organisation in which the system is embedded finds adequate solutions for the organisational problems, two building blocks needed to solve the initial problem are available. But the problem is even more complex because managing flexible teams needs a lot more management functionality. This functionality is supported by different IT-systems which are available and in use today. For example, document management systems can be used for the filing and administration of all project-related documents. Groupware systems can be used for communication and co-operation between the project members. Workflow management systems can be used for the co-ordination and controlling of repeatable project processes and project management systems can be used for the administration of resources, the control of project time and project budget. Combining skill management systems with these management systems can generate significant added value.

While [2] recommend an analysis of the organisation's requirements and the selection of either a personalised knowledge management strategy *or* a strategy that bases on encoding knowledge, it is our opinion that integrating different systems may enlarge functionality. For example, a simple organisational memory system that manages frequently asked questions gets more functionality (in case the question could not be answered) if it offers a skill management component to identify a competent expert and groupware functionality to get in contact with the expert directly. Another example is a project management system that itself is necessary to get information about who is available for a certain task but could be combined with a skill management system to select the available persons by their qualifications. Even more functionality could be added if the following question could be solved: 'What qualification leaves the project if a given employee changes to another project?'.

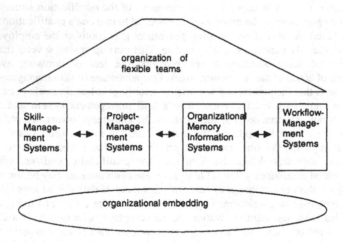

Figure 1. Skill management systems integrated into a complete approach

5. Conclusions

The problem of project management by flexible teams cannot be solved by an isolated information system. To get a solution, a complete skill management approach is needed that includes organisational and system integration aspects. The path to achieving this overall aim is a long one, but skill management systems can play a central role in this scenario if they can fulfil the described requirements. Existing solutions must therefore be adapted and extended or new products have to be developed that enable qualification profiles to be administrated and updated in an effective way but which also enable the management of expert links and the integration of interfaces to existing systems used for the management of teams.

References

1. Angus, D. Behavior modification. *Knowledge Management*, 7, 1999.

2. Hansen, M. T., Nohria, N., Tierney, T. What's your strategy for managing knowledge? *Harvard Business Review*, 1999, pp. 106-116.

3. Liao,   Abecker,   Sintek,   Hinkelmann.   *A   Competence   Knowledge   Base   System   as   Part of the Organisational Memory*. German Research Centre for Artificial Intelligence (DFKI), Universität Karlsruhe, 1999.

4. Libowitz, J. Key ingredients to the success of an organizations' knowledge management strategy. *Knowledge and Process Management*, 6, 1999, pp. 37-40.

5. Markowitsch, H. J. *Neuropsychologie des Gedächtinsses*. Hogrefe Verlag, 1992.

6. McDonald, D., Ackermann, M. Just Talk to Me: A field study of expertise location. *ACM Computer Supported Cooperated Work (CSCW)*, 1998, pp. 315-324.

7. Nonaka, I., Takeushi, H. *Die Organisation des Wissens*. Campus Verlag, 1997.

8. Stein, Zwass. Actualizing organisational memory with information systems. *Information Systems Research*, 6(2), 1998, pp. 85-117.

Model of Reports Based Information System

Donatas Ciuksys, Antanas Mitasiunas, Saulius Ragaisis

Faculty of Mathematics and Informatics, Vilnius University
Naugarduko 24, 2600 Vilnius, Lithuania
Phone: +370 2 333 922
Fax: +370 2 236 191
E-mail: donatas.ciuksys@maf.vu.lt, antanas.mitasiunas@maf.vu.lt, saulius.ragaisis@maf.vu.lt

Abstract

Traditionally the purpose of information system is to collect the organisation's data and present it for analysis. Such information systems are using structured data as a model of the application domain. When application domain is wide and unstructured, document oriented model of information system is usually applied.

There are some specific organisations, whose activities are based on analysis of statistical data collected in other organisations during some period. As some of the organisations providing data do not have information systems, the initial data is available only as a set of reports in table form.

The necessity for the special type - reports based - information system is presented. Requirements for such system are discussed. Model of reports based information system, including domain independent data model and main functionality of the system, is proposed.

Keywords: information systems, domain independent data model, statistical reports based input.

1. Introduction

Traditionally one of the two approaches is applied for information system development. In the cases, when application domain is sufficiently defined, the model of application domain is expressed by structured data model. There are entities corresponding to the concepts of application domain in the structured data model. Therefore information systems that use structured data model operate with the concepts of application domain also [5].

When application domain is wide and the scope is not clearly defined, it is impossible to develop a specific application domain model based on the concepts of the application domain. In these cases, the document-oriented model of information system is applied. Application domain is expressed by the set of some documents. There are functions operating with words, sets of words, and also with general structured attributes of the documents such as author, date, etc. Such a model consists of documents that are different for various application domains mostly because of the fact that various application domains are expressed by different words. Consequently, information systems using document oriented data model also operate with the sets of words and in general they do not employ specific concepts of the application domain.

When the application domain is "poorly" defined, the following question reasonably arises. Is it possible to work out some other data model that would be more subject oriented than the one based on documents and words, is it possible to develop corresponding information system having more specific application functions than the functions with the sets of words? Before answering this question, let's discuss another related problem that has been faced in this work.

Traditionally automation of organisation activity starts with the creation of the operational information system that gathers detailed data about the facts or events and provides required

307

J. Barzdins and A. Caplinskas (eds.), Databases and Information Systems, 307–316.

summary information for analysis. Collection of detailed data requires large investments, therefore organisations often gather only information about the results of their activity during some period especially in the cases when they do not use information systems. Data for some period is presented as statistical reports in table form. These reports are used for production of the summary reports that are used for analysis, comparison, and decision making.

Dealing with statistical reports is substantially widespread in the activity of the diverse type organisations. These reports are even treated as initial data. The first impression is that from the point of view of information technologies such approach is not "right" and can not be applied - first of all information about the activity should be collected and subsequently required statistical data should be produced as reports on the basis of detailed data. Such "right" approach forces organisations to establish processes that fix and gather the detailed information about the primary facts of activity or events. But this method requires wide range changes in the overall activity of the organisation that always causes serious problems.

So the second question arises: is it possible to provide some information service, to develop some information system without significant changes of the organisation's activity, without initiating the processes that fix and gather detailed information. This question is even more important for the specific organisations, whose activities are based on the analysis of statistical data collected in other organisations. It is practically impossible to influence the activity of all organisations that would provide required data.

In fact both questions - concerning possibility of information system development in "poorly" defined application domain and possibility of information system development without restructuring of the organisations activity - can be answered positively in some grade by introducing such data primitive as report and defining information system functions dealing with reports.

This paper presents innovative model of information system based on statistical reports. Dimensional data model as statistical reports abstraction and required functions are defined in the proposed model.

Further the requirements for such a system are briefly discussed. Then corresponding data model, including the system of concepts and conceptual data model oriented to implementation using RDBMS, is introduced. The information system functions that facilitate construction of the queries are presented. Finally the main features of the model are highlighted and compared with data warehouse approach.

2. System Requirements

Information system should enable analysis of data collected in various organisations. The level of computerisation in the organisations that provide data may be very different. Some of them have operational information systems that gather detailed data of the activity. The others have no information systems at all; they collect required statistical data about the organisation's activity manually using only simple tools such as spreadsheet programs. Nevertheless all the organisations prepare official statistical reports about their and their subdivisions activity during some periods irrespectively of the presence of the information system.

Attention should be paid to fact that the value of the indicator for the fixed period even in the past can alter due to objective reasons also. For example, the values of the same indicator for the first month of the last year can be different in the last year and current year reports, and the reason is that some facts were treated differently depending on information available at the time when each report was produced.

As it was mentioned above, some of the organisations presenting data may have operational information systems and there is a possibility to use detailed primary data. But in this case it is not enough to acquire primary data, the proprietary methods of calculation of necessary indicators should be also obtained and implemented. These methods are employed in different information systems of various organisations. Sometimes the exact method exists only in the program that produces required reports. Of course, there is a possibility to develop a set of basic functions and provide the user with the possibility to define formulas for calculation. However such approach requires a user to have deep knowledge of the application domain, and it is not acceptable even for the professional users that have been using paper reports and indicators presented in them for a long time.

The subdivisions of the organisations are geographically distributed in the whole country and each subdivision activity covers some territorial unit, i.e. the report provided by the subdivision presents situation in this territorial unit. It is important to highlight two facets. First, the distribution of subdivisions may be different for various organisations. Therefore in order to obtain the possibility to compare data provided by various organisations unified territorial classification should be introduced. Second, even subdivisions of one organisation may deal with the territorial units of the different levels and the units of the higher level can include other ones. There may be two cases concerning the data provided by the subdivisions dealing with higher level territorial units and by the subdivisions dealing with partial units. The data provided by a higher level subdivision might or might not include data provided by the lower level subdivision. For these reasons both possibilities should be foreseen in the information system.

It is important to emphasise that presented statistical reports are official, i.e. they have legal status, and the organisations presenting reports are responsible for the accurateness of data. Normally it should be equal alternatives to use the indicators from the summary report or to calculate required total indicators from the detailed reports of subdivisions. But in fact the results possibly will be different because of various reasons, e.g. if report of some subdivision could be not presented or even if some miscalculation exist. In any case the information system should give priority to official status of information rather than to calculations.

The investigated statistical reports have a table form, i.e. they consist of rows and columns. The organisations and their subdivisions at regular intervals produce the reports and present them. The periodicity of different reports may alter from one month to the whole year. The reports of one type provide data describing activity during some period. Other reports are accumulative in a sense that their data describe activity from the beginning of the year to the end of the period. In fact such reports are even more often used in many organisations. Thus information system should provide the possibility to calculate non-accumulative data also, i.e. corresponding only to presented period. Depending on the situation and the data included in the certain report each subdivision may present individual report or the data corresponding particular subdivision is presented in the rows or columns of one report.

The information system should function properly even in the cases when not all required information is provided. Actually it is quite possible that the reports of some subdivisions are not presented or the set of some reports for the period is missing at all.

Not only the required collection of data but also the set of organisations that are providing the data is not predefined for information system development. So it is very important to have possibility to expand the functioning information system incorporating new data (reports) and the new organisations also. Fundamental requirement is that information system should allow introducing extensions at the descriptive level without additional programming. These features should be implemented in such a way that even non-IT professionals could be able to accomplish data administration tasks.

The scope of the supposed users of the information system is not clearly defined. It is evident that the users will be geographically distributed. Part of the users will be the professionals that will use information system in their everyday work for data analysis, comparison, and decision making. Therefore the information system should provide a set of different data visualisation formats, including tables, diagrams and maps. In addition possibility to receive required data for more complicated analysis should be implemented.

Also the information system should be open and one of the goals is public dissemination of the information world-wide. This requires the information system to have multilingual interface.

In both cases most of the users will have minimal knowledge and experience of information technologies usage, so the information system should be user friendly and easy to use.

3. Data Model

Similarly to information systems that use unstructured data model and are based on the conception of document, the model of the proposed information system refers to the concept of report. Let us consider system of concepts presented bellow.

3.1 REPORTS

The following concepts have been utilised for definition of the reports.

• **Report**: the pattern of a table form that has attributes of the period and the territorial unit (i.e. organisation's subdivision that presents report) and also defines the collections of rows and columns (i.e. set of indicators that values should be presented in the cells). Remark: some actual reports may have no territorial unit assigned (e.g. *2-dimensional reports*); in such case it is treated that the value of the territorial unit attribute is the whole country.

• **Set of subdivisions presenting report**: set of the organisation's subdivisions that present specified *report*. This set defines all possible values of the territorial unit attribute for specified report.

• **Report instance** (or simply **instance**): *report* filled with data for some period (the value of the period attribute) and presented by the organisation's subdivision that belongs to the *set of subdivisions presenting report* (the value of the territorial unit attribute).

• **Package of instances**: the collection of instances that have the same values of the period attribute, the *set of subdivisions presenting report* defines this collection (one *instance* corresponds each subdivision from the *set of subdivisions presenting report*).

• **Periodicity**: the *report* attribute that defines the regular time intervals at which the *packages of instances* of the *report* are presented. The periodicity of the *report* may be monthly, quarterly, half-yearly, annually.

• **Accumulative report**: the *report* with the data describing activity from the beginning of the year to the end of the period. E.g., quarterly *accumulative report* for 2nd quarter should present data for six months, from January to June.

• **Simple report**: the *report* having data that describe the activity during the period. E.g., quarterly *simple report* for 2nd quarter should present data for three months, from April to June.

• **Difference column**: the column is suitable for difference calculations, i.e. the column's data describing the activity during the period may be calculated by subtracting the corresponding data presented in the *instance* of the same *report* provided by the same subdivision for the previous period. Remark: *difference column* makes sense only in *accumulative report*, but not all columns of the *accumulative report* are *difference columns*.

• **Additive by time column**: the column having data that may be summed up with the same column's data presented in the *instance* of the same *report* provided by the same subdivision for the other period. As a result the data for longer period should be obtained. Remark: *additive by time column* makes sense in *accumulative report* only when the required period is longer than one year.

• **Additive by area column**: the column having data that may be summed up with the same column's data presented in the *instances* of the same *report* provided by the other subdivisions for the same period. As a result the data for territorial unit of higher level should be obtained. Remark: a column may be *additive by area column* but not *additive by time column*.

• **Territorial row**: the row having data that corresponds to some territorial unit (i.e.

organisation's subdivision that presents report). All rows of one *report* are *territorial rows* or not *territorial rows*. Remark: if the columns of the *report* are territorial, information system keeps this report in transposed form (*Transposed report*).

- **Transposed report**: the *report*, in which rows act as columns and columns act as rows. Such report should be kept in the database transposed, i.e., the columns should be kept instead of rows, and the rows should be kept instead of columns. Remark: only the rows of the *report* may be *territorial rows*, and only the columns of the *report* may be *additive by area columns* and *additive by time columns*.

- **3-dimensional report**: the *report* having *instances* that are provided by more than one organisation's subdivision. Such *reports* are called 3-dimensional for the reason that omitting of the period attribute that is the same for all *instances* of one *package of instances* the *reports* have three dimensions: rows, columns, and territorial units. Remark: the rows and columns of the *3-dimensional report* can not be *territorial*.

- **2-dimensional territorial report**: the *report*, having *instances* that are provided only by one organisation's subdivision with rows that are *territorial rows*. If the columns of the *report* are territorial, information system keeps this report as *Transposed report*. Such *reports* are called 2-dimensional for the reason that except period attribute the *reports* have two dimensions: rows (territorial units) and columns.

- **2-dimensional non-territorial report**: the *report*, having *instances* that are provided only by one organisation's subdivision and neither rows nor columns of the report are *territorial*.

- **Territory**: the territorial unit, restricted by the boundaries of a certain region and including the region together with a city (cities) located within the boundaries of that region. For instance in Lithuania, Vilnius territory is the territorial unit, including Vilnius region and Vilnius city; Klaipeda territory is the territorial unit, including Klaipeda region together with Klaipeda and Neringa cities.

- **Single period**: the period specified by a definite date with the precision of the *report periodicity*. E.g., for a *report* with quarterly periodicity the *single period* could be "2nd quarter of 1995".

- **Period range**: the sequence of *single periods*, specified by starting date, ending date, and periodicity. Starting date and ending date are considered *single periods*, specifying the starting and ending date of the *period range* accordingly, periodicity is equal or multiple to report *periodicity*, specifying the periodicity of location of *single periods* within the *period range*. E.g., the *period range* (2nd quarter of 1995, 4th quarter of 1996, 6 months) for a report with the periodicity of three months specifies the following sequence of *single periods*: 1st half-year of 1995, 2nd half-year of 1995, 1st half-year of 1996, 2nd half-year of 1996.

- **Summary period**: the *period range*, for which summary data are provided.

3.2 UNIFIED TERRITORIAL CLASSIFICATION

Data of every territorial report has its territorial distribution that matches the territorial structure of organisation's subdivisions presenting report. In order to obtain the possibility to keep in the database the data of all reports in standardised form and to compare data presented in different reports, unified territorial classification should be introduced. Such classification is also important for summing up data by area.

As the foundation for the territorial classification the administrative-territorial division of a country may serve. For instance, let's discuss the unified territorial classification proposed for Lithuania.

The territorial classification of Lithuania should consists of the following levels:
- **Country level**: corresponds to the whole country and consists of Lithuania.
- **District level**: consists of five Lithuanian districts; division into districts is used for distribution of subdivisions in many Lithuanian organisations. Every district consists of territories.

- **County level**: consists of ten Lithuanian administrative counties. Every county consists of territories.
- **Territory level**: consists of 44 territories (ref. concept *territory*); the Lithuanian administrative regions define the number and the territories themselves.
- **City-region level**: consists of 12 Lithuanian administrative cities and 44 Lithuanian administrative regions.
- **Subdivision level**: consists of the subdivisions of certain organisation.

Notes:

- Notion *region* represents the region without a city (cities) located within the boundaries of that region.
- Divisions into districts and counties are independent; i.e. one part of the county may belong to one district and other part – to the other district.
- Organisation's subdivision may correspond to any other territorial level; e.g., there may be some subdivisions in one city; certain subdivision may deal with the whole district or the whole country.
- As it was stated, subdivisions of the organisation may correspond to the territorial units of the different levels and the units of the higher level can include other ones. And if there is no subdivision that corresponds to certain territorial unit and provides complete information, the data for this territorial unit should be calculated (summed up) on the basis of data presented for partial (lower level) territorial units. Therefore the subdivision should contain references to all territorial units that deal with data provided by this subdivision. For example, the data provided by subdivision should be used in calculation of data corresponding to city, territory, and county, but it should not be used in calculation of data corresponding to district and the whole country, because there are subdivisions that present complete data at the district level.

3.3 CONCEPTUAL DATA MODEL

When the concepts of the system are defined, the creation of matching data model is quite straightforward. The Entity Relationship Diagram of the system is presented in *Figure 1*. The IDEF1X (Integration DEFinition for Information Modelling) [1] notation has been used.

The basic concepts proposed are represented by entities.

The following entities correspond to the territorial classification: *Country, District, County, Territory, Region, City,* and *Subdivision*.

The definition of the reports is expressed by the entities: *Organisation, Report, Row, Column,* and *Report's subdivision (set of subdivisions presenting report)*.

The data of the reports is represented by the entities: *Package of instances, Instance,* and *Data*. The entity *Data* is multiple entity; i.e. there is one entity of type *Data* per report. The data is kept by rows, so each entity *Data* has as many attributes *columnX* as there are columns in the corresponding report.

Other concepts are represented by attributes.

Presented conceptual data model is oriented to implementation using RDBMS.

4. Functionality

The system should consist of two subsystems: information presentation for end users and data administration. In such order the required functionality of the system is further discussed.

The users formulate their queries for information concerning statistical reports of the organisations as well as on administrative-territorial division terms and they can visualise and download data in the form of table, bar diagram, line diagram and administrative-territorial division map.

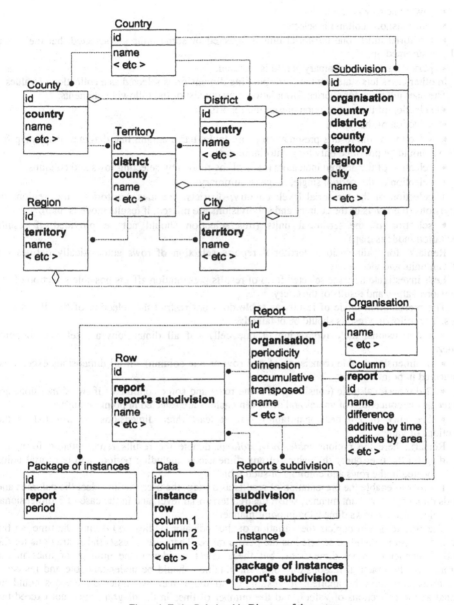

Figure 1. Entity Relationship Diagram of the system

For the uniformity reason, in the definition of the system functionality the period should be treated as additional attribute of the report. Consequently 3-dimensional reports are objects that have four dimensions: rows, columns, territorial units, and periods, while 2-dimensional reports - three dimensions: rows (territorial units for territorial report), columns, and periods.

Lets state that the corresponding dimension is selected in point manner if for:

- rows: one row is selected;
- columns: one column is selected;
- territorial units: one territorial unit is selected or some units are selected, but their data should be summed up;
- periods: single or summary period is selected.

In other cases lets state that the corresponding dimension is selected as a collection of values.

The user interface for queries' formulation may consist of the following elements:

- selection of the organisation presenting reports;
- selection of the report;
- selection of the results presentation form: table, bar diagram, line diagram, map (map for selection should be provided only for territorial report);
- selection of the desired indicators (cells of the report) by selecting rows and columns;
- selection of the period: single, range or summary;
- selection of the territorial level: country, districts, counties, territories, cities-regions or subdivisions (the levels of the country and subdivisions are missed, if results mode is map);
- selection of the territorial units (this selection should not be provided, if results presentation mode is map).

Remark: for 2-dimensional territorial reports selection of rows automatically defines the territorial units and vice versa.

Let's investigate how the selected form of results presentation affects possible selection of the dimensions values and results of the query.

The presentation mode of results as **table** does not restrict the selection of the dimensions values. The following results should be obtained:

- 0-dimensional table (consisting of one cell) - if all dimensions are selected in point manner.
- 1-dimensional table (consisting of one row or one column) - if all dimensions except one are selected in point manner.
- 2-dimensional table (consisting of some rows and some columns) - if two dimensions are selected as the collections of values and other dimensions are selected in point manner.
- Sequence of 2-dimensional tables - if at least three dimensions are selected as the collections of values.

Remark: here the notions *table*, *row*, *column* denote the results representation form, i.e. depending on the user query the values of any dimensions, including periods and territorial units, may be located in the rows and columns of such table.

In order to enable the presentation of results as a **map**, the user should select the columns and periods dimensions in point manner, select desired territorial level, and in the case of 3-dimensional report select also the rows dimension in point manner.

The **line diagram** depicts the variation of the indicator (indicators) during the time, so the periods dimension should be selected as the period range. There are no essential restrictions for the selection manner of other dimensions, but these selections define the number of lines in the diagram. For the practical reasons that diagram obtained should be understandable and readable, some restrictions may be applied: for example, no more than two other dimensions could be selected as the collections of values, and the number of lines in the diagram must not exceed the number specified in the system configuration.

The presentation mode of results as a **bar diagram** also does not cause the essential restrictions. From the practical point of view the possibility for the user to obtain the following results should be ensured:

- variation of one indicator during the time - all dimensions except the periods dimension should be selected in point manner;

- distribution of one indicator by territorial units - all dimensions except the territorial units dimension should be selected in point manner;
- values of some indicators in certain territorial unit and period - the periods and the territorial units dimensions should be selected in point manner.

As it was mentioned the accumulative reports (having data that represents the activity from the beginning of the year) are often provided by many organisations, therefore the information system should supply the functions that facilitate the user to obtain the data for a certain single period. Necessary data should be calculated by subtracting the corresponding data of the required periods. These calculations cause additional restrictions for the selection of the dimensions values: in order to enable the calculation only the difference columns should be selected, in addition solely such periods and territorial units should be selected that have pairs of report instances required for difference calculation.

The information system is devoted for world-wide geographically distributed users, so it should be Internet based and accessible via standard WWW browsers.

The data administration subsystem would provide following functionality:

- definition of the report structure by description of the report attributes;
- configuration of report data import by mapping the data source structure to the report structure defined;
- import of the report data according to configuration defined;
- modification of the report structure definition.

The implementation of these functions should be user friendly, oriented to the use by non-IT professionals.

5. Model Features

The proposed model of the information system can be applied for analytical processing in any application domain in the case when input data about facts and activity exist as statistical reports presented in the table form for the certain area and the certain period.

The meaning and dimension of the reports rows and columns depend on particular application domain and even on particular report. The model requires unified period classification (i.e. month, quarter, half-year, year) and unified territorial classification for all input statistical reports, but it does not require the classification of domain attributes (indicators) expressed by rows and columns of the reports. It is impossible to introduce unified attributes classification, because application domain is unspecified. Also actual reports include specific classifications of domain attributes thus definition of unified classification should require restructuring of data presented in the reports.

Introduced data model is the same for any application domain, i.e., the model is domain independent. Domain dependence is expressed by the values of domain attributes (rows and columns) only.

Such invariable data model enables to develop the statistical reports processing functions only once for any application domain. Also it allows implementing data administration functions so that new input reports and minor changes of incorporated reports can be made at the descriptive level. This possibility is crucial in practice.

Proposed model of information system belongs to OLAP solutions and it presents dimensional data model with facts and dimensions [4] as statistical reports abstraction. Dimensional data model is expressed by relational data dependencies model to satisfy implementation needs using RDBMS.

Report based model as OLAP solution has common features with data warehouse approach [2, 3, 4]:

- it organises and stores the data needed for informational, analytical processing;

- it is a method for combining information from a number of different systems;
- it is a central access point for an organisation's data;
- it is populated by data from otherwise incompatible information systems;
- it is presented in a relevant format that enables reporting across many applications;
- the information presented is "read-only" that means the information sources can not be affected.

Bill Inmon, the acknowledged father of the data warehouse, defines it as an integrated, subject-oriented, time-variant, non-volatile database that provides support for decision making [2].

The principal differences between report based information system and data warehouse are following:

- proposed model is domain independent when data warehouse is subject-oriented;
- presented information system deals with specific objects - statistical reports.

Data warehouse approach suggests creation of a dimensional data model for some application domain. Contrary, in the model of report based information system dimensional data model and required functions are developed.

The adequacy of the model has been proved by its implementation in the Crime prevention information system in Lithuania.

6. Conclusions

The model of information system based on statistical reports is proposed. These reports have a form of table that presents information for the certain period and the certain area in rows and columns. The comprehensive definition of the reports is presented. There are introduced the information system functions that facilitate formulation of the queries using notions of reports and visualisation of the results in the form of table, bar diagram, line diagram and administrative-territorial division map. Information system of such a kind can be applied when initial data about the activity of the organisation is described as set of reports in table mode.

The proposed model is rather aligned with the concept of data warehouse. It also emphasises the capture of data from diverse sources for useful analysis and access, but it utilises specific objects - statistical reports and specific operations with them.

The presented ideas have been proved in the development of the Automated Statistical Information System that provides open crime-prevention related information of the following Lithuanian institutions: Department of Courts, General Public Prosecutor's Office, Department of Statistics, Prison Department, Police Department under the Ministry of Internal Affairs, Department of Informatics and Communications under the Ministry of Internal Affairs. The information system has been developed using Java™ Servlets, Apache HTTP server with Allaire JRun servlet engine, and Informix Dynamic Server™ DBMS. It can be accessed at http://www.nplc.lt:8000/asis/.

References

1. *Federal Information Processing Standards Publication 184: Integration Definition for Information Modeling (IDEF1X)*. http://www.idef.com/Complete_Reports/idef1x/idef1x.htm.

2. Inmon, W. H. *Building the Data Warehouse*. 2nd edition, New York, John Wiley & Sons, 1996.

3. Inmon, W. H., Welch, J. D., Glassey, K. L. *Managing the Data Warehouse: Practical Techniques for Monitoring Operations and Performances, Administering Data and Tools, Managing Change and Growth*. New York, John Wiley & Sons, 1997.

4. Kimball, R. *The Data Warehouse Toolkit: Practical Techniques for Building Dimensional Data Warehouse*. New York, John Wiley & Sons, 1996.

5. Teorey, T. J. *Database Modeling & Design: The Fundamental Principles*. 2nd edition, Morgan Kaufmann Publishers, 1994.

A New Approach to the Modelling, Design, and Implementation of Business Information Systems

Kuldar Taveter

Department of Informatics, Tallinn Technical University, Tallinn, Estonia
VTT Information Technology, Espoo, Finland
kuldar.taveter@vtt.fi

Boris Tamm

Cybernetica Ltd., Tallinn, Estonia
btamm@is.cyber.ee

Abstract

We are proposing an approach where the modelling, design, and implementation of business information systems is based on the notion of agent. By using an example of car rental, we show how the process of agent-oriented modelling and design could look like. It starts from modelling autonomous functional units of an organisation by agents, and continues by analysing business rules of the organisation and modelling a common understanding of the problem domain for the agents by creating an ontology. We show how business rules can be further operationalised through beliefs and action and reaction rules of the agents, and how business processes can be described through repetitive execution of (re)action rules and high-level communication between the agents.

Keywords: requirements' engineering, agent, ontology, business rule, business process.

1. Introduction

Agent is an emerging abstraction that the field of business information systems may also benefit from. Agent is understood as an *active* entity, possessing the features of *autonomy*, *proactiveness*, *responsiveness*, and *social behaviour* in contrast to a passive entity meant for representing information – *object* [19]. Agents thus promote *autonomous action and decision-making* which enables peer-to-peer interaction, while objects are better suited to the more rigid client-server model [3]. *Agent-Orientation* is therefore highly relevant for business information systems, because business processes are essentially interactions of human or artificial agents. In the agent terminology, the information possessed by an agent or an agent's knowledge is referred to as *beliefs* of an agent.

According to the emerging paradigm of *cooperative information systems* [22], information systems are viewed as consisting of agents who relate to each other as a social organisation. Agents cooperate when they share goals and work together to fulfil those goals. The process of requirements' capture for cooperative information systems includes the steps of *identifying the agents in the environment, mapping business goals to system goals*, and *operationalising these system goals by reducing them into constraints that agents can be responsible for through their actions* [22]. We have followed these steps in our work. Under the paradigm of cooperative information systems, once captured organisational objectives and systems requirements must also be "kept alive" and remain a part of the running system, due to ongoing evolution of the system. An

317

J. Barzdins and A. Caplinskas (eds.), Databases and Information Systems, 317–335.
© 2001 *Kluwer Academic Publishers*.

adequate objectives' and requirements' representation language should support a *declarative* style of specification which offers the possibility to model requirements adopting an *aerial view* perspective. For example: "the borrowing of a book should be followed by its return within the next three weeks" [22]. In our opinion representing organisational objectives and systems requirements as *business rules* that define and constrain the actions of *business agents* is a step towards this kind of language. We will also try to support representation of business rules by integrating adequate graphical modelling techniques.

2. Traditional Requirements' Engineering

Traditional requirements' engineering for business information systems can be described by the so-called "triangle" model [25]. The "triangle" consists of three interrelated components: *data model* of the problem domain, relevant *events* taking place in the external world, and *actions* of the system that are triggered by the corresponding events and operate on the instances of entity types (object classes) of the data model (Figure 1).

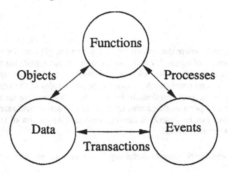

Figure 1. The "triangle model"

The main shortcoming of the "triangle"-based business modelling, including object-oriented modelling is that it doesn't explicitly deal with *actors* that perform different functions of the business. For example, the data flow diagram, which is one of the most popular ways of modelling the vertex of functions of the "triangle" model [25], views functions as transformers of data flows that are not attached to any actors performing these functions. True, on workflow diagrams functions are attached to actors, but these actors do not belong to the business model created for the information system. Actors are usually represented as instances of entity types of the data model, but there they are *passive* entities to be manipulated with rather than true *active* performers of business functions. This is reflected by the existing methodologies of modelling and designing object-oriented systems like e.g. UML [29]. It has also been noticed by the others [33] that in UML actors are only considered as users of the system's services in "use cases", but otherwise remain external to the system model. Due to this business rules defining and constraining the functions of the business remain up in the "air" and are not attached to any processors/executors.

On the other hand, business rules have a *global nature*, i. e. they possibly involve objects of several object classes. This doesn't fit with the principle of encapsulation that we have in object-oriented modelling. For example, the rule "product of the type A should never be cheaper than product of the type B" involves two different object classes: it cannot be expressed within just one class. The rule "when the payment of a bill is two weeks overdue, it is required to send a reminder to the customer" involves several object classes, an action, and time, and cannot therefore be encapsulated within one specific class [15].

There have been proposals to express business rules in an object-oriented fashion by using metamodelling [5, 23], but we are not aware of their any further consequences. The rule-modelling approach described in [24] and [12] enables to model global business rules in a natural way. This approach is, however, data-centred, and doesn't therefore include any semantics for actions. We have widened this approach by viewing data as agents' beliefs, and expressing business rules in terms of agents' beliefs and actions. This may constitute a powerful paradigm for the modelling, design, and implementation of business information systems. Followingly we will take a closer look at the approach proposed by us.

3. The Business Rules' Approach

Our solution to the problems mentioned in section 2 is adding the *Agent Layer* to the top of Object and Implementation Layers (Figure 2). We understand the *Object Layer* in a wide sense of the term as either some relational, object-relational, or object-oriented database, or as some object-oriented framework such as COM™ or CORBA™. The *Implementation Layer* provides lower-level implementation support for objects and agents.

In the Agent Layer, the three vertexes of the triangle in Figure 1 are reflected at a higher level of abstraction as follows:

- *data* is information possessed by an agent;
- (business) *functions* are performed by an agent;
- *events* represent receiving of high-level typed messages, such as "ASK", "TELL", "REQUEST", and "PROPOSE", by an agent.

From the modelling point of view, we apply the metaphor of an agent as a natural and convenient *anthropomorphic abstraction* of a functional business unit/actor and also of an external unit/actor like a customer or supplier. From the technical point of view, we see a software agent in business information systems as *a rule-based intelligent distributed unit that implements business logic. We are interested in how agents understood this way could be utilised in business information systems, and how they could facilitate the modelling, design, and development of such systems.*

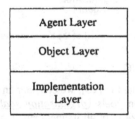

Figure 2. Adding the Agent Layer

3.1 METAMODEL OF THE BUSINESS RULES' APPROACH

We have worked out a preliminary methodology how requirements for business information systems could be engineered at a high level of abstraction by expressing business rules as a combination of events perceived by agents, and beliefs and actions of agents where the events and beliefs respectively constitute triggering conditions and preconditions for the actions. This methodology consists of *modelling functional organisation units by agents, analysing the business rules of the organisation, modelling the problem domain by ontology, mapping the business rules to (re)action rules of the agents,* and *modelling business processes from the perspectives of different agents by using (re)action rules and from an objective observer's point of view through the agents' interactions.* These steps should be applied in an iterative manner. The metamodel depicted in Figure 3 will be referred to throughout this paper.

For evaluating the methodology proposed by us, we have made use of the case study of a *car rental company where customers make rental reservations via Internet, and pick up and drop off cars by using chip cards* (Figure 4). The geographical distribution of such an enterprise over a headquarter and a number of branches suggests to view and model it as a group of interacting agents represented by their respective information systems.

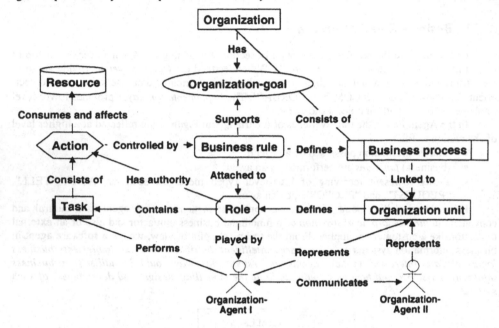

Figure 3. The metamodel of the business rules' approach

3.2 ORGANISATION MODELLING

Following the definition presented in [20], we consider an *organisation* as a social unit which lastingly strives to achieve common goals (*organisation-goals* in Figure 3), and has a formal structure which co-ordinates the activities of all its members in order to achieve the goals.

According to our methodology, firstly functional organisation units of the organisation to be modelled are found. A *functional organisation unit* (Figure 3) can be defined as an entity for managing the performance of activities to achieve one or more goals of the organisation [30]. Each functional organisation unit maintains knowledge about a certain *functional subfield* of the problem domain that has *common business rules and goals* [8]. In our example case study of a car rental company, such functional organisation units are the *branch, headquarter*, and *automotive service station*. Each functional organisation unit can be represented by one or more organisation-agents (Figure 3). An *organisation-agent* is an individual processing entity that may be of human or automated nature [9]. Each functional organisation unit defines a set of *roles* that are played by the organisation-agents representing the given unit (Figure 3), or their *subagents* (i.e. the agents subordinated to them). In the example of a car rental company, the roles "rental reservation manager", "manager of handovers and returns", and "manager of walk-in rentals" are played by the automated *Branch Agent* (Figure 3), while the role "managing automotive service" is played by a human subagent called the *Car Handling Agent*. Each role contains one or more prototypical job functions - *tasks* - in an organisation (Figure 3). For example, in a car rental company the tasks corresponding to the role "rental reservation manager" are "checking the capacity of the pick-up branch on the pick-up day", "checking that the customer is not blacklisted", "creating a rental reservation", and "allocating a car for the rental reservation". Organisation-agents *interact* with each other according to the roles played by them (Figure 3). Each task consists of one or several actions. The role containing a task has an authority to perform the actions the given task consists of (Figure 3). An *action* is an atomic unit of work done by an organisation-agent. We view an agent's action in a broader sense as something that the agent *does*: a human may make a decision, an agent wrapping a database may execute certain retrieval primitives, a statistical computation agent may run certain mathematical procedures, and one agent may send a message to another agent [26], while in the "triangle" model (Figure 1) action is understood narrowly as something that changes the state of a data object. Example actions in our car rental company are "sending a car to service", "asking another agent to transfer a car", and "creating an instance of the *RentalOrder*".

    Other organisation-agents besides *Branch Agents* in our example are the *Automotive Service Agent*, representing the automotive service station, and the *Headquarter Agent*, representing the headquarter of the car rental company and mediating the database of rental orders and customers (Figure 4). Additionally there are *external agents* – Customers and Bank. The *Customers* reserve

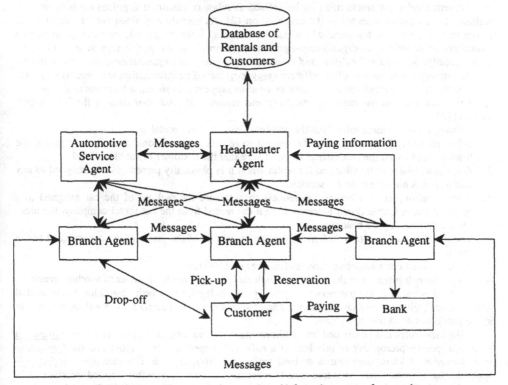

Figure 4. The architecture of an agent-oriented information system of car rental

cars via Internet, and pick up and drop off cars by using chip cards that are sent to them by mail. They pay for rentals by using the services of an external institutional agent – *Bank* (Figure 4). Each *Branch Agent* has his own database of the cars at his disposal. As we will see in section 3.4, agents of all the types mentioned are also explicitly represented in the corresponding agent-oriented information system of car rental.

3.3 ANALYSIS OF BUSINESS RULES

When we take a look at the requirements' description for some business, we find that the organisation-goals of the business are supported by a big number of different business rules (Figure 3). *At the business level*, a *business rule* is defined as a statement that defines or constrains some aspect of the business [12]. A business rule is based on a *business policy*. An example of a business policy in a car rental company is "only cars in legal, roadworthy condition can be rented to customers" [12]. A business rule is also subject to one of the following enforcement levels: *mandate* (must be followed), *requirement* (may be deviated from only with permission), and *guideline* (suggestion) [13]. Business rules are of *declarative nature*: they describe certain states of affairs that are either required or prohibited, or result from actions, while not prescribing the steps to be taken to achieve the transition from one state to another, or the steps to be taken to prohibit a transition [12]. It is a duty of the system analyst to attach these rules to certain roles played by certain organisation-agents so that the rules would control the actions of the agents. In other words: each rule should be attached to its *processor*.

Alternatively, a business rule may be defined as a law or custom that guides the behaviour or actions of the actors connected to the organisation [2]. As already explained earlier, we view all actors connected to the business, which can be humans, software agents, or external units like customers or suppliers, as organisation-agents and external agents, and assign actions to them. Consequently, *business rules define and constrain the actions of organisation-agents and external agents*. Actions consume and affect different *resources*, including information resources (Figure 3).

At the level of an information system created to support a business, a business rule expresses specific constraints on the creation, updating, and removal of *persistent* data in the information system [12].

Examples of business rules from the problem domain of car rental are:

1. When receiving from a customer the request to reserve a car of some specified car group, the branch checks with the headquarter to make sure that the customer is not blacklisted.
2. A car is available to be allocated for rental when it is physically present, is not assigned to any rental, and is not scheduled for service.
3. Upon receiving from a branch the request to authorise the pick-up of the car assigned to a rental, if the customer doesn't already have a car rented from the car rental company, the pick-up is authorised by the headquarter.
4. The rental rate of a rental is inferred from the rental rate of the group of the car assigned to the rental.
5. Each car must get automotive service after every 10,000 km.
6. Only a branch manager of the "donor" branch may assign a car for transfer to another branch.

Rule 5 is based on the business policy "only cars in legal, roadworthy condition can be rented to customers", given as an example above. The business rules of Examples 1 – 5 will be referred to in the sections 3.4 – 3.6 of this paper.

Business rules can be divided into authorisations, derivations, and action rules. *Authorisation* defines a specific prerogative or privilege of a *role* with respect to one or more actions. *Derivation* is a statement of knowledge that is derived from other knowledge in the enterprise. *Action rule* specifies that if some condition is true, a certain action with certain (possibly implied) results should be performed. The rules of Examples 1, 3, and 5 are action rules, the rules of Examples 2 and 4 are derivations, and the rule of Example 6 is an authorisation.

3.4 DOMAIN MODELLING BY ONTOLOGY

We abstract away from a specific composition of the Object Layer (Figure 2), which can be a relational, object-relational, or object-oriented database, or some object-oriented framework such as COM™ or CORBA™, by representing the Object Layer in the form of an ontology. With our approach, ontology provides a common framework of knowledge for the organisation-agents and external agents connected to the organisation. A _problem-oriented ontology_ is a description by truth values of the concepts and relationships of the problem domain that exist for an agent or more commonly for a community of agents [11]. An ontology consists of the *concepts* (*classes*), *relations* between them like e.g. subsumption (inheritance), aggregation, and association, and *axioms* of the problem domain. Ontology should provide all the data structures, relations, and axioms that are necessary for the agents for performing their actions. Ontology should also represent agents themselves. Each agent of the problem domain can see only a part of the ontology, i.e. each agent has a specific *view* of the ontology.

We used the Ontolingua [11] formalism for creating the ontology of car rental, because the Ontology Editor [28] for Ontolingua enables to check the logical consistency of an ontology created by its use.

Ontologies can be viewed as extensions of object-oriented (OO) models of problem domains described e.g. in [38]. However, most OO modelling techniques neither provide the necessary axioms that constrain the interpretation and well-formed use of the terms defined by them, nor support other ontological constructs, such as metamodels (i.e. defining a model by using the model itself) [21]. Therefore we modelled the Object Layer by an ontology instead of a set of OO models.

Ontologies can be graphically represented using different notations. We have chosen to represent the ontology of car rental by using a combination of Agent-Object-Relationship (AOR) diagrams [31, 32] and Ross Notation [24] because it enables a straightforward modelling of business rules.

A simplified and partial version of the ontology of car rental is represented in Figure 5. In AOR diagrams [31, 32], a *subclass* is visualised as a rectangle within its superclass. A *component class* is visualised as a rectangle with dotted lines drawn within the superior class it belongs to (recall that a component cannot exist independently of the whole; if the whole ceases to exist, all of its components also cease to exist).

An *agent class* is visualised as a rectangle with rounded corners. In order to distinguish an internal agent (*subagent*) class from an external agent class and from an agent subclass, it is visualised by such a rectangle with a dotted line (like *BranchAgent* and *CarHandlingAgent* in Figure 5).

Since the *state* of an entity can be interpreted as a subclass of the entity (see e.g. [17]), we use the notation for subclasses also for representing states. For example, an entity of the class *RentalOrder* in Figure 5 can be in the state *reserved*, *allocated*, *effective*, or *dropped-off*. States can also have *substates*, like in Figure 5 the state *present* of *CarForRental* has the substates *available*, *requires-service*, and *scheduled-for-service*.

Different conditions evaluated by agents are represented by an ontology using the Ontolingua [11] formalism as shown in the second column of Table 2 for the business rules of Examples 1 - 5. According to the semantics of Ontolingua, all free variables that appear in the examples have implicit universal quantification.

In Figure 5 the Ross Notation [24] is used for representing the same conditions as intensional predicates. The Ross Notation enables to represent both *materialised* (i.e. instantiated) and *computed-on-the-fly* views of intensional predicates. According to the Ross Notation, each business rule consists of an anchor, rule symbol, and correspondent. _Anchor_ is a data type or another rule for whose instances a rule is specified. In the graphical representation of the Ross Notation, the anchor connection *exits* the anchor and *enters* the rule symbol. _Correspondent_ is a data type, another rule, or action whose instances are subject to the test exercised by the rule. In the graphical representation of the Ross Notation, the correspondent connection *exits* the rule symbol and *enters* the correspondent. Both the anchor connection and correspondent connection are dashed.

Every rule produces a value, called the <u>*Yield Value*</u> (abbreviated YV), at any point of time. Usually this value is hidden. It is used internally by the rule to achieve the appropriate truth value for the rule. Sometimes, rules require testing the Yield Value of a rule directly. To satisfy this need, the Yield Value of a rule may be externalised. When externalised, the Yield Value appears as an attribute type for the rule itself.

The symbols of the Ross Notation, used in our ontology of car rental, and their basic meanings are given in Table 1.

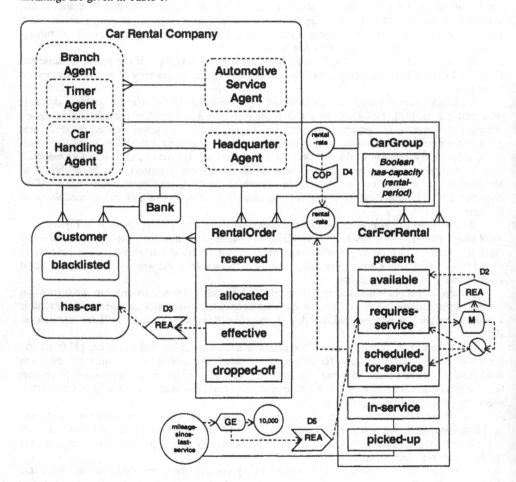

Figure 5. A part of the ontology of car rental

Table 1. A selection of rule symbols and other graphical symbols according to the Ross Notation

Symbol	Basic meaning
M	Given an instance of the anchor, do instances of all the correspondent types simultaneously exist for that instance?
GE	Is the value of the anchor greater or equal than the value of the correspondent?
EA	Creates an instance of the correspondent
REA	Creates an instance of the correspondent, but does not materialise it (i.e. terminates such an instance when the instance of the anchor is deleted)
COP	Requires propagation (i.e. copying) of the value of an instance of the anchor to instance(s) of the correspondent.
⊘	Negation
rental-period	Attribute type

The action part of the action rule of Example 1 in section 3.3 simply checks that an instance of *Customer* does not belong to the subclass *blacklisted*. Its ontological representations in row 1 of Table 2 and in Figure 5 are therefore straightforward.

The business rule of Example 2 is a derivation rule defining how to determine the set of cars that are available to rent. This rule can be expressed as an axiom of Ontolingua that looks like shown in row 2 of Table 2. The axiom determines that a given car *?Car* is available if it is physically present at the branch (i.e. belongs to the subclass *present* of *CarForRental*), is not allocated for any *RentalOrder*, doesn't require service (i.e. does not belong to the subclass *requires-service* of *present*), and is not already scheduled for service (i.e. does not belong to the subclass *scheduled-for-service* of *present*). Figure 5 depicts the visualisation of the business rule of Example 2 by using the Ross Notation (rule D2).

The precondition part of the action rule of Example 3 is a derivation rule prescribing that a customer belongs to the class *has-car* if and until any *RentalOrder* related to it is in the state *effective*. It is represented by Ontolingua as shown in row 3 of Table 2. With the help of the Ross Notation this derivation rule can be visualised as shown in Figure 5 (rule D3).

The derivation rule of Example 4 can be expressed in Ontolingua as shown in row 4 of Table 2. This rule determines that the rental rate of a *RentalOrder*, expressed by its attribute *rental-rate*, is copied from the rental rate of the *CarGroup* that the car allocated for the *RentalOrder* belongs to. In Figure 5 this corresponds to the rule of the type *copier* (COP) (Table 1) of the Ross Notation (rule D4).

The triggering condition of the action rule of Example 5 is a derivation rule that can be expressed as an axiom of Ontolingua shown in row 5 of Table 2. This rule says that if the mileage since the last service of a car physically present at the branch, represented by the value of the attribute *mileage-since-last-service* of the corresponding instance of *CarForRental* in the state *present*, is greater or equal than 10,000 km, the substate of the instance of *CarForRental* changes to *requires-service*, and stays that until the car is scheduled for service (because the substates *requires-service* and *scheduled-for-service* of *present* are mutually exclusive). The visual representation of this derivation rule can be seen in Figure 5 (rule D5).

Since the Ross Notation does not allow for graphical modelling of intensional predicates whose values depend on the values of parameters, such intensional predicates should be represented textually rather than graphically. In our case study, the intensional predicate *has-capacity* of the object class *CarGroup* determines the existence of rental capacity in the given *CarGroup* during the requested rental period (Figure 5). Therefore the truth value of this intensional predicate is also dependent on the value of the parameter *rental-period*.

Table 2. Correspondences between business rules, formal representations of their conditions in Ontolingua, and operational rules of agents

Rule	Ontological Representation of Condition	Operational Rule
1	(blacklisted (?Customer))	**sendMsg** (ASK-IF (blacklisted (*customer*)), HeadquarterAgent) ← **recvMsg** (REQUEST (reserve (*car-group* ...)), *customer*), CarGroup.has-capacity (*car-group rental-period*)
2	(<=> (available ?Car) (And (present ?Car) (Not (Exists (?Rental) (And (RentalOrder ?Rental) (= (Car-Of ?Rental) ?Car)))) (Not (requires-service ?Car)) (Not (scheduled-for-service ?Car)))))	available(*x*) ← CarForRental.present(*x*) ∧ ¬∃*y* (RentalOrder(*y*) ∧ *y*.CarID = *x*) ∧ ¬CarForRental.requires-service(*x*) ∧ ¬CarForRental.scheduled-for-service(*x*)
3	(<=> (has-car ?Customer) (Exists (?Rental) (And (effective ?Rental) (= ?Customer (Customer-Of ?Rental)))))	**sendMsg** (REPLY-IF (has-car (*customer*), **no**), BranchAgent) ← **recvMsg** (ASK-IF (has-car (*customer*)), BranchAgent), ¬Customer.has-car (*customer*)
4	(=> (RentalOrder ?Rental) (= (rental-rate ?Rental) (rental-rate (Car-Group-Of (Car-Of ?Rental)))))	RentalOrder.compute_rental_rate (*rental-ID*)
5	(=> (requires-service ?Car) (And (present ?Car) (>= (mileage-since-last-service ?Car) 10000))))	**sendMsg** (REQUEST (schedule_for_service (*car* OF *rental-ID*)), AutomotiveServiceAgent) ← **recvMsg** (dropOffCar (*rental-ID*), *customer*), CarForRental.requires-service (*car* OF *rental-ID*)

3.5 MAPPING BUSINESS RULES TO OPERATIONAL RULES OF AGENTS

Business rules should be *operationalised*, i.e. represented procedurally, in order to facilitate their enforcement by either artificial or human agents. Therefore at the next step of the methodology proposed by us, business rules are mapped to their *processors*, i.e. to the organisation-agents representing functional organisation units introduced in section 3.2. We have chosen to model organisation-agents by using the *vivid agent* model defined in [35] because of the relative straightforwardness of this kind of mapping and the effectiveness of the vivid agent model needed for business applications in comparison with other candidate agent architectures like e.g. the BDI-architecture [10, 16]. With the vivid agent architecture, business rules are mapped to action, reaction, and derivation rules of agents.

According to the vivid agent architecture introduced in [34, 35], we define an *agent* to be consisting of three components:

- a *virtual knowledge base X*, consisting of the agent's *beliefs*;
- an *event queue EQ*, i.e. a buffer receiving messages from other agents or from perception subsystems of the agent running as concurrent processes;
- a set of *action rules AR* and *reaction rules RR* respectively determining the agent's reactive and communicative behaviour.

An agent's *virtual knowledge base* (VKB) is called "virtual" because it is not necessarily implemented as a classical knowledge base. With our approach, an agent's VKB belongs to the Object Layer (Figure 2), and is modelled conceptually by an ontology.

Action rules have the general form of *Action* ← *Condition* where *Condition* refers to the agent's information state represented in its VKB.

According to the actions prescribed by action rules, action rules are divided into [35]:

- *epistemic action rules* of the form *Eff* ← *Cond* where *Eff* is an epistemic effect formula specifying a corresponding update of the agent's VKB;
- *physical action rules* of the form **do**(α), *Eff* ← *Cond* where **do**(α) calls the procedure α affecting some actuators available to the agent;
- *communicative action rules* of the form **sendMsg**[*m(c)*, *i*], *Eff* ← *Cond* where **sendMsg**[*m(c)*, *i*] is a procedure call to send the message *m(c)* to agent *i*.

Agents communicate in some high-level *agent communication language*, such as ACL proposed by FIPA [20], that is based on *typed messages* like "ASK", "TELL", "REQUEST", and "PROPOSE". In contrast to the application-specific messages in OO-programming, message types of an agent communication language are application-independent and therefore, *in combination with an ontology*, defining the semantic vocabulary of a problem domain, allow for true software interoperability [34].

Reaction rules encode the behaviour of an agent in response to perception events created by the agent's perception subsystems, and to communication events created by communication acts of other agents. Both perception and communication events are represented by incoming messages of an agent [34].

There are three types of reaction rules [34]:

- *epistemic reaction rules* of the form *Eff* ← **recvMsg**[*m(c)*, *j*], *Cond* where the event condition **recvMsg**[*m(c)*, *j*] is a test whether the event queue *EQ* of the agent contains the message *m(c)* sent by agent *j*;
- *physical reaction rules* of the form **do**(α), *Eff* ← **recvMsg**[*m(c)*, *j*], *Cond*;
- *communicative reaction rules* of the form **sendMsg**[*m'(c')*, *i*], *Eff* ← **recvMsg**[*m(c)*, *j*], *Cond*.

Notice that while reaction rules are triggered by the occurrence of specific events, and thus represent automated business functions performed by artificial software agents, action rules are applied when an agent decides to perform an action of that type and thus represent business functions recorded in the enterprise information system but performed by *human (sub)agents* such as the *Car Handling Agent* (Figure 5).

Additionally there are *derivation rules* of the form *Conclusion* ← *Premise* which correspond to intensional predicates in the agent's virtual knowledge base [34]. At the previous step of our methodology (section 3.4), intensional predicates were modelled by the ontology of the problem domain without attaching them to specific agents.

Table 2 shows how business rules of Examples 1 - 5 in section 3.3 are mapped to reaction rules and derivation rules, i.e. to *operational rules*, of vivid agents. The business rule of Example 1 is mapped to the reaction rule of a *Branch Agent* in response to the communication event (reservation request) originating from an external agent *Customer*. The business rule of Example 3 is mapped to the reaction rule of a *Headquarter Agent* in response to the communication event (query whether the customer already has a car) originating from a *Branch Agent*. The business rule of Example 5 is mapped to the reaction rule of a *Branch Agent* in response to the environment event (*dropOffCar*) caused by an external agent *Customer*. The reaction rules described respectively evaluate the intensional predicates *has-capacity*, *has-car*, and *requires-service*. The rules are presented in rows 1, 3, and 5 of Table 2, respectively. The conditions of Examples 2 and 4 are straightforwardly mapped to the corresponding derivation rules of a *Branch Agent*, respectively shown in rows 2 and 4 of Table 2.

Action and reaction rules can be graphically modelled by AOR diagrams defined in [31, 32]. *Events* on AOR diagrams have a concave (incoming) rectangle side, while *actions* have a convex (outgoing) rectangle side. Communication event rectangles and communication act rectangles have a grey background colour.

In a business environment different *commitments* and the corresponding *claims* between parties involved emerge. It is extremely important to represent them explicitly in the virtual knowledge bases of the organisation-agents. The explicit representation and processing of commitments helps to establish coherent behaviour in the information system.

There are two kinds of commitments: commitments to perform an action and commitments to see it that some condition holds. From the perspective of an organisation, commitments are commitments towards other agents, while commitments of other agents are viewed as claims against them. A commitment towards another agent (such as a commitment towards a customer to provide a car) is coupled with the associated action (such as a *provideCar* action). It is visualised as a rectangle with a dotted line on top of the associated action rectangle like shown in Figure 6. A claim against another agent (such as a claim against a customer to return a car) is coupled with the associated event (such as a *returnCar* event). It is visualised as a rectangle with a dotted line on top of the associated event rectangle like shown in Figure 7.

In AOR diagrams, a (re)action rule is visualised as a named circle with incoming and outgoing arrows. The incoming arrows start from the graphical symbols representing the triggering event of a rule and the epistemic condition to be evaluated. The epistemic effects of a rule are visualised as update arrows from the circle representing the rule to the entities or their specific (sub)states affected. The communicative and physical effects of a rule are represented as arrows from the rule symbol to the symbols representing communicative and physical actions. For example, the triggering event of the reaction rule R1 in Figure 6 is the reception of the reservation request message from the *Customer*, the condition to be checked is evaluating the intensional predicate *has-capacity (rental-period)*, and the communicative effect is sending the query message with the content *?blacklisted (customer)* to the *Headquarter Agent*. The mental effect caused by the reaction rule R2 in Figure 6 is the creation of a *RentalOrder* in the state *reserved*. The physical effect of the action rule A1 in Figure 8 is the execution of the action *sendCarToService* by a human subagent *Car Handling Agent*.

3.6 MODELLING BUSINESS PROCESSES

Business rules define and control business processes (Figure 3). A <u>business process</u> can be defined as a collection of activities that takes one or more kinds of input, and creates an output that is of value to the customer [7, 17, 25, 38]. A business process describes from start to finish the sequence of events required to produce the product or service [38]. Business processes typically involve several different functional organisation units (Figure 3). Often business processes also cross organisational boundaries.

With the approach proposed by us, business processes are modelled from the perspectives of different organisation-agents involved in them, that is, we take the *design perspective*. We model each business process by a set of related reaction and action rules representing single process steps. In order to offer a better overview of business processes, we model them also from an objective observer's point of view. The business processes of the car rental company modelled by us are those of *rental reservation, allocating a car for a rental order, picking up a car, dropping off a car,* and *scheduling a car for automotive service*. So far, we have omitted from our case study the business processes related to paying for a rental. Business processes can have subprocesses, like e.g. the business process of allocating a car for a rental order has different subprocesses depending on the availability of a car. A selection of the business processes of the car rental company modelled from different perspectives by AOR diagrams follows. In the diagrams reaction rules are denoted by R_n and action rules by A_n. The reaction and action rules described make use of the intensional predicates defined by the ontology of car rental (Table 2 and Figure 5).

In Figure 6 the business process of *rental reservation* is modelled *from the perspective of a BranchAgent*. It contains the following reaction rules:

R1.   Upon receiving from a *Customer* the request to reserve a car of some specified *CarGroup* for
        some specified rental period, if that *CarGroup* has enough rental capacity during the rental
        period requested (found by evaluating the intensional predicate *has-capacity (rental-period)*
        of *CarGroup*), the *Branch Agent* sends a query to the *Headquarter Agent* to make sure that
        the *Customer* is not blacklisted (also Operational Rule 1 in Table 2);
R2.   Upon receiving from the *Headquarter Agent* a reply telling that the *Customer* is not
        blacklisted, the *Branch Agent* creates the corresponding rental reservation (i.e. an instance of
        RentalOrder in the state *reserved*), commits towards the *Customer* to provide a car, sends to
        its subagent *Timer Agent* a request to remind about the allocation time of a car for the given
        RentalOrder (a car is allocated for the rental reservation 12 hours before the pick-up-time),
        and sends an acknowledgement to the *Customer*.

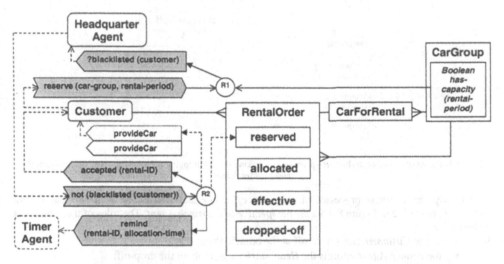

Figure 6. The AOR model of the business process of rental reservation from the perspective of a Branch Agent

        12 hours before the pick-up-time a car is allocated for the *RentalOrder* by executing the
corresponding reaction rule where the *Branch Agent* searches its virtual knowledge base for an
available car with the required parameters, and if the car has been found, allocates the car for the
RentalOrder. While searching for an available car, the *Branch Agent* makes use of the intensional
predicate *available* (Operational Rule 2 in Table 2).
        Figure 7 depicts the business processes of *picking up a car* and *dropping off a car from the
perspective of the Headquarter Agent*. The reaction rules represented in Figure 7 are:
R3.   Upon receiving from a *Branch Agent* a message about the new effective *RentalOrder*, the
        Headquarter Agent inserts into its VKB the corresponding instance of *RentalOrder* in the
        state *effective* (as a result of which the intensional predicate corresponding to the rule D3 in
        Figure 5 changes the state of the *Customer* to *has-car*, see also the condition in row 3 of
        Table 2), and inserts a claim against the *Customer* to return the car;
R4.   Upon receiving from a *Branch Agent* a message telling that the car of the given *RentalOrder*
        has been dropped off, the *Headquarter Agent* changes the state of the corresponding instance
        of *RentalOrder* to *dropped-off*.
        In order to save space, we have omitted the reaction rules describing the standard behaviour
for answering by the *Headquarter Agent* queries with the contents *?blacklisted (customer)* and
?has-car (customer) (Operational Rule 3 in Table 2).

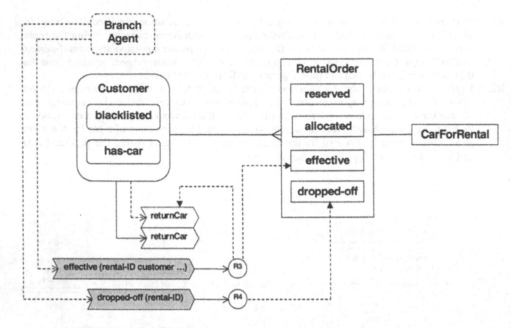

Figure 7. The AOR model of the business processes of picking up and dropping off a car from the perspective of the Headquarter Agent

And finally, the business processes of *dropping off a car* and *scheduling a car for automotive service* are modelled in Figure 8 *from the perspective of a Branch Agent*. The rules of these business processes are:

R5.   When the *Customer* drops a car off at the branch, then:
- the *Branch Agent* informs the *Headquarter Agent* about the drop-off;
- an instance of *CarForRental* in the state *present* is created for that car, or if *pick-up-branch = drop-off-branch*, the state of the corresponding instance of *CarForRental* is changed from *picked-up* to *present*;

R6.   When the *Customer* drops a car off at the branch, then if the car requires service (i.e. the corresponding instance of *CarForRental* is in the substate *requires-service*, determined by evaluating the intensional predicate corresponding to the rule D5 in Figure 5, see also the condition in row 5 of Table 2), the request to schedule the car for service is sent to the *Automotive Service Agent*;

R7.   Upon receiving from the *Automotive Service Agent* the automotive service confirmation, the *Branch Agent* changes the state of the corresponding instance of *CarForRental* to *scheduled-for-service*, and inserts into its VKB the commitment to send the car to service;

A1.   In order to fulfill the *sendCarToService* commitment, the human subagent *Car Handling Agent* of the *Branch Agent* sends or takes the car himself to the *Automotive Service Agent* for service which results in the change of the state of the corresponding instance of *CarForRental* to *in-service* and in the insertion of the claim against the *Automotive Service Agent* to return the car from service.

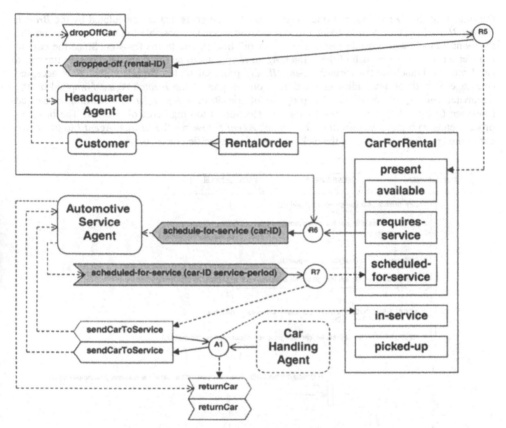

Figure 8. The AOR model of the business processes of dropping off a car and scheduling a car for automotive service from the perspective of a Branch Agent

As an example of modelling business processes from an objective observer's point of view, the process of negotiations between three *Branch Agents* about transferring a car is depicted in Figure 9. Please note that since agent communication languages are based on well-defined, small sets of general communicative actions, whereas objects communicate through unrestricted and idiosyncratic messages with ad hoc semantics, UML diagrams [29] can only limitedly be used for modelling agent-oriented information systems as it is done in Figure 9.

The requirements for the car rental company contain a business rule according to which if more cars have been requested than are available in a car group at a branch, the branch manager may ask other branches whether they have cars they can transfer to him. This business rule can be automated with the help of automated *Branch Agents*. The *Branch Agent* of the branch in need of a car starts the business process by initiating a *contract net* for performing the action *transfer_car* with the lowest possible cost in the interests of the car rental company, as a whole. In our example, this is reflected by the Call-For-Proposals message that the *Branch Agent I* broadcasts to other branch agents (messages 1 and 3, UML doesn't enable to represent broadcast messages!). The parameters' parts of these messages contain the car group and the rental period a car is required for. The *Branch Agents II and III*, whose branches happen to have a suitable car, respond with the PROPOSE messages where each of them specifies the cost of transfer of the car from his branch to the branch of the *Branch Agent I* (messages 2 and 4). The costs that are calculated by the *Branch Agents II and III* take into account the distance between the possible "donor" branch and the receiving branch, and possible losses of the "donor" branch due to the transfer. Since the cost to transfer a car from the branch of the *Branch Agent II* appears to be lower than the cost to transfer a car from the branch of the *Branch Agent III*, the proposal of the *Branch Agent II* is accepted (message 5) without any additional conditions on the part of the *Branch Agent I* implied by the parameter *true* of the message. The proposal of the *Branch Agent III* is accordingly rejected (message 6) by stating that the reason for the rejection is too high cost of transfer. The business process ends with the *commitment* of the *Branch Agent II* towards the *Branch Agent I* to transfer a car of the specified car group by the pick-up time of the specified rental period.

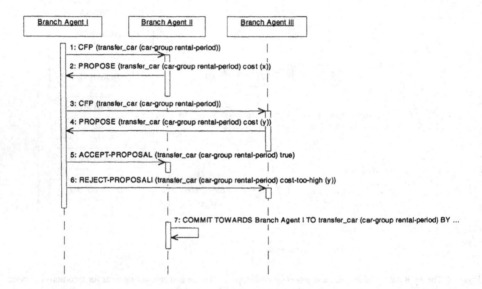

Figure 9. Negotiations between Branch Agents about transferring a car modelled from an objective observer's point of view

4. Related Work

We have integrated our approach with an extension of Entity-Relationship modelling, called Agent-Object-Relationship (AOR) Modelling, proposed in [31] and [32], where an entity is either an *object, event, action, commitment, claim,* or *agent*. The integration is further elaborated in [27].

In the paper [37] a general methodology for agent-oriented analysis and design is presented. The methodology proposed deals with both the macro-level (societal) and the micro-level (agent) aspects of systems. In the analysis phase of the methodology, the *roles* in the system are identified and the patterns of interaction that occur in the system between various roles are recognised. The functionality of each role is defined by its liveness and safety responsibilities. *Liveness responsibilities* are those that say "something will be done", e.g. "whenever the coffee machine is empty, fill it up". *Safety responsibilities* relate to the absence of some undesirable condition arising, e.g. "the coffee stock should never be empty". In the design phase, the liveness and safety responsibilities are respectively mapped to agents' *services* and *pre-* and *postconditions* on each service. Liveness and safety responsibilities thus bear a close resemblance to business rules. The difference from our work is that the methodology proposed in [37] is a software engineering approach, while our approach is aimed at creating business information systems.

In the work described in [18] agents are directly applied to managing business processes. The main difference from our work is that [18] focuses on the interaction and negotiation aspects of business processes, and does not explicitly treat conceptual models of the problem domain, and agents' beliefs and (re)actions.

The paper [27] also concentrates on the interaction aspects of agents in the domain of integrated supply chain management, and particularly on the agents' mutual obligations and interdictions.

Conceptual modelling of the problem domain is included in the paper [6] where concepts and relations between concepts are defined in hierarchies for modelling multi-agent systems. That approach also includes rules that are used for automatic generation of prototype agent applications directly from their specifications. The latter is also one of our future intentions.

The Enterprise Knowledge Development (EKD) approach described in [7] also addresses most of the issues present in our approach such as goals, business rules, concepts, business processes, actors, and resources. The EKD approach does not, however, bring these notions straightforwardly to the operational level like we do in our approach.

As was already mentioned in section 2, object-oriented modelling techniques, such as described in [25, 29], and [38], do not support the concept of an actor (agent), and are therefore not relevant to be discussed here.

5. Conclusions and Future Work

The main contribution of the approach proposed by us is explicit adding of the *Agent Layer* to the top of the Object and Implementation Layers (Figure 2). By doing so, we have *increased the level of abstraction* business information systems can be created at. With our approach, *agents are viewed as meta-level entities that represent business actors and control the behaviour of data objects by implementing business rules*. Moreover, we map the notion of an agent used in modelling straightforwardly to an operational agent architecture.

Another contribution of our approach is the integration and adaptation of different modelling techniques to be used for the modelling and design of agent-oriented information systems. In particular, we have integrated the AOR Modelling proposed in [31, 32] with the rather well-developed methodology of capturing information systems' requirements in the form of business rules (see e.g. [12, 14, 24])).

Implementation of business rules has been traditionally connected to (active) databases [36]. We have widened the sphere of using and implementing business rules by showing that they can also be interpreted and implemented as agents' "rules of behaviour" operating on the beliefs and actions of the agents.

Based on the case study of car rental that we have used for evaluating our work, we can conclude that the approach where we first model the functional units of an organisation, then create the model of the information they deal with, and after that design the ways the agents process the information at their disposal seems to be a pretty natural one from the *cognitive point of view*. True, further formalisation, verification, and validation of our work needs to be done, but these will be important subjects for our future work.

We think that our approach can make the design and implementation of complicated information systems considerably easier by raising the level of abstraction. We believe that just like object-oriented programming has given rise to object-oriented modelling and design, agent-oriented programming [26], that is programming in terms of agents' beliefs and (re)actions, may give rise to the proper agent-oriented modelling and design. We hope that our work has taken a step towards that.

We think that agents are well-suited to be used in cooperative information systems [22] where both data and application logic are distributed like e.g. in our experimental information system of car rental. We hope our work to be a step from the currently predominant client/server systems [4] towards the peer-to-peer systems of the future.

Like it was mentioned before, our future aims also include further *formalisation, verification,* and *validation* of our work. We also plan to model interaction protocols for agents by reaction rules, and to add models for exception handling. Another important aim is to work out the environment that would enable *semiautomatic generation of object-oriented implementations of agent-oriented business information systems* from their high-level (graphical) descriptions by ontologies and agents' "rules of behaviour". Since many business rules in real life are essentially of a "fuzzy" nature, we plan to introduce *fuzzy business rules for agents.* Another aim is modelling business rules for inter-organisational setting and particularly for *business-to-business automated e-commerce.* We also plan to extend the functionality of artificial software agents in agent-oriented information systems by "intelligent" features such as planning and predicting.

References

1. *Agent Communication Language,* FIPA 97 Specification. Available at http://www.fipa.org/.

2. van Assche, F. et al. Information systems development: a rule-based approach. *Knowledge-Based Systems,* 1(4), pp. 227-234, 1988.

3. Barbuceanu, M., Gray, T., Mankovksi, S. Roles of obligations in multiagent coordination, *Applied Artificial Intelligence,* 13(1), pp. 11–38, 1999.

4. Berson, A. *Client/Server Architecture.* McGraw-Hill, 1992.

5. Blanchard, T. Meta model elements as a foundation for implementation of business rules. *Proceedings of the OOPSLA'95 Workshop on Metamodeling in OO,* October 15, 1995. Available at http://saturne.info.uqam.ca/Labo_Recherche/Larc/MetamodelingWorkshop/Blanchard.

6. Brazier, F. M. T., Dunin-Keplicz, B. M., Jennings, N. R., Treur, J. DESIRE: Modeling multi-agent systems in a compositional formal framework. *International Journal of Cooperative Information Systems,* 6(1), pp. 67-94, 1997.

7. Bubenko, J. A., jr., Brash, D., Stirna, J. *EKD User Guide.* Kista, Dept. of Computer and Systems Science, Royal Institute of Technology (KTH) and Stockholm University, Stockholm, Sweden. Available at http://www.dsv.su.se/~js/ekd_user_guide.html.

8. Farhoodi, F., Graham, I. A practical approach to designing and building intelligent software agents. *Proceedings of the First International Conference and Exhibition on the Practical Application of Intelligent Agents and Multi-Agent Technology (PAAM'96),* London, UK, April 1996, pp. 181-204.

9. Fox, M. S., Barbuceanu, M., Gruninger, M., Jinxin Lin. An organizational ontology for enterprise modeling. M. J. Prietula, K. M. Carley, and L. Gasser, (eds.), *Simulating Organizations: Computational Models of Institutions and Groups,* AAAI Press / The MIT Press, 1998.

10. Georgeff, M. P., Lansky, A. Reactive reasoning and planning. *Proceedings of the Sixth National Conference on Artificial Intelligence (AAAI-87),* Seattle, Washington, USA, 1987, pp. 677–682.

11. Gruber, T. R. A translation approach to portable ontologies. *Knowledge Acquisition,* 5(2), pp. 199-220, 1993. Available at http://ksl-web.stanford.edu/knowledge-sharing/papers/README.html#ontolingua-intro.

12. *GUIDE Business Rules Project, Final Report,* October, 1997. Prepared by D. Hay and K. A. Healy. Available at http://grace.evergreen.edu/businessRules/br01c0.htm.

13. Hay, D. C. Business policies, means and ends. *Data To Knowledge Newsletter,* 27(4), 1999.

14. Herbst, H. *Business Rule-Oriented Conceptual Modeling* (Contributions to Management Science). Springer-Verlag, 1997.

15. Høydalsvik, G. M., Sindre, G. On the purpose of object-oriented analysis. OOPSLA'93 Conference Proceedings, *ACM Sigplan Notices,* October 1993, pp. 240-253.

16. Huber, M. J. *Jam Agents in a Nutshell.* Available at http://members.home.net:80/marcush/IRS/.

17. *Information Integration for Concurrent Engineering (IICE) IDEF5 Method Report.* Prepared by Knowledge Based Systems, Inc., 1994. Available at http://www.idef.com/downloads/Downloads.htm.

18. Jennings, N. R. et al. Using intelligent agents to manage business processes. *Proceedings of the First International Conference and Exhibition on the Practical Application of Intelligent Agents and Multi-Agent Technology (PAAM'96)*, London, UK, April 1996, pp. 345-360.

19. Jennings, N. R., Sycara, K., Wooldridge, M. A roadmap of agent research and development. *Autonomous Agents and Multi-Agent Systems*, 1(1), pp. 7-38, 1998.

20. Kieser, A., Kubicek, H. *Organisation*. 3rd edition, Berling/New York, De Gruyter, 1992.

21. Mahalingam, K., Huhns, M. N. Ontology tools for semantic reconciliation in distributed heterogeneous Information environments. M. Kamel M. and Jamshidi, (eds.), *Intelligent Automation and Soft Computing, Special Issue on Distributed Intelligent Systems*, 1998.

22. de Michelis, G., Dubois, E., Jarke, M. et al. *Cooperative Information Systems: A Manifesto.* Available at http://www.sts.tu-harburg.de/projects/EUCAN/manifesto.html.

23. Odell, J. Meta-modeling. *Proceedings of the OOPSLA'95 Workshop on Metamodeling in OO*, October 15, 1995. Available at http://www.info.uqam.ca/Labo_Recherche/Larc/MetamodelingWorkshop/Odell/metamodeling/.

24. Ross, R. G. *The Business Rule Book: Classifying, Defining and Modeling Rules.* Second Edition, Boston, Massachusetts, Database Research Group, Inc., 1997.

25. Rumbaugh, J., Blaha, M., Premerlani, W., Eddy, F., Lorensen, W. *Object-Oriented Modeling and Design.* Prentice-Hall International, 1991.

26. Shoham, Y. Agent-oriented programming. *Artificial Intelligence*, 60(1), pp. 51-92, 1993.

27. Taveter, K., Wagner, G. Combining AOR diagrams and Ross Business Rules' diagrams for enterprise modeling. *Proceedings of the Second International Bi-Conference Workshop on Agent-Oriented Information Systems* (AOIS-2000), 5-6 June 2000, Stockholm (Sweden) and 30 July 2000, Austin (Texas, USA).

28. *The Ontology Editor.* http://www-ksl-svc.stanford.edu:5915/.

29. *UML Resource Center.* http://www.rational.com/uml/index.jtmpl.

30. Uschold, M., King, M., Moralee, S., Zorgios, Y. The enterprise ontology. *The Knowledge Engineering Review*, 13(1), pp. 31-90, 1998.

31. Wagner, G. Agent-Object-Relationship modeling. *Proceedings of the Second International Symposium "From Agent Theory to Agent Implementation" (AT2AI-2)*, Vienna, Austria, April 2000.

32. Wagner, G. Agent-oriented analysis and design of organizational information systems. *Proceedings of the Fourth IEEE International Baltic Workshop on Databases and Information Systems*, 1–5 May 2000, Vilnius, Lithuania, pp. 196-210.

33. Wagner, G. Agent-oriented enterprise and business process modeling. *Proceedings of the First International Workshop on Enterprise Management and Resource Planning Systems (EMRPS'99)*, Venice, November 1999.

34. Wagner, G. *Foundations of Knowledge Systems with Applications to Databases and Agents.* Kluwer Academic Publishers, 1998.

35. Wagner, G. Vivid agents - how they deliberate, how they react, how they are verified. Extended version of: Wagner, G. A. Logical and operational model of scalable knowledge- and perception-based agents. W. Van de Velde, J. W. Perram, (eds.), *Agents Breaking Away, Proceedings of MAAMAW'96*, Springer Lecture Notes in Artificial Intelligence 1038, 1996.

36. Widom, J. and Ceri, S. (eds.). *Active Database Systems: Triggers and Rules for Advanced Database Processing.* Morgan Kaufmann Publishers, Inc., San Francisco, 1996.

37. Wooldridge, M., Jennings, N. R., Kinny, D. A methodology for agent-oriented analysis and design. *Proceedings of the 3rd International Conference on Autonomous Agents (Agents-99)*, Seattle, Washington, USA, May 1-5, 1999.

38. Yourdon, E., Whitehead, K., Thomann, J., Oppel, K., Nevermann, P. *Mainstream Objects: An Analysis and Design Approach for Business.* Yourdon Press, 1996.

Integration of GIS and Expert Systems

Viktoras Paliulionis

Institute of Mathematics and Informatics,
Akademijos 4, LT-2600 Vilnius, Lithuania
E-mail: vikpal@ktl.mii.lt

Abstract

The purpose of this paper is to analyse the possibilities of the integration of geographic information systems (GIS) and rule-based expert systems, and propose an outline of the integrated system architecture, based on client-server techniques. Expert systems are one of intelligent system technologies that enables to make use of expert knowledge for solving problems. The integration of GIS and expert systems is an important activity that enhances the value of GIS. An example of integrating a GIS and expert system is presented.

Keywords: intelligent GIS, software integration, software architecture, expert systems.

1. Introduction

The purpose of this paper is to analyse the possibilities of extending the possibilities of geographic information systems (GIS) by integrating them with expert systems (ES), and propose the outline of the integrated system architecture. GIS are computer-based tools to capture, manipulate, process and display spatial or geo-referenced data. They contain both geometry data (co-ordinates and topological information) and attribute data, i.e., information describing the properties of geometrical objects such as points, lines, and polygons. Expert systems are one of intelligent system technologies that enables to make use of expert knowledge for solving problems. The knowledge is encoded in a computer program in the form of IF...THEN rules. New generation expert system tools combine rule-based and object-oriented knowledge representation, message passing, graphical user interface, and the ability of integrating with other systems. Usually, GIS enables to analyse quantitative spatial information, while expert systems enable to operate qualitative information, including incomplete knowledge. In qualitative reasoning, a situation is described by parameters that have a rather small predefined set of values, and by rules that use these symbolic values instead of numeric values. Linking an expert system with a GIS enables both the expert system and the GIS to perform new tasks, and opens the way for a more flexible and complex analysis of spatial data, based on rules and logical inference.

Expert systems can be used in many GIS application domains. A number of examples from different domains of natural resources and environmental management are presented in [4]. Such systems combine models, GIS, and expert systems in a number of customised implementations for specific decision support problems.

Expert systems are often used to help configure models and estimate parameters. A number of these "intelligent front end systems" or model advisors have been developed in the environmental domain [10].

The expert system technology can be useful in implementing spatial intelligent agents that would help to solve such problems as locating and retrieving spatial information in large networks

337

J. Barzdins and A. Caplinskas (eds.), Databases and Information Systems, 337–342.

(and specifically the Internet), facilitate the handling of a GIS user interface, implementing improved spatial tasks and creating interfaces between GIS and specific software packages [9].

In [1], it is proposed to use rule-based knowledge for more intelligent visualisation of maps. According to the authors, an intelligent GIS should assist the user in the analysis, and this presupposes the following capabilities: the capability to understand user's information-seeking goals, the capability to select and visualise appropriate data in a way productive for achieving these goals, and the capability to support the user's analytical activity with the use of the generated presentations.

Depending on the problem addressed, on uses and users, various levels of integration are possible, ranging from the simple exchange of data files to a complete integration within one common environment, framework, and user interface.

Section 2 overview the methods of integrating GIS and intelligent system technologies. In section 3, the outline of an architecture for integrating a GIS and expert system based on client-server techniques is proposed, and an example of integrating a GIS and expert system is presented. In section 4, conclusions are presented.

2. GIS Integration with Artificial Intelligence Technologies

The problem of integrating GIS and different intelligent systems technologies (including expert systems) was investigated in many works [7, 11]. It can be summarised, that existing approaches to addressing the problem of integrating GIS and other software range from tightly coupled systems to loosely coupled systems.

In *tightly coupled* systems, expert system components exist as specially coded modules within the framework of a GIS. Such modules might be written in a language provided by the GIS. This effectively extends the functionality of GIS and provides seamless integration from a user interface viewpoint.

Loosely coupled systems interact by using files to exchange data between a GIS and other systems. The expert system application may read some of its input data from GIS files, and produce some of its output in a format that allows processing and display with GIS. It requires little if any software modifications but the speed of data transfer between the expert system and the GIS is low and it is difficult to implement a common user interface (for example, point-and-click operations).

To integrate independently developed software systems, wrappers are often used. A wrapper is a kind of software that is used to attach software components one to another. The wrapping software provides a shell around the software to be integrated, providing a point of access to the integrated software. It may encapsulate a system to make it usable in some new way that the unwrapped system was not. Wrappers are common components in a number of software architectures used for integrating software [6, 8].

Recent GIS implementations have begun to support the use of client-server techniques as an effective means of transferring data while retaining data structure. This has presented the possibility of linking other systems with GIS by using these techniques. In [10], a *co-operative* approach is described, based on client-server technologies. The authors present two types of this approach. First, with *direct co-operation*, systems being integrated are directly linked via interapplication communication. Secondly, *indirect co-operation* is characterised by the existence of an intermediate interface between systems. A workbench would be an example of such an interface.

3. Architecture

We propose an architecture for integrating a GIS and expert system that is based on client-server techniques. Servers are components that provide a response to a specific client request for service or data. Clients can also be servers by providing service to higher order clients. Every construct in this architecture is an object. Each has specific interface methods, which allow it to communicate with other objects.

The architecture is compatible with the OGIS (Open Geodata Interoperability Specification) model and supplements it with an expert system shell and knowledge bases. The OGIS model [2] enables application domains to interoperate with geodata stores and geoprocessing services. The OGIS guide identifies several software layers in the design of integration software. These include the presentation layer, the application layer, the application server layer, the spatial data access provider layer, the database layer, and the hardware and network layer. OGIS unify geodata models and geoprocessing services.

The components of the integration scheme are (Figure 1):

- GIS applications,
- GIS service providers,
- Expert system shell,
- Spatial data access providers,
- Spatial databases,
- Knowledge bases.

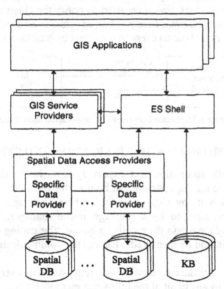

Figure 1. The general integrated system architecture

Spatial (geometric and attribute) data can be stored in databases of different types or in files of different formats. To process them, intermediate software, called "spatial data access providers", is used. *Spatial data access providers* standardise data access. They bidirectionally translate application semantics and database semantics. For example, an application will be able to send the query to the database in terms of a particular geodata model, whereas the database understands only SQL or a proprietary query language. *GIS service providers* are software components that provide a response to a specific client request for service. They include a set of common GIS functions to access, search, analyse, visualise and process in other ways spatial data.

The *expert system shell* makes inferences using knowledge stored in knowledge bases. It includes an inference engine, and interface modules that ensure interaction with spatial data access providers and GIS service providers. Besides, the expert system shell provides its clients with the programming interface. This architecture enables to implement specialised GIS applications that use an appropriate part of GIS services and the expert system shell with appropriate knowledge bases. Filling the expert system shell with knowledge makes it an expert system in a certain field. By replacing knowledge bases, we get another expert system, which uses the same knowledge representation methods and inference engine.

In the proposed architecture, there are two ways to implement the GIS and expert system integration: an expert system shell can be embedded into a GIS application, or a GIS application and expert system can run in separate processes.

3.1 EMBEDDED EXPERT SYSTEMS

One or more objects of the expert system shell can be created in a GIS application. It can operate the expert system shell by using the shell object's properties and methods, and receives notifications from the expert system shell in the form of events. Figure 2 demonstrates this interaction. *Properties* allow the client change certain values of the expert system shell, or make requests of the shell, thus accessing a specific piece of data that the expert system shell maintains. A *method* is a procedure that is exposed by the expert system shell and performs a specific action (for example, runs the inference engine). *Events* are used to notify the client when something important happens in the shell (for example, event fires just before a fact is asserted). The expert system shell can send additional information about an event to the client by attaching parameters to the event.

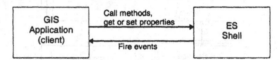

Figure 2. Interaction between a GIS application and ES shell

3.2 COMMUNICATION BETWEEN A GIS APPLICATION AND EXPERT SYSTEM

In some cases, a GIS application and expert system should run in parallel in separate processes. In such a case, the message passing can be used for the interaction of the GIS and expert system. Each application has its own queue of the received messages and retrieves them when ready. Message passing is managed by a message queue manager. Messages are being sent asynchronously, just putting them into the receiver's queue. The calling system is free to continue processing or wait depending on its own needs. Hence, the communication can be synchronous or asynchronous.

A client's process initiates the conversation and requests certain services from the server. The applications exchange data by any or all of the following methods:

- *Manual link*: the client must request data from the server (or send command).
- *Warm data link*: the server notifies the client that specified data have changed.
- *Hot data link*: the server automatically sends data whenever data change.

Depending on which one is a server and which one is a client, there are two possibilities (see Figure 3). If the GIS application is a client, and the expert system application is a server (Figure 3a), then the expert system can monitor external events and notify the GIS application. For example, in the automatic vehicle location system, it can receive and process data from external devices, identify from what vehicle the message is received, determine its co-ordinates and other parameters (time, course, speed, etc.) and pass data to the GIS application, which visualises changes of the vehicle location.

If the GIS application is a server and the expert system application is a client (Figure 3b), then the GIS application can pass messages about events to the client. For example, when a user selects an object on the map or clicks a button, the expert system application is informed about these events and can react to them. This makes it possible to integrate the GIS user interface with the expert system.

In case of the complete integration, a GIS and expert system should act as both a client and a server, depending on the situation.

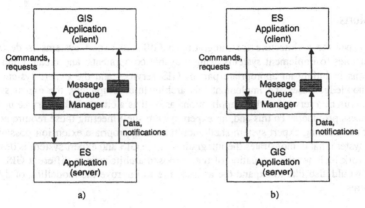

Figure 3. Two directions of communication

3.3 AN EXAMPLE OF IMPLEMENTATION

We developed some experimental systems that demonstrate the GIS and expert system integration. These systems integrate GIS "Akis" and expert system shell CLIPS. "Akis" is a simple GIS program with the main GIS functions (map visualisation, creating of layers and objects, search, measuring, etc.). CLIPS is a forward chaining, multiparadigm, expert system shell that provides support for rule-based, object-oriented, and procedural programming [5]. Basic elements of expert systems, also provided by CLIPS are a fact and instance base, a rule base, and an inference engine. The rules are of the following form:

IF [*conditions*] THEN [*actions*],

and specify a set of actions to be performed for a given situation. There can be such actions as the creating of a new fact, function call, message sending to an instance, and so on. The following CLIPS extensions were implemented:

- Definitions of classes used in the GIS data model (Geoobject, Point, Line, Polygon, etc.) were created. They are stored in the knowledge base and their instances can be created.
- A communication subsystem was developed. It includes two modules: a server part and a client part. The server part processes client's queries and commands, answers queries and sends messages about events. The client part sends queries and commands to the server, processes answers and messages about events.
- External functions were attached that enable to use GIS functions.

One of the integrated systems was developed to analyse radio waves propagation. In this system, the expert system component is embedded to help user in selecting an appropriate calculation model and parameters, analysing the terrain profile, etc. For the prediction of field strength, it takes into account the terrain models, data of cover type (open area, forest, urban area, or water), and transmitter features.

Another example is a real-time automatic vehicle location system. In this system, the expert system component runs in a separate process. It communicates with vehicles via GSM or radio, receives and processes their data. These can be the data from the GPS receiver (the position, direction, speed, time) as well as various sensor data and alarm signals. The location and operational status of the vehicle are displayed on the map.

4. Conclusions

In this paper the architecture for integrating a GIS and expert systems is described. The architecture enables to implement systems using reusable components, and create domain-specific GIS applications including an appropriate part of GIS services and the expert system shell with appropriate knowledge bases. To implement this architecture completely, the expert system shell must be able to run as a server for client applications as well as a client of GIS service providers and spatial data access providers. To this end, an expert system shell meeting these requirements should be created, or the existing expert system shell should have appropriate extension possibilities. The experimental system that demonstrates the integration of the GIS and expert system is described.

Future work includes the evaluation of the proposed architecture in different GIS application domains. We would also like to expand the architecture to improve the modelling of dynamic and temporal features.

References

1. Andrienko, G., and Andrienko, N. Making a GIS intelligent: CommonGIS project view. *AGILE'99 Conference*, Rome, April 15-17, 1999, pp.19-24.

2. Buehler, K., McKee, L. *The OpenGIS Guide. Introduction to Interoperable Geoprocessing and the OpenGIS Specification*. OGC Technical Committee of the Open GIS Consortium, Wayland (MA), 1998.

3. Fedra, K. Decision support for natural resources management: models, GIS and expert systems. *AI Applications*, 9(3), 1995, pp. 3-19.

4. Fedra, K. Expert systems in water resources simulation and optimization. In J. B. Marco et. al., (eds.), *Stochastic Hydrology and its use in Water Resources Systems Simulation and Optimization*, Kluwer Academic Publishers, The Netherlands, 1993, pp. 397-412.

5. Giarratano, J. C. *CLIPS User's Guide*. NASA/Lyndon B.Johnson Space Center Information Systems Directorate, Software Technology Branch, 1993.

6. Ishikawa, Y., Furudate, T., and Uemura, S. A wrapping architecture for IR systems to mediate external structured document sources. In R. Topor and K. Tanaka, (eds.), *Database systems for advanced applications '97*, Advanced Database Research and Development Series, 6, World Scientific Publishing Co., Singapore, pp. 431-440.

7. Lam, D. C. L., Swayne, D. A., Mayfield, C. I., Cowan, D. D. Integration of GIS with other software systems. *Proceedings of the Third International Conference/Workshop on Integrating GIS and Environmental Modeling*, Santa Barbara, CA, National Center for Geographic Information and Analysis, 1996.

8. Papakonstantinou, Y., Gupta, A., Garcia-Molina, H., and Ullman, J. A query translation scheme for rapid implementation of wrappers. Lecture Notes in Computer Science, 1013, 1995, pp. 161-186.

9. Rodrigues, A., Raper, J., Capitao, M. Development of spatial intelligent agents. *Proceedings of the First International Conference on Spatial Multimedia and Virtual Reality, Museum of Water*, Lisbon, Portugal, 18-20 October 1995.

10. Sandhu, R. and Treleaven, P. Client-server approaches to model integration within GIS. *Third International Conference/Workshop on Integrating GIS and Environmental Modeling*, January 21-25, 1996, Santa Fe, New Mexico, USA. http://www.ncgia.ucsb.edu/conf/SANTA_FE_CDROM/sf_papers/sandhu_raghbir/clientserver.html.

11. Sandhu, R. and Treleaven, P. Intelligent geographical information systems. *GISRUK'95 (working notes)*, Newcastle upon Tyne, England, UK, 1995.

Author Index

Subject Index

activation record, 6
agent, 111-124, 157-160, 317, 319-334
  business, 111, 318
  institutional, 117, 119, 322
  intelligent, 113, 337
  organisation, 320-322, 326, 328
  UniCat, 157-159, 161
  user, 157-159, 161
agent class, 117-118, 120, 122, 323
agent communication language, 111,
  114, 327, 331
agentified information system, 113-114
agent-object-relationship modelling,
  114-121, 323, 332-333
agent-oriented information system,
  114-115, 321-322, 331, 333-334
agent-oriented modelling, 317, 333
algebra,
  object, 4
  probabilistic temporal, 59
  recursive NF^2, 63
  relational, 4, 66
  relational/object 3-4
annotation,
  conceptual, 45-48, 54-55
attribute,
  adding, 12
  atomic-valued, 62-63
  complex-valued, 112, 121
  grouping, 89
  high order, 63-65
  location, 47
  multi-valued, 29, 31, 38
  object-valued, 112
  period, 310-311
  relation-valued, 62, 64
  renaming, 4, 8, 12
  restricting, 12
  set-valued, 30
  temporal, 48
  territorial unit, 310
  uncertainty validity, 49
  virtual, 4, 12-13
  zero-order, 62, 64-65

binder, 6, 8-9
business
  agent, 111, 318
  information system, 125, 317-319,
   333-334
  modelling, 317-318
  object, 112-113, 125
  process, 111, 113, 317, 328-333
  rule, 122, 317-323, 325-334
  transaction, 111
commitment, 111, 113-119, 120-122,
  328, 330, 332
component,
  CORBA, 125, 128, 135-136
  Java, 135-136
  reusable, 135-137
  software, 125-137, 157, 221-233
component-based development, 125,
  221-223, 237
component-oriented information
  system, 125
component system, 224, 227-228, 230
component view class, 20, 23
  dependent, 20
  independent, 20
component view object, 20-21, 23-24
  dependent, 20
  independent, 20, 24
conceptual
  annotation, 45-48, 54-55
  data model, 308, 312
  modelling, 57, 60, 97, 99, 105, 107,
   112, 333
database,
  distributed, 15, 17, 140, 148
  federated, 3
  fuzzy, 58
  heterogeneous 3, 11
  object, 4
  object-oriented, 3, 15-16, 29, 34-35,
   319, 327
  object-relational, 29, 112, 115, 121,
   319, 323
  on-line transaction processing, 97,